Intellectual Property Rights and the Protection of Traditional Knowledge

Nisha Dhanraj Dewani
Guru Gobind Singh Indraprastha University, India

Amulya Gurtu
Austin E. Cofrin School of Business, University of Wisconsin-Green Bay, USA

A volume in the Advances in Knowledge Acquisition, Transfer, and Management (AKATM) Book Series

IGI Global
PUBLISHER of TIMELY KNOWLEDGE

Published in the United States of America by
IGI Global
Information Science Reference (an imprint of IGI Global)
701 E. Chocolate Avenue
Hershey PA, USA 17033
Tel: 717-533-8845
Fax: 717-533-8661
E-mail: cust@igi-global.com
Web site: http://www.igi-global.com

Library of Congress Cataloging-in-Publication Data

Names: Dewani, Nisha Dhanraj, 1985- editor. | Gurtu, Amulya, editor.
Title: Intellectual property rights and the protection of traditional knowledge / Nisha Dhanraj Dewani and Amulya Gurtu, editors.
Description: Hershey, PA : Information Science Reference, 2020. | Includes bibliographical references and index. | Summary: “”This book explores the protection of traditional knowledge and indigenous peoples’ rights through intellectual property”--Provided by publisher”-- Provided by publisher.
Identifiers: LCCN 2019034102 (print) | LCCN 2019034103 (ebook) | ISBN 9781799818359 (hardcover) | ISBN 9781799818366 (paperback) | ISBN 9781799818373 (ebook)
Subjects: LCSH: Intellectual property. | Traditional ecological knowledge--Law and legislation.
Classification: LCC K1401.5 .I58 2020 (print) | LCC K1401.5 (ebook) | DDC 346.04/8--dc23
LC record available at https://lccn.loc.gov/2019034102
LC ebook record available at https://lccn.loc.gov/2019034103

This book is published in the IGI Global book series Advances in Knowledge Acquisition, Transfer, and Management (AKATM) (ISSN: 2326-7607; eISSN: 2326-7615)

British Cataloguing in Publication Data
A Cataloguing in Publication record for this book is available from the British Library.

All work contributed to this book is new, previously-unpublished material.
The views expressed in this book are those of the authors, but not necessarily of the publisher.

For electronic access to this publication, please contact: eresources@igi-global.com.

Advances in Knowledge Acquisition, Transfer, and Management (AKATM) Book Series

ISSN:2326-7607
EISSN:2326-7615

Editor-in-Chief: Murray E. Jennex, San Diego State University, USA

MISSION

Organizations and businesses continue to utilize knowledge management practices in order to streamline processes and procedures. The emergence of web technologies has provided new methods of information usage and knowledge sharing.

The **Advances in Knowledge Acquisition, Transfer, and Management (AKATM) Book Series** brings together research on emerging technologies and their effect on information systems as well as the knowledge society. **AKATM** will provide researchers, students, practitioners, and industry leaders with research highlights surrounding the knowledge management discipline, including technology support issues and knowledge representation.

COVERAGE

- Cognitive Theories
- Cultural Impacts
- Information and Communication Systems
- Knowledge Acquisition and Transfer Processes
- Knowledge Management Strategy
- Knowledge Sharing
- Organizational Learning
- Organizational Memory
- Small and Medium Enterprises
- Virtual Communities

The Advances in Knowledge Acquisition, Transfer, and Management (AKATM) Book Series (ISSN 2326-7607) is published by IGI Global, 701 E. Chocolate Avenue, Hershey, PA 17033-1240, USA, www.igi-global.com. This series is composed of titles available for purchase individually; each title is edited to be contextually exclusive from any other title within the series. For pricing and ordering information please visit http://www.igi-global.com/book-series/advances-knowledge-acquisition-transfer-management/37159. Postmaster: Send all address changes to above address.

Titles in this Series

For a list of additional titles in this series, please visit:
http://www.igi-global.com/book-series/advances-knowledge-acquisition-transfer-management/37159

Developing Knowledge Societies for Distinct Country Contexts
Nuno Vasco Lopes (University of Minho, Portugal) and Rehema Baguma (Makerere University Uganda)
Information Science Reference • © 2020 • 280pp • H/C (ISBN: 9781522588733) • US $185.00

Knowledge Management Practices in the Public Sector
Vasileios Ismyrlis (Hellenic Statistical Authority, Greece) Theodore Tarnanidis (University of Macedonia, Greece) and Efstratios Moschidis (University of Macedonia, Greece)
Information Science Reference • © 2020 • 263pp • H/C (ISBN: 9781799819400) • US $195.00

Current Issues and Trends in Knowledge Management, Discovery, and Transfer
Murray Eugene Jennex (San Diego State University, USA)
Information Science Reference • © 2020 • 450pp • H/C (ISBN: 9781799821892) • US $185.00

Handbook of Research on Implementing Knowledge Management Strategy in the Public Sector
Yousif Abdullatif Albastaki (Ahlia University, Bahrain) Adel Ismail Al-Alawi (University of Bahrain, Bahrain) and Sara Abdulrahman Al-Bassam (Arabian Gulf University, Bahrain)
Information Science Reference • © 2019 • 583pp • H/C (ISBN: 9781522596394) • US $195.00

Big Data and Knowledge Sharing in Virtual Organizations
Albert Gyamfi (Aalborg University, Denmark) and Idongesit Williams (Aalborg University, Denmark)
Engineering Science Reference • © 2019 • 313pp • H/C (ISBN: 9781522575191) • US $215.00

For an entire list of titles in this series, please visit:
http://www.igi-global.com/book-series/advances-knowledge-acquisition-transfer-management/37159

IGI Global
PUBLISHER of TIMELY KNOWLEDGE

701 East Chocolate Avenue, Hershey, PA 17033, USA
Tel: 717-533-8845 x100 • Fax: 717-533-8661
E-Mail: cust@igi-global.com • www.igi-global.com

Table of Contents

Detailed Table of Contents

People at large do not have the capacity to transform their knowledge into formal specification and consequently into wealth. Some people who are hampered because of their poverty illiteracy, isolative habitat, lack of information and technological gadgets are unable to convert their knowledge into wealth. In this background, the chapter has critically evaluated traditional knowledge in the context of the challenges it faces. Further, it analyses the protection given to traditional knowledge under different laws and its international perspective. Moreover, efforts are taken at both the national and regional levels. Lastly, the chapter has come up with certain suggestions for its improvement and protection.

This chapter aims to trace the development of patent law regime in India and analyze its evolution in response to globally-influential intellectual property framework, such as TRIPS and pressure from the developed countries US and Europe to open up her markets to permit cash-rich pharmaceutical companies to sell their drugs and receive patent protection in India. An observation of the legislative actions and judicial responses reveal that both the parliament and the supreme echelons of the judiciary have been tediously careful in protecting the healthcare needs of the poor by promoting the generic drug industry through a guarded interpretation of Section 3(d) of Patents Act, 1970. The objective of the chapter is to critically analyze the legislative reforms and judicial interpretations of patent law in light of the socio-economic needs of the country.

The chapter seeks to explore the extent to which copyright law impedes the fulfillment of the right to education and discuss the alternatives that seek to balance these conflicting rights. The chapter is divided into three parts: the first part of the chapter discusses the embodiment of the right to education in several national and international instruments, the extent of problem of the lack of access to educational materials due to copyright protection. The next part of the chapter discusses the flexibilities provided in international copyright law and efficacy of the same, primarily the doctrine of fair use. The last part of the chapter discusses alternatives to fair use and impact of these supplementary mechanisms.

The commercial disputes between business entities to boost international trade and technology will increasingly involve an aspect of patents. Among various modes of ADR, the arbitration is preferred more over litigation. Still, various arguments have been presented both in favor and against arbitration in patent disputes. Thus, this chapter deals with the scope of patent disputes that can be referred to arbitration, which needs to be analyzed and defined, keeping in mind the consequent advantages of arbitration in case of patent disputes over traditional litigation. Additionally, there are various procedural aspects related to arbitration that might be specifically relevant to an arbitration involving patents and may require special attention by parties involved in such arbitration have also been made subject and discussed in detail.

The unique requirements of the Indigenous people with respect to the intellectual property are very different. There are many conflicts regarding the questions of culturally appropriate usage, sharing of knowledge, and proper attribution. The process followed by courts may not resolve their issues. They have distinct social, cultural, and economic needs. The redressal system should be such that it helps to maintain and protect their position. ADR is one of the best to resolve their disputes as it offers a number of possibilities. The main methods of ADR are negotiation, mediation, and conciliation. WIPO plays a role in providing ADR arbitration rules in regards to the Indigenous people and local communities. The WIPO Arbitration and Mediation Centre was established in 1994 providing the resolution among the private parties regarding their international commercial disputes across borders. Through this chapter, questions such as the extent of ADR in resolving these issues and can this centre be considered as an appropriate forum for addressing the issues and settling them are presented.

The protection of indigenous/aboriginal resources is one of the important aspects of biodiversity justice. Many international treaties and conventions legitimised natural rights and privileges of tribal societies and indigenous communities. But some interventionist practices like a conflict of interest in bioprospecting agreement and biopiracy have become major concerns for prospering third-world countries. Strategic application of prior-informed consent and benefit-sharing procedures will definitely meet socio-environmental sustainability in the country. The responsibility and liability of state biodiversity authority and local biodiversity committee at village level need to be fixed to maintain transparency and accountability. Conservation of ethnobiological resources is also important in the view of increasing patent infringement. That's why issues of patentability must include complete disclosure of specification claims even in the case foreign natural resources.

Bio-piracy indicates unauthorized use of bio-resources of a country either by the individuals or institutions or companies of other countries. The countries with enormous bio-resources, like India, become the victims of biopiracy. The paper highlights different issues relating to biopiracy in the context of food security of India. It has been argued that the distress of farmers has increased a lot after the emergence of GM seeds. First of all, GM seeds raise the cost of cultivation by monopolizing the seed business in the hands of a few. Secondly, taking monopoly control over the market by the MNCs became easier because technology allowed them to develop seeds which can be used once-for-all. The farmers, therefore, have to give up their traditional practice of saving and sharing of seeds. The paper cites various instances of biopiracy in India and explains how biopiracy jeopardizes the food security and health security of the people in India. Events of piracy of plants with medicinal values and medicinal knowledge of traditional healers are also on increase at a rapid pace in India. This trend also poses challenges health security of India. More initiatives need to be taken at different levels including government and NGOs need to be taken in documenting codified and non-codified traditional knowledge (TK).

The crop genetic diversity has been sustainably maintained by the farmers of different regions for generations through cross-breeding. Competition among commercial ventures has placed these traditional varieties under severe exploitation and pilferage. The Indian government, to preserve these traditional varieties, has established PPV and FRA (Protection of Plant Varieties and Farmers Rights Act), which are on par with Intellectual Patent Rights (IPR). This gives the rights and ownership of the crop breed and its characterization to the traditional farmers who developed it. The researchers along with VAANGHAI, an NGO, have represented the traditional farmers, who are growing and maintaining traditional crops in Cauvery River's coastal delta region in Tamil Nadu to characterize and register their varieties under PPV and FRA. This study has identified around 69 rice varieties and characterized them based on their uniqueness, distinctiveness, stability, uniformity, test trials, and adaptability potential. Most potential rice varieties were registered under this act.

Hidden in the obscure spirals of rural subconscious of Bihar are vast memories of history, culture, and tradition. These memories are invoked and brought forth by the subtle nuances of folklore, song, and painting by women. A sub-stratum of women memories of power and energy has existed since the ancient past where women were the repositories and sustainers of heritage. Madhubani painting can be said to be a creation of communal spiritual experience. It can be comprehended not just as an aesthetic wonder but also as a representation of collective mind, expressing millennia of traditional knowledge of the women artists and a form of transmitting a series of ancestral motifs. The uniqueness of this beautiful art form along with its specific geographical location has led to it being conferred its own geographical identification or GI tag by the government. The region has evoked the interest and appreciation of art connoisseurs, scholars, and tourists from all over the world, thus creating a niche for itself in the world of art.

The aim of this chapter is to show that innovation can only produce value once it is legally protected. Indeed, the law is involved throughout the entire life cycle of innovation. Thus, legal protection helps to transform innovation into an intangible asset for the company (patent, trademark, designs and models, databases, etc.). The chapter presents the different legal choices that allow the firm to develop innovation internally or externally. The authors explain that the firm, as a taxpayer, must optimize its accounting and tax choices in relation to innovative activities. Moreover, legal management implies an optimization of the legal and tax structure of the corporate structure in the sense that it is important to choose the most suitable form for an innovative activity. They also show that protecting innovation helps to exploit it through several legal techniques of different natures, such as contractual assignment or concession tools (licenses) or other judicial tools. The legal management of innovation appears as one of the key factors for the success of the innovative firm.

Foreword

It is my pleasure to write a foreword for this book, contributing significantly to the literature which ties between culture, Traditional Knowledge (TK), and Intellectual Property Rights (IPR). Knowledge is undoubtedly the main contributing factor in determining how humanity can maintain sustainable development on this earth. Apart from some anthropologists and scholars, not many have acknowledged "science" is rooted in other people's cultures and civilisations around the world. Globally researchers and policymakers are recognising the importance of diverse systems of local and cultural knowledge systems in addressing development and environmental problems. The United Nations declared 1993 as the "International Year of Indigenous People of the World" and from 1995 to 2004 as the "Decade of the Indigenous Peoples of the World". Indigenous and local peoples have developed a tremendous wealth of TK worldwide. People have started using traditional medicine for improving their health in many countries, including India. This has increased the awareness for such medicines, and people now have access to these alternative medicines too. Therefore, the interest in documenting such TK is on the rise.

Interestingly, this book not only concentrated on intellectual propositions but also on problems of the real world such as biopiracy, health and essential medicines, education, environmental protection, food safety, TRIPS, Arbitration and sustainable agricultural activities with or without IPRs. This work has also emphasised the ways to promote and facilitate the practice of sustainable development, access to genetic resources, and fair and equitable benefit sharing arising out of the utilisation of TK.

Sustainable management of biodiversity under the umbrella of IPR and TK is a topic of contemporary significance. This book examines the conflicts and compatibility between cultural legacy and the protection of intellectual property. This work further helps to understand the vital role of cultural and indigenous expertise in the commercial, medical and social domains of our lives. It is a welcome addition to this valuable area for humanity as a whole. The chapters in the book are explained comprehensively. The book has incorporated specific case studies with cutting-edge research on IPR and TK. Traditional Knowledge and attempted to address the various important cases such as access to medicine, protection of indigenous culture, TK, and bio-piracy, among others. This work would find broad appeal among academicians, researchers, policymakers and those who are promoting new ideas in their capacity. My congratulations to Professors Nisha Dhanraj Dewani and Amulya Gurtu for editing this book and including worthy authors from industries.

Kishan S. Kardam
Indian Patent Office, Government of India, India

Kishan S. Kardam, *after working for 37 years in the Indian Patent Office at various positions, retired in July 2019 from the post of Senior Joint Controller of Patents & Designs. As the Senior Joint Controller of Patents & Designs, he was the chief at the Delhi Patent Office. He also led the Indian Patent Office at International Searching Authority (ISA) and Indian International Preliminary Examining Authority (IPEA) under the Patent Cooperation Treaty. He has a Master degree in Organic Chemistry from Agra University and a Bachelor's and a Master's Degree in Law from Delhi University. Dr. Kardam's Ph.D. is in Intellectual Property Law from Delhi University. He has published several papers in the various journals on intellectual property. He participated in the revision and amendments to the Patents Act 1970 in the years 1999, 2002, and 2005. He also contributed to creating the Traditional Knowledge Digital Library (TKDL) in India as one of the members of the task force. He designed the structure for electronically capturing the information in the Traditional Knowledge Digital Library (TKDL) and created the Traditional Knowledge Resource Classification (TKRC) to make the TKDL searchable. He conducted a research study in Japan about the utility model and its economic and technological significance to India under WIPO sponsored program. He studied International patent systems such as the United States Patent and Trade Mark Office, European Patent Office, Japan Patent Office, the State Intellectual Property Office of China, German Patent and Trade Mark Office and Intellectual Property Corporation of Malaysia. He delivered several lectures in seminars, workshops, and symposia on Intellectual Property Rights in India and abroad. He was involved in the preparation of Manual of Patent Office Practice and Procedure (MPOPP), Patent Office Practice (POP) for internal working, Examination guidelines for the inventions relating to Biotechnology, Traditional Knowledge, Pharmaceuticals and Computer Related Inventions (CRI).*

Preface

Over recent years, the world has experienced a massive change whereby knowledge has increasingly become one of the most significant aspects of every country's development and success through Intellectual Property Rights (IPR). These rights are the rights that individuals are given to secure socially valuable human intellectual properties or knowledge, as same as privileges that are required in the forms of physical property in order to defend products and services from duplication or copied by others. Notwithstanding recognising the importance of traditional form of innovation and creativity, the subjects of Traditional Knowledge (TK) and Traditional Cultural Expressions (TCEs) have become more crucial areas of research in the development of IPR. About six per cent of the world's population is composed of traditional indigenous people who live in seventy-two nations worldwide. Also, developing countries are the source of 90 per cent of the world's biological resources.

Nonetheless, for abundant purposes, numerous fraudulent entrepreneurs and businesses around the world have taken advantage of and misappropriated their intellectual properties, traditional knowledge, and traditional cultural expressions. Although they are actual owners of this experience, they still have not the chance to leverage their heritage and knowledge. Henceforth TK is urgently needed to be protected and strengthened against debauched snags such as bio-piracy, illegal bio-prospecting and violation of indigenous people's rights which is precisely the theft of natural products (plants, seeds, leaves among other, which are available freely) that people or communities use every day or the use of copying techniques used by pharmaceutical companies, cosmetic and agro-food firms as bio pirates. Such pharmaceutical companies set up their strong precincts and unethically abuse hegemony in order to extract their beneficial properties. This is how the cultural heritage and related information are gained by a third entity against the interest of indigenous persons. Biopiracy poses a severe threat to our ecosystem. The protection of the indigenous people's traditional rights is, therefore, of great importance in ensuring justice. It is only when their TK is protected, they would be able to preserve their heritage and use their skills to propagate the growth of vital areas such as food security and the development of agriculture and medical treatment. In emerging economies like India, South Africa, China, Indonesia, and the Philippines, a rich heritage of biodiversity can be used in order to achieve a higher degree of sustainability. In order to promote sustainable development and the protection of IPR, traditional knowledge must be preserved. Moreover, the substantial scale equity, conservation, preservation of traditional practices and culture, prevention of appropriation by unauthorised parties of components of TK, and promotion of its use and its importance in development also make this subject more enthralling for this research.

As of now, traditional knowledge does not have an internationally accepted definition. Notwithstanding, many countries have adopted sui generis system to preserve the knowledge base that has been rooted in the mainstream cultures for decades through the use of IPRs. There are three areas of TK where this book pacts with and makes the fascinating gesticulation: firstly, technical know-how, skill, practices and innovation relating to biodiversity, agriculture or health; secondly, traditional cultural expressions of folklore (including cultural manifestations such as music, art, designs, symbols and performances); and finally, genetic resources (genetic material of actual or potential value found in plants, animals and micro-organisms). All these fields demand protection through IPR. Therefore, this book addresses some of these challenges and brings forth valuable insights for dealing with them.

Furthermore, this work makes a humble attempt to take a holistic view of this longstanding but unattended problem by taking two subjects together. The one is IPR, and the other one is TK. Also, this book makes a thorough study of different National and International laws, regulations, declarations, treaties and other International Legal Instruments to protect and preserve the same through various authors' contributions. The book includes a discussion on TRIPS and has a few case studies to show the Dispute Settlement Mechanism.

ORGANISATION OF THE BOOK

The book is organised into 11 chapters. A brief description of each chapter is as follows:

Chapter 1, titled "Critical Evaluation of Law on Traditional Knowledge," indicates the significance of TK and analyses laws thereon. The IPR system is inimical to protect TK. The chapter demonstrates that the protection of TK for commercial use without sharing of benefits is appropriate, and it is the violation of the rights of indigenous cultures. It is not fair that TK is patented and used for commercial purposes without sharing its benefits with the indigenous people. The chapter helps to explain that traditional knowledge of medicines from plants and herbs may benefit India in the development of drugs. India also needs legislation on protecting TK. This chapter helps in enacting concrete laws on TK by sharing the position of other countries on this crucial issue. This chapter takes a systematic discussion for developing policies on sharing the benefits of using TK commercially. The chapter shares similar initiatives taken at other places for the protection of TK.

Chapter 2, titled "Access to Medicines in the Light of Patent Law Regime in India: A Legacy of Legislation or Lease of the Judiciary," aims to trace the journey of law relating to patenting of scientific and technical works in India. It has also explored the influence of the international undercurrents, and the judicial response for its development. The patent law in India and the Supreme Court of India have established a patent regime that serves the society. The flexibilities under international intellectual property law agreements were intended to provide affordable healthcare to the people of India. The chapter highlights the significant contributions made by the Indian judiciary for upholding and preserving the rights of the Indian citizens for access to affordable healthcare, which is highly influenced by patents introduced by the Indian legislature in response to international IPR developments.

Chapter 3, titled "Interface Between Right to Education and IPR: Does Copyright Law Inhibit the Enjoyment of Right to Education?" analyses the interpretation and application of the fair use of copyright materials by the Indian judiciary. It is essential because the cost of educational materials is high. The right to education is recognised as a fundamental human right in international and domestic legal regimes. It is considered an integral part of the Right to Life in the Indian Constitution. A landmark judgment, *The Delhi University Copyright Case*, reveals that the Indian judiciary has favoured the right of "users" rather than "copyright holders." Internationally, courts continue to support the "copyright holders" more than the "users." Pro-user movements such as the Creative Commons licensing and other open-access learning tools have ensured access to copyright materials. Open-access learning tools can also receive legislative recognition enabling authors to reach more readers, providing them access to copyright works for educational and training purposes. This chapter also provides a comparison of the interpretation of "fair use" by the judiciary of other countries such as the USA and the UK.

Chapter 4, titled "Arbitration in Patent Disputes: To What Extent Is It Possible," looks at different issues involved in the arbitration of patent disputes and then examines to what extent arbitration in patent disputes can be allowed. Arbitration is a method of alternative dispute resolution wherein parties choose neutral third parties (arbitrators) to resolve their differences. More often than not, commercial and business disputes arising out of contracts are resolved through arbitration. It is a party-driven process where parties choose arbitrators, procedure, and parties decide how the proceedings are to be conducted. Issues related to criminal cases or constitutional questions are not resolved through arbitration except courts having jurisdiction. A patent dispute could be classified as a contractual dispute, as it involves issues of payment, licensing, and public considerations, among others. A patent is a sole right granted to the patent holder against the general public to manufacture and/or sell the invention. Hence, questions involving the validity of patents will inevitably have public consequences, and the decision will impact more people than just the parties to the dispute. Herein lies the problem-whether to permit arbitration of patent disputes or not? It analyses various approaches adopted by some countries; where some countries allow only contractual disputes related to patents (such as payment issues) to be arbitrated, and the validity is decided by courts. Some countries do not allow patent disputes to be arbitrated at all. Some countries allow all aspects of a patent dispute to be referred to arbitration. After examining the issues that might arise in arbitration of patent disputes, this chapter suggests solutions and means through which arbitration in patent disputes can be allowed and manners in which the existing concerns can be taken care.

Chapter 5, titled "Traditional Knowledge and Arbitration Dispute Resolution: In the Context of Indigenous People and Local Communities," challenges in dispute resolution related to traditional knowledge. There is no universal definition of Indigenous People and Local communities, which poses a problem. The term indigenous is used for inheritors and practitioners of unique cultures and ways relating to people and the environment. The requirements of these people are different and somewhat unusual for Intellectual Property Rights. Indigenous people face many difficulties in resolving their issues and accessing the legal system due to a lack of knowledge and financial resources. In some cases, the process of a court does not even resolve the issues involving traditional knowledge, traditional cultural expressions, and genetic resources. Arbitration Dispute Resolution (ADR) is an alternate process of settling a dispute on the ownership of intellectual property rather than using a court for the same. The main methods of ADR are Negotiation, Mediation, and Conciliation. ADR, especially in the form of mediation, is very advantageous in resolving issues on Traditional Knowledge because it recognises the differences in cultural value systems of indigenous people and local communities. Thus, their grievances can be addressed in a sensitive way of providing a neutral procedure. ADR is an effective form of dispute resolution due to the speed of the proceedings, cost, privacy, and the unbiased approach provided to the parties, to name a few. ADR facilitates and encourages the parties to choose their experienced mediators who are neutral and have expertise on the issues. WIPO plays a vital role in providing rules for ADR to indigenous people and local communities. The WIPO Arbitration and Mediation Centre was established in 1994, providing the resolution to private parties regarding international commercial disputes. The one part of this chapter is devoted to WIPO Arbitration and Mediation Centre functioning for addressing the indigenous dispute settlement relating to Traditional Knowledge.

Chapter 6, titled "Challenges Related to Protection of Indigenous Resources Against Biopiracy," talks about the intrusion and unauthorised access to biological resources, traditional knowledge, cultural knowledge, and other indigenous practices. It becomes a significant challenge against integration and combined approach of contemporary and traditional medicine. The purely economic perspective of bioprospecting indeed includes blatant usage of the patent process and other IP frameworks to enhance the practice of biopiracy affecting indigenous and customary rights of indigenous people and the conservation of natural resources. The pioneering commitment of the CBD to the juristic interpretation of genetic & biological resources is the remarkable acknowledgement of the commitments of indigenous societies and local people, especially ladies, to the preservation and genetic development of biological resources. It also promotes regulation and management of access procedures to biological assets to check the unauthorised act in the form of theft. It is necessary to build a strong inter-relationship between biodiversity process and IPR regime, keeping the interest of natural resources and indigenous communities. Indigenous communities usually face a significant challenge in the form of societal alienation, disempowerment and struggle for socio-cultural cognisance of their rights. It is always desirable to have assimilation of their ethnic and customary rights into the legal system. Hence this chapter suggests various remedies such as a systematic protocol for bio-society should be created where indigenous rights for farmers, non-farmers regarding claim and entitlement over biologically enriched natural resources be logically undertaken.

Chapter 7, titled "Biopiracy: Challenges Before India," addresses the challenges of unauthorised use of bio-resources. The events of biopiracy are occurring more frequently than before all over the world. The victims, in most of the cases, are the countries with enormous bio-resources, like India. It is a mere coincidence that the economically weak or emerging countries possessed a significant share of global bio-resources. These countries not only own rich biodiversity but also possess the knowledge regarding the use of these bio-resources. Multinational companies of economically developed countries are siphoning this knowledge base misusing IPR laws to their advantage. Emerging economies, like India, have consolidated their food security with the help of their richness in bio-resources and associated knowledge regarding their use. Biopiracy is pushing these countries towards plausible food insecurity. Global leaders need to address this challenge.

Chapter 8, titled "Protection of Indian Traditional Rice Varieties: Role of PPV and FRA," talks about the protection of agrarian diversity in India. This diversity had been the source for Indian farmer's contribution to its food security by developing new crop varieties or breeds by adopting indigenous or traditional methods. Indian farmers have been sharing their indigenous farming knowledge for centuries. Their approach has played a significant role in conserving, developing resistant varieties, and sharing resources among farming communities. This rich and time-tested knowledge is facing extinction due to the rapid development of non-traditional methods of crop breeding and its adoption by the farming community. The government of India is collecting them from traditional farmers, identifying and authenticating them, and documenting them, under the aegis of "The Protection of Plant Varieties and Farmers' Rights (PPV & FR) Act, 2001." This is being done to conserve the indigenous methods and crop varieties. This chapter identifies the potential Traditional Paddy Varieties (TRVs) of the Cauvery delta region in South India. It subjects them to various tests to establish their homogeneity and credible characterisation, i.e., distinctiveness, uniqueness, stability, uniformity, purity, and adaptability potential. Later the selected crops are registered under the PPV & FR Act. This study has identified around 69 TRVs after rigorous field tests and deposited them in the respiratory maintained by NBPGR. Also, six crop varieties have been registered under the PPV & FR Act on behalf of the farming communities. The methodologies used for this work are scalable to bring more traditional crops under Intellectual Properties laws as a security to protect Indian farmers and their indigenous methods.

Chapter 9, titled "Women Custodians of Tradition," talks about the need to preserve the priceless heritage, glory, and aesthetic wonder of a beautiful traditional art popularly known as Madhubani Paintings exclusively from Mithila. The women of Mithila have acted as the custodians of the tradition of Madhubani paintings. These women portray the history of Mithila in India through paintings. These paintings are the visual expressions of the common folks of the countryside. The region of Mithila has a legacy of rich intellectual and cultural heritage. One of Mithila's traditional and cultural heritage is Madhubani paintings, which are an expression of the traditional knowledge of local women artists presented in a distinct form of arts exclusive to this region. These paintings are celebrations of nature, love, and life illustrated through flowers, trees, fish, and birds, among others. Many features distinguish Madhubani painting from other paintings, such as the use of simple outlines, bright colours, and directness of expressions, proportionate sizes, and designs. Madhubani paintings play an essential role in Mithila's traditions and provide a voice to the creativity of the women artists of this region. Madhubani paintings evoke the interest and appreciation of art connoisseurs, scholars, and tourists from all over the world, thereby creating a niche for itself in the world of art. The uniqueness of this beautiful art form and its association with a region led to receiving its Geographical Identification (GI). This traditional art form needs to be preserved in its authentic, traditional form. The commercialisation and mass production of these paintings has eroded the purity and authenticity of these paintings.

Chapter 10, titled "Intellectual Property Management by Innovative Firms: Evidence From Tunisia," talks about the intertwined nature of innovation and entrepreneurship. Nevertheless, innovation does not always lead to success, and the innovator is not always a good entrepreneur. That being said, a savvy entrepreneur can understand the value of innovation better than those who have truly innovated. It is, therefore, the management of innovation is crucial that provides added value. Management is multi-disciplinary and has invaded many old disciplines which were once in different disciplines. Law is also becoming a managerial tool, specially adapted to innovative companies. Nowadays, we talk about the legal management of an innovative company. In this context, the legal managers must start by preparing the company to support innovation. Optimising the legal choices offered to the company helps to prepare it to better support the innovation by transforming it into wealth. It is, therefore, necessary to make the right choices regarding the legal form of the company, its legal status, tax structure, and social arrangements. A company poorly adapted to innovation can bury the most promising projects. Subsequently, the legal management department has to focus on the innovation itself. Legal protection is part of the company's overall strategy. There are several options: the innovator can patent, register a trademark, a design or a model, bounce back from a patent to a trademark, or simply keep the innovation secret. The choice to be made must respect the eternal quality/price ratio. Better protection allows for better value. An idea can be transformed into money. Innovation is an immaterial and intangible asset which can provide the company with a much higher income than material assets.

Chapter 11, titled "Traditional Knowledge and States' Compliance: The Case Study From New Zealand," talks about the exploitation of indigenous knowledge for economic reasons. The global society has evolved through great wars, misunderstandings, crimes, and reparations. Indigenous people have multi-dimensional rich cultural past and knowledge. This indigenous knowledge is widely exploited for economic reasons. Their claims on the economic value of their Traditional Knowledge (TK) are legitimate and justified. For others to appreciate rightful ownership of the TK, it requires a change in the thinking of world business leaders. The chapter shows how difficult it is for a Western legal system to include and address the interests of minorities that were never included in its initial legal reasoning. The chapter shares that the world intellectual property law regimes still represent an unsuitable avenue to safeguard the TK held by indigenous peoples. Further, it analyses indigenous TK in the context of the world's economy, highlighting the scenario set by the TRIPS Agreement in the global market. The chapter describes the compromises made by developing countries to comply with TRIPS high-minimum standards, and the self-interested demands and political manipulations made by strong economies which moulded TRIPS. The analysis of a very famous New Zealand case shows how countries often use TRIPS as an excuse to avoid any serious and successful protection of indigenous TK nationally and internationally. The Waitangi Tribunal Report on the Wai 262 claim includes examples of discussions, considerations and recommendations about indigenous TK and Bioprospecting and how and why the claim did not succeed in bringing 'effective' measures nationally, or the implementation of new 'sui generis' legal norms for the protection and safeguard of indigenous TK.

This book is an excellent addition to the contemporary challenges in protecting and preserving the knowledge of tradition and culture and sustainable entrepreneurship through the canopy of IPR. It also highlights some of the successful cases across the world in preserving and safeguarding TK. This work is targeted toward graduate students, researchers, and corporate leaders who either appreciate these challenges, want to learn more, or who want to expand their horizons on these challenges. We hope that readers would benefit from the insights of authors from various geographies and continue to grow and share their knowledge in this area.

Nisha Dhanraj Dewani
Guru Gobind Singh Indraprastha University, India

Amulya Gurtu
Austin E. Cofrin School of Business, University of Wisconsin-Green Bay, USA

Acknowledgment

I wish to express my first and special gratitude to Prof. Amulya Gurtu, who joined me as a co-editor and sincerely acknowledge his valuable suggestions and guidance at various stages for completion of this book. The production of this book has been a great team effort. I would like to express my deep appreciation to all of the contributors whose insights, experience, understandings and interpretations are at the core of every chapter in this book. I sincerely thank my doctoral supervisor, Prof. S. Z. Amani, for his guidance and practical advice on the issues of IPR. Also, I would like to express my profound gratitude to Dr. K. S. Kardam, for his insightful observations on the subject of Traditional Knowledge, along with his invaluable support. I wish to thank the following experts who peer-reviewed one or more book chapters: Ms. Carishma Singh (Delhi University), Ms. Aarushi Agarwal (GGSIPU), Dr. Mamta Sharma (Gautam Budhha University). I would also like to thank the administration and editorial support staff of IGI Global that have supported us in getting this book from inception through to the publication. Finally, yet importantly, I thank my family for their patience, love and support for this venture. My special thanks to my-in-laws, parents and of course, my husband, Mr. Sumit Dewani, a source of my strength.

Nisha Dhanraj Dewani

I would like to thank Nisha Dhanraj Dewani for involving me in this project. I learned a lot about the need for protection of traditional knowledge and patent laws. I thank the contributors for helping with multiple reviews of book-chapters and providing constructive feedback to fellow authors. I thank corresponding authors for working as a conduit between the editors and co-authors, working on their chapters, and submitting the revisions in the editorial system. Last but not least, I thank my wife, Neeta Gurtu, for her support in completing this book.

Amulya Gurtu

Chapter 1
Critical Evaluation of Laws on Traditional Knowledge

Unanza Gulzar
The NorthCap University, India

ABSTRACT

People at large do not have the capacity to transform their knowledge into formal specification and consequently into wealth. Some people who are hampered because of their poverty illiteracy, isolative habitat, lack of information and technological gadgets are unable to convert their knowledge into wealth. In this background, the chapter has critically evaluated traditional knowledge in the context of the challenges it faces. Further, it analyses the protection given to traditional knowledge under different laws and its international perspective. Moreover, efforts are taken at both the national and regional levels. Lastly, the chapter has come up with certain suggestions for its improvement and protection.

INTRODUCTION

Most of the people in the world do have the capability to convert their traditional knowledge (TK) into formal arrangements and eventually it into wealth. The reason may be illiteracy, poverty, awareness of technological advancements and handling of gadgets. Some of the cases (Singh, 2008). Some of the cases, though illustrative, are:

- The big business houses, hoteliers, film industries and music tycoon are using cultural expressions of nomadic, tribal and village community.
- The pharmaceutical industry widely uses the rich heritage of TK. TK is used in allopathic and Ayurveda medicine.

DOI: 10.4018/978-1-7998-1835-9.ch001

- Village community, tribal and indigenous people have TK of biodiversity. They are conserving knowledge of biodiversity, which serves the largest genetic resource for breeding activities, but gene giant or seed giant (MNC's) through the IPR regime may make huge profits.

Hence, the research has four objectives:

- To evaluate existing laws on TK.
- To understand the international and regional perspectives on TK.
- To evaluate the challenges to the protection of TK and efforts taken for the protection of the same.
- To suggest measures for the protection and preservation of TK.

TK is defined as "the indigenous people of world possess an immense knowledge for their environment based on centuries of living close to nature "(Mayor, 1994). Living in and from richness and variety of complex ecosystems, they have an understanding of the properties of the plants and animals, the functioning of the ecosystem and the technique of using and managing them that is particular and often detailed.

In rural communities of developing countries, locally occurring species are relied on many sometimes, all foods, medicines, fuels, building materials and other products. The essential attribute of the cultural identity of any place is the knowledge of its people, their understanding of it and relationship with it (Ellen, 2000).

TK has the potential of being transformed into wealth by providing leads/clues for the development of useful practices and processes for the benefit of humanity. The valuable leads/ clues provide by TK can save time, money investment of modern technology and other industries into research and product development (Tripathi, 2003). Existing Intellectual property rights (IPR) system is based on individual private property rights. TK is incompatible with IPR because it emphasises collective creation and ownership. The information is classified into four groups in TK:

- Knowledge possessed by society about TK with or without records and is inconsistent use by people, e.g. everyday use of neem and turmeric.
- Information public holds through texts for use and its examination, e.g. Ayurveda text, the information in the palm leaves.
- Information that is not documented or commonly unknown outside a small group of people and not revealed outside the group, for example, tribal knowledge.

- Information known only to individuals and members of families, e.g. cure of asthma by the Bathini Goud family using a specific fish variety as a means for a dispensing anti-asthma drug.

The knowledge possessed by the public does not satisfy IPR criterion viz. new, non-obvious innovation (Gopalakrishnan, 1998). Thus, the IPR system is inimical to protect TK. The only protection of TK is appropriated for commercial use without the sharing of benefits. It will violate native cultural teachings by strengthening them to commodify same. It is not fair that TK is appropriated for commercial use without the sharing of benefits. The defence of TK will prove beneficial in pleading fake claims on intellectual property. TK base of plant-based medicine may enable India to accelerate drug development.

PROTECTION OF TRADITIONAL KNOWLEDGE AT NATIONAL LEVEL

Indian NGO's Effort

The Society for Research and Initiatives for Sustainable Technologies and Institutions (SRISTI), Ahmedabad has been for several years developing databases of TK and innovation in close collaboration with local community members. A global registration system is proposed so that individual and collective innovators can receive acknowledged and rewards for commercial application of their knowledge and practices. With a view to achieving the following objectives, People Biodiversity Register has been recommended for:

- To provide a record of local knowledge for the use of present and future generations of village community people.
- To promote the revitalising of the local community by
    - rewarding outstanding knowledge, skills, techniques and conservation practices.
    - recognising the range of such knowledge.
    - validating and promoting sound local knowledge and resource management traditions.
    - promoting inter-community transfer knowledge for capacity enhancement.
- To alert conservationists about the need for action concerning threatened resources and the need for protection of local resources rights.

- To protect local biodiversity and knowledge from misappropriation by companies such as through patenting of modified products, process and biological resources. The first people's biodiversity register was prepared and released in 1997. According to the proposal, this register should be kept at panchayat.

Governmental Efforts

The government of India has prepared TK in the digital library on Traditional medicinal plants and systems, which will also lead to TK resource classification. The Important Characteristics of this library are-

1. It records approximately 35,000 Ayurvedic medicinal formulations based on TK.
2. The details of formulations include descriptions, methods of preparation and claim, the botanical name of plant and disease, which can be cured.
3. Sanskrit text of formulations is translated in many foreign languages.
4. This will be available to almost all patent offices over the world to search and examine any prevalent use and prior art. This will help in preventing bio-piracy.
5. This will eliminate the problem of the grant of wrong patents since its knowledge is available to the patent examiner.

Apart from above the Regional Tribal Research Centres and Indian Council of Agricultural Research is also working very hard in documenting TK. In many universities and research institutions eth-no-botanical researchers have been carried out. It will be a useful document for protecting TK. These researches should be compiled and documented (Antons, 2009).

Jawaharlal Nehru Tropical Botanic Garden & Research Institute (TBGRI) Palode, Thiruvananthapuram, set an example to demonstrate respect for TK. TBGRI has entered into an agreement with a local Kani tribe to share the benefit of new herbal medicine (Jeevani). Scientists have learnt the properties of a plant "Trichopus Zeylanicus" for its health benefits from the member of the tribal Kani, who inhabit the forested western ghat region of the state. The TBGRI agreed to give initial fees and regular royalties.

LEGISLATIVE INITIATIVES FOR THE PROTECTION OF TRADITIONAL KNOWLEDGE IN INDIA

Patent Law

Patent Amendment, 2002 reflects concerns for TK. The following provisions are supportive of the protection of TK:

1. Innovations based on TK or aggregation or duplication of known properties of TK is not patentable.
2. Patent applicants must disclose the source and the geographical origin of biological material used in an invention.
3. Failure to disclose the source and geographical origin of biological material used in the invention would be good ground for opposing the patent application.

Biodiversity Legislation

The main objective of biodiversity legislation is to provide for the conservation of biological diversity, sustainable use of its component and equitable sharing of the benefits arising out of the use of biological resources and for matters connected in addition to that or incidental to it. National Biodiversity Authority (NBA) is constituted. It is empowered to check bio-piracy and to regulate transfer the result of any research.

Section 4 of the Act provides "no person shall without previous approval of the NBA transfer the results of any research relating to any biological resources occurring or obtained from India for monetary consideration or otherwise to any person who is not a citizen of India or body corporate or organisation which is not registered or incorporated in India or which has any non-Indian Participation in its share capital or management." Section 6 of the Act provides that no person shall apply for any IPR by whatever name called in or outside India for any invention based on any research or information on a biological resource obtained from India without previous approval of the NBA. The NBA, while approving may impose benefit sharing fees or royalty. The NBA has been given the power to oppose the grant of IPR in any country outside India on any Biological resources derived from India.

This Act seeks to constitute State Board Biodiversity to promote and protect biodiversity as "No Indian citizen or person, or body corporate is allowed to obtain biological resource for commercial utilisation without obtaining prior intimation of State Biodiversity Board" (SBB). However, this recognises TK of the local people and communities, including Vaids and Hakims practising indigenous medicine. They are kept out of intimation restrictions. The Act also provides a post-intimation strategy. The SBB is empowered to prohibit and restrict if it is of the opinion that such activity is detrimental or contrary to the objectives of conservation and sustainable use of biodiversity.

Instead of sending a notice, there should have a prior approval arrangement. The time gap between intimation and post intimation enquiry may be wide enough. The large number of bio-diversities will be easily removed if the time gap between intimation and prohibition order is wide.

Protection of Plant Variety and Farmers Right Act`

This is sui generis law with respect to plant variety and farmers' rights. The breeding activities move around genetic resources. The Act covers the interplay of breeding, genetic resources and TK. The Act has the following provisions for recognising TK.

1. "The Act recognises the concept of benefit-sharing between provider and recipient of the plant genetic resources."
2. "An applicant seeking registration of variety must disclose Geographical location from where genetic material has been taken while evolving new variety."
3. "If the applicant fails to disclose the contribution of the farming community and the source of genetic resources, his registration will be cancelled."

The Indian TK (Preservation and Protection) Bill, 2000 has been drafted by N.S. Gopal Krishnan "School of Legal studies, Cochin, University of Science and Technology" (Sachin, 2000).

The Features of the bill are as under:

1. Definition of TK existing known and used by the members of the Indian society from generation to generation, excluding knowledge used in secret by individuals and groups.
2. "The formation of a community TK trust, which will have the exclusive right to manage TK of the community."
3. "Commercial exploitation of TK trust by persons outside the community, whether in collaboration with members of the community or not, shall be with the prior informed consent of the committee."
4. The civil remedies such as injunctions, damages and accounts of profits. The Bill also provides for a maximum imprisonment of three years with a maximum fine of 0.2 million INR.

"The Geographical Indications of Goods (Registration and Protection) Act, 1999"

The Act was established to secure the precious geographical indications of the country. It is applicable to the agricultural, natural, handicraft goods, industrial goods and manufactured goods. In a certain manner, this Act provides security to the goods of a particular region or locality with reference to special characteristics, reputation, process and method of production and quality. Geographical Indications helps to identify the geographical location of the stuff. The authorised users and the geographical indications registered under this Act are entitled to get protection under this Act.

This Act can become one of the effective ways to secure TK if the statutory conditions are satisfied. In this manner, it would prevent misuse of the geographical indication. Although this Act is not that old, it has registered many TK acting as the geographical indications under the Act.

The Scheduled Tribes and Other Traditional Forest Dwellers (Recognition of Forests Rights) Act, 2006

In India during the pre and post-independence, the forest-dwelling tribes were there. They owned ancestral lands and their habitats, but their rights were not correctly identified. This resulted in injustice with them and also with other forest dwellers who have been a fundamental part and responsible for the continuous and correct usage of the forest ecosystem.

When Indian Government recognised that there is a need for a legislation to address the rights of forest dwellers then they came up with The Scheduled Tribes and other Traditional Forest Dwellers (Recognition of Forests Rights) Act, 2006 recognises the rights of the forests, the rights of forest-dwelling scheduled tribes and the rights of other traditional forest dwellers. These dwellers have been residing on the forest land from generations. The Act provides a structure for documenting forest rights so conferred along with the pieces of evidence needed for the identification. The Act provides that the rights which have been recognised for the forest-dwelling tribes and further international forest dwellers comprise the authority and responsibilities for sustainable usage, maintenance and preservation of biodiversity to make a balance ecologically to strengthen the conservation activities of forests by making sure that it is in benefit for the livelihood and food security of the forest dwellers.

This Act has an authority in the hands of Gram Sabha to initiate the process for determining the nature and the extent of the rights. The consolidation and verification of the rights are determined by Village Committee (commonly called in India Gram Sabha). Under this Act, the sub-divisional and district level committees have also been established to resolve the matters and to seek a solution to the petitions. The State level Monitoring Committees have the function to scan the way of identification of the rights and conferring the rights and to comply with respective agencies.

Analysis of Constitutional Provisions Relating to Traditional Knowledge

To safeguard the TK and the rights of the local people and groups, there is no specific provision under the Constitution of India. The minorities are protected under Part III of the constitution, which states the fundamental rights. Later, Article 371 read with schedule 6 states the special protection for people who belong to the tribal areas. Other than India, the government of the respective country has the authority to establish planned areas for the protection of tribal communities. Therefore the Constitution of India not directly but indirectly recognises the indigenous people's rights regarding their cultural knowledge.

CONTEMPORARY BILLS PENDING ON TK

Human Genome Regulatory Bill, 2009

India has a rich multicultural background and with great genetic diversity. Jarawa's and Onges from Andaman have been entitled with the longest unbroken chains of genetic heritage across the globe. The genetic material is an essential element that is important for our immune structure. The investigators have established that in some Indian tribes, the cardiovascular and diabetic problems are absent. Thus many international industries want to do research work on Indian genes (Indian Council of Medical Research, 2009). Many incidents have been occurred until now where outside or other country's researchers have used Indian genes in their agricultural industries and pharmacy.

The Bill has been planned because the guidelines given by the Indian Council of Medical Research of biotechnology are often not followed. The Bill focuses mainly on documenting human genetic samples and controlling access for the purpose of research. To make sure that the profits made out of the research are shared with the community that allows to access the information and lending the sample. Another benefit from this Bill is to preserve the samples and allow the affiliated hospitals and laboratories under this programme to use samples for research. Currently, there is an absence of any legislation that regulates the export of samples of plants and animals genes for research. The proposed Bill will act as a bank of samples of genes which will probably fill up the space of empty legislation and prevent misappropriation of genetic resources.

Traditional Knowledge Bill, 2009

The Bill here was the result of a round table conference on Protection of Traditional Knowledge at National Law School of India University, Bangalore. The focus of the Bill is to provide protection and proper management of Traditional Knowledge (Traditional Cultural expression, 2002). The bill also aims at protecting the strength of togetherness against the misuse or the exploitation of Traditional Knowledge (WIPO report, 2009). The bill comprising of nine chapters focuses on creating a safeguard mechanism. The features of the Act are:

- It tries to define the word TK.
- Recognition of the origin and documenting TK.
- Establishes the concept of prior informed consent.
- Restriction on the exploitation of TK.
- Creating a TK Board.
- Establishing an appellate mechanism.

The Biotechnology Regulatory Authority of India Bill, 2013

The Biotechnology Regulatory Authority of India Bill, 2013 focuses on the establishment of a National Biotechnology Regulatory Authority of India which regulates and supervises the Research, importation, production and the utilisation of products belonging to modern biotechnology. The focus is on the questions relating to the impression of biotechnology and its impact on agriculture by genetically altered organisms, health, production, food, climate change, sustainable development and protection of the environment (prsindia, 2013). The Bill tries to create a bond between biotechnological activities and ecological values. The Bill does not directly deal with the matter of TK but indirectly secures the natural resources of local people. It will make sure that the environment does not get affected by the activities which are connected to biotechnology and genetically altered micro-organism.

People Biodiversity Register

India had come up with People's Biodiversity Registers. The registers comprise of the data and information of the knowledge of the people about biodiversity, trade, use and efforts for the sustainable utilisation along with the conservation. They are set up at village levels by the local teachers of schools and colleges, students or Non-

Governmental Organisations researchers and by the villagers also (NBA India, 2013). These registers are later converted into computerised data at the level of talukas, districts, states and the entire country. This helps in providing data and information to the Government, industries and public. The registers have got recognition by the Indian Biological Diversity Act to perform prior art for the evaluation of patent applications along with ensuring equitable benefit sharing.

Intellectual Property Rights Policy for Kerala, 2008

Kerala came up with an Intellectual Property Rights Policy in 2008 for the conservation and safety of TK specifically. It goals at securing the wealthy foundation of Ayurveda and other natural drug originated from Kerala (WIPO, 2008). The policy classifies two types of TK:

1. The knowledge that has been protected by specific communities, majorly the tribal people and communities or specific families or institutions situated in particular areas and has transferred from many generations in a variety of traditional methods.
2. Any kind of knowledge which is responsible for the living of many people all over the state that does not belong to any special community or family.

The policy states that the owners of TK under the first classification of TK will be in the hands of TK under a single authorisation. Through this license holder of the right gives permission to others to use their heritage over which the right is given for non-business purposes. Under the heading of the second category, Kerala is supposed to carry the rights over the prestigious knowledge. Nobody will have any rights over TK if they are registered as medium or large enterprises. The second category provides two kinds of rights to its holders:

(i) The right to a brand name or a name associated with the unique practice of a community, institution or family.
(ii) Right to use the knowledge

No one can use TK other than the right bearer cannot use knowledge without the authorisation. Further use of TK violating the law of common license inside or outside the state is said to be the breach of the rights of the owner of the TK that will ultimately introduce to legal proceedings. Kerala TK Academy has been set for registration of the original TK. TK owners have to prove the authenticity of TK. They need to disclose all the important information about the nature of the family or group which is involved and know the knowledge that will make them the custodian of the practice (Jha, 2011).

Kerala has become the first state of India, which has an intellectual property policy. But the policy does not have the status of a legally recognised document. Therefore, the policy needs to be converted into a legal instrument.

Innovation Patent and Registration

The process includes developing a path for registration for novel and useful experiments and products invented by inventors for a specific period. It is given to the inventor so that it can help the inventor in case there is any use of the innovation without the prior permission of the rights holder. India has taken limited efforts in this context. One of the examples is the Honey Bee (National Agricultural Library, 2013). It is an advantage for getting the innovations registered by respective inventors. The system can be used to add information about innovations and to share benefit with the actual knowledge owners. This arrangement provides documenting, experimenting and disseminating of native knowledge. For innovators at a lower level this network can be considered as the largest database all over the world (Sengupta, 2019).

All the discussions stated that India had initiated some steps for the protection of TK through various legislations, bills and policies. However, there is still a need for comprehensive legislation and a mechanism to strengthen the roots of TK. This will empower the indigenous community and people to stand for their rights.

CHALLENGES FOR THE PROTECTION OF TK

Lack of Definition

There have been a lot of attempts to define the term TK. However, these definitions are just illustrations because none of them has been accepted universally. In all these attempts, there are few efforts to recognise indigenous communities' rights on their native knowledge; still, there is no extent of rights. So, the first problem which needs to be resolved is to develop a universally recognised definition of TK. TK is something which is multi-dimensional and includes various definitional aspects. So, it is not possible to bring a single definition of TK.

Subject Matter

The subject matter of TK is mainly variable and dynamic and designed by native and traditional factors than other forms of intellectual property. The first challenge which is faced in the matter of TK is that it is not clear anywhere that what exactly can be written under the category of TK. We do talk about protecting TK, but it is essential to know the subject matter that belongs to TK. The meaning of subject matter includes (a) creation of an acceptable and clear definition of the TK (b) putting together the inclusions of the rights in a correct method and which suits the domestic needs and demands of the State.

A number of standing definitions of TK states various features of the world of TK, which are connected at the same time different in nature. The Convention on Biological Diversity has comprised of Article 8(j) which legislation, respect, preserve and maintain knowledge of the local people. It gives a wider application option and makes it flexible for the parties to place their directives into action. Hence this broad inclusion in the definition of TK does not make a functional method. It will be right if the parties define the TK according to the national and domestic aspects following the spirit of the Convention on Biological Diversity (Robinson, 2017).

Since we have a wide variety in the subject matters which need protection, therefore a single method to protect them may not work. In the wide variety of TK, every kind of TK demands a special treatment. As many components of TK and practices connect to commercial use and exposure may also need some protection from the intellectual property side. On the same note, the knowledge and practices which relate to biodiversity conservation and management need a specific approach in regard to protection.

Similarly, TK related to farming communities, medicinal communities and various other forms of practices may vary in the kind of protection they require. The distinct methodology may be taken in to safeguard and safeguard TK under Intellectual Property Rights, along with the sui generis system or a mixture of both. Acknowledgement of some types of proprietorship of TK can also be achieved through the enforcement of customary laws (Gordon, 2012).

Identification of the Benefit Holders

Collective Rights

One of the important challenges that need to resolve is to entitle the correct person as the beneficiary. As TK is the knowledge that belongs to a particular community or the indigenous community of the region, it becomes very difficult to make one person as the beneficiary of the TK. These rights are held collectively by the group of people which generally belongs to economically backward classes and educationally weaker sections. So these people don't have enough courage or knowledge to come in the front and stand to seek protection for their knowledge. They don't know about the rights they are entitled to. The native people have a lot of connectivity among themselves. So they don't approach for individual rights, they want to secure the rights as a whole community. Every state should try to describe the rights as elaborately as possible so that the indigenous people can be described as the beneficiaries.

Mixed up Communities

Broadly, TK includes knowledge related to science, medicine, and agriculture, ecological and other knowledge related to biodiversity. In India and many other nations, natural medicines have always been preferred in case of curing any disease. Earlier this knowledge was known to specific people, and they used to be considered a master in it. With the evolution of time, all the communities have mixed up and there is no specific community or group of people assigned with a particular work. Now anyone can do any job according to their needs and interests. So this is also another reason by which it becomes difficult to find out the real community or people who have actually gained that knowledge from their forefathers.

Absence of Law

The issue which needs to be looked into is the implementation and enforcement of a specific Law. There is no agreement or legislation among the international community related to the implementation mechanism that can aid to apply sui generis rights.

Intellectual Property Rights

Many nations preserve and provide security to their TK through the Intellectual Property Rights system, which actually does not include TK. It is because it fails to fulfil the requisites of novelty, single owner etc. so there are problems to secure indigenous knowledge under the intellectual property system. Issues of protection under the Intellectual Property mechanism is that indigenous knowledge is not new, and it is known to the people in their local area and has been carried from many generations. Therefore, it moves out from the ambit of novelty which is one of the essential elements to protect under the intellectual property regime.

Another issue is that TK is not assigned to any one individual or any one institution. So, when a group approaches under Intellectual Property Rights for protection, they need to clarify the identity of each and every individual of the group, which is not possible in case of TK. In the case of music and folk dances kind of TK, one may be able to get protection under intellectual property regime whereas it is different in case of medicine, food and other kinds of bio agricultural knowledge.

Access and Benefit Sharing

The current laws in the practice to protect TK do not facilitate proper security to the farmers or breeders of TK. They have only been developed a bit by assigning them the right to get compensated as the indirect acknowledgement of their involvement in this research and expansion. Section 26 and 41 of the Protection of Plant Varieties and Farmer's Rights Act, 2001 states the Determination of Benefit-sharing and compensation, respectively. Gopalakrishnan considers that these sections overlap each other, which results in economic stress on the breeder states. The breeder while using TK is entitled to pay more than once.

Benefit Sharing Agreements

Various pharmaceutical companies use TK and medicinal plants as the base of their products. It is observed that the people who have gained knowledge from generations are not very rich people. Whereas, in many cases, it has been reported that people who take away the information for bioprospecting do not provide any kind of share to the TK holders. However, in contrast, the developing nations, the native place of the knowledge and the biogenetic resources have to capture in heavy price legal fights to grasp their rights over the TK which they own (Manupatra, 2019). For example, in the case of neem and turmeric related patents issued by the USA, India had to spend millions of dollars.

Benefit Sharing is an innovative protocol which has been recently established because there have been changing prototype concerning claims over TK and biogenetic resources. Benefit-sharing is an indirect mechanism through which the holders of TK can settle down when their knowledge becomes the essential base of the product protected under Intellectual Property Rights law. It is a way of compensation which has been introduced as a method to have an indirect control that provides access to knowledge. It stands on the compensatory obligation methodology, which targets providing for a certain form of appropriate compensation for the use of knowledge.

There is also the opposite side of the whole scenario. Presently, in the era of biotechnology, it would be widely unreasonable to prohibit inventions based on TK. However, the village communities should also be given the right to own their TK, which they have well-preserved from years. So, in the present agenda of intellectual property, that does not give any security to farmers, breeders, or TK holders, there must be a mechanism to compensate and to give at least acknowledgement of their participation to progress in the technological field and contribute in new lines of investment (Parkes, 2000).

On the basis of the above discussion, it would be sagacious and most effective, than to litigate, to develop legal structures for protection and recognition of TK containing guidelines for benefit sharing. Accordingly, in addition to the conclusion of the Convention on Biological Diversity and the World Summit on Sustainable Development arose plan (2002), the numerous techniques of benefit sharing are the major attention of international discussions associated with TK. The principle of benefit-sharing states that there should be just and reasonable benefit sharing with the TK holders, which arises from the usage of TK.

Overall benefit-sharing is a method which is nice for developed and developing nations. Kani- TBGRI Kerala Model Act as a very nice model for benefit sharing, which in fact shared the benefits with the tribal people for helping in bioprospecting. Therefore, what happened was there was an unintended discovery made by the scientists of Tropical Botanical Garden and Research Institute during the Ethnomedico-Botanical investigation to the Agastya valley areas of Trivandrum, Kerala, India. The plant Trichopus zeylanicus, also known as Arogyaoacha, was at a massive scale in that area. It has the anti-fatigue and restorative properties into it. The unique property which was discovered was based on the revelations provided by the people of the Kani tribe accompanied by porters and guides. Kanis is the local community, which was an earlier nomadic community, but most of them are stable now.

The unripe fruits of Arogypacha are consumed fresh to stay healthy and able to move quickly during the long trekking trips by Kani tribespeople. So while screening of Arogyapacha, it was found that it has properties related to anti-fatigue, anti-gastric ulcer, anti-tumour, anti-allergic, anti-stress, anti-oxidant, immune-modulatory and aphrodisiac. The researches ended in bioprospecting and developing a new drug known as Jeevani. Out of four patent applications, two were granted. The Government discussed for benefit sharing. After discussions and consultations with the involved parties, the know-how for the production of the drug Jeevani has been provided through a manufacturing license to the Arya Vaidya Pharmacy, for a fee of Rs.10 lakhs for a period of 7 years with 2.0% royalty at ex-factory sales price. Norms of the Council for Scientific and Industrial Research were accepted for the transfer of technology in Nov 1995. According to this arrangement, Tropical Botanical Garden and Research Institute had agreed to share half of the licence fee, and royalty with Kani tribes which allowed them to utilise the original content for the making of the Jeevani. Later Kani tribe made registered a trust called 'Kerala Kani Samudaya Kshema Trust', under the supervision of Tropical Botanical Garden and Research Institute and the benefits received by the technology assignment and royalty were remitted to the Trust's account. After, in discourse with the Institute, the executive committee finalised three Kani tribes who will provide the data about Arogyapacha. This Tropical Botanical Garden and Research Institute were awarded the UN Equator Initiative Award in 2002.

According to the Convention on Biological Diversity, benefit-sharing must be equitable and fair. It defines benefit-sharing as just allocation of the benefits which are gained through the use of genetic resources, including proper access to genetic resources and through proper transfer of material technologies, making into the thought that all rights over the resources and technologies are by suitable funding. As benefit sharing principle seems clear, it is that difficult in the implementation. Benefit-sharing has developed in different ways in various countries. Till now also very few benefits sharing have been successfully claimed by the countries against their genetic resources and TK. In the wide-ranging acceptance of the benefit-sharing which now is accepted at the International level, the major debate which is left out is what is known as exact benefit-sharing, or under what situations the benefits should be shared and in which filed they should be taken place (Rosendal, 2000).

One of the biggest difficulties faced is to adapt benefit-sharing at the national level exclusively. This is because the nations of the source are not in such a situation where they can execute extra-territorial actions on user countries. So, an actual way of benefit sharing for transboundary dealings must comprise of legal framework or must be synchronised among all nations. Nations of the source can take steps at the point of access to the resources, but it is most difficult to judge that what exactly be considered as the use of the capitals and what benefits finally be obtained. Also, when an approximation is made, if there is no arrangement made for the benefit sharing condition of commercialisation of products, it will ultimately become hard to imply benefit-sharing (Sreedharan, 2004).

Access to Traditional Knowledge

Access to TK means the conditions through which the users would get the resources they need. Access here means access across different borders. Access includes revealing all the information related to the origin of the knowledge and benefit-sharing. A highly controlled access regime should be provided to the TK holders to contribute a better way of protection to TK. Somehow it may disappoint many bio-prospectors. A method involving a balance between the right holders and the bio-prospectors should be there. So that it leads to a potential increase in overall economic gain and does not lead to the reduction of control of the TK holders.

According to article 15.7 of the Convention on Biological Diversity, the benefit earned from the results of the research and development have to be shared in a fair and equitable manner with the country allowing them to access the resources. Its concept of benefit-sharing is what is considered fair and equitable. These terms that are kept before while sharing the resources should be kept mutually. But in case of any dispute, there is no International Arbitration established to solve the dispute (Rosendal, 2000).

Prior Informed Consent

Prior informed consent enables the state to set up the conditions through which access is to be granted. Nations such as India that is rich in biological resources and TK, prior informed consent is the method to control the use of their resources and knowledge. Article 15(5) of the Convention on Biological Diversity, 1992 says that to access any genetic resources there is need to take prior informed consent and under Article 15(7) there is a need to enact legislation and set up an administrative body to keep a check on the fair benefit-sharing system. In India under The Biological Diversity Act, 2002, the national and state authorities have the right to make decisions related to access to resources. For prior informed consent, India has a Biodiversity Management Committees who plays the advisory role to determine access to biological resources.

In India, it can be observed that there is an absence of proper mechanism or prevalent initiatives that are required while taking prior consent of the indigenous knowledge. Most of the time, knowledge is unknown from our own system. Due to which many foreigners take unwanted advantage of it. Therefore, there is a need for documentation of the knowledge present in the country. And after the registration of TK, there is a need to create a contract that provides all the terms and conditions while disclosing knowledge to someone else. This will ultimately prevent bio-piracy and misappropriation to some extent.

Non-Monetary Benefits

It is one of the important issues which states about the benefits which are other than monetary in nature. It is not important that the benefits shared should be in the form of money only. It can even be allotted in the form of "kind". Kind includes:

1. Technology transfer
2. To participate in sample collection
3. To participate in bioprospecting in all stages
4. Employment opportunities for locals.
5. Improvement of the infrastructure
6. Creating genuine funding schemes

The problem which arises in the matters of non-monetary benefits is the lack of knowledge and education. People here are still not that educated that they can understand the complicated legal language. Sometimes it becomes an advantageous point for some people who fraudulently states providing non-monetary benefits to the knowledge holder and actually gives nothing in return (Secretariat of CBD, 2001).

There is a need to create awareness among the people and to provide free legal aid to such circumstances so that the knowledge holders can well understand the clauses under the agreement and can give consent where the deal falls into their favour.

ISSUES UNDER A SUI GENERIS SYSTEM

TK is part of heritage and culture. It is an essential share of the native communities' lifestyle diligently connected with their land, culture and economic and socio-political systems. The major issue related to this matter is that the protection of the communities originally means the protection of their lifestyle and cultures and not just protecting the TK (WTO, 2009).

The next issue which may occur is deciding the incentives. Many people carry their TK as a sacred value and will not share it for the sake of money. They actually just want to preserve their knowledge from being robed. The knowledge holder should be rewarded for taking care of the knowledge along with sharing the idea. Such people should be encouraged more to continue the preservation of TK. Sui generis system has another issue to examine and decide what needs to be protected and what not. It is to be determined that in which form the protection should be done. The system has a financial plunge that would point at securing the knowledge contrary to unauthorised use and preserving it from further diffusion. Hence these are some issues which are needed to be recognised and addressed properly at the international level.

The importance of securing and prevent TK from being misused was first recognised in the Convention on Biological Diversity in 1992 at the International level. Later it was also realised that Convention was not able to secure TK properly. Convention proved to be a failure in including TK into Trade-Related to Intellectual Property Rights Agreement. Next in Doha round in 2001, through World Trade Organisation a review was ordered to reconsider the link between Trade-Related to Intellectual Property Rights and Convention on Biological Diversity to understand the way to protect TK.

As it is not possible to secure TK into the Intellectual Property Rights system, it is necessary to come up with a specific law that will be designed specially according to the needs of TK. To achieve bigger aims to uplift the position of local and native people and communities, there is a requirement of a well-structured implemented plan that does not mix up with the other property rights. Even after many exemplary cases set out in the past in which foreign countries have tried to capture the TK of our country, the nation's government has not even tried to create a policy that especially looks after TK.

Until unless we don't have any law at the national level, we cannot expect something to happen at an international level. If all the nations come up with their own set of rules and regulations in their own respective countries. This will lead to the creation of a mechanism at an International level too. Even after having its own laws of the countries, the International level legislation can be expected in some kind of standard clauses which can be easily undertaken by all the nations.

In conclusion, there is no International System until now, which has planned and applied in favour of preserving the rich heritage knowledge (Malhan, 2001).

TRADE RELATED INTELLECTUAL PROPERTY RIGHTS (TRIPS)

TRIPS has failed to strengthen the aims of the Convention on Biological Diversity. Because of the presence of Intellectual Property Rights under TRIPS, it totally out skirted TK and the offerings shared by the indigenous people through their TK. The initiation taken up by the various countries, according to the TRIPS directs to have a second glance at the laws of their nations on intellectual property, so to carry them in one line with their commitment under the TRIPS agreement which is actually increasing the misappropriations and bio-piracy activities. The gap in the TRIPS, now allows the patent system, which is thought to give back in-genuine creativity or invention, to properly avoid piracy leads contrasting to it. If the patent system is not applicable to TK, then there is a need for the revision of TRIPS.

REGIONAL INITIATIVES

Ardean Community Common system on Access to Genetic Resources

This is adopted by Ardean community member countries. This system recognises the historical contribution to bio-diversity, its conservation by the traditional community. This system has introduced the concept of "intangible component" which means and knowledge, innovation or practice of an individual or collective of actual or potential value associated with genetic resources or derivative whether or not it is protected by the IPR system (Dutfield, 1999).

An agreement between Aguarunas "people of Peru and Searle demonstrates a case of TK." the Aguarunas and their know-how agreement with Searle show how TK is respected through the non-IPR system. In Peru, the Aguruna people have negotiated, a know-how license with Searle. The Agurunas agreed to pass on medicinal plants and knowledge to the company in exchange for a know-how license fee (Dutfield, 2000).

This fee will increase to reflect success in research and development even before a product reaches the market. This license is non-exclusive in that it does not affect the right of any Aguarunas communities to use share or sell or otherwise transfer plants or knowledge, whether or not they are parties to an agreement. A trust fund is created with Aguraunas people, including representatives of both participating and non-participating communities. Legal ownership of biological resources is not a pre-condition for communities to benefit.

Costa Rica Biodiversity Law

The objective of the law, among others is the protection of scientific and TK of biodiversity and awareness of the public. The law protects every kind of information that are equally entitled to claim protection. It is an obligation on NSO (National Seed Office) and IP registers to consult the NBM Commission to assure that innovations should not fall within the purview of intellectual property. Also, the native people have the right to refuse to share their resources or other knowledge connected to it.

African Unity Draft Legislations

Article 5 of the draft model exclusively deals with local communities. It provides that local communities are recognised as lawful and sole custodians of the relevant knowledge, innovations and practices. And the state is required to recognise and protect the rights of local communities to collectively benefit from their knowledge, innovations and practices and to receive compensation for the conservation of biological as well as genetic resources (The Hindu, 2003). The communities have given to veto access to their knowledge, technology and sources.

The United Nations Declaration on the Rights of Indigenous Peoples (UNDRIP) is an international instrument adopted by the United Nations on September 13, 2007, to enshrine (according to Article 43) the rights that "constitute the minimum standards for the survival, dignity and well-being of the indigenous peoples of the world." The UNDRIP protects collective rights that may not be addressed in other human rights charters that emphasise individual rights, and it also safeguards the individual rights of Indigenous people. In the four years since the World Conference on Indigenous Peoples, there have been several positive developments by the Member States, largely in the African and Latin American regions, to fulfil commitments made in the event's outcome document. Also, it is well-known that when the United Nations Declaration on the Rights of Indigenous Peoples (UNDRIP) was being voted on in the United Nations General Assembly in 2007, only four states voted against it: the infamous CANZUS countries (Canada, Australia, New Zealand, and the United States). They have all since changed their position and shown varying degrees of support for the UNDRIP and what it contains. The expected result of the project would be improved capacity among local and national government officials in the four participating countries to develop and/or implement policies, plans of action or strategies, in close consultation and collaboration with indigenous peoples, their representative institutions and other relevant stakeholders, to advance inclusive development in the framework of the UNDRIP (UNDRIP report, 2019).

Also, the Nine Tribes of Mataatua in the Bay of Plenty Region of Aotearoa New Zealand convened the First International Conference on the Cultural and Intellectual Property Rights of Indigenous Peoples (12-18 June 1993, Whakatane). The Conference met over six days to consider a range of significant issues, including; the value of indigenous knowledge, biodiversity and biotechnology, customary environmental management, arts, music, language and other physical and spiritual-cultural forms. On the final day, the following Declaration was passed by the Plenary. The member states of United Nations affirm that the knowledge of the Indigenous Peoples of the world is of benefit to all humanity; Recognise that Indigenous Peoples are capable of managing their TK themselves, but are willing to offer it to all humanity provided their fundamental rights to define and control this knowledge are protected by the international community; Insist that the first beneficiaries of indigenous knowledge (cultural and intellectual property rights) must be the direct indigenous descendants of such knowledge; Declare that all forms of discrimination and exploitation of indigenous peoples, indigenous knowledge and indigenous cultural and intellectual property rights must cease. (The Mataatua Declaration, 1993).

Lack of International Cooperation

Protecting TK cannot be gained solely on the municipal laws or the law of the country. The issue of protection is actually at the global level and that requires a solution by an international association. The convention on biological diversity also needs international exposure and cooperation, which will provide aid in the protection of the resources and identifying the agreements for the proper utilisation of resources. There is a vacant space which is needed to be filled by developing the nations untidily in one direction. These nations have to build up a united community that will set down patent or form of Intellectual Property Rights on the inventions based upon TK. The nations should make sure that they provide unique identification to the TK and should always conduct "prior art" before committing any invention.

Even after facing many cases related to bio-piracy of TK, the government has neither made any policy nor implemented it. Hence it is necessary to recognise and protect TK lawfully. India is a hub of this kind of knowledge. It is high time that

India should set up national-level protection reaching straight to the basic grounds of the local communities.

Non- stability among Conflicting Notions

The acknowledgement of the rights of the native people over their native knowledge, practices and innovations related to genetic and biological resources under Article 8(j) of the Convention on Biological Diversity has been understood as a way of breaking turning point in international law. The continuous arguments over the existing questions state various degrees of interest associated with protecting TK. The main issue lies in the query of how to bring together the tough, unconventional patenting system of the grown world with the community-owned knowledge systems of developing and developed nations. On the international level, there is a great influence from North and West in contradiction of any optimistic security of TK (Bubela, 2012).

At the national level, it can be seen that in countries that are rich in greens, they comprise a long term interest in procuring and protect biogenetic resources. The nations which own the biogenetic resources and TK should use their shared concern to build up the laws at national levels. The laws will govern the use of TK and will allow equitable benefit sharing. In contrast, it is seen that the countries have diverse and different opinions in regard to the protection and conservation mechanism. There are differences even in the terms and conditions in the benefit-sharing agreement. It is, therefore, leading to parted ways in establishing successful legislation. At the level of the local communities the interest of indigenous people has to be a part of any kind of legal framework and make sure that the use, exchange and benefit-sharing should uphold their habitual laws and foundations.

One section that fuses among all the levels is scientific research in the biotechnology industry that chiefly relies on access to biogenetic resources in the territories which is exclusively owned by ancestors and later taken further by the local community. Another ambivalence, which is observed mostly, is the conflict among the existing Convention on biological diversity and TRIPS. Convention provides positive protection to TK. Its objectives are based on the identification of the rights of the community. Whereas, TRIIPS excludes TK from its ambit and to don't find it eligible for protection. Its objective is based on the private monopoly rights of an individual. Therefore, it has become one of the biggest challenges for the TK-rich countries which need to be reviewed and amended by TRIPS.

The bedrock is that Convention on biological diversity is not included in the TRIPS agreement, while Convention on biological diversity takes care of the sovereign rights over biological resources and the TRIPS provides patents over the biological resources. Presently, there is no provision that prevents bio-piracy acts under TRIPS, through which an individual can claim patent rights in one country over genetic resources that are under the rule of another country. TRIPS has no provision that allows a member's claims to impose its national commands for fair and equitable benefit sharing from the patenting its own resources in another country. Hence, it certainly acts as a barrier today in the enactment of the convention on biological diversity.

The relation between TRIPS and convention on biological diversity is managed by the secretariat of the World Trade Organisation. The relation that includes the guard of TK was investigated by the CTE, i.e. committee on Trade and Environment at the World Trade Organisation. This committee was made in 1995 by the World Trade Organisation General Council to look into the relationships amongst the allocation of the multilateral trading system and trade measures for environment-related purposes. This also included MEAs, i.e. Multilateral Environmental Agreements. The committee contemplated the provisions of the TRIPS agreement applicable to its work on the environment whereas few developing nations have argued upon asking amendment to be done in TRIPS in the light of article 8(j) of the convention on biological diversity.

CONCLUSION AND RECOMMENDATIONS

Many proposals have been laid down inside and outside the Intellectual Property Rights system, as to secure TK. Many times these proposals fail to describe the logic behind its safeguard. The expansion of a mechanism for the security of TK must comprise of such definitions which provide a qualified way to meet the objectives. There is no clear method that has reached to develop the strategies which can protect all the forms of TK. There are many complex issues that need to be legally recognised, along with the protection and enforcement of the rights attached.

It is highly desirable to have a universal path for the nations who are interested in protecting their ambit of TK. The nations have basically two ways:

1. Define TK as an umbrella term lato sensu (Broad Sense)
2. Define TK as stricto sensu – (Specific Sense)

Other than this, we need to identify a formula with the unified consent which describes the nature and content of the "knowledge" that we want to secure.

In other words, the definition should include all the main features such as

1. The context in which creation had been done
2. From where does it exists, i.e. its origin

3. The link to the community
4. The community to which it belongs

As all these blank spaces will be filled up with the information, the countries will have a wide variety of options of Intellectual Property, including choices for sui generis security, to select the right choice.

By understanding the scenario of accessing the TK and later misusing it for personal benefits, the government of India should take major steps to change the picture:

Establishing stringent laws to Prevent Fraudulent use of the Knowledge

India should not forget that the nation is a developing nation and many people here have still not gained the minimum level of education. So the people here are very gullible, and people from the other nations can easily take advantage of this nature of them. Legislations should be stringent enough to stop any kind of fraudulent or misuse of TK.

Allocating people and creating awareness about TK

The government should make sure that they authorise representatives who would specifically work towards creating awareness among such people. The knowledge holder will be taught better ways to take their knowledge to the outer world of their region. They would also be taught that from whom they have the threat and how the knowledge can be prevented from theft.

Provide fair rights and benefits to real Holders of Knowledge

People in the backward areas practice the knowledge gained from a generation so as to earn their livings. So in case when any other person or community wants to use their practice or knowledge for research, innovation or commercialisation, then the original holders should be provided with fair benefits either in the monetary form or even in a non-monetary form such as involvement in the commercialisation affairs.

- Creating a holistic integration of all the legislations

India has the Biological Diversity Act, 2002, Geographical Indications Act, 1999 and various other laws also. These numerous Laws ultimately yields to a lot of confusion to a common man. In spite of having various incomplete Laws, there is a need to come up with one single legislation that is an integration of various laws and become a complete law. Complete law means the legislations which have a wider scope and a bigger arena to cover all the rights, duties and illegal acts related to TK.

REFERENCES

Christoph, A. (2009). *Traditional Knowledge, Traditional Cultural Expressions*. New York: Kluwer Law International.

David, G. M. (2012). *Indigenous Knowledge and the Environment in Africa and North America*. Ohio University Press Athens.

Dutfield, G. (1999). *Project on the Convention on Biological Diversity and the International Trade Regime*. Oxford University Press.

Dutfield, G. (2000). *IPRs and Biodiversity: Conflict or Synergy?* Oxford University Press.

Ellen. (2000). *Indigenous Environmental Knowledge and its transformation: Critical Anthropological Perspectives*. Amsterdam: Alan Psychology Press.

Gopalkrishnan, N.S, (1998). Impact of Patent System on Traditional Knowledge. *Cochin University Law Review,* (1), 219.

Indian Council of Medical Research. (2009). Retrieved from: https://www.icmr.nic.in/

Jha, A. (2011). *Traditional Indian Medicine with Specific Reference to Buddhist and Tribal Medicine*. Research India Press Publisher.

Kingsbury, B. (2005). The Emergence of Global Administrative Law. *Law and Contemporary Problems*, (68), 15–62. Retrieved from https://scholarship.law.duke.edu/lcp/vol68/iss3/2

Malhan. (2001). Protecting Traditional Knowledge Systems. *Indian Journal of Environmental Law*, *2*(1), 85–91. Retrieved from https://www.ecolex.org/details/literature/protecting-traditional-knowledge-systems-ana-067982/

Mayor. (1994). The D.G of UNES and Cultural Organization.

National Agricultural Library. (2016). Retrieved from: https://data.nal.usda.gov/dataset/holobee-database-v20161

People's Biodiversity Registers. (2019). Retrieved from: http://nbaindia.org/uploaded/pdf/PPT_PBRs_Guidelines.pdf

Protection of Traditional Knowledge. (2019). *Traditional Cultural Expression*. Retrieved from: https://www.bananaip.com/ip-news-center/round-table-on-protection-of_25/

Robinson Daniel, F. (2017). *Protecting Traditional Knowledge*. Abingdon: Routledge. doi:10.4324/9781315666358

Rosendal. (2000). *The Convention on Biological Diversity and Developing Countries*. Springer.

Secretariat of CBD. (2001). *Handbook of the Convention on Biological Diversity*. Rio: Earthscan Publications Ltd.

SenGupta, N. (2019). *Traditional Knowledge in Modern India*. Shimla: Springer. doi:10.1007/978-81-322-3922-2

Shiv Shai Singh. (2000). *The law of Intellectual Property Rights*. New Delhi: Deep and Deep.

Sreedharan, T.P. (2004). *Biological Diversity of Kerala: A survey of Kalliasseri Panchayat*. Kannur District: Deep and Deep.

Tania & Gold. (2012). *Genetic Resources and Traditional Knowledge: Case Studies and Conflicting interests*. Edward Elgar Publishing Limited.

The Biotechnology Regulatory Authority of India Bill. (2013). Retrieved from https://www.prsindia.org/billtrack/the-biotechnology-regulatory-authority-of-india-bill-2013- 2709/

Traditional Knowledge Digital Library. (n.d.). Retrieved from https://www.wipo.int/meetings/en/2011/wipo_tkdl_del_11/about_tkdl.html

Tripathi, S. K. (2003). Traditional Knowledge Significance and Implication. *Indian Journal of Traditional Knowledge*, *2*(2), 102.

WTO. WT/CTE/W/156. (2009). *Protection of Biodiversity and Traditional Knowledge – the Indian Experience*. Retrieved From: https://docs.wto.org/dol2fe/Pages/FE_Search/FE_S_S009DP.aspx?language=E&CatalogueIdList=6651,53767,40823,73024,14069,45767,47562&CurrentCatalogueIdIndex=6&FullTextHash=&HasEnglishRecord=True&HasFrenchRecord=True&HasSpanishRecord=True

ADDITIONAL READING

Intellectual Property and Traditional Knowledge. (2009). Retrieved from: http://www.legalserviceindia.com/article/l98-Intellectual-Property-and-Traditional-knowledge.html

Mgbeoji, I. (2006). *Global Bio piracy: Patents, Plants, and Indigenous Knowledge*. UBC Press.

Sengupta and Nirmal. (2018). *Traditional Knowledge in Modern India*. New Delhi: Springer Publishers.

KEY TERMS AND DEFINITIONS

Benefit Sharing: It defines fair and equitable sharing of benefits arising from the use of genetic resources. It recognises the communities that hold such knowledge are entitled to a share of the benefit arising from commercial utilisation.

Bio-Piracy: the practice of commercially exploiting naturally occurring biochemical or genetic material, especially by obtaining patents that restrict its future use, while failing to pray fair compensation to the community from which it originates.

Bioprospecting: The search for plant and animal species from which medicinal drugs and other commercially valuable compounds can be obtained.

Geographical Indication: It is a sign used on products that have a specific geographical origin and possess qualities or a reputation that are due to that origin and sign must identify a product as originating in a given place.

Human Genome: It is a complete set of nucleic acid sequences for humans, encoded as DNA within 23 chromosome pairs in cell nuclei and in a small DNA molecule found individual mitochondria.

Indigenous Medicine: It is a traditional medicine that comprises medical aspects of TK that developed over generations within various societies before the era of modern medicine.

Chapter 2
Access to Medicines in the Light of Patent Law Regime in India:
A Legacy of Legislation or Lease of the Judiciary?

Akanksha Jumde
Deakin University, Australia

Nishant Kumar
Central University of Punjab, Bathinda, India

ABSTRACT

This chapter aims to trace the development of patent law regime in India and analyze its evolution in response to globally-influential intellectual property framework, such as TRIPS and pressure from the developed countries US and Europe to open up her markets to permit cash-rich pharmaceutical companies to sell their drugs and receive patent protection in India. An observation of the legislative actions and judicial responses reveal that both the parliament and the supreme echelons of the judiciary have been tediously careful in protecting the healthcare needs of the poor by promoting the generic drug industry through a guarded interpretation of Section 3(d) of Patents Act, 1970. The objective of the chapter is to critically analyze the legislative reforms and judicial interpretations of patent law in light of the socio-economic needs of the country.

DOI: 10.4018/978-1-7998-1835-9.ch002

INTRODUCTION

Infectious diseases kill over 10 million people each year, more than 90% of whom are in the developing world (World Health Organisation, The World Health Report 2001). The leading causes of illness and death in Africa, Asia, and South America-regions that account for four-fifths of the world's population-are HIV/AIDS, respiratory infections, malaria, and tuberculosis (World Health Organisation, The World Health Report 2001). The magnitude of the disease crisis has drawn attention to the fact that millions of people in the developing world do not have access to the medicines that are needed to treat these diseases or alleviate suffering (UNAIDS: Reports on the Global HIV/AIDS Epidemic, 2001).

In India, Hepatitis-B is one of the most common diseases in India. There are over 40 million infected patients, and India is second only to China in the highest number of Hepatitis-B (HBV) infected patients by country (NCBI Report, 2013). Every year, nearly 600,000 patients die from HBV infection in the Indian sub-continent. In addition, around 20,000 people die of typhoid fever in the country (UNAIDS: Reports on the Global HIV/AIDS Epidemic, 2001).

Among vector-borne diseases, malaria is the most common killer in the country, with 40,297 deaths reported per year. In 2006, India reported 1.39 million cases of Chikungunya with no attributable deaths (NCBI Report, 2007). Ahmedabad alone reported around 60,777 cases. Since 1985, India has reported an estimated 25, 000–30, 000 human deaths from rabies annually. The current statistics stand at 20,565 deaths per year (NCBI Report, 2013).

Besides these common infections, India, with 2.1 million patients, has the 3rd highest number of HIV patients in the world, behind only South Africa and Nigeria (Sonowal & Goswami, 2015). On a brighter note, the 2012 UNAIDS Report stated that new HIV cases among adults declined by half in India since 2000, while praising India's contribution to AIDS response through the manufacture of generic antiretroviral drugs (Sonowal & Goswami, 2015).

The reasons for the lack of access to essential medicines are manifold, however, in many cases, the high prices of drugs are a barrier to needed treatments (Hoen, 2002). Such exorbitant, and thus, prohibitive drug prices are often the result of strong intellectual property protection (Pecoul et al., 1999). Despite the enormous burden of disease, drug discovery and development targeted at infectious and parasitic diseases in emerging countries has ground to a standstill because drug companies in developed and developing nations cannot recoup the cost of R&D for products to treat diseases that abound in developing countries (Pecoul et al., 1999). A number of new medicines vital for the survival of millions are already too costly for the vast majority of the people in emerging countries. Further, the investment in Research and Development (R&D) towards the health needs of people in developing countries has almost come to a standstill. Developing countries, where three-quarters of the world population lives, accounts for less than 10% of the global pharmaceutical market (Hoen, 2002).

The TRIPS Agreement, effective from January 1, 1995, is the most comprehensive multilateral treaty on intellectual property rights to date (TRIPS, 1994). This Agreement sets out the minimum standards for the protection of intellectual property, including provisions to be made for product patents for drugs and pharmaceuticals (Article 27.1), which member states must comply with. The Agreement, keeping in mind the needs of the developing countries, have afforded certain flexibilities, which may be harnessed by developing and under-developed countries, in order to control over-pricing of the drugs, so that medicines are within reach of the economically disadvantaged sections (Hoen, 2002).

The Indian patent regime cleverly employs these flexibilities to curb monopolistic tendencies of the large pharmaceutical industries, the gates for which were opened post-TRIPS, with the introduction of product patents (Verkey, 2005). Also, the judiciary, with the manner of its legislative interpretation, has also played a key role in access to medicines in India.

This chpater seeks to explore the evolution of patent law in India, the socio-economic, political and international undercurrents that sculpted the law over the period of time, from 1911 to 2005 and the kind of role the judiciary has played in access to medicines in India.

EVOLUTION OF INDIA'S PATENT LAW

Patents Act, 1911: a Legacy of the British Raj

The beginnings of the Indian Patent law may be traced back to 1856 when the Protection of Inventions Act was enacted based on the British Patent Law of 1852. Under the Act of 1856, exclusive privileges were granted to the inventors of new manufacturers for a period of 14 years (Verkey, 2005).

This Act was modified in 1859, under which patent monopolies, called as exclusive privileges were granted for a period of 14 years from the date of filing of the specification. Subsequently, the Patents and Designs Protection Act was adopted in 1872. These acts were consolidated as the Inventions and Designs Act. In 1911, the Indian Patents and Designs Act was enacted. The 1911 Act had provisions for both product and process patents (Verkey, 2005).

A need was felt for a comprehensive law on patents when the 1911 Act was found inadequate to respond to the needs of the society and keeping pace with the industrial development of the nation (Mueller, 2006). At this point in time, foreign firms controlled about 70 per cent of the Indian market, and Indian drug prices were among the highest in the world (Verkey, 2005). Foreign firms could use colonial-era patent laws to their advantage to suppress competition from local companies. It was generally felt that the patent law had done little good to the people of the country. The way the Act was designed benefited foreigners far more than the Indians. It did not help at all in the promotion of scientific research and industrialisation in the country, and it curbed the innovativeness and inventiveness of Indians (Ahuja, 2009).

Therefore, shortly after Independence in 1949, a committee was constituted under the Chairmanship of Justice (Dr.) Bakshi Tek Chand, a retired Judge of the Lahore High Court, to undertake a comprehensive review of the working of the 1911 Act (Ahuja, 2009). The Committee submitted its interim report on August 4, 1949, and the final report in 1950 making recommendations for the prevention of misuse or abuse of patent rights in India. It also observed that the Patent Act should contain a clear indication that food and medicine and surgical and curative devices were to be made available to the public at the lowest price commensurate with giving reasonable compensation to the patentee. Based on the committee's recommendations, the 1911 Act was amended in 1950 (by Act XXXII of 1950) in relation to the working of inventions, including compulsory licensing and revocation of patents (Verkey, 2005). In 1952, a further amendment was made (by Act LXX of 1952) to provide for compulsory licence in respect of food and medicines, insecticide, germicide or fungicide, and a process for producing substance or any invention relating to surgical or curative devices. The committee's recommendation prompted the Government to introduce a bill (Bill no. 59 of 1953) in Parliament, but the bill was not passed, and it was allowed to lapse (Verkey, 2005).

JUSTICE AYYANGAR COMMITTEE REPORT AND ITS IMPLICATIONS

In 1957, Justice Rajagopala Ayyangar was appointed by the Government of India to examine afresh and review the patent law in India and advise the Government on the changes required to be made in the law. Justice Ayyangar analysed and pointed out that during the period 1930-37, the grant of patents to Indians and foreigners was roughly in the ratio of 1:9. Even after Independence, though a number of institutions for post-graduate training were set up and several national laboratories were established to encourage rapid growth of scientific education, the proportion of Indian and the foreign patents remained substantially the same, at roughly 1:9 (Ayyangar, 1959).

Justice Ayyangar further pointed out that this ratio does not take into account the economic or industrial or scientific importance of the inventions. If these factors

Table 1.

Year	MNCs (%)	Indian Companies
1952	38	62
1970	68	32
1978	60	40
1980	50	50
1991	40	60
1998	32	68
2004	23	77

are taken into account, Indians would appear to be lagging even further behind. Further, taking into reckoning the number of inventions for which renewal fees were paid beyond the 6th year, which would give a rough idea of the value attached to the invention by the patentee, the patents taken by Indians would appear to be of little worth as compared with patents held by foreign nationals (Ayyangar, 1959).

The book titled, *The WHO and the Indian Pharmaceuticals Industry (2005),* describes the market shares of multi-national companies and Indian companies in India as under (Chaudhari, 2005):

The fall and rise of the Indian pharmaceutical industry are explained as the result of certain factors, not the least important of which was the change in the patent law in the country, which made medicines and drugs and chemical substances non-patentable. Chaudhuri explains that before the introduction of sulfa drugs (1930s) and penicillin (1940) that brought about the therapeutic revolution, drugs of natural origin were more important than synthetic ones (Chaudhuri, 2005).

By the time the Second World War started (1939), several indigenous firms were engaged in manufacturing drugs, and indigenous producers met 13 per cent of the medicinal requirements of the country. Indigenous firms and producers still had a long way to go to attain self-sufficiency, but in terms of the range of operations, they were already manufacturing all types of drugs. By the early 1950s, because of the spread of manufacturing activities, the indigenous sector dominated the pharmaceutical industry in India. It accounted for about 62 per cent of the market in 1952 (the table above). However, the rise and growth of multinational corporations (MNCs) worldwide in the post-Second World War period, as well as the therapeutic revolution changed these dynamics (Chaudhuri, 2005). The MNCs started research for developing new drugs in the 1930s-40s. As a result, in the late 1940s and during the 1950s and even after that at a slower rate, new drugs discovered by the MNCs began to be available for medical use. The indigenous sector was not equipped for research for developing new drugs, that is, for developing a new chemical entity. With the introduction of new drugs at a rapid rate by the MNCs, the role of patents became important. Because of the patent regime under the 1911 Act and the unsupportive industrial policy, the indigenous sector lost its status in the 1950s and the 1960s (Chaudhuri, 2005). In contrast to 62 per cent of the market in the early 1950s, the market share of the indigenous sector declined to 32 per cent by 1970. In contrast, the market share of the MNCs increased from 38 per cent in 1952 to 68 per cent in 1970 (the table above).

However, according to Chaudhuri, the situation changed in the 1970s. Several official initiatives were taken in the 1970s, of which the most important one was the enactment of the Patents Act, 1970, which changed the environment in favour of the indigenous sector.

Observing that industrial countries and under-developed countries had different demand and supply requirements, Justice Ayyangar pointed out that the same patent law would operate differently in two countries at two different levels of technological and economic development, and hence the need to regulate the patent law in accordance with the need of the country (Ayyangar, 1959).

Justice Ayyangar observed that the provisions of the Patent law have to be designed with special reference to the economic conditions of the country, the state of its scientific and technological advancement, its future needs and other relevant factors, and so as to minimise, if not to eliminate, the abuses to which a system of patent monopoly is capable of being put. Bearing in view the matters set above, he recommended retaining the Indian patent system, but with a number of improvements (Ayyangar, 1959).

One of the improvements suggested was to define, with precision, those inventions which should be patentable and equally clearly identify certain inventions, the grant of patents to which would retard research, or industrial progress, or be detrimental to the national health or well-being, and to make those inventions non-patentable.

In regard to patents for chemical substances, he examined the history of the law in other countries and pointed out that Germany was the first to adopt the system of confining the patentability of inventions relating to chemical products or substances to process claims. The law was then followed in many other countries in the world, for instance, Austria, Brazil, Czechoslovakia, Holland, Hungary, Japan, Mexico, Norway, Poland and the U.S.S.R. Products produced by chemical process were not patentable though processes for making such products were patentable, if they satisfied the other tests of patentability, e.g., novelty of subject matter. In light of the experience of the other countries, Justice Ayyangar recommended that only process claims should be permitted for the chemical and pharmaceutical industry (Ayyangar, 1959).

Coming to the patents for inventions relating to food and medicine, Justice Ayyangar pointed out that barring the US, there was hardly any country that allowed unrestricted grant of patents in respect of articles of food and medicines, or as to the licensing and working of patents in this class. In none of the countries of the European Union were patents granted for product claims for articles of food or medicine, and in a few (Denmark for articles of food; and Italy, under the law of 1957, for medicinal products) even claims for processes for producing them were non-patentable. He explained that the reason for this state of law is stated to be that the denial of product claims is necessary in order that important articles of daily use such as medicine or food, which are vital to the health of the community, should be made available to everyone at reasonable prices and that no monopoly should be granted in respect of such articles. Refusal of product patents would enlarge the area of competition and thus result in the production of these articles in sufficient quantity and at the lowest possible cost to the public (Ayyangar, 1959).

Ayyangar Committee Report advised against patenting of products in the case of food, medicines, drugs and chemical substances, as the Committee found that foreigners held between eighty and ninety patents in India, and more than 90 per cent of these patents were not commercially worked in India. In light of its conclusions, the Committee concluded that the system was exploited by multinationals to achieve monopolistic control over the market. This recommendation of the Committee saw its light of the day in the Patents Act, 1970, which came into force on 20 April 1972 (Ayyangar, 1959).

PATENTS ACT, 1970

The 1970 Act introduced the definition of "patent" as a right granted for an invention as a new product or a process involving an inventive step and capable of industrial application (Patents Act, 1970). The Act further defines an invention as a new product or a process involving an inventive step and capable of industrial application. On a combined reading of Section 2 (j), (ac) and (ja), in order to qualify as an invention, a product should satisfy the following tests:

1. It should be novel, or "new"
2. It should be an outcome of inventive activity,
3. It should have utility, or "capable of being used in an industry"
4. It should not be contrary to law and morality,
5. It must come into being as a result of an invention which has a feature that:
    - (a) Entails technical advance over existing knowledge;
    - (b) Or has an economic significance
6. Makes the invention not obvious to a person skilled in the art

The 1970 Act served as a substantial driver of three decades of growth in the domestic pharmaceutical industry (Kapczynski, 2009). One of the significant changes made by the 1970 Act was prohibiting product patents on medicines. In the years that followed the enactment of the Act, the number of patents granted in India dropped significantly (Kapczynski, 2009). Although the law permitted process patents related to medicines, they were very limited in scope and rarely sought. The law thus created significant space for the entry of local pharmaceutical firms, and they rapidly increased their share of the Indian market (Lanjouw, 1998). Indian companies became skilled in reverse engineering and developing new processes for drug production. In the mid-1970s, Indian firms became more technically sophisticated, producing active pharmaceutical ingredients (APIs), with production steadily increasing over the next three decades (Aggarwal, 2006). Over time, the Indian industry also evolved to become extraordinarily competitive and diverse. Numerous surveys indicate that Indian drug prices by the 1990s were among the lowest in the world (Chaudhari, 2005).

In regard to the Patents Act, 1970, Chaudhuri maintains that Patent "reforms" contributed directly to the transformation of the pharmaceutical industry. He points out that under the Patents Act, 1970, articles of food, medicines and drugs and chemical substances could be patented only for a new method or process of manufacture, not for the products as such (section 5 of the 1970 Act).

Further, unlike in the previous patent regime, for each particular drug only one method or process – the best known to the applicant - could be patented (sections 5 and 10 of the 1970 Act). Also, even in case of a process patent for an article of food, medicine or drug, the term of the patent was brought down from fourteen (14) years to five (5) years from the date of sealing of the patent, or seven (7) years from the date of patent whichever was earlier. Until the early 1970s, the industry was dominated by MNCs, who commanded 68% of the market share. India was dependent on imports for many essential bulk drugs. This import dependence constricted consumption in a country deficient in foreign exchange and inhibited the growth of the industry. Drug prices in India were very high. In the late 1970s and 1980s, Indian companies started large-scale production of bulk drugs (Chaudhari, 2005). The development of the bulk drugs sector is actually the most important achievement of the pharmaceutical industry in India. This led to the transformation of the industry (Chaudhari, 2005).

The most rapid growth of the Indian pharmaceutical industry took place from the 1990s onwards. Both production and exports grew remarkably fast. The production of both bulk drugs and formulations started increasing sharply and steadily. (Chaudhari, 2005). From Rs.6, 400 million in 1989-90, bulk drug production increased to Rs.77,790 million in 2003-04; and from Rs.34,200 million in 1989- 90, formulation productions increased to Rs.276,920 million in 2003-04. (Chaudhari, 2005). The growth was most remarkable from 2000 to 2005, when production increased much more than it had in the last two decades. Indian companies further consolidated their domination in the domestic market. Their market share increased from 60 per cent in 1991 to 68 per cent in 1998 and 77 per cent in 2003 (Chaudhari, 2005).

The growth was also very fast in the export markets. India became a net exporter by 1988- 89, and since then there has only been an increase in the Indian exports. As a result, net exports as a percentage of exports have increased from 4.4 per cent in 1988-9 to about 50 per cent in the early 1990s and more than 75 per cent in the early 2000s. More than three-fourths of bulk drug production and almost one-fourth of the production of the formulations are exported. The USA, which has the toughest regulatory requirements, has emerged as India's largest export partner in pharmaceuticals (Chaudhari, 2005).

Dealing with the growth of the Indian pharmaceutical industry after the change in the patent law, Chaudhuri writes,

"Because of the rapid growth and structural transformation in the last three decades or so, India now occupies an important position in the international pharmaceutical industry... India has received worldwide recognition as a low-cost producer of high-quality bulk drugs and formulations. India produces about 350 bulk drugs ranging from simple pain killers to sophisticated antibiotics and complex cardiac products. Most of the bulk drugs are produced from basic stages, involving complex multi-stage synthesis, fermentation and extractions. For more than 25 bulk drugs, India accounts for more than 50 per cent of the international trade. India is a major force to reckon with in the western markets for such drugs as ibuprofen, sulphamethoxasole..."

WTO AND TRIPS: THE TWIST IN TALE

In 1995, India joined the WTO and the TRIPS Agreement as a consequence (Kapczynski, 2009). TRIPS had the effect of altering the terrain of international law (Kapczynski, 2009). The treaty was a product of intensive lobbying and concerted efforts by the multinational firms in information-intensive industries that persuaded the United States, the European Union, and Japan that their national trade supremacy depended on stronger protection for IP abroad, especially in the developing countries. The "single undertaking" nature of the WTO ensured that countries would have to accept TRIPS if they wanted to be part of the WTO (Kapczynski, 2009).

TRIPS has caused the most controversy in the domain of access to medicines because it requires patents on pharmaceutical products. India opposed TRIPS, and particularly its patent provisions, as did the bulk of the Indian pharmaceutical industry. Faced with the alternative of remaining entirely outside the WTO framework,

India nonetheless acceded to the Agreement, negotiating in the process for certain flexibilities that would limit the effects of the changes it required (Kapczynski, 2009).

The TRIPS Agreement also provides for a built-in mechanism for review through the biennial Ministerial Conference (vide Article 71). The Ministerial Conference is the highest decision- making body of the WTO and it can make decisions on all matters under any of the WTO agreements, including the TRIPS Agreement (Kapczynski, 2009). The fourth WTO Ministerial Conference in Doha on November 14, 2001, adopted the Doha Declaration on the TRIPS and Public Health.

TRIPS AND ITS CONSEQUENCES ON INDIAN PATENT LAW

Under the TRIPS Agreement, developing countries that did not provide patent protection for pharmaceutical and agricultural chemical products were given a 10-year transition period to establish such protection. In the interim, however, these countries were required to establish a "mail box system" to receive and date patent applications. In addition to the grant of mail applications, as designed to preserve the novelty of the inventions and priority of the applications during the transition period, the TRIPS Agreement also required the countries to grant Exclusive Marketing Rights (EMRs) to certain products that are subject to mail box applications (Verkey, 2005).

India was required to comply with the product patent requirements of TRIPS until 2005, although it did have to create a "mailbox" for filing of patent applications that would be examined when the 2005 changes came into effect. (Article 70.5, TRIPs). While the full legal effects on India were nonetheless substantial, because of its impact on the behaviour and thinking of industry and health advocates. In order to meet the December 31, 2004 deadline for the introduction of product patents, India passed an ordinance that temporarily brought its law into compliance (Verkey, 2005). The Ordinance, set to expire in approximately three months, set the stage for intense debating and protests from several advocacy groups (Verkey, 2005). The exceptionally globalised advocacy efforts around the bill resulted in several consequential changes in the new law: The Patents (Amendment) Act, 2005.

PATENTS (AMENDMENT) ACT, 2005: SALIENT FEATURES AND RESULTANT CHANGES IN THE LAW

The changes brought about by the 2005 Amendment, included most insignificantly, new subject matter exclusions, and the resurrection of full pre-grant opposition system (Kapczynski, 2009). One of the most significant amendments was the deletion of Section 5 of the Act, which prohibited patenting of products in case of food, drugs, medicines, chemical substances. With the amendment, it is now possible to obtain product patents in the case of drugs, food, medicines, and chemical substances. This was, without hesitation, the single most important change brought about by the Amendment of 2005, as it opened doors for product patents in areas of food, medicines, and agrochemicals in India. The removal of Section 5 was also accompanied by amendments in clauses (j) and (ja) of Section 2(1), apart from some other ancillary clauses of Section 2(1), as well as amendments in Section 3, which redefined the concepts of invention and patentability (Kapczynski, 2009).

The reintroduction of the product patents was a cause of concern not only for the country but also for other developing countries and international agencies, as the earlier patent system which had barred patent products for pharmaceuticals, food and agro-chemicals, had led to exponential growth of the indigenous drug industry, which scaled great heights and became a major supplier of affordable medicines to a number of developed and other developing countries.

Another cardinal amendment was the inclusion of Section 3(d), which states that "mere discovery of a new form of a known substance, which does not result in the enhancement of the known efficacy of that substance is *not* (emphasis added) an invention, and therefore not patentable. Therefore, under this clause, salts, esters, polymorphs, metabolites, pure form, particle size, isomers, mixtures of isomers, complexes, combinations and other derivatives of known substances are to be considered to be the same substances, unless they differ significantly in properties with regard to efficacy (Section 3(d), Patents Act, 1970). Further, Section 21 of the 2005 Amendment removed Chapter IV A of the 1970 Act, dealing with provisions related to Exclusive Marketing Rights (EMRs). Since the grant of pharmaceutical patents was a particularly controversial issue, developing and Least Developed Countries (LDCs) were required to grant EMRs to certain products that are subject to mail box applications under the TRIPS Agreement (Article 70(8), TRIPS). According to Article 70 (9) of the TRIPS Agreement, a grant of EMRs is contingent on two pre-conditions:

1. The issuance of a patent to another WTO member state for the product that is subject of mail box application;
2. The securing of marketing approval for the product in the country where the mail box application is filed.

In order to bring India in line with the obligations of Article 70(8) and (9), the President of India promulgated an amendment to the Indian Patents Act, 1994 (Kapczynski, 2009). However, the ordinance failed to receive an endorsement from the Parliament when it resumed the session. As a result, India had no explicit, published legal basis for receiving mail box applications or for granting of EMRs for pharmaceutical and agricultural chemical products (Verkey, 2005). On request filed by the US, the WTO established a panel to hear a dispute filed by the USA regarding India's non-compliance of Article 70 (8) and (9) of the TRIPS Agreement. The Panel found that India had violated Article 70(8) and (9) of TRIPS. India's appeal was rejected by the appellate body on the grounds that its administrative mechanisms for accepting "mail box applications" were insufficient to establish legally tenable provisions (Verkey, 2005). In addition, India had also failed to institute a legal mechanism for granting of EMRs by January 1, 1995.

Section 3 (p) of the Patents Act, 2005 excludes the patentability of traditional knowledge. Section 3(p), The Patents Act, 1970, "an invention which in effect, is traditional knowledge or which is an aggregation or duplication of known properties of traditionally known component or components." The legislative objective of excluding traditional knowledge is to protect the traditional wisdom of India against misuse and misappropriation. The *neem* and *turmeric* case is a case in point. The patent for Neem was first filed by W.R. Grace, Department of Agriculture, USA in the European Patent Office. The said patent is a method of controlling fungi on plants comprising of contacting the fungi with a Neem oil formulation. A legal opposition has been filed by India against the grant of the patent. The legal opposition to this patent was lodged by the New Delhi-based Research Foundation for Science, Technology and Ecology (RFSTE), in co-operation with the International Federation of Organic Agriculture Movements (IFOAM) and Magda Aelvoet, former green Member of the European Parliament (MEP). A tree legendary to India, from its roots to its spreading crown, the Neem tree contains a number of potent compounds, notably a chemical found in its seeds named azadirachtin. It is used as an astringent in so many fields. The barks, leaves, flowers, seeds of neem trees are used to treat a variety of diseases ranging from leprosy to diabetes, skin disorders, and ulcers. Neem twigs are used as antiseptic toothbrushes since time immemorial. The opponents' submitted evidence of ancient Indian Ayurvedic texts that have described the hydrophobic extracts of neem seeds were known and used for centuries in India, both in curing dermatological diseases in humans and in protecting agricultural plants form fungal infections. The EPO identified the lack of novelty, inventive step and possibly form a relevant prior art and revoked the patent. Apart from this, several US patents were recently taken out Neem-based emulsions and solutions protecting agricultural plants form fungal infections. The EPO identified the lack of novelty, inventive step and possibly form a relevant prior art and revoked the patent. Apart from this, several US patents were recently taken out for Neem-based emulsions and solutions.

Turmeric is a tropical herb grown in east India. Turmeric powder is widely used in India as a medicine, a food ingredient and a dye to name a few of its uses. For instance, it is used as a blood purifier, in treating the common cold, and as an anti-parasitic for many skin infections. It is also used as an essential ingredient in cooking many Indian dishes. In 1995, the United States awarded a patent on turmeric to the University of Mississippi Medical Center for wound healing property. The claimed subject matter was the use of "turmeric powder and its administration," both oral as well as topical, for wound healing. An exclusive right has been granted to sell and distribute. The Indian Council for Scientific and Industrial Research (CSIR) had objected to the patent granted and provided documented evidence of the prior art to USPTO. Though it was a well-known fact that the use of turmeric was known in every household since ages in India, it was a herculean task to find published information on the use of turmeric powder through oral as well as a topical route for wound healing. Due to extensive researches, 32 references were located in different languages, namely Sanskrit, Urdu and Hindi. Therefore, the USPTO revoked the patent, stating that the claims made in the patent were obvious and anticipated, and agreeing that the use of turmeric was an old art of healing wounds. Therefore, the TK that belonged to India was safeguarded in Turmeric case.

Certain Indian traditional systems of medicines such as Ayurveda and Unani have been using plants and plant extracts to treat and cure diseases. Given that these systems of medicines have been practised since time immemorial, its wisdom and conventions are known to one and all in India. The excludability of traditional knowledge demonstrates the traditional culture and ethos of the country.

PATENTS (AMENDMENT) ACT, 1999

Subjected to intense international pressure, India introduced the first amendment to the Patents Act, 1970, in 1999 (Verkey, 2005). Two key aspects of this amendment were: "provision for mailbox", and the "provision for EMR" for products related to drugs, pharmaceuticals and agrochemicals, effective from January 1, 1995.

Under the Patents (Amendment) Act, 1999 which established EMRs for mailbox applications in India, the following conditions were laid down:

a. The product must be patentable, that is, it must be an invention as per the Patents Act 1970.
b. The invention must have been made in India or in a WTO Convention country. If made in a convention country, the invention must have been:
    (i) Filed on or after January 1, 1995, and
    (ii) Before getting a patent in India, the applicant must have obtained such a patent in the Convention country.
    (iii) If the invention has been made in India,
c. The application for a patent for the method or process of production of such a substance should have been filed on or after January 1, 1995, and

i. The patent must have been granted on or after the date of filing of such EMR (Patents Amendment Act, 1999).
ii. The Patents (Amendment) Act, 2005 removed this provision for EMRs, after the patent law of India was brought fully in line with TRIPS, at the end of the 10-year transition period (Patents Amendment Act, 2005).

THE PATENTS (AMENDMENT) ACT, 2002

The 2002 Amendment to Patents Act, 1970 was particularly significant because it inserted Section 104A, dealing with the burden of proof in case of infringement. In the case of *Glenmark Pharmaceuticals Ltd. versus Symead Labs Limited,* a single judge of the High Court of Delhi had granted an interim injunction in favour of Symead, which had filed this application on the alleged infringement of two of its patents, API linezolid, a synthetic compound used to treat infections of the skin and blood, and also pneumonia. Thus, Glenmark was restrained from manufacturing Linezolid using the process patented by Symead. Thus, on January 19, 2015, Glenmark appealed before the Division Bench of the High Court, requesting the setting aside of the temporary order. The Court set aside the single judge's order because the Division Bench found that the Single Judge had failed to come to the conclusion that Linezolid API manufactured by the Plaintiff using its patented process was identical to the Linezolid API manufactured by the defendants/appellants. This judgment is particularly significant because the Division Bench of the High Court set aside the erroneous application of Section 104A, which states that in case of alleged infringement of process patent, the Burden of Proof lies upon the Defendant to prove that process used for obtaining the product, identical to the product of the patented process, is different from the patented process.

IMPLEMENTING TRIPS: INDIA'S RESPONSE TO TRIPS AND ITS FLEXBILITIES

Patent granted to Roche India, the Indian branch of the Swiss Hoffman La Roche, for Pegasys, or pegylated interferon alfa-2-a, a drug used for the treatment of Hepatitis-C (Duggan & Goyal, 2016), was the first product patent for medicines in India. Roche, thus, earned for itself the distinction of being the first MNC to be granted a product patent for medicine in India, under the TRIPS mandated product patent for medicines in India. However, in 2007, concerned with the impact of this patent on public health and accessibility of the medicine in the country, as patients with Chronic Hepatitis-C, who need a six-month course, have to purchase it at a discounted price of Rs. 3, 14, 496, Wockhardt, Indian generic major, and Sankalp, an NGO that provides treatment and rehabilitation support for injecting drug users, filed post-grant opposition, which as invalidated by the Patent Office. Generic versions of another drug, interferon (alpha 2b) are also available in India. The cost of this treatment regimen varies from Rs 1.5 to 2.5 million or the same period. Sankalp appealed against the order before the IPAB. The IPAB revoked the patent, more than six years after it was granted.

The IPAB revoked the patent on the grounds that a "person" skilled in the art could have easily predicted the claims made by the patent, since, the pegylated form of interferon to improve the activity of protein-based drugs had been recognised since the 1970s. Impliedly, the respondent could not show "increased efficacy over known substances" as required under Section 3(d). More importantly, the Court said that the appellant has valid *locus standi* because patient groups working for persons who are in dire need of the medicine are definitely "persons interested" under Section 64 of the Act.

The IPAB decision spelt a major victory for public health activists and interest groups. The decision was an epitome of the IPAB recognising the interests of the patients, which outweighed the private monopolistic interests of the pharmaceutical giant. The decision also implied the efforts of the judicial bodies to make essential drugs more affordable and easily accessible in the country (Duggan & Goyal, 2016). The order also implies that the generic version of Pegasys may become available in the near future. However, that depends upon whether Roche India decides to appeal the ruling. Furthermore, the decision specified that a patient group is considered to be an interested party in patent opposition cases, raising the possibility of additional patent challenges in the future.

While TRIPS includes many relatively clear obligations, such that the duration of protection for patents should be minimum twenty years, it also includes many vague and undefined commitments, such as the requirement to engage in "reasonable" efforts to negotiate with the patent holders before overriding a patent (Kapczynski, 2009).

In the process of interpreting the TRIPS Agreement, and exploiting sustainably its flexibilities, in response to the intervention of local industry and health advocates, India introduced robust versions of the compulsory licensing mechanism, one of the most significantly utilised flexibilities to TRIPS till date, but also some entirely new flexibilities (Kapczynski, 2009). Among those flexibilities are novel limitations on the subject matter, and exceptionally high inventive step standard, procedural requirements that could decrease the patent grant rate, and limitations on injunctive remedies. Therefore, India was able to fully embrace TRIPS, instead of rejecting its terms (Kapczynski, 2009).

Compulsory Licensing

The provision for compulsory licensing is reflected under Section 84(1) of the Act. The Patents (Amendment) Act, 1999 added a full chapter for the grant of compulsory licenses and the revocation of licenses. After the 1999 amendment, the grounds on which a compulsory licence could be granted were:

1. Reasonable requirements of the public with respect to the patented invention have not been satisfied; or,
2. The patented invention is not available to the public at a reasonably affordable price; or,
3. The patented invention is not worked (i.e. not used or performed) in the territory of India.

The Amendment of 2005 added an Explanation to Section 84 (6), which states that the Controller while examining the application for the grant of compulsory licence, "shall take into consideration that the Applicant has made efforts to obtain a license from the patentee… and such efforts have not been successful within a reasonable period of time." The Explanation states that a "reasonable period" shall be construed as a period not ordinarily exceeding six months. The Explanation also added under what conditions "reasonable requirements of the public shall not be deemed to have been satisfied".

In addition, Section 90 (1) (vii) was added to the Act, which states that in settling the terms and conditions of the compulsory licence as required under Section 84 of the Act, the Controller shall "secure that the licence is granted with the primary purpose of supply in the Indian market, and the licensee may also export the patented product, if need be".

Another significant insertion to the Act by the 2005 Amendment was the inclusion of Section 92A, which states that "Compulsory licence shall be available for the manufacture and export of patented pharmaceutical products to any country having insufficient or manufacturing capacity in the pharmaceutical sector for the concerned product to address public health problems, provided such a country permits importation of pharmaceutical products from India." This provision is particularly significant because India is one of the most important exporters of generic, low-cost medicines to African and other low-income countries. For instance, in an order (C.M.A. No. 879 of 2014) dated December 5, 2014, the AP/Telangana High Court denied the appeal of Bristol Myers Squibb (BMS) against Mylan Laboratories, in a patent infringement suit and allowed Mylan to export its generic anti-retroviral drug "Atazanavir" in pursuance of its agreement with the Pan American Health Organisation (PAHO) to sell and distribute "Atazanavir" to Venezuela, a WHO-recommended, essential drug for treatment of HIV. BMS is actively engaged in the research, formulation and development of "Atazanavir", sold under the brand name of Reyataz. Atazanavir is used for the treatment of HIV and has been approved by 57 countries throughout the world and is included in WHO's List of Essential Medicines. It is interesting to note that the trial court had denied the interim injunction to BMS because Mylan had raised the defence of "public interest" in its arguments. Mylan had argued that the export of a drug to a sovereign government in pursuance of a WHO order does not strictly constitute "sale for commercial purpose" due to the larger interests at stake. Against the rejection of their injunction application by the local Hyderabad trial court, BMS filed an appeal before the AP/Telangana High Court.

The case set itself out as an example of a series of cases of voluntary licence agreements between branded and generic drug companies in an attempt to promote access to medicines (Samuel, 2016). Voluntary licences may limit the scope of the sale, use and distribution of the essential drug to certain territories while excluding those where the patent application is pending or denied. The judgment in the above case shows that Courts across the country are keen to protect the interests of the domestic generic drug manufacturing industry.

In the case of *Natco Pharma Ltd. Versus Bayer Corp.*, for the first time, the Indian Patent Office granted a compulsory licence to Indian generic major, NATCO for the drug Nexavar, used for treating kidney and liver cancer in March 2012. Nexavar was manufactured and sold by the Germany-based pharmaceutical company, Bayer, which had received regulatory approval for importing and manufacturing the drug in India. In July 2011, the applicant, NATCO had filed for a compulsory licence, after a voluntary licence request was rejected by Bayer. NATCO proposed to sell the drug at Rs. 8800/- for a month's treatment, as compared to Rs. 2, 40, 425 charged by Bayer. The Patent Office granted a compulsory licence to NATCO for selling the generic version of Nexavar in India, on condition that NATCO shall pay a royalty to Bayer at the rate of 6% for selling generic versions of Nexavar. On appeal before the IPAB, the Board increased the royalty rate from 6% to 7%. On appeal to the Supreme Court, the decision of the IPAB was upheld. One of the grounds for granting the compulsory licence is that the requirements of the public should be satisfied. Bayer was able to meet the requirements of only 2% of the 8,842 patients of kidney and liver cancer. Hence, the reasonable requirements of the public were not being met to an "adequate extent" as laid down under Section 84(7) of the Act. The decision reflected that the needs of the public were the driving force for the Supreme Court's decision. The Supreme Court decision implied the desire of the Court to make the anti-cancer drug easily accessible and affordable to the patients. The Order also marked a watershed in the development of the jurisprudence of compulsory licensing in India.

In the case of *M/s. BDR Pharmaceuticals International Pvt. Ltd. versus M/s. Bristol Myers Squibb Co.,* second compulsory licence application in the country, the Applicant, BDR Pharmaceuticals International Pvt. Ltd., had requested the patentee, Bristol Myers Squibb Co.(BMS), for a voluntary licence to manufacture and market its anti-cancer active pharmaceutical compound, Dastanib, sold under the trade name, Sprycel and used for treatment of myeloid leukaemia, vide letter dated 2nd February 2012. On 13th March 2012, the patentee replied to the voluntary licence request with a number of queries that impliedly spelt rejection of the request. On 4th March 2013, in response to this letter, BDR filed an application for a compulsory licence under Section 84(1) of the Act. On 16th September 2013, the application for the compulsory licence was heard. The Controller of Patents, Mumbai rejected the application for a compulsory licence on the grounds that the applicant did not try to obtain a voluntary licence from the patentee on reasonable terms and conditions.

In addition, the Court said that a compulsory licence could not be granted as a matter of right, but it a remedy to be resorted to only when all attempts to secure a voluntary licence from the patentee have failed. In addition, the Court ruled that the objections raised by the patentee were reasonable, and the applicant failed to adequately answer its queries. Further, the applicant failed to make any communication after the initial request failed to bear fruit. The Applicant deliberately waited for time to pass by in order to invoke Section 84. Thus, the applicant did not follow the scheme of the law and make a *prima facie* case for making an order under Section 84 of the Act. Thus, the application for a compulsory licence was rejected.

Section 3(d): Restriction of Patentability for new forms of known substances

The most important subject-matter exclusion under Section 3(d), has significant implications in the area of pharmaceuticals. This section forbids patents on both new uses of known substances and on new forms of known substances that do not enhance the "efficacy". The *Explanation* to the section makes it clear that salts, esters, ethers, polymorphs, complexes, combinations, and other derivatives of known substance shall be considered to be the same substance unless they differ significantly with regard to efficacy. This is in stark contrast with the United States and Europe, where patents for a new form of a known substance are fairly common and do not cover a compound, but rather a compound's use in a particular way (Kapczynski, 2009). New forms of known substances that have pharmaceutical applications are also commonly patented. These "new forms" could be structural forms of a compound with different properties, such as polymorphs (Kapczynski, 2009).

Pharmaceuticals are typically administered in the salt form, as salt forms dissolve more easily into the bloodstream. Salts are formed by adding different acids to bases to produce different forms with different properties. Patents for pharmaceutical salts have been granted for decades in the United States, upon showing that the salt differed from the previously disclosed compound in an unexpectedly beneficial way (Kapczynski, 2009).

Section 3(d) imposes substantial limits on these claims, limiting the claims on new forms of known substances to those that have "increased efficacy." The section aims to prevent "ever-greening" of patents, by providing only those pharmaceutical derivatives that demonstrate significantly enhanced efficacy are patentable. The underlying assumption behind section 3(d) is that derivatives such as salt forms, polymorphs, isomers, that are structurally similar to known pharmaceutical substances are likely to be functionally equivalent as well, and if that is not the case and the new form works better than the old form, it is up to the patent applicant to demonstrate this and justify the claim to a patent (Kapczynski, 2009).

To this extent, Section 3(d) draws a distinction between "ever-greening" and incremental innovation. Here, S. 3(d) draws a distinction between "ever-greening" and incremental innovation. By supporting incremental innovation, the improved products help achieve better results, S. 3(d) is trying to address unmet health needs. The definition, meaning and scope of the term "increased efficacy" has enormous implications on the pharmaceutical industry in the country, as is demonstrated in the *Novartis* judgment. Novartis, the Swiss pharmaceutical giant, developed beta-crystalline form of Imatinib mesylate, an anti-cancer drug used for the treatment of Chronic Myelogenous Leukemia (CML), a debilitating form of cancer. To date, 40 patents covering this polymorph have been granted to Novartis in various countries. Owing to the unavailability of drug patents in India until 1st January 2005, Novartis filed for a patent for this polymorph under the "mail box application". Pursuant to the 2005 Amendment to the Patents Act, 1970, which introduced product patents for pharmaceuticals, the Novartis application was opened and examined. The grant of the patent was opposed by several generic drug companies on the grounds of lack of novelty, lack of "significantly enhanced efficacy" under Section 3(d), and obviousness. In 2006, agreeing with the arguments raised by the Assistant Controller of Indian Patent Office rejected the patent application of Novartis covering Glivec, or "Gleevec" as it is known as in the United States, under Section 3(d). On an appeal to the Madras High Court, Novartis challenged the constitutionality of Section 3(d) and its compatibility with TRIPS. The Madras High Court ruled that Section 3(d) was constitutional and that it was also compatible with TRIPS. Pursuant to a government notification, the High Court transferred the first petition to the Intellectual Property Appellate Board (IPAB), a specialist tribunal set up to deal with appeals from the various intellectual property offices across the country. The IPAB held that the patentability of the product is hit by Section 3(d) of the Act. Reiterating the High Court's observation, the IPAB also referred to the pricing of the drug Gleevec while the appellant held EMRs over the drug, and used to charge Rs. 1,20,000/- per month for a required dose of the drug from a cancer patient, not disputed by the Appellant, which was in view of the Madras High Court too expensive to the poor cancer patients in India. Thus, the Court observed that the grant of product patent to the appellant could create havoc to the lives of poor people and their families affected with cancer for which this drug is effective. So in the light of public interest and effect of the patent on the drug on the society, the Court held that grant of the patent would also be hit by Section 3(b) of the Act, which prohibits the grant of the patent on inventions, exploitation of which would create public disorder. Thus, the IPAB allowed process patent for Imatinib Mesylate in beta crystal form and disallowed the product patent on the same.

Aggrieved by the order of the IPAB, Novartis filed a writ petition under Article 136 of the Constitution before the Supreme Court of India. The Supreme Court ruled that Imatinib Mesylate is a known substance, and thus does not qualify the test of "invention" as laid down under Section 2(1)(j) and Section 2(1)(ja) of the Patents Act, 1970. Further, the beta-crystalline form of Imatinib Mesylate is a polymorph of Imatinib directly ran into Section 3(d) of the Act. Thus, a beta-crystalline form of Imatinib Mesylate was a new form of a known substance which bore similar pharmacological properties of Imatinib Mesylate, thus, there is no "enhance therapeutic efficacy" as required under Section 3(d). The Court further states that while the beta-crystal form of Imatinib Mesylate has the following enhancing properties Imatinib Mesylate: (1) better thermodynamic stability (2) more beneficial flow properties (3) lower hygroscopicity, but these properties have nothing to do with therapeutic efficacy. Therefore, the beta-crystalline form of Imatinib Mesylate failed the test of both inventiveness under Section 2(1)(j) and (ja) and Section 3(d) respectively. Finally, the Court dismissed the Appeal of Novartis, in what was a 7-year long litigation saga that had gripped the country from start to end. This case is widely touted as landmark judgments in the history of pharmaceuticals in the country. Moreover, this case made the general public, health advocates sit up and take notice of the raging access to medicines debate in the country. In addition, the case is also interpreted with the intent to protect the generic drug industry of the country.

In another landmark judgment (*F. Hoffmann-La Roche Ltd. And Anr. versus Cipla Limited)* involving Section 3(d), Roche, along with Pfizer (as a joint applicant), claimed that it had been granted a patent in February 2007 for "Erlotinib', the molecular [6, 7-bis (2-methoxyethoxy) quinazolin-4- y (3-ethynylphenyl) amine hydrochloride. The patented product, which Roche introduced into the Indian market in 2006, was marketed under the brand name TARCEVA. In December 2007 and January 2008, Indian newspapers reported Cipla's plan to launch a generic version of 'Erlotinib', and soon after, Roche commenced patent infringement proceedings. In response to Roche's claims, Cipla filed a detailed defence and counterclaim arguing that

Roche's patent was invalid because 'Erlotinib' was a derivative of Quinazolin, which had been used in cancer treatment. Pursuant to S.3(d) of the Indian Patents Act, a derivative of a known compound is not patentable. In addition, the huge difference in price between Roche's drug (Rs. 4,800 (approx. US$ 100) and Cipla's drug (Rs. 1,600 (approx US$ 33) should be taken into account when deciding whether or not to grant an interim injunction. Cipla strongly argued that because the drug in question was a life-saving drug, the public interest issue was an important factor to be taken into account. While hearing the case, the judge noted that the generic drug version of 'Erlotinib' manufactured and marketed by Cipla is available at one-third the price of Roche's drug, Tarceva. Further, the Court noted that Tarceva is not manufactured in India, it is imported. The Court noted that the right to access to life-saving drugs, and the need for secure long term supplies, is a serious issue in India. In cases of this sort, the injury that would be caused to the general public if the generic version of the drug were not available is a strong point for the court to rule in favour of a refusal to grant an injunction.

The doubts about the validity of the patent raised by Cipla on the ground of obviousness, and 'Erlotinib' being a derivative of a known compound which did not meet the 'increased efficacy' requirement provided for in S. 3(d) of the Patents Act, were dismissed by the judge as having been adequately dealt by the Patent Office at the opposition stage. The Court reviewed the observations that had been made by the Controller while granting the patent and concluded that Cipla had not substantiated this objection. Overall, the judge was of the view that while Roche had established a strong case in support of its patent infringement claim, the 'public interest' and lower pricing of Cipla's drug made the court to rule in favour of Cipla. Roche filed an appeal against the Order of the single judge, primarily arguing that since it had made out a prima facie case of infringement, an injunction should have been granted. Roche further argued that a failure to protect the rights of the patentee is contrary to the public interest of encouraging further research in the pharmaceutical field. The Court dismissed Roche's appeal and upheld the order of the single judge. The Court did not fully elaborate the public interest point relating to the pricing of the drugs, basing its judgment instead of on the ground that Cipla had raised a credible challenge to the validity of the patent.

However, in a case that is the flip side of the coin, the Patent Office has recently granted a patent for the polymorph of a known compound, notwithstanding the objections raised under Section 3(d) of the Act. An application was filed for "Polymorphic Forms of Rixamixin, Process for their production and use thereof in medicinal preparations," on January 3, 2008. Some of the procedural objections raised by the Controller of Patents were "some of the claims fell under Section 3(d) as they are defined as merely a new form of a known substance without any enhancement in known therapeutic effect thereof". Following the arguments of the Applicant's counsel in favour of the amended claims, the Controller held that the invention under consideration comprises a synergistic composition and has improved pharmaceutical properties. The enhancement in efficacy lay in the fact that the polymorph had an in vivo absorption level of about 100 times slower than the original form, resulting in a reduction of the toxicity 100 times due to absorption. Therefore, the Controller was of the opinion that the disclosure by the Applicant for proving the efficacy (i.e. same therapeutic value with 100 times less toxicity of the new polymorph of this invention) was appropriate until someone interested proved contrary to it. Hence, the claims were set free of the clutches of S. 3(d), with the qualification that they might be examined in a stricter sense in the proceeding if arising out of the opposition u/s. 25 and/or revocation. The other technical and procedural objections by the Examiner were also set aside by the Controller. The patent was granted to the polymorph on the basis of the amended claims.

This decision may well indicate the beginning of a trend by the Patent Office to be willing to overlook S. 3(d) objections to the grant of a patent to a polymorph in the presence of proven enhanced efficacy of the original form. This would be welcome news indeed for the proponents of the school of thought firmly believing that polymorph patents will increase cost-efficiency.

In *Ajanta Pharma versus Allergan Inc. and Controller of Patents and Designs,* Allergan, the US-based drug company had obtained patents for combination derivatives of the Bimatoprost and Timolol, and Brimonidine and Timolol, used for the treatment of Glaucoma. The Appellant sought to revoke the patents on the grounds of obviousness. The combination showed advantages over single therapy of either of the drugs (Bimatoprost, Timolol, or Brimonidine). The Court held that derivatives of either of the drugs were not unknown and hence indicated that the invention was an obvious one. Also, since the combination of the drugs had only significant advantages over single therapy, and thus, "efficacy" could be shown in the respondent's combination derivative. Section 3(d) excludes the patentability of "derivatives of known substances, unless they differ significantly in properties with regard to efficacy." On the stated grounds, the patent of the respondent was revoked. This decision may have also encouraged the generic ophthalmological drug industry, in competition with the pharmaceutical MNCs.

In another case of *Gilead Pharmasset, LLC versus Union of India and Anr.*, Gilead, a US-based pharmaceutical company, had filed for a patent application for their product Sovaldi, a Hepatitis-C drug, more effective against the disease than the existing prior art, and sold at an extremely high rate in the USA. The complete course of Sovaldi was expected to cost around $84, 000 in the USA, and approximately $ 60, 000 worldwide. As the Times of India reported, Sovaldi would be available at a price of $900 for 12 weeks in India. It is estimated that 3% of the world's population is infected with the disease, and 170 million chronic carriers at risk of developing liver cancer, Hepatitis-C (HCV) is fast-overshadowing HIV/AIDS in urgency and severity. India alone has an estimated 12 million people who are chronically infected with HIV, with 96,000 deaths annually due to the infection. Coupled with the fact that the majority of the HCV patients are poor and uninsured, the issue of access to medicines for patients becomes more acute. Due to the extremely high costs associated with the drug, Gilead had voluntarily licensed and allowed seven Indian generic manufacturers to market the drug, while the patent application was still pending. The patent application was opposed by NATCO Pharma and patient interest groups Delhi Network of Positive People, Initiatives for Medicines, Access, and Knowledge. In spite of the voluntary licence made by Gilead Sciences to Indian generic companies, the cost of the drug was still very high due to the number of restrictions imposed upon these drug companies. The patent application was rejected under Section 3(d), as Gilead could not show "therapeutic efficacy" as compared to the closest prior art. On appeal before the Delhi High Court, the Court ruled in favour of Gilead Sciences, however, not on the grounds of Section 3(d), whereas the Patent Office had rejected the application under Section 3(d). The Court, while allowing the writ petition, held that when the appellant's petition under Section 14 of the Act was pending, two pre-grant oppositions were filed by NATCO and IMAK. The appellants were not issued any notice under Section 25 of the Act. The Court also accepted Gilead's claim that the Patent Office's order was influenced by the pre-grant oppositions, including the typographical errors made in them. In view of the elements of bias and flouting of procedural requirements as laid down under the Act, the order of the Patent Office violated principles of natural justice, and thus, the Court remanded the case back to the Patent Office for fresh proceedings, and decision be made only after holding hearings for both Section 14 and 25, and issuance of prior notice to all the parties.

In another case (*Merck Sharp and Dohme Corporation and Anr. versus Glenmark Pharmaceuticals*) dealing with Section 3(d), US-based Schering Corporation (now Merck Sharp), sought to patent Vorapaxar, a crystalline polymorph of bisulfate salt of thrombin receptor antagonist, which was yet to be fully developed. In 2009, the Assistant Controller of Patents and Designs dismissed the application view of the absence of "therapeutic efficacy" as required under Section 3(d) and Section 2(i)(j)(a) on the grounds of lack of "inventive step" as required under Patents Act, 1970. On careful consideration of the order passed by the Assistant Controller of Patents and Designs, the IPAB ruled that the Controller passed a cryptic and non-speaking order; and the claims raised by the appellant were not properly considered. Under Section 15 of the Patents Act, 1970, the Controller has the option to either afford an opportunity to the applicant to make amendments in the Application or refuse the application on failure to submit any amendments. However, as mandated under Section 15 of the Act, the Applicant was given an adequate opportunity to make his submission. Secondly, the Controller rejected the claims of the appellant on the grounds of "lack of inventive step". However, no substantial reasons were given, without going into details of the entire document. In view of the above reasons, the order of the Assistant Controller was set aside, and ordered the Controller to hear the matter afresh, and dispose of the matter within three months from the date of receipt of the amended claims of the appellant. Foreign applicants typically seek patent protection by filing PCT applications designating India. Since proof of efficacy relating to the crystalline form of pharmaceutical drugs is a unique requirement under Indian patent law, many patent applications belonging to foreign MNCs, are either refused or invalidated, as often the specifications do not include data showing proof of enhanced "therapeutic efficacy".

Section 8: Requirement of Details in Case of Foreign Applications

As required by Section 8, Applicants must also "disclose the source and geographical origin of any biological material in the specification, when used in the invention." According to Section 8, "an application filed for grant of patent in India, the Controller may require the applicant to furnish the details related to the processing of the application in any country outside India, within the prescribed period of time." This provision was added to the Act in 2005. In *Ajanta Pharma versus Allergan Inc. and Controller of Patents and Designs,* Ajanta Pharma, an Indian pharmaceutical company dealing with drugs used for the treatment of Glaucoma filed an application before the IPAB to revoke the patents for drugs to achieve enhanced treatment of ocular hypertension with reduced side effects, as granted to Allergan Inc., a branch of the U.S. pharmaceutical major, Allergan. Allergan had been granted a patent for "Ganfort," a patented fixed-dose combination of bimatoprost and timolol, and "Combigan," patented fixed dose of brimonidine and timolol. Both combinations were used for topical ophthalmological treatment. Ajanta sought to revoke the patents on the grounds of obviousness and non-compliance with Section 8 of the Act. In the present case, the Court found that the respondent failed to furnish information regarding any of its foreign applications for the same invention, even when it had agreed to do so. On the grounds of non-compliance with Section 8, the patent of the respondent was revoked.

Role of Judiciary: Recent Trends and Interpretation of Patent Law by Leading Courts

Several judgments of the High Courts and the IPAB show their inclination to protect the generic drug industry of the country. In *Ajanta Pharma versus Allergan Inc. and*

Controller of Patents and Designs, Ajanta Pharma succeeded in revoking the patents for drugs for ophthalmological treatments of Allergan, a U.S. based pharmaceutical company. Thus, the decision proved to be a boon for generic companies of the country vis-à-vis medicines for the treatment of eyesight and blindness.

However, judgments have also been given in favour of the leading pharmaceutical giants and thus, protect the rights of the patent holders. In a recent judgment of the IPAB, Novartis was granted an interim injunction against Indian generic company Wockhardt (Novartis AG & Ors versus Wockhardt Ltd.CS(OS) 646/2014). Novartis is the patent holder of the anti-diabetic pharmaceutical ingredient, Vildaglipitin, and its combination with Metformin Hydrochloride. The defendant, Wockhardt, filed a petition for revocation of the patent before the IPAB. The plaintiff was granted an interim injunction as a strong prima facie case had been made out for the grant of the injunction and the balance of convenience in favour of Novartis. While the case has not reached its conclusion, the interim injunction granted by the judge of the Delhi High Court indicates the intention of the judiciary to protect the rights of the patent holders.

In *Abraxis Bioscience LLC versus Union of India and Ors.,* a U.S. based biotechnology company, had filed for a patent for its invention, "composition and method for delivery of pharmacological agents", or protein-based nanoparticles chemotherapeutic cancer treatment clinically approved in several countries. NATCO, the respondent in the present case had launched Albupax, generic bio-similar drug, and thus, filed a pre-grant opposition. Based on this opposition, the Assistant Controller of Patents and Designs had rejected the application. Abraxis appealed against this rejection before the IPAB. The order of the Patent Office was set aside and the matter was remanded by the Board to the Assistant Controller of Patents for fresh consideration as the order was found be given with blatant violation of the principles of natural justice. Under Section 25 of the Act, both the parties should be heard before an order is passed under any pre-grant opposition proceedings. Moreover, an order under Section 14 and 15 of the Act is an appealable order. However, the appellant was deprived of his right to appeal. Based on the above grounds, the order was set aside and the matter was remanded for fresh consideration.

For the first time, a court has granted a *quia timet* injunction in a case involving the Indian pharmaceutical giant, Ranbaxy *(Novartis AG and Ors. versus Ranbaxy Laboratories Ltd.),* in favour of Novartis, in one of the six suits filed by the company against six Indian generic companies to guard its patented anti-diabetic compound Vildagliptin, marketed under the name, Galvus. On the question of whether the injunction should be granted or not, the Court noted that the Defendant has applied for revocation of the patent in the year 2014, showed that the Defendant wanted to launch its own patented compound. The Court also considered the fact that the balance of convenience also lies in preserving the status quo as the Defendant is yet to launch Vildagliptin. Thus, the Defendant was restrained from manufacturing, selling, or offering for sale either through its website or by any other means, directly or indirectly dealing with active pharmaceutical ingredients, compounds or formulations containing Vildagliptin or Vildagliptin in combination with any other compound as may amount to infringement of the plaintiff's patent. However, the Court did not lay down the standard of proof required for what constitutes "proof of imminent threat." Therefore, this is still a grey area in India.

In another case, Pfizer/Sugen was granted a patent on anti-cancer drug Sunitinib on October 5, 2007. Five years later, Cipla initiated a post-grant opposition, and the patent was revoked by the Patent Office. After patentees (Pfizer/Sugen) filed a writ petition before Delhi High court, the first revocation decision was set aside, on the grounds that the recommendations of the opposition board were not furnished to the patentee.

The Sunitinib patent was revoked by the Controller of Patents for the **second time** around in mid-February this year. On 5th April 2013, the IPAB stayed the revocation of Sunitinib patent. Sugen's appeal against the revocation was fixed for hearing on 14th May 2013, subject to the undertaking given by the appellant (Sugen) that they will not use the revoked patent against the second respondent (Cipla) in other proceedings. Sugen argued that Section 25(2) (b) should have not been taken into account by the Controller since that ground was not specifically pleaded by Cipla (respondent); and hence the decision of the Controller based on prior publications wasn't valid. The IPAB, however, held that S 25(2)(e) had been raised by the respondent, and Section 25(2)(e) is a ground for revocation if that *the invention so far as claimed in any claim of the complete specification is obvious and clearly does not involve any inventive step, having regard to the matter published as mentioned in clause (b) or having regard to what was used in India before the priority date of the applicant's claim*; The IPAB thus held that Section 25(2)(e) clearly and unambiguously takes Section 25(2)(b) within its ambit and rejected this ground. It also held that if the ground has been pleaded in the written statement, but not listed on the grounds, then the Controller may apply it provided the patentee is in the know.

The IPAB expressed disapproval at the manner in which the Controller had dealt with the opposition proceedings and reiterated the importance of providing sound reasons for arriving at conclusions. The IPAB then held that the Opposition Board should be constituted again and a different Controller should hear the matter afresh within a strict time-frame.

CONCLUSION

The evolution of patent law in India is the changes made in the law is largely a response to international developments. Since the enactment of the 1970 Act, the government has consciously tried to enact a patent regime that serves best the interests of the society. Even after accession to WTO and resultantly, the TRIPS Agreement, India cleverly enacted provisions that caters to the health-care needs of the society, maintaining its position as the "pharmacy of the developing world", while fulfilling its international obligations. The judiciary, too, has played its part in interpreting the provisions of the patent law which manifests the intention of the legislature to protect the public health needs of the society. As stated by a leading author, Amy Kapczynski, the Indian example shows that TRIPS leaves developing countries with a wide-ranging set of flexibilities, and India has been able to adopt and implement its flexibilities to their full potential. Because of India's leading role as a generic supplier in the world pharmaceutical market, and given the novelty and expansiveness of the implementation approach it has taken, the flexibilities adopted in the Indian patent context may well become central to new interpretive conflicts over TRIPS.

Indian firms and health activists were drawn into the terms of IP law through their encounter with TRIPS, and played an important role in recasting the terms of TRIPS as they pressed India to adopt the substantial flexibilities that it chose. Rather than reject TRIPS, Indian government actors have engaged in creative acts of legal interpretation that take extensive advantage of known TRIPS flexibilities, and that have also generated new ones. In the process, India has paved the way for new interpretive disagreements over the meaning of TRIPS. The dynamic has clearly operated beyond India as well. The process of TRIPS implementation has more generally led developing countries to make new demands with regard to TRIPS reform and to become more active participants in global IP debates.

REFERENCES

Abraxis Bioscience LLC v. Union of India and Ors. M.P.NO.57/2010 IN OA/3/2010/PT/DEL; OA/3/2010/PT/DEL.

Aggarwal, A. (2006). Strategic Approach to Strengthening the International Competitiveness in Knowledge Based Industries: The Indian. *Die Pharmazeutische Industrie*.

Ahuja, V. K. (2009). *Intellectual Property Rights in India*. LexisNexis Butterworths Wadhwa Nagpur.

Ajanta Pharma v. Allergan Inc. and Controller of Patents and Designs, Order No. 172 of 2013.

Ayyangar, N. R. (1959). *Report on the Revision of the Patents Law*. Manager of Publications.

Chaudhuri, S. (2005). *The WTO and India's pharmaceuticals industry: Patent protection, TRIPS, and developing countries*. Oxford University Press.

Dinesh, B. (2013, February 14). *India's Patent Office Revokes Sutent cancer drug patent*. Retrieved from http://www.worldipreview.com/news/india-s-patent-office-revokes-suten-cancer-drug-patent.

Duggan, M., Garthwaite, C., & Goyal, A. (2016). The market impacts of pharmaceutical product patents in developing countries: Evidence from India. *The American Economic Review*, *106*(1), 99–135. doi:10.1257/aer.20141301 PMID:31178595

Gilead Pharmasset, LLC v. Union of India and Anr., WP(C) 687/2015 and CM No.1222/2015.

t. Hoen, E. (2002). TRIPS, pharmaceutical patents, and access to essential medicines: A long way from Seattle to Doha. *Chi. J. Int'l L.*, *3*, 27. PMID:15709298

Kapczynski, A. (2009). Harmonisation and its discontents: A case study of TRIPS implementation in India's pharmaceutical sector. *California Law Review*, *97*, 1571.

Lanjouw, J. O. (1998). *The Introduction of Pharmaceutical Product Patents in India: Heartless Exploitation of the Poor and Suffering? (No. w6366)*. National Bureau of Economic Research.

Merck Sharp and Dohme Corporation and Anr. v. Glenmark Pharmaceuticals, 201 126 DLT (2013).

M/s. BDR Pharmaceuticals International Pvt. Ltd. v. *M/s. Bristol Myers Squibb Co.*, CLA No. 1 of 2013.

Mueller, J. M. (2006). The tiger awakens: The tumultuous transformation of India's patent system and the rise of Indian pharmaceutical innovation. *U. Pitt. l. Rev.*, *68*, 491.

Natco Pharma Ltd. v. Bayer Corp., C.L.A.No.1 of 2011 (ICPD 2012)

Natco Pharma Ltd. v. UoI & Ors.; *M/S Cancer Patients Aid Association v. UoI & Ors.*, Civil Appeal No. 2706-2716 of 2013

Novartis AG & Ors v. *Wockhardt Ltd.* CS (OS) 646/2014.

Novartis AG And Ors. v. Ranbaxy Laboratories Ltd., I.A. No. 17139/2014 in CS.

Novartis AG v. Union of India (UOI) and Ors.

Patents (Amendment) Act, 1999.

Patents (Amendment) Act, 2005.

Pecoul, B., Chirac, P., Trouiller, P., & Pinel, J. (1999). Access to essential drugs in poor countries: A lost battle? *Journal of the American Medical Association*, *281*(4), 361–367. doi:10.1001/jama.281.4.361 PMID:9929090

Pharmaceuticals Ltd. v. Symead Labs Limited, I.A. No. 5908/ 2013 (Order XXXIX Rules 1 and 2 CPC) and I.A. No. 5417/ 2013 (Order VII Rules 10 and 11 CPC) in CS (OS) No. 678/ 2013.

Sonowal, R., & Goswami, A. (2015). Opportunistic Infections in HIV Seropositive Patients: A Study in a Tertiary Hospital in Assam, Northeast India. *Tuberculosis (Edinburgh, Scotland)*, *53*, 65–43.

The Patents Act, 1970.

UNAIDS. (n.d.). *UNAIDS: Reports on the Global HIV/AIDS Epidemic*. Retrieved from www.unaids.org/epidemic_update/report/Epi_report.pdf

Verkey, E. (2005). *Law of Patents*. Eastern Book Company.

Vishwanathan, M. (2013, June 8). *The Sunitinib Saga Continues: Third Time's the Charm?* Retrieved from http://spicyip.com/2013/06/the-sunitinib-saga-continues-third.html

World Health Organisation. (2000). *The World Health Report 2001*. WHO.

Chapter 3
Interface Between Right to Education and IPR:
Does Copyright Law Inhibit the Enjoyment of Right to Education?

Akanksha Jumde
Deakin University, Australia

Nishant Kumar
Central University of Punjab, Bathinda, India

ABSTRACT

The chapter seeks to explore the extent to which copyright law impedes the fulfillment of the right to education and discuss the alternatives that seek to balance these conflicting rights. The chapter is divided into three parts: the first part of the chapter discusses the embodiment of the right to education in several national and international instruments, the extent of problem of the lack of access to educational materials due to copyright protection. The next part of the chapter discusses the flexibilities provided in international copyright law and efficacy of the same, primarily the doctrine of fair use. The last part of the chapter discusses alternatives to fair use and impact of these supplementary mechanisms.

DOI: 10.4018/978-1-7998-1835-9.ch003

INTRODUCTION

The First Copyright Statute, the Statute of Anne of 1709, was entitled "An Act for the Encouragement of Learning" (Copyright Act, 1709). Thus, copyright law was founded on the belief that it shall promote the progress and dissemination of ideas and information (Helfer and Austin, 2011). Similarly, the U.S. Constitution empowers Congress to "promote the progress of science" (or in modern parlance, "knowledge" (Article 1, Section 8, Clause 7). By virtue of this power bestowed upon the Congress, Congress devised a national copyright system for according protection to scientific and creative works.

Copyright seeks to protect "original and creative works" and this includes literary, artistic works, which was later extended to musical and cinematographic works. With the invention of the printing press, copyright protection came about to incentivise authors and publishers to derive commercial or financial benefit from their "creations" (The British Statute of Anne, 1710). In light of the underlying principle of copyright law embodied in the Statute of Anne (1709) to incentivise authors, copyright protection has been extended to educational materials as well (Jaszi, 1991). A right to benefit financially from work is articulated, and court rulings and legislation have recognised a right to control the work, such as ensuring the preservation of its integrity. (Masson, 1995). An irrevocable right to be recognised as the work's creator appears in some countries' copyright laws. Copyright law is based on the idea that the flourishing of the private markets in copyright-protected works will promote learning. On the other hand, the human right to education imposes an obligation on the States and their governments to provide free education for all, and this, in turn, means the easy and cheap access to educational and learning materials (Masson, 1995).

During the nineteenth century, the state's role expanded to participate in providing education in the public sphere with the rise of the concept of the welfare state, and its accompanying obligations (Nowak, 1995). The provision of learning materials is an integral part of the human right to education. Copyrights affect the prices at which textbooks and learning materials are provided, and therefore, tensions may arise between the right to education and the monopoly private right of the author owning to that copyright (Nowak, 1995). With the rise of socialist conceptions of the welfare state and its accompanying obligations, specific government responsibilities to provide education in the public sphere developed (Maskus, 2000). Therefore, along with the right to work and the right to social security, the right to education featured prominently in the socialist constitutions and the socialist theories of human rights (Maskus, 2000).

This led to a radical transformation in worldview regarding the scope of the role of the state and its human rights obligations, and thus, the emphasis shifted on the commitment to a universal right to education that is outlined in modern international human rights instruments (Claude & Weston, 1992). This, in turn, required a reconsideration of the relationship between education and intellectual property (Claude & Weston, 1992).

RIGHT TO EDUCATION: EMBODIMENT IN DIFFERENT LEGAL REGIMES

Internationally, several instruments recognise the right to education as an "inherent right" to secure the "dignity" of all the people, and thus, the right to education stems from human rights (Beiter, 2005). As embodied in Article 26 of the Universal Declaration of Human Rights (UDHR), the Preamble of which emphasises the "the inherent dignity and of the equal and inalienable rights of all the members of the human family…" A more direct connection between human dignity and the right to education is made in Article 13(1) of the International Convention of Economic, Social and Cultural Rights (ICESCR), which states that "that education shall be directed to the full development of the human personality and the sense of its dignity, and shall strengthen the respect for human rights and fundamental freedoms" (Beiter, 2005).

Education also furthers other human rights values. In its *General Comment No. 13,* the Committee on Economic, Social and Cultural Rights characterised education as the "primary vehicle by which economically and socially marginalised adults and children can lift themselves out of poverty" (Scott, 1999). Education is also closely tied to public health and individual survival; as is widely acknowledged, a strong positive relationship exists between education and health outcomes, whether measured by death rates (mortality), illness(morbidity), health behaviours, or health knowledge (Beiter, 2005). Basic literacy and numeracy can provide a means for an individual to secure employment and, thereby, to satisfy other needs such as food and shelter (Higgins *et al.,* 2008). Education is also critical to development programs, and the realisation of sustainable development. As Ruth Okediji observes, "A well-informed, educated, and skilled citizenry is indispensable to the development process" (Okediji, 2006).

Education is also connected to the idea of self-realisation (Houston, 2008). Article 26(2) of the UDHR, for example, states that "education shall be directed to the full development of the human personality." The Universal Convention on the Rights of the Child (UNCROC) refers to education in the context of "the development of the child's personality, talents and mental and physical abilities to their fullest potential." The Committee on Economic, Social and Cultural Rights has also emphasised that "education is not just practical: a well-educated, enlightened and active mind, able to wander freely and widely, is one of the joys and rewards of the human existence."

The right to education is also characterised as an empowerment right, as even basic education empowers the citizens to participate more effectively in political systems of any state. Thus, the right to education is consistent with civil and political rights (U.N. Committee on Economic, Social, and Cultural Rights, 1999). For example, education provides citizens with the tools to question and challenge government orthodoxy. Education enables the citizens to gain better understanding of the political questions at issue, thus makes basic democratic commitments, like the right to vote more meaningful, as educated citizens are able to make more informed decisions in electing the right candidate to be their political leader (U.N. Committee on Economic, Social and Cultural Rights, 1999).

The U.S. Supreme Court decisions reflect several of the ideals sought to be achieved with the conferring of the right to education to citizens of a state, as embodied in many international instruments elucidated above. In *Brown v. Board of Education (*347 U.S. 483, 1954), the Court characterised education as the "most important function of the local and state governments", the "very foundation of good citizenship" and the "principal instrument in awakening the child to cultural values…"

The Hon'ble Supreme Court of India has expanded the right to education in the right to life, as manifested under Article 21 of the Indian Constitution. In India, the right to education was conferred with the status of Fundamental Right under Part III of the Constitution in 2002 (*Bandhua Mukti Morcha v. Union of India*, (1984) 2 S.C.R 67, Bhagwati J). The Constitution (Eighty-sixth) Amendment Act, inserted Article 21A, which made education a Fundamental Right for Children in the age group of 6-14 years, by providing that:

"The State shall provide free and compulsory education to all children of the age of six to fourteen years in such manner as the State may, by law, determine" (Right to Education Act, 2009).

This Act, enforceable from 1st April 2010, makes it obligatory for the appropriate governments to ensure that every child gets free elementary education. In addition, the Act mandates that even private educational institutions have to reserve 25 per cent seats for children from weaker sections. The Act says no school can deny admission to a student, and all schools need to have trained teachers. In the case of schools not having trained teachers, they will have to comply with the provision within three years (Right to Education Act, 2009). As per the new law, the schools need to have certain minimum facilities like adequate teachers, playground and infrastructure. The government has also evolved some mechanism to help marginalised schools comply with the provisions of the Act. The government has already prepared model rules which have been circulated to the states for preparing their own rules for implementation of the Act. The Centre has also prepared separate rules for the Union Territories, which will be notified by the Law Ministry next week (Right to Education Act, 2009).

Moreover, the Act mandates that the state governments and local authorities establish primary schools within walking distance of one km of the neighbourhood. In the case of children for Class VI to VIII, the school should be within walking distance of three km of the neighbourhood. As per the government's estimate, there will be a requirement of INR 1.71 Trillion (lakh crore) in the next five years for the implementation of the Act.

COPYRIGHT IN TEXTBOOKS AND LEARNING MATERIALS: LAW OF COPYRIGHT V/S RIGHT TO EDUCATION

The critical problem of potential conflicts arises from the fact that the educational materials, in which authors may have a material interest, are critical to the realisation of the right to education (Helfer & Austin, 2012).

The price of textbooks is influenced by a number of factors, which is relative to the per-capita income of the country (Chon, 2006). For example, textbooks are typically distributed to the students "for free" in the United States, one of the most developed countries, as a part of the system on public education (Foster, 2008). In contrast, States do not provide textbooks, and students must purchase them out of their own in the majority of the developing countries (Chon, 2006). In the case of state-owned or assisted publishing, these reasons include inefficient manufacturing methods, state monopolies, and favouritism (Heyneman, 2006). In the case of market-based textbook publishing, these reasons may include industry consolidation and lack of competition. Higher prices may also be caused by the failure of multinational publishers to engage in differential pricing, so that a student in a developing country may pay a relatively high price for a book as a per centage of per capita GDP compared to a student in a developed country (Heyneman, 2006).

Many developing countries are also dominated by major international languages, and this dominance puts further strain on limited publishing and other resources (Farrell& Heyneman 1989). This also makes these countries dependent on the nations which publish in major international languages (Farrell & Heyneman 1989). Moreover, the existence of minority languages within developing countries requires either *de novo* content creation or translation of existing materials that add to the cost of textbook development (Foster, 2009).

Reliance on trade books rather than textbooks does not solve the pricing or access issues (Albatch, 2013). A literature-based approach to basic education is costly compared to a textbook-based approach. This is due to a lack of capacity and infrastructure to publish supplementary books, the expense of teacher training, and language difficulties, including the challenge of multilingual nations. However, limited book supply is "the biggest obstacle to literacy using non-textbook reading materials alone" (Albatch, 2013).

A combination of all these factors has led to severe access problems with respect to basic educational materials protected by copyright.

The Provision of Learning Materials and the Human Right to Education

A 2009 study affiliated with UNESCO found that "in many cases, children and teachers lack access to basic learning materials. Over half of Grade 6 pupils in many countries, including Mozambique, Malawi, Uganda, Zambia, did not have a single book.

In its concluding observations on member state reports, the Committee on Rights of the Child has often identified problems with the provision of education materials. Of Barbados, the Committee said in 1999 that it "remains concerned about practical implementation of the educational reforms and of policy to provide textbooks to all schoolchildren (U.N. Comm. on the Rights of the Child, 1999).

In 2001, the Committee said of Dominic Republic: "The Committee welcomes the State party's efforts in the field of education but it remains concerned about children's limited access to materials and textbooks" (U.N. Comm. on the Rights of the Child, 2000).

In the same year, the Committee expressed concern regarding "the limited availability of learning materials" in Georgia (U.N. Comm. on the Rights of the Child, 2000).

A drastic shortage of textbooks in India was noted in 2000 (U.N. Comm. on the Rights, 2000), and reiterated in 2004, when the Committee referred to "the insufficient number of trained teachers, schools, classrooms, and the lack of relevant learning material, which affect the quality of education" (U.N. Comm. on the Rights of the Child, 2004).

The Doctrine of Fair Use

Prevailing copyright practices and policies in the global publishing industry have fostered inequality rather than addressed the need to build domestic capacity in publishing or greater access to books published outside the small national market (Chon, 2007). Resultantly, rules on copyright of began to be shaped according to the needs and requirements of the developing countries. The principal international instrument that addresses these accommodations is the Appendix to the Berne

Convention (Helfer & Austin, 2006). The Appendix facilitates "bulk access" of certain types of copyrighted material, including educational materials, in developing nations (U.N. Comm. on Rights of the Child, 2006). The Appendix allows nations to adopt a compulsory licensing scheme that limits copyright owners' control over reproduction and translation rights in these works (1971 Appendix to the Paris Act Revision of the Berne Convention). Under the Appendix, a national of an eligible developing country may apply for a compulsory license to translate or to reproduce covered works at a price that is reasonably related to that normally charged in the country for comparable works. However, the circumstances in which may issue such licences are quite confined and highly complex. Firstly, a translation licence may be issued only after three years from the date of first publication of the work and can be granted only for teaching, scholarship, and research purposes (Ginsburg, 2006).

For a reproduction licence, the waiting time is generally five years after the publication of a particular edition of a copyright-protected work and is granted only for "systemic instructional activities" (Ginsburg, 2006). The Appendix also requires an applicant for a licence to show that the copyright owner denied permission to reproduce or translate, and imposes record-keeping and reporting obligations on parties who have attempted to locate the owner of the copyright, in case the copyright owner cannot be located (Berne Appendix, 1971). The Appendix also gives a "grace period" beyond the waiting period to copyright owners, in which no compulsory licence can be issued if, during this grace period, the work is distributed in the developing country at reasonable prices (Berne Appendix, 1971). Article 10 of the Convention states that countries of the "Union" are permitted to use copyrighted works for teaching purposes, provided that such utilisation of the work is compatible with "fair practice" (Berne Convention, 1886). However, these provisions have been a "dismal failure owing to the unduly complex and burdensome requirements associated with its use" (Chon, 2010).

Moreover, Article 13 of TRIPS allows for exceptions or limitations to exclusive rights to "certain special cases which do not conflict with normal exploitation of the work and do not unreasonably prejudice the legitimate interests of the rights holder." (Trade Related Aspects of Intellectual Property Rights, 1999). Consequently, copyright laws of TRIPS member states are designed to provide flexibilities that allow the use of copyrighted works that do not result in infringement and allows use for specific purposes. This is generally known as "fair use" (US), or "fair dealing" (India, UK).

In India, as in the UK, the concept of fair dealing has been adopted in the Copyright Act, 1957, instead of the fair use of the USA (Singh & Kumar, 2005). One of the purposes that are within the ambit of fair use is making copies of the copyrighted work for educational, research and teaching purposes (Section 52(1), Copyright Act, 1957). This exception further entails the right to reproduce a literary, musical, or artistic work by the teacher or the pupil in the "course of instruction". Fair Use or Fair Dealing is one of the most jurisprudentially ambiguous doctrines found in the law, and has consequently seen the widest and varied interpretation from courts all around the world. Seemingly, interpretations of this legal doctrine have also been influenced by the per-capita income of the country.

In Canada, educational institutions and persons acting under their authority may make copies and give performances of works for educational purposes, with restrictions where such works are commercially available. This is not an infringement of copyright to publish in a collection, mainly composed of non-copyrighted matter, intended for use in schools, if not more than two passages from works by the same author are published by the same publisher within five years, and the source from which the passages are taken is acknowledged (Section 32.2 (1) (e), The Copyright Act of Canada, 2012).

In the USA, the fair use doctrine allows a person to use copyrighted material in a reasonable manner without the copyright owner's consent and irrespective of the monopoly granted to the owner (Section 107 of the USA Copyright Act).

While statutes in many copyright laws of the world allow copying or reproduction of copyrighted works for educational, research and training purposes, limited to classroom instruction, and benefit of the students, courts have given strict interpretation to the scope and ambit of the term "educational purposes".

The Indian DU Copyright case epitomises this conflict between statutory language for fair use under copyright laws, and the interpretation of "fair use for educational purposes" by the leading courts of the country. In this case, a consortium of publishers, which included the likes of Oxford University Press, and other publishing giants such as Cambridge University Press (CUP) and Taylor and Francis, for alleged copyright infringement against Delhi University and Rameshwari Photocopy Service. On 14 August 2012, the Delhi High Court issued an order appointing a local commissioner to visit, without any prior notice, the premises of Rameshwari Photocopying Service. Under this search and seizure order, permitted under Section 64 of the Copyright Act, 1957, an inventory of all the infringing or pirated copies was made to be seized and handed over to the defendants only on the basis of a surety (Sheikh, 2012). The allegedly infringing materials were course packs containing extracts from different books that are selected by the relevant faculty teaching the course at Delhi University, which students routinely procure from Rameshwari Photocopy Service. It is common knowledge that in most academic disciplines, textbooks are extremely expensive and unaffordable for the average student, and if one attempted to buy all the books which are prescribed for a course, it would mean only a few privileged students would afford education in India (Sheikh, 2012). In a landmark decision granted in favour of the teachers and students of Delhi University, the Delhi High Court upheld that "copyright is not an absolute right or a natural right, which may be claimed by each and every individual or an author. Copyright must be balanced with the needs of the society and public purpose." (*The University of Oxford and Others v. Rameshwari Photocopy Services,* 2013). The publishers such as Oxford University Press, Cambridge University Press among others, appealed against the decision of the Delhi University, but later, on their own accord withdrew the case due to a petition made by their own students to let the students of Delhi University use the materials without any roadblocks on them.

In the United States, the first infringement litigation against photocopying for educational uses arose in 1980-81. In 1980-81, publishers brought copyright actions against two for-profits shops that were copying materials for student use (*Association of American Publishers v. New York University*, 2013). The parties settled both the cases, and the settlement included an agreement that the shops would adhere to the Classroom guidelines as a limit on fair use.

However, in a major court decision, course packs were held to be illegal and amount to copyright infringement, as evident from the 1991 case of *Basic Books Inc. v. Kinko Graphics Corp*. The plaintiffs in this case, all major publishing houses, alleged that Kinko's infringed their copyrights when they copied excerpts from books, whose rights were held by the plaintiffs, without permission and without payment of required fees and sold the copies for a profit. The Court found that Kinko's did not convincingly show that the excerpts it appropriated without seeking permission were a fair use of the works in question and concluded that they violated the Copyright Act (*Basic Books, Inc. v. Kinko's Graphics Corp*., 2008). The Court granted the plaintiffs injunctive relief, as well as statutory damages in the amount of $510,000, attorney's fees and costs. The Court further held that plaintiffs did not misuse their copyrights, nor are they estopped from asserting their rights under copyright law.

The case of *Princeton University Press v. Michigan Document Services (MDS) Inc*., further demonstrates the lack of resolution on common fair use issues, and the case reveals the struggle even among federal judges over the meaning of fair use in general (Singh and Kumar, 2009). In this case, a private shop created and sold course packs under the circumstances similar to Kinko's and the copy shop was found to have acted outside the limits of fair use.

In *American Geophysical Union v. Texaco Inc*., Chickering, an employee of Texaco, engaged in conducting scientific research to improve commercial performance of petroleum products, placed six photocopied articles from the *Journal of Catalysis* in his files for future reference, as he believed that the material and data found within these articles would facilitate his current professional research. The issue was whether the photocopying of individual articles by Chickering for his own research was fair use. The Court held that photocopying of individual general articles by a Texaco scientist for his research needs was not fair use.

In *Marcus v. Rowley*, the plaintiff wrote a 35-page booklet on cake decorating and used it to teach adult education classes. Rowley, the defendant, enrolled in one of Marcus' classes, purchased a copy of the booklet, and used it to develop her own booklet for her own classes, and eleven of twenty-four pages in her work were copied directly from Marcus' original work. Rowley neither gave the plaintiff credit for her work nor acknowledged her copyright. The Ninth Circuit rightly ruled that Rowley's use was not fair use. This was a clear-cut case of the use of copyrighted work for commercial purposes, as the students who enrolled in her classes paid fees, and Rowley was able to make profits from copying Marcus' original work.

However, in a more recent case with striking similarities with the DU Photocopy case, a case was filed against Georgia State University against Cambridge University Press, Oxford University Press and Sage Publications. The defendants were indulging in digital dissemination of these course packs through two on-campus systems as maintained by them: E-Res (E-Reserves) and U-Learn. Both these systems allowed students to obtain a digital copy of the designated course material, as against paper course-packs like in the DU case. The issue was whether the defendant was required to take licences or "permissions" to post an excerpt from the plaintiff's work at E-Res or U-Learn. The District Court applied fair use analysis on each individual claim of copyright infringement. Thus, the Court ruled in favour of the Defendants in five out of seventy-four claims of copyright infringement. On appeal to the 11TH Court of Appeals, however, the Court held that District Court did not apply the fair use test correctly, and the legally flawed methodology adopted by the Court, and thus, the Court reversed the decision of the district court.

The Court of Appeals held that the four factors for fair use need to be applied on a case-to-case basis as a whole, and one or more factors may be given less weightage than the other factors. The decision of the Court of Appeals was a blow to the University and the students.

The Delhi High Court also adopted a similar approach in the Delhi Photocopy case. In this case, the defendant was engaged in the business of selling course packs to the students of Delhi University, which contained excerpts from textbooks for humanities subjects, of which the plaintiff had copyright. These course packs were prescribed by the faculty of Delhi University for the students. Publishing Houses like Oxford and Cambridge University along with the Press of Cambridge University sued the photocopying shop along with Delhi University and sought an order to permanently restrain the plaintiffs from selling the course packs and compensation for the loss of sales due to the alleged infringement of the copyright of the plaintiff. The Delhi High Court ruled in favour of the publishers and granted an interim injunction (temporary order) to restrain the defendants from selling the course packs. The Judgment, however, fails to provide expound reasons for the grant of an injunction under the provisions of the copyright law.

Under the Indian Copyright Law (Section 52 (1)(i), Indian Copyright Act, 1957), reproduction of a copyrighted work by a teacher or a pupil is permitted if so done for the course of instruction. Therefore, the creation and selling of course packs, containing excerpts of academic textbooks, prescribed by the teachers of the University themselves, are well within the domain of "fair use" under the tenets of Indian law. The fact that the Copyright Act in India does not lay down any quantitative restrictions when it comes to personal use or educational use even though such restrictions operate for other kinds of usages is indicative of the intention of the policymakers to ensure that there is adequate access to learning materials (Sec. 52(1) (a) Indian Copyright Act, 1957). The Delhi Photocopy case epitomises the debate between the right of the publishers to be recompensed for their intellectual and creative output, on the one hand, and the rights of the students, including those from impoverished sections of the society, for whom full and functional enjoyment of the right to education is beyond their reach without the cheap access to exorbitantly priced learning and educational material (Mohanty, 2014).

While reproduction, including in the form of photocopying, and using or distributing parts of a copyrightable work, without permission or making payments to the copyright holder, is permissible under Indian as well as international copyright instruments, also known as "fair dealing," for determining whether distribution of extracts to students, constitutes "fair use," a reference may be made to the Canadian case of *Alberta (Education) v. Canadian Copyright Licensing Agency (Access Copyright)*. In this case, the court ruled that copying material for teaching in classrooms would pass the permissible purpose test. One could arguably restrict the scope of this decision to *'teaching in the classroom'* alone. Arguably, the Canadian copyright law runs on similar lines with the Indian Copyright law (Section 29, Canadian Copyright Act).

The "fair dealing" exception may also be examined under the "four factor test" under U.S. Copyright law:

1. The purpose and character of the use, including whether such use is of a commercial nature or is for nonprofit educational purposes;
2. The nature of the copyrighted work;
3. The amount and substantiality of the portion used in relation to the copyrighted work as a whole; and
4. The effect of the use upon the potential market for or value of the copyrighted work.

The actions of the photocopy shop do satisfy the first test: the purpose is clearly identifiable as the course packs have been made available for the study and research purposes of the students (Mohanty, 2014). Thus, the use of the allegedly infringing

Table 1.

BOOK	Total pages in book	Pages copied	% of book copied	Publisher
COURSE PACK I				
Transforming India: Social and Political dynamics of Democaracy	456	36	7.89	OUP
The BJP andCompulsions of Politics in India	402	26	6.46	OUP
Parties and Party Politics in India	584	33	0.05	OUP
Ethno-nationalism in India: A reader	576	36	6.25	OUP
Nehru and the Language Politics of India	280	27	9.64	OUP
The Political Economy of Federalism in India	432	14	3.24	OUP
Politics in India	618	19	3.07	OUP
The Production of Hindu-Muslim Violence in Contemporary Indi	500	21	4.2	OUP
The New Cambridge History of India (IV) The Politics of India sin	428	21	4.9	Cambridge
COURSE PACK II				
The New Cambridge History of India III: 4 Ideologies of the Raj	256	32	12.5	Cambridge
Capitalism: A Very Short Introduction	160	48	30	Cambridge
Post-Colonialism: An Historical Introduction	512	57	11.1	OUP
A Concise History of India	372	16	4.3	Cambridge
Oxford Journals: The Past and Present Society	204	39	19.1	OUP
An Anthropologist among the Historians and other Essays	682	18	2.63	OUP
COURSE PACK III				
Issues in Political Theory	416	141	33.8	OUP
Practical Ethics	352	31	8.8	OUP
Political Philosophy	Not Available	Not Available	Not Available	Routledge/Taylor & Franci:

work is lividly non-commercial. Under the second factor, there are two questions to be seen: is the copyrighted work original and creative, or it is mostly factual in nature? As a general principle, facts and compilation of information are accorded less strong protection than purely creative works. Thus, it needs to be seen whether the copyrighted textbooks were mostly factual or creative in nature.

Further, on the question of "the extent of permissible copying," in the case of *Cambridge University Press v. Becker*, it was decided that the University would not require a licence for reproduction of less than 10% of the total page count of the book.

As Amlan Mohanty states, in the table reproduced below, the average per centage of the entire book copied is only 8.81%, which meets the threshold level of *Becker*.

With respect to the third factor, as already seen, the "amount" of pages copied as compared to the total number of textbooks was on average 8.1%. Thus, the third test is also satisfied. However, the Delhi High Court has failed to analyse "how many" pages have been copied from the entire books for creating the course packs.

As regards the fourth factor, how the course packs affected the sales of the textbooks needed to be analysed. If the effect on the net sales of the textbooks was minimal or negligible, the fourth factor is also fulfilled.

The extent of fair use was also discussed in the celebrated Hathi Trust Case. In a suit filed in 2011, Authors Guild sought to restrain Hathi Trust from digitalising literary works for the purpose of creating a full-text database to provide access to the print disabled through the creation of image files of the text, and general preservation of the texts. In June 2014, the Court of Appeals ruled in favour of Hathi Trust allowing

Hathi Trust to digitalise the works on the grounds that it constituted fair use. Thus, the Court also considered public interest as a factor to determine "fair use".

In summary, it may be said that the Court failed to consider the jurisprudential aspects of copyright law for delivering its judgment. The Court, unlike the Court of Appeals in the Hathi Trust Case, did not consider public interest aspects as well, for deciding whether the course-packs are covered under the ambit of "fair use" or not.

HOW CAN LEARNING MATERIALS BE MADE MORE ACCESSIBLE?: OTHER ALTERNATIVES TO DOCTRINE OF FAIR USE

The Open Access System

Simply put, the Open Access System deals with free access to and reuse of scholarly works. So far, it's been primarily concerned with scholarly journal articles, digital books, electronic theses, and dissertations, and research data (Pandey & Pandey, 2014). Open Access (OA) accords users to read, copy, download, print and distribute, search or link to the complete textbooks, permitting use for any lawful purpose, as long as internet access to the material is feasible.

Creative Commons

Creative Commons is a nonprofit organisation that enables the sharing and use of creativity and knowledge through free legal tools (Creative Commons, 2015). The organisation allows authors to give permission to make their works publicly accessible for use and share, by providing customised copyright licences, which may be chosen by the authors themselves. CC licences let authors easily change their copyright terms from the default of "all rights reserved" to "some rights reserved."

Creative Commons licences are not an alternative to copyright. They work alongside copyright and enable authors to modify their copyright terms to best suit the authors' needs.

The following kinds of licences are granted by Creative Commons:

1. **Licence of Attribution:** This licence lets others distribute, remix, tweak, and build upon the authors' work, mostly non-commercially and even commercially, as long as there is attribution and crediting of the original creation. This is the most accommodating of all the licenses offered.
2. **Licence of Attribution-ShareAlike:** This licence lets others remix, tweak, and build upon the author's work even for commercial purposes, as long as

the users credit the authors and license their new creations under the identical terms. This licence is often compared to "copy-left" free and open-source software licences. All new works based on the original works will carry the same license, so any derivatives will also allow commercial use.

3. **Licence of Attribution-NoDervis:** This licence allows for redistribution, commercial and non-commercial use, as long as it is passed along unchanged and, in whole, with credit to the author.
4. **Licence of Attribution-NonCommercial:** This licence lets others remix, tweak, and build upon the author's work non-commercially, and although their new works must also acknowledge the author and be non-commercial, and others do not have to licence their derivative works on the same terms.
5. **Licence by Attribution-Non-Commercial-ShareAlike:** This licence lets others remix, tweak, and build upon the author's work non-commercially, as long as users credit the author and licence their new creations under the identical terms.
6. **Licence by Attribution-Non-Commercial-No Derivs:** This licence is the most restrictive of Creative Commons' six main licences, only allowing others to download the authors' works and share them with others as long as they credit the author, but they cannot change them in any way or use them commercially.

Creative Commons is a novel concept that allows creators to retain copyright while allowing others to copy, distribute, and make some non-commercial, and to some extent, commercial use, of their work, through a system of customised licenses.

Number Crunching: Understanding the Impact of Creative Commons

From the figures obtained from the Creative Commons website, many authors around the world are using Creative Commons (CC) licences from making their works more accessible worldwide. Encouragingly, more authors themselves are opting for more liberal and open of the CC licences than they did four years ago. This demonstrates the attitude of the authors themselves to make their works more easily accessible and the desire to reach millions of people through their creative contributions, rather than enjoying their monopoly copyright accorded to their works. Of all the CC-Licenced works, the highest number of the works is published in North America. Further, around 9 million websites use CC Licences.

Significantly, openly-accessible textbooks have saved students 100 million dollars.

Thus, one may conclude that open access movements such as Creative Commons have not only made textbooks and other kinds of reading materials more accessible through the medium of internet, but also have saved students, and other users alike, truckloads of money, which they would otherwise have to shell out because of higher costs associated with copyrighted materials while enabling authors to retain copyright over their creative works.

Realising the impact open access movements, including Creative Commons, has had on sharing of educational and reading materials to the students, and other users of the world, UNESCO has launched Open Access Repository under Creative Commons, making more than 300 digital reports, books and articles available under Creative Commons Licences (Green, 2015). This clearly shows that open access policies that increase access and reduce costs to education, research, scientific and cultural resources have also grabbed the attention of international forums such as the United Nations (UN), and the days are not far behind when open access and policies are adopted by and committed to by most countries of the world.

Countries around the world, such as US, UK, Argentina, Scotland, India, China, New Zealand, Australia, have adopted legislation or policies that lead to the creation, increased use, or improvement of open educational resources by requiring an open licence like CC BY (Marzetti, 2015).

CONCLUSION

One of the ways in which educational materials may be made more accessible if the Courts around the world sought more clarity on the extent and objective of fair use provisions. The success of movements like Creative Commons is evidence that authors are willing to reach to millions of readers. Such efforts should be encouraged with the legislative implementation of open access provisions within domestic copyright laws. Governments should also commit themselves to make learning materials more accessible, particularly developing countries, where education is an important tool to alleviate the socio-economic conditions of the country.

REFERENCES

Copyright Act, 1709, 1710, 8 Ann., c. 19 (Eng.).

Albert, K. M. (2006). Open access: Implications for scholarly publishing and medical libraries. *Journal of the Medical Library Association: JMLA*, *94*(3), 253. PMID:16888657

Alberta (Education) v. Canadian Copyright Licensing Agency (Access Copyright), 2012 SCC 37

American Geophysical Union v. Texaco Inc., 60 F.3d 913 (2nd Cir. 1994).

Australian Government: Australian Research Council-Open Access Policy. (n.d.). Retrieved from https://www.arc.gov.au/pdf/Open_Access/ARC_Open_Access_Policy_Version_2015.1.pdf

Authors Guild, Inc. v. Hathi Trust, 755 F.3d 87 (2d Cir. 2014).

Bandhua Mukti Morcha v. Union of India, (1984) 2 S.C.R, 67.

Basheer, S. (2017). *A Fair Education in a Copyright World?* Retrieved from https://spicyip.com/2012/09/a-fair-education-in-copyright-world.html

Beiter. (2019). *The Protection of the Right to Education by International Law 19.* Academic Press.

Beiter, K. D. (2005). *The protection of the right to education by international law: Including a systematic analysis of article 13 of the International Covenant on Economic, Social and Cultural Rights*. BRILL.

Berne Convention, 1886

Brown v. Board of Education of Topeka, 347 U.S. 483 (1954)

Cambridge University Press et al. v. Patton et al.,769 F.3d 1232 (11th Cir. Ga. 2014).

Cambridge University Press v. Becker, 863. F.Supp.2d 1190 (N.D.Ga., 2012).

Campbell v. Acuff-Rose Music, 510 U.S. 569 (1994).

Chon, M. (2006). Intellectual property from below: Copyright and capability for education. *UC DAViS l. reV., 40*, 803.

Claude, R. P., & Weston, B. H. (Eds.). (1992). *Human rights in the world community: issues and action*. University of Pennsylvania Press.

Creative Commons. (n.d.). *About*. Retrieved from https://creativecommons.org/about

Eide, A., Krause, C., & Rosas, A. (1995). *Economic, social and cultural rights. In Economic Social and Cultural Rights A Textbook*. Kluwer Academic Publishers.

Farrell, J. P., & Heyneman, S. P. (1989). *Textbooks in the Developing World: Economic and Educational Choices*. EDI Seminar Series. Publications Sales Unit, The World Bank.

Feist Publications, Inc. v. Rural Telephone Services Co., 499 U.S. 340 (1991).

Foster, S. E. (2008). Prelude to compatibility between human rights and intellectual property. *Chi. J. Int'l L.*, *9*, 171.

Ginsburg, S. J. (2006). *International Copyright and Related Rights: The Berne Convention and Beyond*. Academic Press.

Global Monitoring Report, E. F. A. (2009). *Overcoming Inequality: Why Governance Matters*. Retrieved from https://unesdoc.unesco.org/images/0017/001776/177683E.pdf

Green, C. (2013, December 18). *UNESCO Launches Open Access Repository Under Creative Commons*. Retrieved from https://creativecommons.org/weblog/entry/41265

Helfer, L. R., & Austin, G. W. (2011). *Human rights and intellectual property: Mapping the global interface*. Cambridge University Press. doi:10.1017/CBO9780511976032

Heyneman, S. (2006). *The role of textbooks in a modern system of education: Towards high-quality education for all*. Academic Press.

Higgins, C., Lavin, T., & Metcalfe, O. (2008). *Health impacts of education: A review*. Institute of Public Health in Ireland.

Houston, S. (2008). Beyond homo economicus: Recognition, self-realization and social work. *British Journal of Social Work*, *40*(3), 841–857. doi:10.1093/bjsw/bcn132

Jaszi, P. (1991). Toward a theory of copyright: The metamorphoses of authorship. *Duke LJ*, 455.

La Viña, A. G., Hoff, G., & DeRose, A. M. (2003). The outcomes of Johannesburg: Assessing the world summit on sustainable development. *SAIS Review (Paul H. Nitze School of Advanced International Studies)*, *23*(1), 53–70. doi:10.1353ais.2003.0022

Liang, L. (2016). *Oxford and Cambridge University Publishers v. Students of India*. Retrieved from https://kafila.org/2012/08/27/oxford-and-cambridge-university-publishers-v-students-of-india/

Marcus v. Rowley, 695 F.2d 1171. Princeton University Press v. Michigan Document Services Inc., 99 F.3d 1381 (6th Cir. 1996).

Marzetti, M. (2016, December 13). *Argentina Passes Open Access Act for Publicly Funded Research*. Retrieved from http://www.ip-watch.org/20

Maskus, K. E. (2000). *Intellectual property rights in the global economy*. Peterson Institute.

Masson, D. J. (1995). Fixation on Fixation: Why Imposing Old Copyright Law on New Technology Will Not Work. *Industrial Law Journal, 71*, 1049.

Mohanty, A. (2014, June 4). *Analysing the Delhi University v. Publishers Photocopying Case*. Retrieved from https://spicyip.com/2012/09/analysing-delhi-university-v-publishers.html

Okediji, R. L. (2006). *The international copyright system: limitations, exceptions and public interest considerations for developing countries*. Academic Press.

Pandey, A. (2016). *Delhi University vs. Publishers: A Critical Appraisal on Doctrine of Fair Dealing Vis a Vis Fair Use*. Retrieved from http://ijlljs.in/delhi-university-vs-publishers-aniket-pandey-b-b-a-ll-b-corporate-law-hons-5th-yr-university-of-petroleum-energy-studies-dehradun-and-apoorv-pandey-b-b-a-ll-b-hons-3rd-yr-itm-universi/

Priyadarshini, S. (2014, December 24). *India Unveils New Open Access Policy*. Retrieved from blogs.nature.com/indigenus/2014/12/india-unveils-new-open-access-policy.html

Right to Education. (n.d.). Retrieved from https://mhrd.gov.in/rte

Scott, C. (1999). Reaching beyond (without abandoning) the category of economic, social and cultural rights. *Hum. Rts. Q., 21*(3), 633–660. doi:10.1353/hrq.1999.0043

Sheikh, D. (n.d.). Fair Use and Course Packs: A Comparative Perspective. Retrieved from https://kafila.org/2012/08/27/fair-use-and-course-packs-a-comparative-perspective-danish-sheikh/

Singh, D. V., & Kumar, P. (2005). *Photocopying of Copyrighted Works for Educational Purposes: Does it Constitute Fair Use?* Academic Press.

The Australian Copyright Act, 1968

The Chancellor, Masters & Scholars of University of Oxford & Ors v. Rameshwari Photocopy Services &Anr., I.A. No. 14632/2012 in CS (OS) No. 2439/ 2012.

The Chancellors, Masters and Scholars of the University of Oxford and Others v. Rameshwari Photocopy Services, CS(OS) 2439/2012, I.As. No. 14632/2012 (of the plaintiffs u/O 39 R-1&2 CPC), 430/2013 (of D-2 u/O 39 R-4 CPC) & 3455/2013 (of D-3 u/O 39 R-4 CPC).

The Constitution of India The Constitution of the USA Universal Copyright Convention U.N. Comm. on Rights of the Child The Federal Research Public Access Act (FRPAA), 2012

The Copyright Act of Canada, 1921 Indian copyright act, 1957

The Newzealand Copyright Act 1994

The UK Copyright, Designs and Patents Act 1988 Right to Education Act, 2009

The United States Copyright Act of 1976 (17 U.S.C. §107)

The Universal Declaration of Human Rights (UDHR), 1948

Tomaševski. (n.d.). *Removing Obstacles in the Way of the Right to Education: Right to Education Primers No. 1,* 5. Tomaševski: Primers.

Unni Krishnan, J.P. v. State of Andhra Pradesh, (1993) 1 SC.R. 594.

Van Noorden, V. R. (2015). *Chinese Agencies Announce Open Access Policies.* Retrieved from http://www.nature.com/news/chinese-agencies-announce-open-access-policies-1.15255

Chapter 4
Arbitration in Patent Disputes:
To What Extent Is It Possible?

Shaharyar Asaf Khan
Amity Law School, Delhi, India

Ashita Alag
Supreme Court of India, India

ABSTRACT

The commercial disputes between business entities to boost international trade and technology will increasingly involve an aspect of patents. Among various modes of ADR, the arbitration is preferred more over litigation. Still, various arguments have been presented both in favor and against arbitration in patent disputes. Thus, this chapter deals with the scope of patent disputes that can be referred to arbitration, which needs to be analyzed and defined, keeping in mind the consequent advantages of arbitration in case of patent disputes over traditional litigation. Additionally, there are various procedural aspects related to arbitration that might be specifically relevant to an arbitration involving patents and may require special attention by parties involved in such arbitration have also been made subject and discussed in detail.

INTRODUCTION

As the world moves towards a high-technology society, it is only natural that the prevalence of patent litigation will increase. Technological innovations are entering almost all aspects of life, and this has resultantly increased competition between manufacturers to gain exclusive rights over new inventions (Paradise, 1995, Edwards,

DOI: 10.4018/978-1-7998-1835-9.ch004

1992, Cooper and Madigan, 1989). This competition would, as a consequence lead to an increase in patent litigation (Paradise, 1995; Kilb, 1993).

Many believe that traditional court litigation does not have the ability to deal with patent disputes, often involving complex issues requiring knowledge of the inventions, which in today's day and age often involve complex technology. This lack of technical knowledge can lead to improper judgments (Paradise, 1995).

Arbitration is an alternative means of dispute resolution and can be understood as "[t]he reference of a dispute by voluntary agreement of the parties to an impartial person for determination on the basis of evidence and argument presented by such parties, who agree in advance to accept the decision of the arbitrator as final and binding." (Goldsmith, 1971)

Many industries have made a paradigm shift towards arbitration, recognising the various advantages that it brings with it. We saw the world of sports take upon arbitration and move towards a Court of Arbitration for Sport. We also saw States adopt arbitration for investment disputes, (Kim and Khalil, 2016) which consequently lead to the rise in investor-State arbitrations.

Despite this, there has been reluctance in referring patent disputes to arbitration. (Paradise, 1995) This chapter will examine the advantages that arbitration brings with it for patent disputes and analyses the various approaches taken by jurisdictions across the world. The chapter will also look into some procedural aspects of the arbitration, which gain particular importance in case of a patent arbitration. This chapter will also analyse the extent to which arbitration can be permitted in patent dispute cases.

Advantages of Arbitration in Patent Disputes

In general, arbitration is said to be the "most neutral, most efficient, most objective, most expert and the fairest means of international dispute resolution" (Born, 2015). As opposed to this, patent litigation has been categorised as complex, expensive and time-consuming (Farley, 1986; Carmichael, 1983).

Being a more flexible dispute resolution process (Paradise, 1995; Brunda, 1987), arbitration brings certain advantages, which are lacking in the traditional court system while tackling patent infringement disputes. It is due to the complex nature of the patent disputes that arbitration may prove to be a more efficient dispute resolution mechanism for such disputes.

In addition to the complexity of patent disputes, the involvement of parties from different jurisdictions only weakens the case of traditional courts as the dispute resolution forum for international patent disputes.

Arbitration is said to have certain distinct advantages over the court system, specifically with reference to the patent disputes. Several features of arbitration can prove to be advantageous in cases involving patent disputes:

Cost

Costs associated with litigating any dispute are high, (Carboni et al., 2018, p.21) especially considering international disputes wherein one party would have to hire local lawyers to undertake proceedings in the other party's jurisdiction. This is more so in case of patent disputes which would naturally involve expert testimonies and their examination. It is widely recognised that patent litigation involves high costs (Farley, 1986). This would in-turn make it extremely difficult if not practically impossible for small businesses or independent investors to enforce or protect their patent-related rights. Arbitration of patent disputes has been said to be less than 85% of the cost of litigating the patent dispute (Paradise, 1995; Arnold, 1993; Eiland, 2009).

Being a party-driven process, the parties can control the cost of arbitration in various ways. They can decide the size of the tribunal, the extent of discovery to be allowed, and the number of hearings required, among others (Kilb, 1993). The fact that the scope of appeal in the arbitration is also limited goes a long way in reducing the cost to be borne by parties.

Arbitration also allows parties to choose the location for the arbitration or the seat. Unlike litigation where a party can sue the other only in certain courts, (e.g., courts where the defendant resides or works, courts of the location where performance is affected) an arbitration can be seated anywhere that is convenient to the parties. Parties can make this choice based on the 'cost' factor and try to reduce the costs of travelling among others. Another advantage of arbitration, especially in case of international disputes is that not all hearings need to be conducted at the seat of arbitration. If in some cases if it is not cost-effective to move mass evidence or witnesses, the hearings can be conducted at different locations to prevent costs from increasing. (Eiland, 2009)

Speed

In technology-driven industries, the dynamics change every day. There are new inventions every day and technologies become out-dated even faster. Hence, it can be devastating for the involved parties if patent disputes from the industry took years to be resolved (Kilb, 1993). It will be in the interest of all involved to have a speedy resolution of the patent dispute. It is well-known that litigation in most jurisdictions takes many years, and a considerable backlog of cases causes delays in the resolution of a dispute (Lew, Mistelis, Kröll, 2003). This will be even truer in cases of complex patent disputes. This extended litigation may also result in the disruption of business for both parties (Farley, 1986).

Arbitration is relatively a faster dispute resolution mechanism and it has been observed that resolution of a patent dispute through arbitration will rarely take more than 12-15 months (Paradise, 1995; Arnold 1993). Though arbitration is being criticised for not being as speedy as it used to be, arbitration institutions are working on rectifying this.

In fact in case of arbitrations many times there is a requirement to complete the arbitral proceedings and pronounce the award within a specific period (Article 31, *ICC Arbitration Rules,* 2017; Section 29A, *India Arbitration & Conciliation Act,* 1996; Rule 32, *SIAC Rules,* 2016). The World Intellectual Property Organisation (WIPO) Arbitration Rules require that ideally the arbitral proceedings should be completed within nine months and the award should be pronounced within three months after that (Article 65, *WIPO Rules*, 2014). In addition to this, parties can themselves contractually stipulate a period as well.

Additionally, since arbitration allows parties to choose the arbitrators and the parties can choose to have the those who are experts in the field to act as arbitrators, the time and cost the parties would have spent in a court of law explaining the technical aspects of the case to a judge or jury are reduced (Kim & Khalil, 2016; Kilb, 1993).

Furthermore, since in arbitration it is the parties who bear certain costs such as the arbitrators' fees, administrative costs related to the tribunal, which are not present in litigation, it can be assumed that it will be in the interest of the parties to complete the proceedings as fast as possible in order to keep the costs to the minimum.

In case of litigation, usually, the scope of appeal(s) is broader from a judgment which also adds to dragging on the litigation for years. In arbitration, the arbitral award is final and can be challenged on very limited grounds. This would also make arbitration as a whole faster than litigation, which may provide for multiple levels appeals with a broad scope.

All these factors together would make arbitration a speedier and less time-consuming process as compared to traditional litigation. It is in the interest of big corporations involved in patent disputes to have their disputes resolved as fast as possible, considering the fact that patent rights are given for a specific number of years.

Expert Determination

Unlike in the court system where the judges cannot be chosen, arbitration gives parties the autonomy to choose the arbitrators. In the case of patent disputes, the parties have the choice to have technical experts act as arbitrators. Since patent disputes involve complex technology, arbitration gives the parties the power to choose experts with knowledge about the technology and even those familiar with the patent regime (Kim & Khalil, 2016). In litigation, judges may struggle to understand the complex technology underlying a patent dispute (Baker, 2009) and this may impact the final judgment delivered.

Patent disputes often require the person making the adjudication to understand the underlying engineering process and the scientific basis for the invention (Kim & Khalil, 2016). The freedom to choose an expert in the field will prove to be a benefit to the parties involved in a patent dispute.

Experts acting as arbitrators will also be able to give adequate time to understand and analyse the technical aspects of the dispute as opposed to judges as the court systems in most countries are already overburdened with heavy dockets (Kim & Khalil, 2016).

Such an arbitrator will be better placed to understand and consequently resolve the dispute (Paradise, 1995; Niblett 1995). The expert determination will not just make the decision more effective but also make the arbitration speedier and cost-effective as time and money spent to explain technical aspects of the dispute to non-expert judges will be saved in patent arbitrations.

Confidentiality/Privacy

As patent disputes often involve complex modern technologies and innovations, many parties to patent disputes for various reasons may wish to keep the proceedings confidential. Many times it is in the interest of the parties to prevent certain aspects of the dispute such as business secrets from becoming public. This privilege is not available to parties in case of court litigation as in many jurisdictions, court proceedings and material are public (Born, 2006).

Arbitrations, unlike court proceedings, are confidential (Paradise, 1995; Brunda, 1987; Kim & Khalil, 2016; Baker, 2009). There is no obligation to make the pleadings, evidence, testimonies, or award public in case of an arbitration (Farley, 1986). For corporations that might want to keep their trade secrets, financial information, technological information away from the public domain, arbitration serves to be a better dispute resolution process as opposed to courts.

However, in some jurisdictions, there might be a statutory requirement to submit some awards from patent arbitrations such as those dealing with the validity of patents to the relevant patent authority (35 U.S.Code §294[d]).

Single Forum and Enforceability

International disputes often lead to litigation in multiple courts. The courts of more than one country may have jurisdiction over the dispute depending on various factors such as the country the parties belong to, the place where performance is to take place. In case of infringement disputes, the territoriality principle will apply. This, in effect, means that a patent is only valid in the jurisdiction in which it is granted. Therefore, disputes related to infringement have to be litigated separately in each state where the infringement has allegedly occurred. In the case of missing an arbitration clause, each party can start proceedings in different jurisdictions leading to parallel proceedings (Kim & Khalil, 2016).

In addition to this, there might also be reluctance on the part of a party to litigate in a foreign forum owing to unfamiliarity with the language, procedure, alleged bias (Kilb, 1993).

The agreement between parties to submit all their disputes to a single arbitration with a neutral arbitral tribunal can avoid parallel proceedings and also the cost of litigating in various states. Though foreign judgments may face issues at the time of enforcement in some jurisdictions (Baker, 2009) as there is no multilateral treaty obligating countries to enforce judgments of foreign courts, this is not the case with arbitral awards as there is a convention for the enforcement of arbitral awards. In light of the Convention on the Recognition and Enforcement of Foreign Arbitral Awards, 1958 (the New York Convention) the enforcement of arbitral awards in another country is easier. It is pertinent to note that more than 150 nations are a party to this Convention.

In addition to these advantages, the arbitration will continue to bring with it, the well-accepted advantages of arbitration such as the flexibility given to parties to effectively 'tailor' the arbitration to suit their specific circumstances (Paradise, 1995). It allows the parties to adopt the procedure best suited to their circumstances (Kim & Khalil, 2016). The arbitration will also avoid multiple litigations in case of an international patent dispute wherein each party may choose to initiate proceedings in its jurisdiction. Such a case will not only lead to an increase in costs and time but also cause confusion and may also result in conflicting and/or unenforceable decisions. Additionally, the likelihood of a business relationship getting spoilt is also less in a mutually agreed to dispute resolution process such as arbitration as it minimises the hostility between the parties and leads to lesser disruption of the business between the parties (Paradise, 1995; Farley, 1986).

Arbitrability of Patent Disputes

Public policy is often cited for not allowing patent disputes to be resolved through arbitration. (Eiland, 2009). This does not mean that in practicality an arbitral tribunal cannot consider or cannot decide patent-related issues, it only means that in many jurisdictions there is a legal bar preventing an arbitral tribunal from doing so.

The prevalent rationale is that it is the State that grants patents and is involved in enforcing the protections. Any decision in relation to grant, validity, enforcement of patents is said to impact the general public (Eiland, 2009) and hence should be in the exclusive domain of the judiciary.

There exists a difference in legal opinions across jurisdictions whether arbitration of patent disputes should be allowed, and if yes, then to what extent. For instance, South Africa does not allow any type of intellectual property (IP) dispute to be resolved through arbitration (Article 18(1), Patents Act, 1978). However, some countries allow contractual disputes related to patents such as those related to payments, licensing agreements to be arbitrated. These countries include the United Kingdom, Germany, and France. Very few countries, such as the United States of America (U.S.A.), Switzerland and Canada, allow for the issues related to the validity of a patent to be considered by an arbitral tribunal. Many countries invoke the defence of public policy to bar arbitral tribunals from considering the issue of the validity of patents even if they permit contractual disputes related to patents to be arbitrated (Briner, 1994). Even among countries that allow for the validity of a patent to be arbitrated, there is a difference in the operation of such an award, that is, whether it should operate against the general public or only between the parties. Broadly, the disputes involving patents will involve contractual aspects and/or issued of infringement and validity of the patent.

Contractual disputes related to patents might be those that relate to non-disclosure agreements, licensing agreements. Such disputes will predominantly deal with contractual aspects and will not call into question the validity of a patent. The controversies in these disputes may deal with issues such as payment of fees, royalty or other payments under the contract, performance of contractual obligations. Many issues arising out of patent licensing agreements are more an aspect of contract law than of patent law (Farley, 1986). In this sense, contractual disputes related to patents are similar to other commercial disputes, which are often referred to as arbitration (Kim & Khalil, 2016; Baker 2009).

Hence, patent disputes that only involve contractual questions should be permitted to be resolved through arbitration, just like any other commercial dispute.

However, more often than not, a dispute in case of patents will involve the issue of infringement. Where an allegation of infringement would arise, it is likely that the other party would take the defence of invalidity of a patent, which would consequently require a decision on the validity of the patent.

There is no uniformity among jurisdictions on whether disputes involving patent validity are arbitrable. Some jurisdictions do not allow for disputes related to validity to be decided through arbitration. However, in some countries patent disputes are fully arbitrable including the question of validity and the decision on validity is not limited just to the parties who were part of the arbitration; while in some other countries the infringement disputes, as well as validity of patent disputes, are arbitrable but the award binds only the parties to the arbitration (Baker, 2009). Some countries like France do not enforce awards that deal with the validity of a patent. However, a civil action for infringement, in theory, may be decided through arbitration. Such a situation will be extremely rare since a dispute for infringement will invariably raise the question of validity (Smith et al., 2006) Infringement disputes will be those wherein the infringement of a particular patent is being alleged and very often as a defence, the other party will question of the validity of the patent involved (Kim & Khalil, 2916). Even a determination of whether a patent has been infringed would require for it to be proved that someone has without a proper license used a patented invention during the term of the patent (Farley, 1986). A valid patent should exist for infringement.

Arguments for Non-Arbitrability of Validity of a Patent

The issue with the arbitration in case of patent disputes arises when the question of the validity of patent arises. It has been believed that the question of the validity of patents is essentially not arbitrable (Goldsmith, 1976). Decades ago U.S. Courts had held that patent validity is not an arbitrable dispute due to the public interest involved and hence it should be adjudicated upon by a court. Courts have held that issues related to validity or infringement of patents are not issues related to commerce (*Beckman Instruments, Inc. v. Technical Development Corp.*,1970; *Zip Mfg. Co. v. Pep Mfg. Co.*, 1930). Though now in the U.S. through a subsequent amendment in 1982, the validity of patents is allowed to be decided through arbitration.

Some countries restrict arbitrations in patent disputes in an attempt to keep issues of public law out of the realm of a private mechanism such as arbitration. These countries may allow for arbitration of contractual issues concerned with patent as property such as those of licensing and even of infringement as long as they do not include the issue of validity. However, citing policy reasons, such jurisdictions will refuse to enforce an award that deals with the validity of a patent (Smith et al., 2006).

Some believe that since laws entrust a specific authority or court of the nation with the exclusive jurisdiction over patents (28 U.S.Code. § 1338 2000; *The Indian Patents Act*, 1970; *Rijksoctrooiwet* [*Patent Act*, 1995], 51 (Neth.), allowing for arbitral awards dealing with the validity of patents to be enforced like a court judgment takes away from this exclusive jurisdiction given to public authorities. To preserve this exclusive jurisdiction, it could be permitted that infringement may be dealt with by an arbitral tribunal while a court deals with the issue of validity (Smith et al., 2006). However, until the court in such a case renders a decision on validity, it will be futile to continue arbitral proceedings on an infringement issue. Waiting for a court decision takes away a lot of the advantages of arbitrating patent disputes. It is bound to cause delays as arbitration cannot commence until the court decision is given, and the courts usually already suffer from long delays. The advantage of a single forum in case of arbitration also diminishes as parties will have to go to litigation for a particular issue, use their resources to fight in court and come back to the tribunal for other issues.

Another way to look at this objection is that since the Sovereign or the State grants the patent, only it should have the right to invalidate it. Essentially this view states that since the State creates the right, only the State has the power to extinguish it. Patent arbitration to function would require the State to give up some of its decision making power in favour of arbitral tribunals. The State would then also have to enforce the awards dealing with the issues of invalidity. However, looking at it in another way, this would be true for all arbitrations. Tribunals have been given the right to adjudicate on private rights, which also in a way are given by the State, and the power to adjudicate and enforce such rights was earlier with the courts. The awards from simple commercial arbitrations would also be worthless without the State ensuring enforceability (Smith et al., 2006).

Another view is that since arbitration is a private process, the parties consent to submit to arbitration. This limits the scope of an arbitrator only to decide issues, which the parties submit to arbitration. Any award given by the arbitrator should impact only the parties that decide to submit themselves to the jurisdiction of the arbitrator. In case an arbitrator decides on patent invalidity. His decision has a 'public effect', (Smith et al., 2006) one which deals with issues beyond the power of an arbitrator affecting non-parties to the arbitration, those who did not submit themselves to the arbitrator's jurisdiction. Some States have overcome this hurdle by allowing for the award to affect the parties, and not against the general public.

If an award from an international arbitration dealing with the validity of a patent is sought to be enforced in a country that does not allow the issue of validity to be arbitrated, then most likely enforcement of such an award will be denied, like it is in France, on the grounds of public policy (Smith et al., 2006).

Another theory that is widely used to keep validity issues away from arbitrations is that of public interest. Public interest has been one of the major considerations while deciding patent disputes, including the validity of patents for years now (Curley, 1976). The Lear Doctrine (*Lear, Inc. v. Adkins*, 1969) laid down by the U.S. Supreme

Court also gives more weight to the public interest involved in case of patents and hence allows the licensee to challenge the validity of the patents and further states that such a challenge should not be blocked by contractual obligations (Curley, 1976). It tried to promote open challenges, in court rather than in arbitrations, which were essentially private proceedings (Farley, 1986). There is a legitimate public interest in ensuring that patents are not misused or used beyond the scope for which they had been granted. It is widely believed that the protector of this interest should be a court. It is also believed that these interests will not be adequately protected if such disputes go to arbitration (Curley, 1976).

However, while dealing with the 'public interest' consideration, it is important to understand what it would mean in real terms, instead of just being an abstract reason. The essential public interest consideration behind the whole patent regime is to provide an incentive for people to invest and put in efforts to come up with innovations as well as provide them with protections so that they disclose what they invent in order for it to benefit the public (Smith et al., 2006). The monopoly is granted as an incentive to the patent holder. Up till this point, it is the sovereign function of the State to grant the patent.

The arbitration will at most deal with the question of the validity of an existing granted patent. The incentive was given the minute the patent was granted and the monopoly commenced. The question of the validity of an existing patent will require an examination of the question that a monopoly granted justifiably exists or not (Smith; et al., 2006). It is an evil that is necessary and a balance the State has to maintain between costs of a monopoly and benefits that will accrue from granting of the patent right. It is this balance that runs the risk of being upset in the case of arbitrations while dealing with questions of validity through incorrect decisions by arbitrators. The question, hence, focuses itself on the competence or the ability of an arbitral tribunal to deal with patent issues (Smith et al., 2006). The inherent faith in letting judges decide on issues that carry the colour of 'public importance' with them is the assumption that judges would hold their position because of their capability to decide these issues correctly.

Such a public-interest bar will not hold too much weight. While dealing with a copyright case, it was said that "[T]here is no reason to think that arbitrators are more likely to err... than state or federal judges are."(*Saturday Evening Post Corp. v. Rumbleseat Press Inc.*, 1987). If anything this public interest will be served better by arbitrators adjudging patent disputes. These arbitrators will not be overburdened by heavy dockets such as courts in case of litigations. Moreover, these arbitrators will be legal experts with technical knowledge in the field to which the dispute relates to and hence will be better suited to understand and resolve the dispute, not to say resolve it faster. The public interest will not be lost. In fact, in the private dispute resolution mechanism that is arbitration, if the public interest is in any way not being served, then the solution (award) will in one way or the other be overturned (Balmer, 1995). This could most likely be at the enforcement stage by the court.

With respect to the other policy considerations stated, the bottom line in cases of patent validity issues would be whether the public interest in the patent regime would be adequately protected and represented in a private dispute resolution mechanism such as arbitration.

In this context, it should be seen that even private rights (for instance, commercial rights) in a way involve some kind of public interest. Commercial disputes arising out of a contract are generally arbitrable as rights out of a contract are considered private rights. However, in the larger scheme of things, it is the interest of the State and the public at large to ensure proper enforcement of private business contracts as per reliable principles for the enhancement of business. In such cases, the public interest is aligned with the private interest in such a manner that it is bound to be adequately represented (Smith et al., 2006).

In case of patents, a holder defends the patent against a claim of invalidity as vociferously in arbitration as in litigation. It is the other party who might allege invalidity as a defence in case of infringement. However, it may be in the other party's interest to pursue a claim for an irrevocable broad license for the invention while keeping the patent valid for its competitors. In cases of validity, if a patent has been held to be invalid, the party to the arbitration alleging invalidity would benefit, but so would its competitors. Hence, it is the public interest in pursuing a claim for invalidating a patent that may not be properly represented. Moreover, since arbitral proceedings are kept confidential, it is possible that crucial material that could pave the way for invalidation is kept away from the public.

However, these concerns can be dealt with easily. Specific laws can be laid down dealing with patent arbitrations. It can be prescribed like it is in Switzerland (where the invalidation award functions as a judgment) and in the U.S. (where the award is valid only inter-se the parties and does not operate against the rest of the world) that where a patent has been held to be invalid the award must be filed with the relevant patent authority. This would leave the party charged with infringement with the same options that it has before a court of law. It could either pursue the defence of invalidity, knowing that its competitors would also become aware of the decision of invalidity, or pursue other arguments with the risk being found guilty of infringement. A course has these two choices as well. It is safe to assume that the public interest would be taken care of in arbitration just as it is in case of litigation (Smith et al., 2006).

Moving Towards Arbitrablility of Patent Validity Issues

Some states, such as the U.S.A, have through statute, allowed the disputes with respect to the validity of a patent to be decided through arbitration (35, *U.S. Patents Act*, 35 USC §294). However, in case of an award dealing with the invalidity of a patent notice has to be given to the Director of the U.S. Patent Office for it to become enforceable (35, *U.S. Patents Act*, 35 USC §294). After this, the award is available to the public. Moreover, the award only binds the parties and if the award holds the patent to be invalid, this only applies to the parties to that arbitration and the patent is still valid against others. Switzerland also in 1975 gave the power to arbitral Tribunals to decide on the validity of patents as well as decide patent infringement disputes. Switzerland goes a step further where an award declaring a patent invalid, will be recognized by the Swiss Institute for Intellectual Property, exactly like the judgment of a court (Lenz & Staehelin, 1994). Canada as well allows for the issue to be arbitrated. However, the award operates *in personam* and binds only the parties to the arbitration (Smith; et al., 2006).

Arbitral institutions are also moving towards creating rules for patent arbitrations. The American Arbitration Association (AAA) also included in its rules voluntary guidelines for arbitration of patent disputes (*American Arbitration Association, Patent Arbitration Rules*, 1992). It has a specific provision for international patent disputes. (American Arbitration Association, Patent Arbitration Rules, 1992). A few lines from a speech given by C. Marshall Dann, then Commissioner of Patents, to the New Jersey Patent Law Association in 1976 before the U.S. made validity and infringement of patents arbitrable are relevant while dealing with the objections raised against the same. He stated:

This seems to me a very important and highly beneficial provision. I think it unfortunate that some courts have concluded that validity and scope should not be subject to arbitration on the basis that these matters are of such great public interest. An agreement to arbitrate is not an agreement not to contest. Arbitration simply changes the forum and the procedure. It can save a great deal of valuable judicial time. (Farley, 1977; Goldsmith, 1976).

It is generally said that arbitration helps avoid parallel proceedings, especially in case of international disputes. Though in many commercial disputes, there is a chance that parties may start proceedings in multiple litigations, in disputes involving patents multiple proceedings are bound to be an inevitable consequence owing to the territorial nature of patents. Patents are registered in particular jurisdictions. In case of infringement, litigation would have to be undertaken in every jurisdiction where the alleged infringement took place. As already discussed, this brings with it issues of retaining multiple counsels, incurring extensive costs in different jurisdictions, dealing with different procedural requirements and most importantly this might lead to inconsistent judgments (Eiland, 2009).

However, even if the objections to making the validity of a patent arbitrable are overcome, the issue of the scope of the applicability of the arbitral award would arise. Being a consensual process, some say, only those who submit themselves to the arbitration should be bound by the award. This happens in countries like the U.S. where the award would bind only the parties, and hence if invalidated the patent would be invalid for the parties to the arbitration and valid against everyone else. On the other end of the spectrum are countries like Switzerland, where the award on validity, once filed with the patent authority functions like a judgment of the court.

Decision Binding Only on the Parties to Arbitration

Arbitral awards have an *in personam* effect (Curley, 1976). Due to this the award only binds the parties to the arbitration and does not bind 'outsiders' to the arbitration. However, since in the case of patents, the huge public interest is involved, the question arises- when a patent is invalidated by an arbitral award, should and if so how can the patent become invalid vis-à-vis everyone?

This approach recognises and respects the contractual freedom of parties to decide to resolve disputes between them through arbitration. This approach allows for the contractual freedom to parties to submit all their patent-related disputes, including those related to infringement and validity to arbitration.

While dealing with patent disputes, in case the patent is held to be valid, the award can be enforced by a court. However, if the patent is held invalid, it will be effective only between the parties to that arbitration, and the patent remains valid against everyone else (Smith et al., 2006). In effect, though this approach allows for parties to submit all patent-related disputes to arbitration, in cases where an award deals with the invalidity of a patent, the award will only apply between the parties. This is to say that the award will only bind the parties who were part of that arbitration and the patent will continue to remain valid against all non-parties to that particular arbitration. This is also the view that has been adopted in the U.S. A decision of invalidity of a patent does not lead to the patent holder losing all the rights as would have happened in case invalidity was held by a court (Eiland, 2009).

Some critics have also argued that if an arbitration between a licensee and a licensor leads to invalidation of the patent of the licensor, it will also benefit the licensee's competitors by the free usage of the invention without having to bear the expenses of the legal proceedings (Curley, 1976).

However, in jurisdictions that adopt to make an award binding only between the parties to the arbitration, the patent will be invalid only with respect to the licensee part of the proceedings and not for the others. For the licensee's competitors, the patent will still be valid and they will still be bound by the payments enlisted in their agreements with the licensor.

Under this approach issue of invalidity dealt with in arbitration should only be considered as a part of contractual rights and obligations. Such an interpretation would keep intact the State's public policy concern in dealing with issues related to patents that affect the general public and will also give the parties the freedom to choose arbitration as a dispute resolution mechanism. The result on the question of invalidity will only bind the parties to the arbitration and may be used to determine their consequent liabilities under the contract.

If valid inter-se between the parties, the public policy concern may require for a decision on the invalidity of a patent to be filed with the relevant patent office, as is the case in the U.S. Such a requirement may contradict one of the major advantages for a party to choose arbitration in case of patent disputes, i.e., confidentiality. A probable solution to this could be to not include the arbitrator's reasoning in the award to be submitted to the authorities. The final decision on validity with the bare minimum information, such as the amount of damages if any could be filed with the authorities without the reasoning of the tribunal and the award with the reasons could be issued separately by the tribunal to the parties (Baker, 2009). Since the award will be binding inter-se the parties, it is natural that a party whose patent has been held invalid by the tribunal would not want the reasons for it to be known to the whole world as the patent would still stand to be valid against others. Simply because the patent was held to be invalid in arbitration does not mean that the patent holder has lost all rights. Since the patent continues to operate against everyone except the other party to the arbitration in which the patent was held invalid, it can be an incentive to parties to submit all patent disputes to arbitration if the reasons for invalidating a patent, if it is finally held to be invalid are not made public.

However, critics of this approach have said that this will enable a licensee, against whom the patent has been invalidated to sell the patented invention at a lower price as compared to his competitors on account of this licensee not having to pay any royalty payments (Curley, 1976).

Another issue which might arise with the award being binding only on the parties to the arbitration is that when the invalidity award is submitted to the patent authority, the fact that the patent has been held to be invalid will be known to all, and this would open the patent holder to more arbitrations (if all agreements entered into by the patent holder includes an arbitration clause) wherein others might want to use the patent without paying the amount alleging invalidity of the patent. This would lead to multiple arbitrations and may confuse if another arbitral tribunal comes to a different conclusion and some tribunals uphold the validity of the patent while others invalidate the patent. Hence, there are certain drawbacks that this approach has.

PROCEDURAL ASPECTS RELATED TO PATENT ARBITRATIONS

Rules

Patent arbitration is a specific type of arbitration, unlike simple commercial disputes. Hence, arbitral institutions can encourage parties to submit patent disputes to arbitration by catering to the special needs of a patent or IP disputes. In furtherance, the WIPO set up an arbitration and mediation centre in Geneva and the WIPO Rules are specially designed for IP disputes keeping mind specifically the confidentiality and evidentiary factors related to IP disputes (Eiland, 2009).

AAA also has the Resolution of Patent Disputes Supplementary Rules, 2006. Additionally, the Arab Intellectual Property Mediation and Arbitration Society was formed in 2003 in Jordan and an IP Arbitration Centre was also formed in China in 2007. While deciding to arbitrate their patent disputes, parties should be careful while choosing an arbitral institution and be mindful of its rules. Parties should consider whether the provisions in the rules suit their needs and accordingly choose the rules they want applicable to their arbitration.

Keeping in mind the nature of patent arbitrations, there are some procedural aspects of arbitration that are bound to be more important and that parties should pay close attention to. These include the questions related to evidence, confidentiality, and interim relief.

Evidence

Arbitration is not bound by traditional rules of evidence, and it is up to the parties to set out any guidelines to be followed in their arbitration with respect to evidence. Based on what the parties have decided and on the rules applicable to the tribunal, it is up to the arbitral tribunal to decide what kind of evidence to entertain and which type of evidence to reject. Predominantly documents and experts will play a crucial role in any patent dispute. There might be documents of communication with patent agents and parties may also wish to introduce evidence by way of experts to explain a certain technical aspect of the invention (Eiland, 2009). The Tribunal may itself, if the rules permit, appoint an expert to assist it. It is imperative that parties decide on these issues beforehand because both can lead to enormous costs and delays.

Documents

While dealing with documents, the tribunal will have to deal with the important issue of privilege. Arbitrators cannot go ahead and examine documents that are privileged as this will open the award to challenges at the enforcement stage (Eiland, 2009). However, despite giving a ruling as to privilege claimed by one party and asking for the document to be submitted, a party may continue to assert its privilege and not submit the document. To this effect, many institutional rules provide for a tribunal to draw a negative inference against such a party (Article 9(4) *IBA Rules on the Taking of Evidence in International Commercial Arbitration*, 1999). It is for the tribunal to decide whether the party's explanation for asserting privilege was satisfactory or not. In many cases in such a scenario, tribunals also have the power to get court assistance in obtaining evidence depending on the national law (Article 27, *UNCITRAL Model Law on International Commercial Arbitration*, 2006).

Another important issue to deal with in relation to documents is that of discovery. Discovery can be a huge factor that can lead to the cost of arbitration mount up fast and also lead to the proceedings becoming lengthy. Hence, it is important for the parties to deal with the issue of discovery beforehand and agree upon the extent of discovery they would like in case of patent arbitration.

It is generally seen that under common law a full disclosure of documents is supported, whereas under civil law a limited discovery is supported. These leanings are very well present in arbitration as well. Common law jurisdictions allow the tribunal to decide on the level of discovery whereas civil law jurisdictions allow for the parties to agree on this issue but do not allow the tribunal to have any power with respect to this issue (Eiland, 2009; Simpson & Kesikli, 2006).

Individual institutions also vary in their rules when it comes to discovery. While some do not specifically deal with discovery, others allow for tribunals to order parties to produce certain documents. The United Nations Commission on International Trade Law (UNCITRAL) Rules provide the tribunal to require the production of documents or other evidence (Article 24(3), *UNCITRAL Arbitration Rules*, revised in 2010). The International Bar Association (IBA) Rules of Evidence proposed to find the middle ground between Common and Civil law with respect to this issue and allow a tribunal to order a party to produce documents, but the tribunal does not have coercive power. However, in case of refusal to submit the documents, the tribunal can draw negative inferences if the documents were deemed to be relevant (Article 3.4-5, 9.4, *IBA Rules on the Taking of Evidence in International Commercial Arbitration*, 1999).

Since national laws and institutional rules may vary significantly in relation to discovery, not agreeing to the extent beforehand may land the parties into an uncomfortable situation where they face either a full disclosure or limited discovery not suited to the dispute. The IBA Rules have had a significant impact and are set to incorporate the best practices in international arbitration (Eiland, 2009; Peppard, 2000; Baker, 2009). The parties will have to agree to the IBA Rules for them to apply. Even if the IBA standard is not suitable, it is beneficial for parties to agree on the discovery issue beforehand in order to avoid unwelcome surprises and costs.

Experts

While arbitration allows the parties to choose arbitrators and they can choose to appoint experts, there can be scenarios where parties may require experts to prove specific points related to the invention, which might be understood better and faster by a tribunal comprised of experts in the field. Additionally, there can also be a scenario wherein, at a particular stage, for some aspect, the tribunal requires the assistance of an expert. Generally, tribunals do have the power to appoint experts where it is deemed necessary. However, this power of the tribunal is subject to the governing law and an agreement between the parties (Redfern, Hunter, Blackaby, Partsides, 2004). Some tribunals' rules, however, do not give the power to the tribunal to appoint experts on its own and leave this power with the parties to appoint experts or to be consulted before the tribunal appoints an expert (Article 20, *International Chamber of Commerce Rules of Arbitration*, 1998).

Expert evidence can also be a factor that increases costs and hence, it must be introduced only where necessary.

However, this expert does not act as an arbitrator and does not adjudicate upon the issue referred to her/him. The expert simply gives her/his opinion. In some cases, an expert is treated as a witness (Rule 28, *Patent Arbitration Rules*, 2005; Supplementary Rules for the Resolution of Patent Disputes). In other cases, the role of an expert is well defined and parties are obligated to assist the expert and provide the expert with relevant documents or goods (Article 22, *International Dispute Resolution Procedures*, 2008).

Rules seem to be more specific, considering they were drawn up keeping in mind IP disputes specifically. The Rules allow for the tribunal to order for documents or other evidence to be made available to the tribunal or the expert. It allows for evidence to be put in control of an expert for testing or inspection (Article 50(b), *WIPO Arbitration Rules*, 2014). This would effectively cover all kinds of evidence and not just documents. This rule is specifically important in case of patent disputes where the opinion of an expert might be needed on technical aspects of evidence submitted or even on inventions. This also takes into account the "battle of experts" which often takes place in patent disputes wherein each party provides its set of experts giving differing views on technicalities of the invention. The WIPO Rules propose to reduce this conflict by allowing the tribunal to assess any and all expert evidence submitted in light of the context of the circumstances of the case. This is subject to an agreement by the parties to treat the expert determination as conclusive on the specific issue referred to the expert (Article 57(d), *WIPO Arbitration Rules*, 2014).

While dealing with experts, it is important to consider the fact that the parties must have a fair opportunity to present their case, if not then the award can be challenged under the New York Convention (Article V(1)(b), *New York Conventions*, 1958) at the stage of enforcement. Since expert evidence plays such a crucial role in patent disputes which are technical and complex, it would be prudent for the parties to consider the aspects related to expert evidence in advance especially when parties may want to introduce expert evidence to prove their cases.

Interim Relief and Injunctions

While tribunals have the power of awarding economic damages at the end of the dispute, patent disputes by their very nature may require other reliefs as well. Especially in cases of infringement, injunctions, including interim injunctions, can play an important role. However, in order to examine whether an arbitral tribunal has the power to grant an injunction, the first step is to look at what the parties have decided. The intention of the parties can be seen from their arbitration agreement. Parties may choose to restrict the remedies available. If the parties are silent, then the applicable rules and the law of the State may also be considered.

However, sometimes the formation of a tribunal may take some time and patent disputes might require immediate interim measures. In some states, courts can grant interim protection until the tribunal is formed. Once the tribunal is formed, some states allow the tribunal to grant the same interim reliefs as courts (Lew, 1994; Section 17, *The UNCITRAL Model Law*, 1985). Many institutional rules also provide tribunals with powers to grant interim reliefs. (Rule 33, *Patent Arbitration Rules*; Art. 28, *ICC Rules*). WIPO Rules also provide for the tribunal to take interim measures (Article. 48, *WIPO Rules*, 2014).

Hence, generally, unless specifically restricted by the parties, an arbitral tribunal will have the power to grant an interim relief necessary in cases of patent disputes. However, parties must take into account the law of the State issuing the patent as well the law of the State where the arbitration is seated, in cases where arbitration is seated outside the State that has issued the patent. If the relevant law of that State limits the injunctive relief to courts, then an arbitral award granting an injunctive relief may be denied enforcement. This would then hold true for any interim injunctive relief as well. Moreover, if the applicable rules and law require the parties to approach courts for interim relief, then this would require the courts in the patent-issuing State to support a foreign seated arbitration through interim measures (Smith et al., 2006). Though this should not be a crippling hindrance as many jurisdictions recognise the power of national courts to grant interim measures in case of foreign-seated arbitrations (Wong, 2017; *Company 1 v. Company 2*, 2017; Section 2(2) r.w Section 9, *Indian Arbitration and Conciliation Act*, 1996). Hence, while drafting the arbitration clause and choosing the seat of arbitration, the parties should consider the laws related to injunctions as well as interim measures.

CONCLUSION

As more and more IP related disputes move towards arbitration, there is hope for the acceptance of arbitration in patent disputes. 375 IP disputes were filed before the AAA in 2007. The International Chamber of Commerce (ICC), Paris estimated that annually 10% of its cases are related to IP. The WIPO Centre was founded in 1994 and has had over 100 requests for arbitration.

The benefits that arbitration brings to the table for patent disputes cannot be disputed. In the fast-moving world of technology, arbitration proves to be a speedy mechanism for resolution of disputes as compared to court litigation. It also allows parties to reduce costs and choose the applicable rules as per their circumstances. Arbitration also allows parties to choose experts in the field of patents and the specific technology in question to decide their disputes. The overall picture painted shows that arbitration may be a better method to resolve patent disputes.

However, jurisdictions across the world remain divided on whether arbitration should be permitted in case of patent disputes. The often-used public interest argument will not hold water in case of contractual disputes arising out of patents. These disputes are just like commercial disputes, and hence should be permitted to be resolved by arbitration in as much as these also represent ‘private rights’. Issues of licenses, payments, royalties. under the agreements related to patents should be arbitrated just like any other commercial dispute. As for infringement disputes, even if in theory, we allow for infringement disputes in themselves to be arbitrated in practicality, they will almost always involve the question of the validity of a patent. Hence, an infringement dispute will be very difficult to arbitrate if the issue the validity is not arbitrable.

One way to resolve this is to let the tribunal have the power to refer the question of validity to the competent authority/court and wait for the decision. The tribunal can then continue the proceedings and decide the remaining issues, including infringement once the decision on validity has been rendered. However, this forces the parties to go back to a system, which often suffers from delays, and delay is one of the reasons the parties chose a speedier method, that is, arbitration. Moreover, parties will have to indulge in two proceedings- one for validity before the courts and another for the remaining issues before the arbitral tribunal. This is bound to diminish the convenience that arbitration would bring to the table for the disputing parties and would also inevitably increase the cost.

The other option is to allow for the arbitral tribunal to decide on validity. Here, certain public interest weighs in which can be taken care of by statutory safeguards. To protect the public interest involved in the patent regime, the law can set down certain statutory qualifications for arbitrators in case of arbitrations involving patents. This could attempt to address the concern of incorrect judgments. As judges are as likely to make a mistake as much as arbitrators, by providing minimum qualifications for patent disputes' arbitrators, it can be ensured that the dispute is being considered by quality minds. In addition to this, since parties' own interests are involved, it is natural that they would appoint the best in the field to decide on their issues. In addition to this, it can be stipulated that an award dealing with patent invalidity has to be deposited with the relevant patent authority. This does take away from the confidentiality provided for in arbitration. However, this would only be in the cases dealing with invalidity, all other patent arbitration which deals with issues other than invalidity will continue to enjoy the confidentiality provided by arbitration. Even in cases of invalidity to balance the public interest involved, simply the final decision on invalidity, damages could be given to the patent authority without the evidence and reasoning of the tribunal. The award with the rationale and reasoning could be provided only to the parties.

The next question deals with the extent of the applicability of the award. If the award holding a patent invalid applies only in relation to the parties and the patent remains valid for the rest of the world, then it allows the party to the arbitration to use and sell the invention/product at a price lower than its competitors as the competitors would still have to pay fees, royalty. Since the patent remains valid *vis-a-vis* the competitors, they still have to abide by their licensing agreement and make payments. The patent being invalidated against the party to the arbitration allows it to provide the product at a lower cost. *Prima facie* this would seem unfair.

This could lead to a case where if a tribunal invalidates a patent and the decision is deposited with the patent authority, others would be encouraged arbitral proceedings for invalidation against the patent holder. This could lead to a case where different tribunals give different rulings on validity- one upholding the validity and another invalidating the patent.

Moreover, the issue of a subsequent ruling by a court still exists. In the U.S., the law provides the parties to allow a court to modify an award, which held a patent to be valid in case the court subsequently finds the patent invalid. However, even as per the U.S. laws, parties have to expressly authorise the court to modify the award to bring it in line with the ruling. It seems unlikely that a party who benefitted from the award would give such permission.

Additionally, in cases where an invalidity award is valid only between the parties and subsequently a court held the patent to be valid, then the rights of the patent holder *vis-a-vis* the licensee are unclear in light of the payments, royalties, fees. The patent holder would have lost in the interim. Similarly, the converse would also be true wherein a patent whose validity was upheld in arbitration was invalidated in court. In this case, the licensee would have made payments as per the agreement in the interim. The situation would get complicated if one patent holder would have multiple awards on the same patent with different licensees and some upheld the validity and others did not.

However, the view which supports the award to bind only the parties to the arbitration seems to be one that supports the concept that arbitration as a consensual process and only those who consent to submit to it are bound by it. This view has the possibility of leading to a certain degree of confusion, which may, in practicality, lead to uncertainty causing parties to steer away from arbitration. If arbitration does not prove itself to be a reliable method of dispute resolution, parties would naturally not choose it. Such a situation could be avoided by adopting an approach such as that of Switzerland. This approach says that an award on invalidity should be submitted to patent authority and would then operate as a judgment of the court. While some might label this approach as slightly extreme, it brings with it a certain degree of uniformity and stability. It can also be that once an award declaring a patent invalid is submitted to patent authority, it gives it cause to *prima facie* look into and rule on invalidity. In case the authority concurs, the award can function as a judgment, and in case the authority differs, the award could be accordingly modified. However, this would bring in the concept of a full-fledged appeal and for the merits of a case to be looked into again, which does not exist in arbitration. The limited grounds on which an award can be appealed is one of the advantages of arbitration. A manner of solving this problem could be to prescribe that an award dealing with invalidity must be reasoned, and the instead of a hearing before the patent authority, the patent authority on the basis of an award could decide to treat it as a judgment if it concurs and in case it does not, there could be a provision for remand of the case to the tribunal.

As patent arbitration develops, and we have experts with prescribed minimum qualifications ruling on validity, there should be no reason to doubt that public interest would not be protected, with statutory safeguards in place. An error can be committed by courts as well, and yet a judgment attains finality after a certain point. After exhaustion of the appeals, the decision of the last court is considered final. There should be no hesitation in giving this finality to an award of an arbitrator rendered on the validity of a patent in arbitral proceedings governed by statutory safeguards. Such an award should be filed with the patent authority for record and like in Switzerland operate like a judgment.

Even in case of investment disputes arising out of Bilateral Investment Treaties (BITs) between a State and the investor, the public interest is involved. Yet, in those cases, due to the advantages of arbitration, a choice was made to move towards a specialised kind of arbitration, that is, investment arbitration with rules and safeguards suited to its needs. With the same stride, we could move towards another special type of arbitration, that is, patent arbitration with its own rules and safeguards to protect the public interest. Additionally, any arbitral award can be set aside and refused enforcement on grounds mentioned in Article V of the New York Convention, and this includes the ground of public policy. Hence, the statutory safeguards coupled with the grounds on which an award will be refused enforcement form a framework, which could keep at bay all the objections, raised against patent arbitration.

As arbitration spreads and grows as a system, it is bound to get strengthened. Many countries that do not allow patent rights to be arbitrated at all are also those where arbitration itself is in its beginning stage. As arbitration develops in all countries, there is bound to be a move to submit more and more types of disputes to arbitration. Moreover, as arbitration strengthens, it is also bound to become more trusted, and with that, the legal bars related to the arbitration of validity of a patent dispute will also start to vanish. It may be that as a beginning step the award may only be valid between the parties, but as arbitration, as a system strengthens along with sufficient statutory backing to protect the public interest involved, patent arbitration is bound to move the Switzerland way where the award on invalidity will function as a judgment of the court.

Like any new idea, patent arbitrations will and are dealing with their fair share of impediments. It takes time for jurisdictions to accept a new concept and overcome the challenges one by one. However, the advantages that arbitration brings with it for patent disputes are a considerable incentive for the world to start looking for ways to overcome the hurdles and accept patent arbitrations. If nothing else, then these advantages are at least a reason for nations to start having a conversation around patent arbitration at a multi-lateral level.

REFERENCES

American Arbitration Association, Patent Arbitration Rules, revised rules and fees for cases filed on or after May 1, 1992 4 (1992).

American Arbitration Association. (2006). *Resolution of Patent Disputes Supplementary Rules*. Retrieved from http://www.adr.org/sp.asp?id=27417

Arnold, T. (1993). Fundamentals of Alternative Dispute Resolution: Why Prefer ADR in Patent Litigation. *Practising L. Inst: Patents, Copyrights, Trademarks, and Literary Property Course Handbook*, 655-657.

Article 20, International Chamber of Commerce Rules of Arbitration, 1998.

Article 22, International Dispute Resolution Procedures, 2008.

Article 24(3), UNCITRAL Arbitration Rules as revised in 2010.

Article 27, UNCITRAL Model Law on International Commercial Arbitration, 2006.

Article 3.4-5, 9.4, IBA Rules on the Taking of Evidence in International Commercial Arbitration, 1999.

Article 50(b), WIPO Arbitration Rules.

Article 65, WIPO Arbitration Rules, 2014

Article 9 (4), IBA Rules on the Taking of Evidence in International Commercial Arbitration, 1999.

Article V(1)(b) New York Convention, 1958.

Baker, H. W. (2009). Arbitrating Patent Infringement Disputes. *Convergence*, *5*(90), 93.

Balmer, L. N. (1995). Alternative Dispute Resolution in Patent Controversies. *Risk (Concord, NH)*, *6*(145), 1–52.

Beckman Instruments, Inc. v. Technical Development Corp. (1970) 433 F.2d 55, 167 USPQ 10 (7th Cir.)

Born, B. G. (2006). International arbitration and forum selection agreements: drafting and enforcing. *Kluwer Law International*, 11.

Born, B.G. (2014). Article. *International Commercial Arbitration, 2*(86).

Born, G. (2015). BITS, BATS and Buts: Reflections on International Dispute Resolution. *ESIL Lectures*. Retrieved from http://www.globalarbitrationreview.com/cdn/files/gar/articles/BITs_BATs_and_Buts2.pdf

Briner, R. (1994). *The Arbitrability of Intellectual Property Disputes with Particular Emphasis on the Situation in Switzerland.* Worldwide Forum on the Arbitration of Intellectual Property Disputes, Geneva, Switzerland. Retrieved from http://www.wipo.int/amc/en/events/conferences/1994/briner.html

Brriner, R. (1994). *The arbitrability of Intellectual Property Disputes with particular emphasis on the situation in Switzerland.* Worldwide Forum on the Arbitration of Intellectual Property Disputes, Geneva, Switzerland. Retrieved from https://www.wipo.int/amc/en/events/conferences/1994/briner.html

Brunda, B. B. (1987). Resolution of Patent Disputes By Non-Litigation Proce-dures. *AIPLA Quarterly Journal, 15*(73), 82–83.

Carboni, A., Humphreys, G., Margellos, T., Bonne, S., Crupi, M, Strümann, S., Müller, P., & Player, J. (2018). Chapter 1: Mediation as a Resolution Method in IP Disputes. In Mediation: Creating Value in International Intellectual Property Disputes. Kluwer Law International.

Carmichael. (1983). The Arbitration of Patent Disputes. *ARB. J*, 38.

Company 1 vs. Company 2 & Anr. (2017) EWHC 2319 (QB).

Cooper, C. J., & Madigan, K. (1989, May 8). The Economy must keep its speed Down to Swerve Away From Inflation Bus. *Business Outlook,* p. 31.

Curley, A. J. (1976). Arbitration of Patent-Antitrust Disputes: Business Expediency vs. Public Interest. *The PTC Journal of Research & Education, 18*(107), 107–108.

Edwards, O. (1992). Technology Meets the Today. *Forbes*, 130.

Eiland, L. M. (2009). The Institutional Role in Arbitrating Patent Disputes. *Pepp. Disp. Resol. Law Journal, 9*(283), 283.

Eisenberg, S. R. (1989). Patents and the Progress of Science: Exclusive Rights and Experimental Use. *The University of Chicago Law Review. University of Chicago. Law School, 56*(3), 1017–1019. doi:10.2307/1599761

Farley, A. M. (1986). The Role of Arbitration in the Resolution of Patent Disputes. *Touro Law Review, 3*(47), 49.

Goldsmith, H. (1971). Patent, Trademark and Copyright Arbitration guide. *Journal of the Patent Office Society, 53*(224), 226.

Goldsmith, H. (1976). Addendum: Patent, Trademark and Copyright Arbitration Guide. *Idea: The PTC Journal of Research & Education, 18*(29), 31.

Gregg, A., & Paradise, G. A. (1995). Arbitration of patent infringement disputes: Encouraging the use of Arbitration through Evidence Rules Reform. *Fordham Law Review, 64*, 247.

ICC Arbitration Rules, 2017

Indian Arbitration & Conciliation Act, 1996.

Judiciary and Judicial Procedure, 28 U.S.C. § 1338, 2000.

Kilb, P. K. (1993). Arbitration of Patent Disputes: An important option in the age of information technology. *Fordham Intell. Prop. Media & Ent. L.J.*, *4*(599), 613.

Kim, Y. K., & Khalil, U. (2016). The Procedural Benefits of Arbitrating Patent Disputes. *J. Arb. Stud*, *26*(51), 52.

Lear, Inc. v. Adkins, (1969) 395 U.S. 653.

Lew, J. (1994). *The Arbitration of Intellectual Property Disputes*. Retrieved from https://www.wipo.int/amc/en/events/conferences/1994/lew.html

Lew, M. D. J., Mistelis, A. L., & Kröll, S. (2003). *Comparative International Commercial Arbitration*. Kluwer International Law.

Niblett, B. (1995). Intellectual Property Disputes: Arbitrating the Creative. *Dispute Resolution Journal*, *64*, 65.

Patent Arbitration Rules § 28, 2005.

Patents Act of 1952, 35 U.S.Code. §294(d) (1952).

Peppard, F.T. (2000). New International Evidence Rules Advance Arbitration Process. *Wis. Law*, *73*, 18.

Redfern, A., Hunter, M., Blackaby, N., & Partsides, C. (2004). *Law and Practice of International Commercial Arbitration*. Thomson/Sweet & Maxwell.

Rijksoctrooiwet 1995 [Patent Act 1995], art. 80, Stb. 1995, 51 (Neth.)

Rule 15, the *AAA Patent Arbitration Rules*,1992.

Rule 32, *SIAC Rules*, 2016

Saturday Evening Post Corp. v. Rumbleseat Press Inc. (1987) 816 F.2d 1191, 1197 (7th Cir. 1987) (Judge Posner).

Section 2(2) r.w. Section 9 of the India Arbitration and Conciliation Act, 1996.

Simpson, S. W., & Omer Kesikli, O. (2006). The Countours of Arbitration Discovery. *ALA. Law*, *67*(280), 280–282.

Smith, A. M., Cousté, M., Hield, T., Jarvis, R., Kochupillai, M., Leon, B., ... Branch, J. (2006). Arbitration of Patent Infringement and validity issues worldwide. *Harvard Journal of Law & Technology*, *2*(19), 333.

South African Patents Act, 1978, Act 57 of 1978.

Supplementary Rules for the Resolution of Patent Disputes (c)(1 2)-(13).

The Indian Patents Act, 1970, Act 39 of 1970

The UNCITRAL Model Law. (1985). Retrieved from https://www.uncitral.org/pdf/english/texts/arbitration/ml-arb/07-86998_Ebook.pdf

U.S. *Patents Act*, 35 U.S. Code §294.

Wong, R. (2012). Interim Relief in aid of International Commercial Arbitration. Singapore Academy of Law Journal, 24(499), 504.

Zip Mfg. Co. v. Pep Mfg. Co., (1930) 44 F.2d 184 District Court, D. Delaware.

ADDITIONAL READING

Bowes, T. (1976). Arbitration of Patent Disputes, 18 *PTC. Journal of Research in Education*, *18*, 49.

Cook, T., & Garcia, A. (2010). *International Intellectual Property Arbitration, Arbitration in Context Series*. Kluwer Law International.

Devitt, T., & Donahey, M. (1983). International Arbitration of Patent Disputes. *Journal of the Patent Office Society*, *65*, 621.

Dresser, J. (1985). Agreements to Arbitrate Patent Disputes. *Journal of the Patent and Trademark Office Society*, *67*, 551.

Field, T. Jr. (1976). Arbitration of Patent and Other Technological Disputes: An Introduction. *PTC Journal of Research and Education*, *18*, 1.

Janicke, P., & Borovoy, R. (1980). Resolving Patent Disputes by Arbitration: An Alternative to Litigation, 62. *Journal of the Patent Office Society*, *62*, 337.

Negm, M., & Bustanji, H. (2018). Particularity of Arbitration in International Intellectual Property Disputes: Fitting Square Peg into Round Hole. *Asian International Arbitration Journal*, *1*(14), 88–116.

Wu, W. (2011). International Arbitration of Patent Disputes. *John Marshall Review of Intellectual Property Law*, *10*, 384.

KEY TERMS AND DEFINITIONS

Arbitrability: Whether a certain dispute or specific types of disputes can be resolved through arbitration; whether a certain dispute is not barred from being resolved through arbitration.

Arbitration: Resolution of a dispute outside of courts wherein the disputing parties refer their dispute to a mutually agreed person(s), and are consequently bound by their decision.

Award: The decision rendered in an arbitration.

Discovery: Process through which a party to a dispute can obtain evidence from the other side through various mechanisms such as requests for admissions, depositions, requests for production of documents.

Litigation: The process of taking and pursuing a dispute in a court of law.

Patent: A sole right given on an invention, for a particular period, which precludes others from making or selling that invention without the right holder's permission.

Seat of Arbitration: Is a legal concept and not a geographical one and refers to the jurisdiction whose national law will govern the arbitration proceedings; it is the legal jurisdiction to which the arbitration is tied.

Chapter 5
Traditional Knowledge and Arbitration Dispute Resolution:
Indigenous People and Local Communities

Venu Parnami Tuteja
Amity University, Noida, India

ABSTRACT

The unique requirements of the Indigenous people with respect to the intellectual property are very different. There are many conflicts regarding the questions of culturally appropriate usage, sharing of knowledge, and proper attribution. The process followed by courts may not resolve their issues. They have distinct social, cultural, and economic needs. The redressal system should be such that it helps to maintain and protect their position. ADR is one of the best to resolve their disputes as it offers a number of possibilities. The main methods of ADR are negotiation, mediation, and conciliation. WIPO plays a role in providing ADR arbitration rules in regards to the Indigenous people and local communities. The WIPO Arbitration and Mediation Centre was established in 1994 providing the resolution among the private parties regarding their international commercial disputes across borders. Through this chapter, questions such as the extent of ADR in resolving these issues and can this centre be considered as an appropriate forum for addressing the issues and settling them are presented.

DOI: 10.4018/978-1-7998-1835-9.ch005

INTRODUCTION

Traditional knowledge is a set of cumulative knowledge, which is handed down from one generation to another generation through cultural transmission. One of the definitions can be "a body of knowledge built by a group of people through generations living in close contact with nature". It is generally described as information, which exists in a society passed by previous members of the society. The information mainly includes the use, the method and even the manner of manufacturing of the products majorly used by the natives or the members of the society (Anderson, 2012).

Traditional Knowledge can be classified into the following categories:

- Information is known to society with or without the documentation and its constant use by people, e.g., the common use of Neem, Turmeric, and Tulsi.
- Information that is adequately documented or commonly known outside the group.
- Information is known only to a few individuals and members of a few families.

The issue of the protection of the Traditional Knowledge of the local and Indigenous communities seems to have become one of the most contentious and complicated nowadays (Simon, 2005).

INDIGENOUS PEOPLE

In International law, the term Indigenous is very open-ended. The UNDRIP (United Nations Declaration on the Rights of Indigenous People) by avoiding a definition stated that the Indigenous People have the right to determine their own identity of membership. UN treaties expand rather than restrict the meaning of these fields. According to Indigenous and Tribal Convention of 1989, "Indigenous People are those who existed as a group prior to an act of conquest or colonisation and restrained at least some of their pre-existing institutions" (Pinel & Evans, 1994).

The unique and exclusive requirements of the Indigenous people and the local communities about Intellectual property are very different. Hence, the protection of traditional knowledge has become one of the most complicated issues. The historical development of the protection of the Intellectual Property in the wake of rights of the enjoyment of the private property by an individual pushed the Traditional Knowledge and the innovative practice based on the practice followed by the communities from the purview of the formal intellectual property protection regime (Arnold & Schuruman, 1991). There are many conflicts and disagreements regarding the questions of the culturally appropriate usage along with the sharing of knowledge and proper attribution of the profits. The process followed by courts may not resolve the issues involving them. Even in most of the cases, Indigenous people face many difficulties in accessing the legal system (Bell & Cahane, 2004).

Due to many legal claims filled with the disputes relating to the Traditional Knowledge, Traditional Cultural Expressions (TCEs) and Genetic Resources (GRs), all these pose severe challenges to the International legal community to set new standards and measures for tackling the problem of the Intellectual Property Protection.

HISTORICAL BACKGROUND ON TRADITIONAL KNOWLEDGE

The holders of Traditional Knowledge, who are trying to protect their knowledge through the Intellectual Property system, have three major constraints. They are as follows:

1. Most traditional knowledge is ancient and does not meet the criteria of novelty or "inventive step".
2. Traditional Knowledge is a collective effort as there is no particular individual who can be termed as the inventor and thus in whose name the application can be filed.
3. The cost involved in drafting and prosecuting the application form, the acquisition, the maintenance and finally, the enforcement of Intellectual Property Rights.

There are various examples in the form of the case studies, which prove that the protection of the Traditional Knowledge of the Indigenous People requires attention and thus, a resolution is the dispute management. Some of the case studies of them are listed below:

Hoodia Cactus and San Tribe of Africa

One of the most primitive inhabitants is the people of San tribe of South Africa. These people used a plant named "Hoodia Cactus" as an appetite-suppressant which was considered as the traditional knowledge of these people (Tellez, 2006). A patent was registered by (SACSIR) South African Council for Scientific and Industrial Research and was expecting to get exclusive rights to make, and sell the drugs commercially and entered in agreement with an international firm to mass-produce a drug which will be an appetite suppressant from the extracts of this plant. With the help of a Non-Governmental Organisation, the San people organised a campaign for the exclusive rights over their Hoodia Cactus Plant, raising the argument that they were not consulted in a pre-grant stage. Because of their efforts, they reached an agreement of benefit sharing with SACSIR. (WIPO PCT Notable Invention, 1999).

Ayahuasca and The Tribes in Amazon

A ceremonial drink, "Ayahuasca" the wine of soul used by the tribesman of Amazon basin using the bark of tree naming, "Banisteriopsis Caapi" during the ceremonies for the treatment of specific ailments of the usage of the drug "Da Vine". The US citizen, Loren Miller in 1986, acquired a patent for this drink. The tribal people came to know of it in 1994 and a huge cry was made. An umbrella organisation named "Coordination Body of Indigenous Organisations" comprising of 400 Indigenous groups took the initiative, and the Centre for International Environmental Law represented the issue before the United States Patent and Trademark Office.

Maca And the Tribes in Peru

Maca is a plant of the family of radish and mustard family, which is believed to be the first used in Junin (Peru) 1300 to 2000 years ago. It is also used as a health drink with or without fruits and vegetables in Junin and Cerro. It is also used to improve fertility and sexual functions. A conflict arose when two US companies were granted two patents which claimed that it possesses chemical secrets and the ones who recognised them as traditional knowledge.

Jeevani and Kani Tribe in Kerela

People of the Kani tribe in Kerala, India have been using the plant "Arogyapaach" for the medical benefits it possesses since time immemorial. The traditional knowledge possessed by these tribal healers called "Plathis" is the only authorised ones by the tradition to transfer the knowledge to their coming generations (Gupta,2001). The traditional knowledge of this plant possessed by the Kani tribe was disclosed by three members to the scientist of the "Tropical and Botanical Garden Research Institute" in 1987 who then isolated twelve active compounds of anti-fatigue from the plant and then a medicinal drug was developed called "Jeevan" in 1955 in Arya Vaid, a Pharmacy. It is an anti-stress, anti-fatigue, revitalising and immune-enhancer drug. Two patents were granted to the scientists for the drug, one of them for the particular use of that plant. A license was granted to an Indian pharmaceutical company for the usage of the plant for manufacturing a drug. A fund was created for the sharing profits among the various stakeholders. TBGRI finally trained the 25 families from the Kani tribe to cultivate the plant around their dwellings in the forest. In the very first year itself, the families earned Rupees 800/- on the sale of leaves.

Turmeric Case

The turmeric plant grown in India is commonly called the "grandmother's remedy' which has been applied to the scrapes and cuts of children from generations. In 1995, a US patent on the "use of turmeric in wound healing" was awarded to the University of Mississippi Medical Centre. The claim covered "a method of promoting healing of a wound by administering turmeric to a patient afflicted with the wound", such wounds including surgical wounds and body ulcers. In mid-1996, the Centre for Scientific and Industrial Research (CSIR) requested the US Patent and Trademark Office to revoke the patent. Their claim was based on the ground that the turmeric powder is famous and widely used in India for the renowned property of wound healing. Further, the scientist that confirms the existence of these properties has carried out more a great deal of scientific research. They claimed that they possessed "prior art," i.e. the existing public knowledge. CSIR also presented an ancient Sanskrit test conducted and a paper published in 1953 in the Journal of Indian Medical Association. The US patent office accepted these grounds and upheld the objections raised and even cancelled the patent. The turmeric case failed to meet the novelty criterion. This is an instant where the possession of traditional knowledge was very well known and widespread. The patent claim made was non-original, thus was easily defeated because of the lack of novelty.

DIFFERENT PLATFORMS FOR THE PROTECTION OF INTELLECTUAL PROPERTY

There are various international instruments, which recognise the importance of Indigenous People and the rights, which they should be entitled. These instruments not only recognise such rights but also provide measures to protect these rights. Some of them are explained hereunder:

UN Declaration on the Right of Indigenous People (UNDRIP)

An international instrument adopted by the UN on 13th September 2007. It was the outcome of an extreme deliberation amongst the Indigenous people and the Human Rights Commission of the Economic and Social Council (ECOSOC) of the UN. These negotiations lasted for almost 25 years (1983-2007).

The first 46 articles of this instrument lay down that, "The Intellectual Property holders have the right to the full enjoyment as a collective or as an individual of all the human rights and the fundamental freedoms as recognised in the United Nation Charter. The Declaration guarantee rights of enjoyment and practice of their culture and customs, the religion they want to follow, the choice of language and even helps in developing and strengthening the economies, their social and the political institutions" (Scheinin, 2003). One hundred and forty-four countries adopted this declaration, four countries voted against it, and 11 of them were in abstentions. Among those who opposed Australia and New Zealand reversed their position later in 2009 and announced their support.

UNEP/CBD- Convention on Biological Diversity

The aim is the promotion of the conversation of biodiversity, sustainable usage and the just and fair and equitable sharing of the profits out of the use of the genetic resources. The parties contracting under Article 8(j) are required to maintain respect and to preserve sustainability, knowledge and the practices of the Indigenous People and the local communities.

UNFAO: Treaty on Plant Genetic Resources

This Treaty on Plant Genetic Resources for Food and Agriculture came in force in June 2004 mainly focused on the conservation and justifiable usage of the resources and focuses on the equal sharing of the profits.

The treaty recognises the various rights of the farmers. It imposes a duty on the Government for the protection and the promotion of the rights of the farmers, including the protection of Traditional Knowledge.

UNCTAD: UN Conference on Trade and Development

It seeks the approach of "to protect, promote and preserve" the traditional knowledge. Although all the aims do not give priority to the interest and rights of Indigenous People.

UNILO- Convention 169 on Indigenous and Tribal People

International Labour Organisation convention 169 majorly concerns about the Indigenous and Tribal Peoples in Independent Countries who entered the convention. It came in force in 1991. The main objective is to protect the rights of Indigenous and tribal people. The convention emphasises on the giving these people the choice of deciding their priorities for developments it plays a significant role in their lives and belief. It also recognises the extraordinary importance, which should be given to the cultural and spiritual values in regards to their lands and territories.

UNESCO

On the International level, the UNESCO and the WIPO took the first initiative to approach the highlighted issue of protection of heritage by the Model Provision for natural laws on the Protection of Expressions of Folklore (1982). The Model provides protection of Intellectual property, which can be extended to musical, verbal, corporal, tangible expressions. It also includes musical instruments, architectural forms.

World Health Organisation

The main target is the protection of Intellectual Property in regards to International Trade. TRIPS agreement focuses on Intellectual Property at territorial and national levels. This agreement has given a wide range of opportunities to the nations to trade freely all across the globe without any fear of their work being stolen, and it provides proper recognition to the traditional knowledge of the Indigenous people in the global trade market.

Universal Declarations of Human Rights

UDHR 1948 is a world-recognised international document, which promotes the ownership rights of the Indigenous people. UDHR does not particularly mention the word Intellectual property right, but there are few articles which recognise such rights like those that Article 27 lays to protect the rights created by Intellectual property. Article 17 also covers the rights of people to own property, which in turn re-enforces Article 27. Article 17 extends its scope to ownership of the Intellectual property rights as well and thus providing protection to Indigenous people to make the decision regarding their own property.

Universal Declaration of Rights of People's (UDRP)

As the knowledge of the Indigenous people is protected by their customs, history, practice and artisanship. This document recognises the traditions followed by the community, the historical art and values among others. This document mainly recognise Intellectual Property Rights

Articles 5 lays that "*all people have the right to sovereignty over the natural wealth and resources within their territories. All people also have the right to Intellectual Property*". Article 14 and Article 15 are also focused on protecting and promoting these rights. These Declarations will promote and converse the knowledge of the Indigenous people by giving them a legal platform for the people who copy their legal/lawful work.

In spite of all these measures in place to protect and promote Traditional Knowledge of Indigenous People, they are still unable to resolve issues relating the Intellectual Property rights.

Protection of Intellectual Property Rights of Indigenous People

Indigenous people are inheritors and practitioners of a unique culture. They have distinct social, cultural and economic needs. Due to their sensitive background, it is pertinent that the importance is given to the complex and polycentric nature of disputes about the historical, political, social and legal dimensions of Indigenous people (Gupta, 1996). Indigenous People have unique and exclusive requirements with regards to Intellectual Property. There are various conflicts and disagreements regarding the questions of culturally appropriate usage, sharing of knowledge and proper attribution of profits.

The processes followed through courts may take a lot of time or may not even resolve the issue involving them. Even in most of the claims in disputes is relating to the Traditional Knowledge (TK), Traditional Cultural Expressions (TCEs) and Genetic Resources (GRs) who in most cases have no legal basis who may, in turn, raise a question of law. The tiresome process of the litigation may further disadvantage these people in getting justice due to various reasons like financial issues. The redressal system should be such which helps to maintain and protect their position. Arbitration allows the parties to an outcome that transcends their individual biases about the strength of their claim. Depending on the mentioned rules of the process, arbitration can offer a good chance of the desired outcome, which can be achieved in a manner, which is less formal and more affordable than the court adjudication. Considering all such factors, Alternative Dispute Resolution (ADR) is one of the most suitable and preferred options as it offers a wide range of possibilities for resolving the issues among the Indigenous people, traditional and the local communities (Nagel, 2005).

Traditional Knowledge is deeply embedded in the local culture of indigenous communities. These are the information that the people in a particular community, possess based on the experience of the previous generation and adaptation done according to local culture and the surrounding environment. It is a continuous process of evolution and development.

ADR is one of the most beneficial forms of the dispute resolution due to its various benefits few of them naming the speed of proceedings, a matter of price, privacy, even the neutral approach provided to both parties, there is a certainty of a forum, expertise of an arbitrator. It is more flexible, consensual and non-binding negotiations and mediation to more formal and binding arbitration (Osi & Carlo, 2008). The main methods of ADR are Negotiation, Mediation, and Conciliation.

Although very different from each other, they provide flexible procedures to achieve resolution in constructive ways alongside being sensitive about the feelings of the parties. It also increases the understanding of the issues at hand by pointing out the key elements at the core of the dispute. Parties here can be an Individual or collectives, a community or a business organisation or they can even be States.

In addition, Arbitration is a more formal process than Mediation. Both Arbitration and Mediation share many principles but different in conceptual ways. In an Arbitration agreement, an arbitrator is appointed in front of whom the dispute is presented who finally make a decision after considering merits and their decisions are final and binding on parties involved, which are known as Award. Thus, the parties on their own will not withdraw from the proceedings of arbitration as it functions as a Tribunal. The Arbitration proceeding provides the option of appointing an arbitrator of his or her own choice. An Award is recognised internationally, and its enforceability is under the Convention on Recognition and Enforcement of Foreign Arbitral Awards (New York, 1958).

Practically, ADR is the most suited for the disputes arising from the Intellectual Property as they include polycentric interest and in most of the cases, the decision given by the courts are in favour of one party. Intellectual Property agreements are license agreements where in exchange for cash a right to use of technology or royalty is granted which means "parties often consider some form of shared rights to be an acceptable or even preferred result" (Blackman & McNeill, 1998).

ADR, especially in the form of mediation, is very advantageous in resolving issues involving Traditional Knowledge (TK), Traditional Cultures (TCs) and Genetic Resources (GRs) as the different cultural value system of the Indigenous people and the local communities are well recognised, and their grievances can be addressed in a sensitive way of providing a neutral procedure dealing with a variety of issues. ADR also facilitates and encourages them by providing an option of the choice of their experienced mediators who acts as neutral and have the expertise regarding the issues in hand. Along with the Indigenous group and local communities, they can be very advantageous to third party users (Wichard & Wend, 2006). ADR provides a number of opportunities to the indigenous people, traditional and local communities by:

- Recognising their varied culture and value system.
- Placing their needs of application of their customary law processes.
- Recognising the various components of the dispute, whether they are legal or non-legal.
- Finally, by providing remedies that are culturally appropriate.

Furthermore, ADR provides third party users like museums, research institutes, and universities with an opportunity to:

- Form a healthy relationship between institutes and communities.
- Remove misunderstandings and enmity among themselves
- Encourage dialogue and provide an environment for understanding the difference in their cultural opinion.

It is well known that many of the Indigenous people still in remote villages with no modern technologies at their ease. In a few of the areas, they are still living without electricity, no running water and no or limited contact with the modern world in which we live. Indigenous people are very private people who prefer to keep their knowledge and sources to themselves, especially for the purpose of medical cures. The cultural heritage depicted in their artwork like paintings and crafts, songs, dances, and potteries, among others. These people are very easily manipulated and exploited due to the limited knowledge and resources to defend them (Theurich, 2009). Eventually, with the recent involvement of companies in regards to the rights of intellectual property, a lot of them have come in the public eyes, which got them the recognition from national as well as international institutions about the validity of their local norms, especially the customs followed by indigenous people.

The United Nations created an advisory body in the year 2000 reporting directly to the Economic and Social Council, which was called the "Permanent Forum for Indigenous Issues". Further, in the year 2007, a UN declaration on the Rights of Indigenous People was adopted, strengthening the claims of Indigenous people over the cultural property and Intellectual property rights. Article 3 of the UN Declaration on the Rights of Indigenous Peoples lays Indigenous People can now invoke the right to self-determination as the right to "freely determine their political status and freely pursue their economic, social, and cultural development" (Sarfaty, 2007).

In addition to the above, a very important document is the Convention on Biological Diversity, 1922 that aims to protect biodiversity, sustainable usage, the just, fair, and equitable sharing of the profits arising out of the utilization of the genetic resources (Morgera & Tsioumani, 2010). This convention together with the Nagoya Protocol on Access to Genetic Resources and the International Treaty on Plant Genetic Resources for Food and Agriculture of the United Nations Food and Agriculture Organisation creates distinctive international legal and policy framework, which includes the protection of indigenous people's interests and mainly focuses on the above-stated benefits.

In modern times, WIPO (2004) also plays an important role in providing ADR arbitration rules in regards to the Indigenous people and local communities. According to an International survey conducted by WIPO on Dispute Resolution in Technology

Transactions, The most favoured methods among Alternate Dispute Resolution is Arbitration (30%), the next is Mediation (12%), Mediation, which is included in Multi-tier clauses, in combination with court litigation, expert determination (17%). Court litigation still stand-alone in dispute resolution (32%) (Sekolec & Getty 2003).

WIPO Arbitration and Mediation Centre

WIPO Arbitration and Mediation Centre is an international neutral and non-profit organisation for dispute resolution. It provides time-effective and cost-effective options. It is based in Geneva, Switzerland with a further office in Singapore. The Centre was established in 1994 to offer ADR options for the resolution of International Commercial Disputes between private parties. It has 184 Member states. WIPO has a history of over 120 years going back to 1883. WIPO administers 24 multilateral Intellectual treaties, including the Patent Cooperation Treaty (PCT) and Madrid system, which facilitate patent trademark applications and registration in different countries.

WIPO provides a database of 1500 experts from 100 countries specialised in Intellectual Property as well as Alternative Dispute Resolution having in-depth knowledge and experience in these fields to act as Neutrals. WIPO, as an ADR Centre, focuses on providing such a procedure, which makes sure that the special, as well as the specific needs of the parties, are met in an Intellectual Property dispute. These Neutrals are not only highly qualified, but they are multilingual legal experts in both Intellectual Property and ADR fields. This centre is an appropriate forum for the cross-border disputes of Intellectual Property, which can be resolved through Mediation, Arbitration, Expedited Arbitration and Expert Determination. (WIPO guide to Arbitration and Mediation).

Role of WIPO Arbitration and Mediation Centre

The main object of the WIPO Arbitration and Mediation Centre is to facilitate Intellectual Property Disputes. It helps in:

1. Parties to resolve the disputes by adhering to the clauses of WIPO in case they have not previously agreed to it
2. Providing a list of neutrals, mediators, it also assists in choosing the right expert.
3. Settling the fees of the neutrals, after the discussion between the neutrals and parties and administers the financial aspect of the proceedings.
4. Sets the procedural efficiency by liaising between the parties and neutrals.

If the procedure is held at the WIPO centre of Switzerland, Geneva, they provide rooms for meetings or support services free of charge. A charge can be imposed only on any other support service, which may be required. Although the charge is separate from the Centres administrative fees. It also provides for WIPO EADR, accessible through the Centre's website.

WIPO-FORUM for ADR Procedures

WIPO centre provides specific rules and neutrals for the following procedures:

- Mediation
- Arbitration
- Expedited Arbitration
- Mediation followed in the absence of a settlement by expedited arbitration.

For the ADR procedures, the WIPO Arbitration and Mediation Centre provides for neutrals, rules, and clauses for the easy determination of the dispute.

As shown in Figure 1, the parties can opt for Negotiation in the form of Mediation, Expert Determination or Expedited Arbitration. Mediation is a more informal process in which a neutral, a mediator, helps in settling their dispute. Mediation can be done only by choice of the parties, which may be done by either party, which may be done either by Arbitration or by Expedited Arbitration or even by an Expert Determination.

Expedited Arbitration is a process in which settlement is done in a short duration and at a reasonable cost. Expedited Arbitration can be followed by mediation or expert determination. Mediation followed in the absence of a settlement by expedited arbitration. If an arbitration process does not settle a dispute, then the procedure of this expedited arbitration and mediation is followed (Moore, 2003).

Expert determination is a process where an issue regarding a technical, scientific or business-related is presented to an expert. The expert may be one or more depending upon the need, which further helps in the determination of the matter.

Cases Filled in WIPO Centre

For all the commercial disputes, WIPO Rules is the most appropriate as they have various provisions for confidentiality. They also provide for the technical and experimental evidence, which may be of special interest to the parties of an intellectual property dispute.

Figure 2 clearly shows the cases filed with the WIPO Arbitration and Mediation Centre, illustrating the choices, which are made by the people. Arbitration has the highest rate of 49%, Mediation being at 41% and lastly Expedited Arbitration at 10%.

Figure 1. WIPO contract clause/submission agreement procedure
(Source: WIPO Guide to Arbitration)

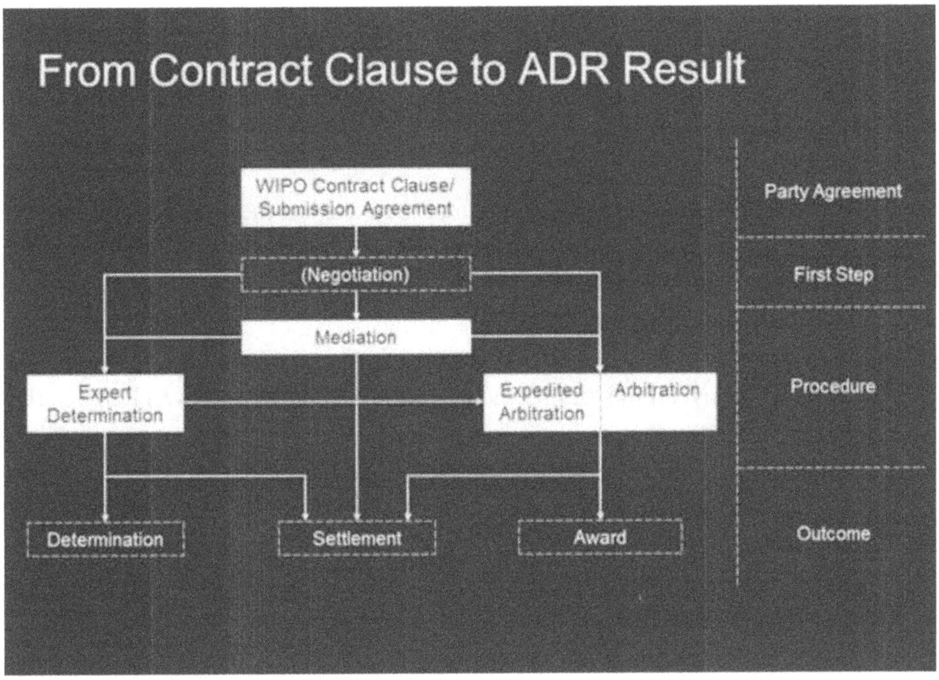

Figure 2. Cases filed with the WIPO arbitration and mediation centre
(Source: WIPO Guide to Arbitration)

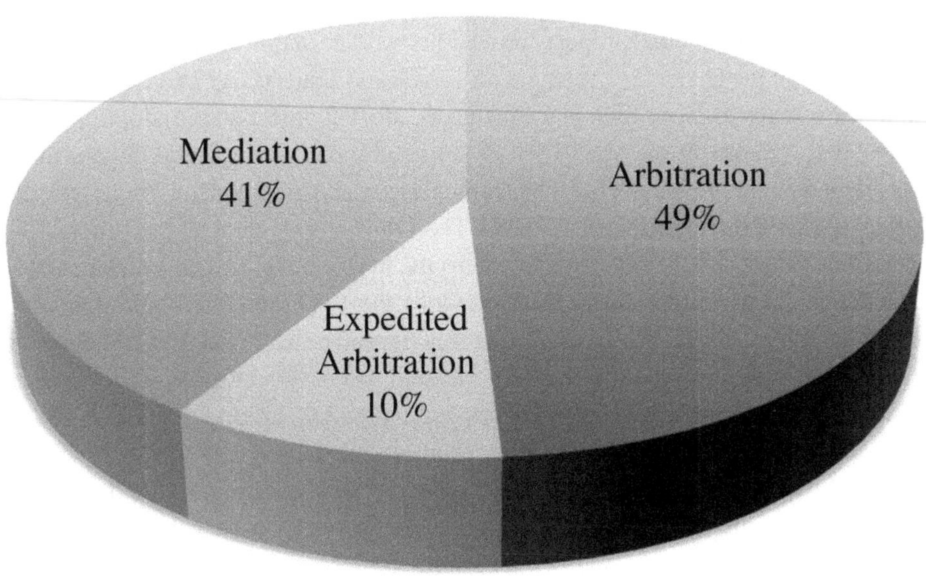

It also provides a brief overview of the different options of the dispute resolutions which are offered by these centre to the parties from which they can choose either one or possible combinations. The aim of the centre is to provide an efficient, fair and just process. (Guide to WIPO Arbitration publication no. 919E).

Priorities of WIPO Centre

To provide a just and an equitable procedure, the centre has the following priorities:

- To provide a flexible procedural framework as the procedure opted are done in the consultation with the parties.
- WIPO centre provides a lawyer who tracks the deadlines of the case, manages communications, all the enforcement of the procedures and even helps in the administrative assistance.
- The main characteristics of the centre are to provide efficiency.
- The success of the proceedings depends on the extent of the experts who are appointed in the tribunal. So it is important to see that the arbitrators have knowledge of the subject matter.
- Integrity is the most important element in providing a fair and just procedure. Great importance is given to the impartiality and independence to the candidates to choose their arbitrator and even change them if they find that there are justifiable doubts.

Settling Disputes through the TRIPS Agreement

Enforcement of intellectual property provisions was one of the main issues negotiated by members of the General Agreement on Tariffs and Trade (GATT) on the Uruguay Round. These discussions took place in the decade that preceded the adoption of the Marrakech Agreement on April 15, 1994, whereby the World Trade Organisation was created including Annex IC, which comprised the Agreement on Trade-Related Aspects of Intellectual Property (TRIPS). The TRIPS Agreement plays a crucial role in facilitating trade in knowledge and creativity, in resolving the trade disputes over the intellectual property, and in turn, provides the WTO members with the extra latitude to achieve their objectives. The agreement can be treated as legal recognition of the significance of links between intellectual property and trade. The extent of protection and enforcement of these rights varied widely around the world; and as intellectual property became more important in trade, these differences became a source of tension in international economic relations. New internationally agreed trade rules for intellectual property rights were seen as a way to introduce more order and predictability and to settle disputes more systematically. The same was achieved in the Uruguay Round.

Under the TRIPS Agreement, WTO members have considerable scope to tailor their approaches to IP protection and enforcement in order to suit their needs and achieve public policy goals. The agreement provides ample room for members to strike a balance between the long-term benefits of incentivising innovation and the possible short-term costs of limiting access to creations of the mind. Members can reduce short-term costs through various mechanisms allowed under TRIPS provisions, such as exclusions or exceptions to intellectual property rights. Moreover, when there are trade disputes over the application of the TRIPS Agreement, the WTO's dispute settlement system is available.

The TRIPS Agreement covers five broad research questions:

1. How general provisions and basic principles of the multilateral trading system apply to international intellectual property?
2. What are the minimum standards of protection for intellectual property rights that members should provide?
3. Which procedures should members provide for the enforcement of those rights in their territories?
4. How to settle disputes on intellectual property between members of the WTO?
5. What special transitional arrangements for the implementation of TRIPS provisions?

There are three basic stages while understanding the view to settling a dispute between members concerning their rights and obligations under TRIPS, namely:

1. Consultation (Article 4, DSU).
2. Establishment of a Panel (Article 6, DSU).
3. Appellate review by an appellate body (Article 17, DSU).

Arbitration and Intellectual Property Disputes

Arbitration is an appropriate tool in resolving Intellectual Property disputes as it provides:

- A single and neutral procedure other than the various kinds of the procedure followed by the different countries in court litigation and even helps in overcoming the jurisdictional issues concerning them.
- As arbitration is a private process, it provides parties with multiple options of choosing the manner they wish to resolve their issues. Thus providing

them complete autonomy of the law applied the place and the language of the proceeding.

- Arbitration proceedings mainly focus on providing a neutral approach towards both parties.
- The option lies with the parties to choose their special experts as arbitrators, who know the respective fields to resolve the issue.
- The parties have the option to keep their dispute and the results confidential, thus protecting the trade secrets, which can be at stake.
- Awards given by the arbitrators are final and are not subject to appeal.
- The recognition of the enforceability of awards across borders is given by the Convention for the Recognition and Enforcement of Foreign Arbitral Awards of 1985, also known as the New York Convention.

PRINCIPAL STEPS

Arbitration proceeding at WIPO follows these key steps. The following sections elaborate them:

Article 6-13: Starting Procedure

The very first step in the Proceedings begins with the submission of the request of the Arbitration at the centre, which contains the summary of the dispute. It also contains the name and the communication details of the parties and their respective representatives.

The WIPO also requires attaching the arbitration agreement, with the brief of the relief these parties sought and any requirements they might have in the appointment of the arbitrators. The respondent is given 30 days to file the answer to the request. It shall include the indications of choice, which the respondent wants to make, whether to file a counterclaim or a set-off.

Article 14-36: Establishment of the Tribunal

The next is to establish the tribunal, the choice of the number of arbitrators lies with the parties. If there is no agreement, then the tribunal has a right to appoint a sole arbitrator except in the cases where the arbitrator finds it appropriate to appoint a panel of three arbitrators. In these three arbitrators, the respective parties select the two arbitrators of their own choice, and the arbitrator chosen by the parties appoints the third arbitrator who presides the tribunal.

Article 53- 55: Conducting the Arbitration

There are 30 days duration given to file the statement of claims from the constitution of the tribunal and further 30 days are given to file the statement of Defence from the date on which the statement of Claims was received. The tribunal may even ask for any other documents or submissions as well. Once the submissions are completed, a hearing of the tribunal may take place either on the request of the parties or at the discretion of the tribunal. In the hearing, evidence from the expert witness is presented, and the oral arguments can be made. If no hearing is conducted, then the decision will be based on the submission of the documents and the other materials.

Article 57-66: Pronouncement of Award

When the tribunal is satisfied that both the parties have had an adequate opportunity to present evidence and their arguments whether oral and through submissions, the proceedings will be declared closed. The entire process shall be completed in nine months either from the time of the submission of the defence or from the time of the establishment of the tribunal, whichever is later. In the next three months, the tribunal shall announce the award. This award pronounced is binding on the parties from the day it is communicated by the WIPO Centre.

Impartiality and Independence of Arbitrators: Safeguards

Article 22 lays great value on the integrity of the arbitrators, whether appointed by the parties themselves. They have to maintain fair and impartial behaviour. No bias can be exercised whether in favour or in against can be practised by them. The arbitrators beforehand shall disclose any information, which may indicate bias. A declaration is to be submitted by the arbitrators.

At any time during the proceedings, maybe if there arises a justifiable doubt in the mind of any of the parties about the arbitrator's impartiality, they ought to challenge it. Article 24 upon such a challenge if the claim is proved valid, the arbitrators may be removed, or they may withdraw voluntarily.

- Awards and Remedies Provided By the Centre

Article 62 (a) provides for the preliminary, interim, interlocutory, partial or final awards. Article 60 provides for monetary compensation, including damages and interest. Article 71and 72 includes costs. Furthermore, the tribunal may also provide:

- Injunctions between parties, but not in regard to the third party.

- Declaratory relief with binding effect on both the parties.
- Specific performance, if the substantive law provides for the same.
- Arbitration Proceeding Cost through WIPO

The centre aims that arbitration proceedings should be cost-effective as compared to court litigation. The cost that the WIPO charges include:

- The fees for the centre and one or more arbitrators.
- Any expense incurred by the arbitrator such as his expenses of travel, meetings done and hearings facilitated by him.
- Legal cost and any other expenses beard by any of the parties.

There are three types of fees, which are applied in the WIPO arbitration proceedings:

1. Article 67 lays down the registration fees of USD 2000 for arbitration and USD 1000 in expedited arbitration.
2. Article 68 lays down the administration fees of USD 10,000.
3. Article 69 lays down the arbitrations fees as agreed by the centre in consultation with the parties and the arbitrators. A wide range can be from USD 300 to USD 600 per hour.

WIPO Electronic Case Facility (ECAF)

A magnificent example of WIPO is the right forum for dispute resolution is ECAF in modern times. WIPO ECAF is an electronic case facility to manage the disputes, which are filled by the parties. With this facility parties, neutrals and the centre can access the submissions and other materials securely anywhere in the world. They can even search, store and retrieve them.

SUGGESTIONS AND CONCLUSION

To conclude, like Tom Arnold, "*As dispute is a problem to be solved, rather than a contest to be won*" (Arnold & Schuruman 1991).

ADR provides an alternate form of resolving conflicts of Intellectual Property, Traditional Knowledge, Traditional Cultural Expressions and Genetic Resources from litigation. The special requirement of their interests, responsibilities that exist within these local communities. The court litigation for Indigenous People in regards to their traditional knowledge gets complex here as ADR can present a forum for a more comprehensive understanding of what is at stake and for whom. The procedure of ADR provides several options and does not replace the present and developing an international legal instrument. Thus providing a complementary tool, that enhances the effectiveness and the applicability of any international instrument.

Indigenous and Local communities as the holders of the traditional knowledge to qualify as a party in Intellectual Property conflicts and can engage in arbitration and can enjoy the benefits of ADR proceedings. Alternative Dispute Resolution offers a preferential framework that addresses the complex nature of the dispute, regarding the traditional knowledge of the Indigenous people and the right to use such knowledge.

ADR is a problem-solving tool, which does not necessarily mean resolving of controversies. It can be treated as a form of social ordering. I t can only be initiated if both parties agree expressly and impliedly (Sajko, 2009). Thus making it a combined effort from both the parties to reach a just settlement benefitting both the parties. It is rightly said that whatever destroys the participation destroys the integrity of adjudication itself (Fuller, Winston, 1978).

In addition to all the benefits that the ADR process provides to the parties, it also provides additional help to the judges on whom there is enormous pressure of their pending caseloads. With this new procedure introduced for dispute settlement, about sixty to eighty per cent of the cases are resolved and thus relieving judges' caseloads. In so many cases, in litigation, judges appointed may not have adequate expert knowledge of the dispute whereas in ADR neutrals are specialized experts and have in-depth knowledge about the matter concerned in Intellectual Property. Thus, ADR especially Mediation, may be the best way to accomplish this goal.

REFERENCES

Anderson, J. (2012). On Resolution, Intellectual Property and Indigenous Knowledge Disputes Prologue. *Landscapes of Violence*, *2*(1), 1–14.

Arnold, T. & Schuruman, G. W. (1991). *Alternative Dispute Resolution in Intellectual Property Cases*. Academic Press.

Bell, C., & Kahane, D. (2004). *Intercultural Dispute Resolution in Aboriginal Contexts*. Vancouver: University of British Columbia Press.

Blackman, S. H., & McNeill, R. M. (1998). Alternative Dispute Resolution in Commercial Property Disputes. *The American University Law Review*, *47*, 709–1734.

Fuller, L. L., & Winston, K. I. (1978). The Forms and Limits of Adjudication. *Harvard Law Review*, *92*(2), 353–409. doi:10.2307/1340368

Geingos, V., & Ngakaeaja, M. (2003). *WIPO, PCT Notable Inventions: "Hoodia" appetite suppressant.* Retrieved from http://www.wipo.int/ pct/en/inventions/hoodia

Gupta, A. (1996). Patent on Neem: Will it deprive Indian farmers of right to use it? *Biotechnology Law Report, 15*(1), 6–14. doi:10.1089/blr.1996.15.6

Gupta, A. (2001). WIPO-UNEP Study on the Role of Intellectual Property Rights in the sharing of benefits arising from the use of Biological Resources and Associated Traditional Knowledge. Kaula Lampur: WIPO-UNEP.

Moore, W. C. (2003). *The Mediation Process: Practical Strategies For Resolving Conflicts*. San Francisco: Jossey-Bass Publishers.

Morgera, E., & Tsioumani, E. (2010). The Evolution of Benefit Sharing: Linking Biodiversity and Community Livelihoods. *Review of European Community & International Environmental Law, 19*(2), 150–173. doi:10.1111/j.1467-9388.2010.00674.x

Nagel, T. (2005). *The Problem of Global Justice, Philosophy and Public Affairs*. Oxford: Blackwell Publishing Inc.

Osi, C. (2008). Understanding Indigenous Dispute Resolution Processes and Western Alternative Dispute Resolution: Cultivating Culturally Appropriated Methods in Lieu of Litigation. *Cardozo Journal of Conflict Resolution, 10*, 163.

Pinel, S. L., & Evans, M. J. (1994). *Tribal Sovereignty and the Control of Knowledge, Intellectual Property Right for Indigenous Peoples*. Kluwer Law International.

Sajko, K. (2009). Intellectual Property Rights and Arbitration: Miscellaneous. In *Patents and Technological Progress in a Globalized World*. Springer. doi:10.1007/978-3-540-88743-0_32

Sarfaty, A. G. (2007). International Norm Diffusion in the Pimicikamak Cree Nation: A Model of Legal Mediation. *Harvard International Law Journal, 48*(2), 441.

Scheinin, M. (2003). *UN Human Rights Committee: Protecting Indigenous Livelihoods and Cultural Rights*. Geneva, Switzerland: Centre on Housing Rights and EvictionsPublishers.

Sekolec, J., & Getty, B. M. (2003). An Emerging Consensus on Mediation and Conciliation. *Journal of Dispute Resolution, 1*, 175-181.

Simon, S. B. (2005). Intellectual Property and Traditional Knowledge: A Psychological Approach to Conflicting Claims of Creativity in International Law. *Berkley Law Journal, 20*(4), 1613–1616.

Taubman, A., Wager, H., & Watal, J. (2012). *A Handbook on the WIPO Trips Agreement*. Cambridge University Press.

Tellez, M. V. (2006). Recognising the Traditional Knowledge of the San People: The Hoodia Case of Benefit-Sharing. Carol Bonnett Publisher.

Theurich, S. (2009). *Art and Cultural Heritage Dispute Resolution*, Retrieved from https://www.wipo.int/wipo_magazine/en/2009/04/article_0007.html

Wichard, J. C., & Wendland, W. B. (2006). *Mediation as an Option foe Resolving Disputes between Indigenous/ Traditional Communities and Industry Concerning Traditional Knowledge*. Cambridge, UK: Cambridge University Press.

WIPO. (2004). *World Intellectual Property Organization (WIPO): Arbitration and Mediation Centre, Guide to Arbitration Centre*. Retrieved from www.wipo.int/amc/en/

Chapter 6
Challenges Related to Protection of Indigenous Resources Against Biopiracy

Zubair Ahmed Khan
University School of Law and Legal Studies, Guru Gobind Singh Indraprastha University, India

ABSTRACT

The protection of indigenous/aboriginal resources is one of the important aspects of biodiversity justice. Many international treaties and conventions legitimised natural rights and privileges of tribal societies and indigenous communities. But some interventionist practices like a conflict of interest in bioprospecting agreement and biopiracy have become major concerns for prospering third-world countries. Strategic application of prior-informed consent and benefit-sharing procedures will definitely meet socio-environmental sustainability in the country. The responsibility and liability of state biodiversity authority and local biodiversity committee at village level need to be fixed to maintain transparency and accountability. Conservation of ethnobiological resources is also important in the view of increasing patent infringement. That's why issues of patentability must include complete disclosure of specification claims even in the case foreign natural resources.

INTRODUCTION

Biodiversity is interpreted as an inexhaustible variety in diverse living creatures. These resources are organic that exists for a very long time. Indigenous communities assume a valuable part in developing and securing natural (aboriginal) assets. We

DOI: 10.4018/978-1-7998-1835-9.ch006

accumulated traditional knowledge for many hundred years in our country. Traditional Knowledge (TK) remains an indispensable piece of ethnic identification and only mode of survival in provincial regions. Evolution, proliferation, and usage of TK took many eras and consistent engagement of indigenous communities. It is closely associated with biological assets accessible to native societies. Though a substantial portion of TK is well documented. However, its translation and comprehension matter become tedious due to the presence of aboriginal content utilised, therefore resulting in patent accord to the individuals who get maximum profit regardless of those not possessing TK in reality. The indigenous people associated with TK are usually disappointed because of the absence of the shared benefits or advantages which are endowed upon them. Misuse of contemporary frameworks of TK is an aftereffect of commercialisation procedure where productivity is more important than sustainability. Thus, TK of the indigenous communities untenably and unjustly misused (Tinker, 2014).

It is backed with ignorance of rights of indigenous people in regards to their security or recompense by contemporary legal frameworks which may result in loss of TK. Many scholars disclose that significant numbers of native and aboriginal peoples possessing TK are not in support of commercialising these indigenous resources, including TK for pecuniary and other substantial profits. The pervasiveness of morals inherent in their cultural life influences them to part with TK and related insight with anyone without anticipating benefits, commercial service from corporate entities. That is why these native societies stay underprivileged and corporate enterprises keep on commercially exploiting and collecting affluent resources. Aside from this predicament which has emerged with the discord of moral and social standards between indigenous people and the overwhelming corporate entities in relation to its insight, legitimacy and significance of fundamental ethics and social codes are also came into purview of deliberation. The indigenous people and societies are usually not recognised for TK and their consistent approach to safeguarding these natural resources. The pertinent deliberation, which was not elaborated before that needs to be discussed as to why these indigenous persons remain anonymous and valueless in the context of TK? Furthermore, the legitimacy of bioprospecting and commercialisation of biological resources achieved through the usage of TK without any endorsement, acknowledgement and recognition of these indigenous communities. The pharmaceutical organisations put significant emphasis on biodiversity since biological resources are crucial for the creation and advancement of many medicines (Dutfield, 2016).

Biological assets have a significant capability for creating chemical products. In spite of the decrease in the utilisation of these biological items for creation of medicinal substances, scholars view biological assets like the precious elements of pharmaceutical companies even today because of having different varieties.

Numerous primary farming products are evolved and flourished by active human engagement through proper variation and adjustment. The advancement of these farming products has developed particular TK to a specific category. Incorporated entities have progressively endeavoured to gather such indigenous information and legitimise their importance by getting appropriate IP law related to patents (Krishnamurthy, 2003).

BACKGROUND

Biodiversity, biotechnology and traditional herbal science are specific subject-matters of knowledge and research which are meant for commercial prospects, trade and IPR application. Biodiversity is such a perspective which has a monetary, environmental, cultivated and enduring quality. Biological resources are indeed commercially useful for many industrial units of domestic and international entities in different pharmaceutical sectors. However, there are many commercial practices of biological resources, which are done with illegally and without permission of the regional competent authority. Biopiracy is one of the illegal and unwarranted commercial practices usually done through patenting procedure (Belsare, 2007).

Biopiracy is a term which is not explicitly defined anywhere in any legalisation or convention. It is characterised as larceny and embezzlement of biological (indigenous) resources whereby different varieties of plants are gathered by native groups and licensed by patent applying groups members or companies without conceding appropriate IP protection against indigenous groups. It is also construed as illegitimate exploitation and misuse of biological resources against its indigenous holders and skilled persons through interpretation of the meaning of seeds, and related TK, in this way expelling the plant materials from patent qualification. This type of definitive character reflects an assortment of resources though the abysmally interpreted conception of biopiracy as it is challenging to exhibit and identify the practical implication of acts of biopiracy. The extraction and the end product of biological and other genetic resources are technological and materialistic treasured and organisations endeavour to apply for patentable claims for such products to legitimise lawful proprietorship by IP principle. On the other hand, the conspicuous absence of formal accord related to the main subject of a patent as to whether it pertains to TK or not often creates ambiguity in the whole matter (Robinson, 2010).

Developing states which are enriched in ecological resources and biodiversity usually put the blame on western states (developed) for evacuating and commercialising such assets and TK where they went for patentability of their creation made of natural resources. The contentious biopiracy issues arise when there is a universal ambiguity as to whether indigenous people own and possess natural resources or these resources are the subject matter of shared legacy of humanity. There is another matter for deliberation to decide the scope and nature of state sovereignty in deciding the level of appropriation. It is important to introspect the ambit of IPR regime in the context of the inventive process and State governed limitations for the rights of indigenous communities (Narasaiah, 2005).

PATENTABILITY ISSUES

Trade-Related Aspects of International Property Rights (TRIPS) 1994 is considered to be one of the sincere attempts for legitimising standard rules on IPR with protective measures and encouragement. It has endeavoured to integrate domestic level for securing IP by orienting its guidelines for a universal standard with the procedures presently utilised by developed states. Protective measures related to genetic and biological resources are described explicitly in the Convention on Biological Diversity (CBD) which came into existence in 1992. CBD is viewed as an important and indispensable covenant for security and preservation of biological and genetic resources and elucidates general issues of prospering states' management on indigenous resources within its territory. It also underlines the deference, protection, subsistence and sustenance of TK along with empowering indigenous people by providing them with a fair standard of shared profit after commercialisation (Suthersanen, 2005).

The International Treaty on Plant Genetic Resources for Food and Agriculture is another important treaty which came into existence in the year 2004 that has a target to preserve plants and diverse genetic assets and encourage agricultural practices including plant breeding (Mgbeoji, 2006). Exclusive rights are recognised and given to Indigenous farmers, namely:

1. Direct engagement in deciding the central level for preservation and ecological sustainability of genetic assets,
2. Right of getting shared benefit coming out from commercialisation of genetic resources in the form reciprocity of research-based data, transferal of technological innovation and competency developmental mechanism. However, the absence of prior-informed consent is a major concern that's why the independent contractual agreement is expected to address the issues of food insecurity, infringement of cultural and customary practices in preserving resources. Protected and conservation rights are also granted to native people or societies of the least prospered nation having weak IP law related to infringement provisions as TK regime are very much diversified rather than collectively recognised and safeguarded. The definition of the

term invention is not explicitly mentioned anywhere in TRIPS. It has been academically debated for long as to what things comprised of the invention and how it is judicially interpreted during the initial development universal patent regime. That is why many countries are indiscriminately interpreting the concept of invention for their vested interest. They ignore the conceptual difference between patent granted on already conceived and disclosed and real innovation capable of patentability.

Presence of dissension and equivocality surrounding rules of accessibility to indigenous resources and shared profit principle are major obstacle against ecological balance and its conservation. As a result, the undue advantage will be taken by corporate entities, including pharmaceutical firms. Old patent regimes explained the nature of invention/innovation by emphasising on its tangible character as a glaring outcome of the efficient scholarly exercise. This intensified phenomenon excludes methodical/experimental disclosure from the purview of patentability. However, there is a paradigm shift in overall perspective in granting patentability with a surge of demand and innovation in the field of biotechnology as well as consortium and cartels among pharmaceutical entities. Accordingly, entities favoured legislations in western states, countries' policy and judicial opinion also changed with time in the socio-economic interest of the State. The assertion that distinguishes patentable innovation/invention and already disclosed methodology/substance does not seem to be satisfactory and acceptable (Gubarev, 2012).

Interestingly, US legislation on the patentable subject is a matter of serious deliberation, especially the definitive character. Patentability criteria include aspects of the innovative invention or mere discovery, new amalgam, new plant assortment, newly discovered seed in the coarse area within Section 161 of US Patent Act, 1930 depending on preconditions. Appropriation of any natural product resulting in invention or discovery with intellectual effort would be qualified for patent protective measures. As a result, commercialisation of offshore/foreign plants is allowed as per universal accessibility and lenient law. However, patentability will not be acceded if alleged patentable issue/ product existed, already utilised before or already documented (printed form) in the country or any different country (Mgbeoji, 2006).

However, the apex court in *Gayler v. Wilder* (1850) made a different observation on the interpretation of section 102 of US Patent law. It has been discussed that any innovation/invention created in another country with a proper printed form or already patented form indicates it has now become a subject matter of global epitome/view for everyone. However, there is a complete possibility that in prospering or least prospering states, subject matter of the invention (if not patented yet) does not exist printed or written form systematically due to diverse, compelling reasons among indigenous societies. It is very much possible that the particular method or product existed there and known there locally for an extended duration. It is further used for different purposes. They may not know the basic rules of accessibility. Their ignorance may result in a case of wrongful loss where their indigenous resources are commercialised by a foreign company without giving any portion of profit or benefit to indigenous people. This case gave an important inference that strict interpretation of Section 102 of US Patent legislation may compromise with rules of justice and eventually denied it. It shows that that patent can be approved to a claimant who might not be the original inventor. There is reasonable apprehension that the particular provision may be misused by the patent claimant where he justifies himself as inventor just bringing few improvements like the already existed process or product.

This issue raises another serious deliberation regarding the validity and nature of specifications claim adopted by the universal patent system. This issue also raises another serious deliberation regarding the validity, criterion and nature of specification claim adopted by the universal patent system. The whole patenting mechanism becomes weak if there is ambiguity exist specification. Specification includes descriptive and evaluative information related to inventions. It also includes every component, main source and another derivation aspect of invented product or action. The main issue is whether every detail needs to be disclosed under specification claim while applying for a patent and if a patented claim does not disclose everything, will it seem to be an encouragement of biopiracy practice? (Robinson, 2010).

Concealment or suppression of facts is always considered as a fraudulent practice. Now if corporate or pharmaceutical entities suppress facts like a source of invented substance so that they can deny sharing mechanism of profits gain through commercialisation among particular indigenous communities. So, it is important that conspicuous absence of absolute application of complete disclosure of source in specification may bring disrepute and discourage the patenting regime. In the case of *Bonito Boats, Inc. v. Thunder Craft Boats, Inc.*, (1989), the patent has a contributive, functional and pragmatic objective of cultivating further improvement of invention. The patent regime is considered to be a mechanism promoting profit by commercialisation with due diligence. Due diligence is required due to massive investment involved, several experienced personnel involved and other risk elements related to advancement step and infringement issues. The intellectual stimulus is inherent in the patentable subject matter, which makes it exclusive by utilising, reproducing, putting on sale by patentee within the domain of the State (Liang, 2011).

The fundamental problem in patenting mechanism is a misconception of interpretation of precise definitions mentioned in any patent law. There is no particular yardstick in defining what is new and non-obvious in a patentable claim as it depends on facts and circumstances of the application content and the kind of documentary evidence to support its scientific approach and peculiarity. It is necessary to introspect and impartially examine the case to uphold the rule of transparency. So, it means that all essential features of a patent are mostly found interrelated and inter-associated during documentation of patent grant or examination for patent grant. There is a major concern regarding the insufficiency of the patent regime is that most of the developed states did not recognise biopiracy concerns because of two reasons, namely:

1. There is no description or definition of biopiracy or a similar concept associated with it in the CBD and Nagoya Protocol. Many western countries view it as a matter of exaggeration on the commercialisation of biological resources. They consider it as encouragement of particular vested interests raised by NGOs or developing states. A major issue of wrongful loss and wrongful gain in the context of a human right violation of indigenous people is not acceptable in this case.
2. Many developed and developing states signed CBD and became a party of the convention. However, there are very less of countries that become a party to Nagoya Protocol which legitimise the practice of benefit sharing. It is undeniable fact that principle of benefit sharing and human rights are closely related. Complete or partial rejection of benefit sharing can be contextualised as a major obstacle against the right of development and right of self -determination of indigenous resources.

Many experts opined that a universal patent mechanism needs to adopt a contemporary approach in dealing matter of patentability which involve sensitive matter related to the rights of indigenous people and societies. It has been further suggested that a substantial change may be brought by encouraging two practices (Dutfield, 2004).

1. Inclusion of patent co-ownership for patentee and indigenous people or group.
2. Inclusion of Compensation or similar concept like reparation.

If we check the feasibility of these two suggested practices as an option, it is clear from the first instance that these two ways are not going to be helpful in preventing the nature of biopiracy.

Interestingly, any non-pecuniary benefit shared with indigenous people can be given in the form of patent co-ownership, which is also discussed under Bonn Guidelines. He further emphasised that this approach can benefit the indigenous community in the long run, and it may harmonise with the basic principle of reinstatement. However, if particular indigenous resources are jointly owned by many native groups in a city or across the city, then it will difficult to apply patent-co-ownership where many groups survive and preserve these resources for ages. However, there is no specific patent theory where describe the merit of co-ownership where indigenous people can get equal patented rights and privileges. The real issue is how to define co-owner in this scenario? How does indigenous people fit into the category of co-owner? Patent co-ownership will be considered as legitimate if every involved claimant has vigorously engaged and participated in developing and creating invention based subject matter for patentability. TK stakeholders or particular indigenous people generally involve themselves only in conserving and securing their knowledge and natural resources. Their intellectual effort in overall preparation stages of the patented product will be very restricted due to many reasons like lack of technical education, poverty, among others. (Blakeney, 2004).

The whole case of patent co-ownership will seem to be more difficult when a foreign company is involved. Even if it is practised, it will be difficult to manage, and utilise the necessary obligations of a patentee and general uncertainty over the security of TK. There are various costs involved in the whole patenting process like sustenance costs, litigation cost that will be difficult to adjust along with regional usages, habitual course of action and legislations (Nwabueze, 2003). The real question is how mode of compensation can be treated as appropriate remedy in case of an illegal granted patent, which it is acquired through scientific formulation and improvement of indigenous resources? An illegal patent is a result of the accessibility of indigenous resources without proper approval from local authorities or State. Compensation is usually granted as remedy when an illegal action of external force resulted into wrongful loss to the aggrieved party. When a considerable quantity of indigenous resources has been utilised illegally, it results in a socio-economic loss for indigenous people and communities as these resources are meant for their livelihood and fulfilling bare necessities. Sometimes, pecuniary interest will not provide proper justice to their loss. That is why reparation can be considered as one of the good options because of certain non-pecuniary benefits like transfer of technological innovation, an opportunity of employment.

The concept of the 'prior art' is originated under the western philosophy of patenting regimes. The literal interpretation of the concept of the prior art is any evidence that the invention was already publicly known or available, in whole or in part, before the effective filing date of the alleged patent application. So, the burden of proof of substantiating and producing prior art is on the party/stakeholder who files the case of opposition against the grant of patent. However, its interpretation changed over time. Now it is not necessary that a product must be entitled to patentability. Even if it is endured in any formal written form like ancient book or literature or something very known public display of mechanism or demonstration. The US legislation also brought specific changes, where general concerns related to prior art needs to be clarified and checked through standard patentability search (novelty) to ensure the character of uniqueness (Richard, 2004).

The utmost viable approach of scrutinising patentability application related to TK will be contemplated when TK is viewed as prior art. Two possibilities where substantial objection can be raised against acceptance of patent namely:

1. Proof to show that alleged invention/innovation already came into existence even before the documentation of patent and it is something very much familiar and accustomed to society in large.
2. Any kind of enhancement and refinement in invented product or method is evident to any simple individual proficiency in craftsmanship and to society that challenges distinct character (Coombe, 2001).

The issue of non-inclusion of overseas societal usage under prior art is a major concern. It is also feasible such prior art exist in local areas in local languages which is not recognised under different western patent office. Now, the real question is whether the establishment and continuous assessment of TK repository mechanism can restrict illegitimate accessibility of foreign entities and applicability of patent.

NATURE OF TRADITIONAL KNOWLEDGE DIGITAL LIBRARY

Traditional Knowledge Digital Library (TKDL) is a progressive mechanism endeavoured in India to stop illegitimate commercialisation and utilisation of TK. Its creation is based upon safety manner and endeavours to include all indigenous resources which were not recognised because it was never put officially on any written register. That is why these TK can be treated as prior art so that it can be available and accessible to the global patent office for scrutiny and check similarity (Bhutani, 2016).

TKDL include digitised information on ancient literature related to traditional medicinal knowledge, and its whole structure is systematically codified and translated in English and numerous dialects around the globe. Its aim is to standardise in such way so that the global patent office find it very convenient to search and identify these TK as prior art. It also aims to make available to all intellectuals, bio-researchers, analysts.

Documentation of TK and ethnobiological information/products in TKDL facilitate efficient scrutiny and veracity of specification claim in a particular patent application through viable patentable search option in different languages. The real issue of deliberation is that whether the systematic mechanism discourages the practice of biopiracy in India? Will it reduce the illegal appropriation and expropriation of indigenous resources? There are many traditional resources (in a different context) which are yet to be documented by TKDL. So, there is always the apprehension that this undocumented traditional texts/information can be secretly misused. So, a contractual collaboration between TKDL and different patent office around the globe will boost commercialisation of genetic resources and bioprospecting with benefit in exchange among concerned indigenous resources, local technical institutes and transnational entities. Benefit in exchange is a principle which promotes sharing of benefit (pecuniary and non-pecuniary as a result of profit gained by a transnational entity) among indigenous communities (Verma, 2004).

SCOPE OF RESOLUTION MECHANISM IN BIOPROSPECTING AND BIOPIRACY DISPUTES

TKDL takes sincere responsibility in securing and safeguarding TK and ancient resources related to Ayurveda. The institution often has to challenge the matter before different international patent office for different issues. Biopiracy is off course an allegation where indigenous resources secretly steal and swindle natural resources without taken formal approval from central level biodiversity board. It may be something associated with illegitimate acquisition, transference and patentability of natural assets that leads to a conflict of interest in the court of law. However, any type of partnership agreement, joint venture and contractual agreement between a foreign entity and biodiversity authority related to commercialisation of natural resources may involve different nature of the dispute (Raghvan, 2001).

There are certain matters of deliberation like as to how the principle of dispute accord can tackle the issue of biopiracy? Secondly, is there any scope of dispute resolution mechanism in Indian biodiversity legislation and regulations? What can be the possible model of dispute accord to bioprospecting agreement and what will be the purpose of its inclusion? The real basis of dispute resolution through mutual agreement is described in Article 27 of CBD. There are three options of conflict resolution discussed, namely, negotiation, mediation, arbitration and admittance of conflict matter before the international court of justice. However, there is no specific provision dealing with conflict resolution between parties to a contractual agreement under the Biological Diversity Act, 2002 and ABS regulation, 2014 except settlement process between state biodiversity boards.

Nagoya Protocol on ABS mechanism provides legitimacy on the compulsory application of formal consensual agreement as Prior Informed Consent (PIC). It exists in the form of formal intimation and approval to be taken by the interested applicant for an appropriation of natural resources. Another important feature like Mutually Agreed Terms (MAT) is legitimised properly in the Protocol. The nature and ambit of MAT depend upon the geographical conditions of indigenous resources, local specification, and nature of commercial business of applicant as a company, quantity of the resources required, the purpose of accessibility of such natural resources (applicability of patent, bioprospecting agreement, and any possible kind bio-survey). Some aspects of negotiation can be included under the contractual agreement involving different stakeholders like Biodiversity Board, Biodiversity management committee, state technical university or technical research institute and the government. The nature of such negotiation can include proper dialogue and discourse between parties to the contractual agreement to fix the type of benefit to be shared and its quantity about time and place with a better channel in the interest of benefit claimer (Pritchard, 2005). Alternative dispute resolution (ADR) provides the best option in contrast to formal litigation established mechanism for addressing IP conflicts which can emerge in different aspects of TK, indigenous societal articulations, aboriginal raw products. These types of conflicts are frequently vulnerable and engage parties that can be exceptionally divergent on social and financial viewpoint. Traditional stakeholders and indigenous group networks have contemporary issues relating to their requirements under IPR. The same is not handled properly by courts due to improper procedure as this mechanism has no explicit legal base. Court established procedure cannot determine various issues of such nature that has no explicit legal base (Tejera, 2001).

The standard form of mediation or arbitration will exclude prolonged conflict and economic upsurge. It also helps indigenous communities to acknowledge their cultural dogma and folklore even though it does not provide any type of legal recognition of such customary exercise. Instead, it works as an additional mechanism to resolve discord (Shiva, 2001). The scheme of ADR methods can be helpful in resolving different conflicts on commercial exploitation of biological assets and TK:

1. Ambiguity on accessibility and acquisition of resources,
2. Complete repudiation of compensation amount (depending on the extent of misappropriation and secretly stealth of resources),
3. Disproportionate dispensation of benefit as a result of commercial utilisation of natural resources, and
4. Complications in dispensing benefits among various indigenous groups to serve the cause of distributive justice.
5. The facility of negotiation can be offered first to the alleged patentee via foreign patent office by a representative of TKDL. This informal negotiation, mediation or other forms of ADR methods can be cost-effective in comparison to litigation costs and helpful in reducing the time required and other inconvenience. There is always a possibility of difference of approach in fulfilling the requirements of the IPR regime in a different country, especially about patentability criteria. The

dispute of commodification of patentable subject matter (indigenous resources) and contradiction in specification claim can be addressed appropriately and efficiently resolved by ADR mechanism (Ciftci, 2012).

SPECIFIC CHALLENGES IN ABS MECHANISM

The concept of benefit-sharing serves a dual purpose. It intends to enhance the preservation and protection of natural resources with numerous varieties. It has been interpreted that benefit-sharing can bring socio-economic sustainability in the ecosystem. It is also advantageous to the indigenous people concerned or group socially and economically as they secure and preserve biological assortments and ecosystem for many generations which provide them natural sovereignty over time. However, there are a few challenges in the overall perspective of the benefit-sharing mechanism:

1. The formality of getting PIC seems to be easy as interpreted explicitly in the legislation. However, the actual fulfilment of PIC norms involves complex situation. It is possible that divergent sample with indigenous resources with different market price can exist among various communities. So, commodification may not be agreeable to various communities who are stakeholders of such resources. It is difficult to comprehend the relationship between indigenous resources and native communities because they inherit symbolic value in such resources which includes their societal, ethical, cultural recognition. They cannot equate the economic value of indigenous resources with such indispensable values that get along from their originality. So, the absence of PIC report can be considered as a proper ground for opposing patent in an international patent office and cancellation of such patent. It is because the absence of PIC would make it clear that illegitimate accessibility and expropriation of natural resources took place.
2. There are numerous native communities whose livelihood depends upon indigenous resources. Their poverty and lack of proper education become one of the reasons for their economic backwardness. It certainly put an adverse impact on the negotiation steps in deciding the criteria of ABS mechanism. It will be very difficult for such communities to maintain, safeguard and enhance such benefits as received in any form of trust based on commodification and commercialisation of the resources. It is because of a lack of efficient managerial skills and other financial resources. The practical notion of ABS mechanism also faces obstacles and remain unsuccessful due to the absence of domestic societal governance (Bhutani, 2016).

CONCLUSION

Ideally speaking, the benefit-sharing aspect should be treated as a matter of right for indigenous people. Now the substantial question is what kind of rights are closely associated with the ABS mechanism and commercialisation of indigenous recourses. Right of self-determination is one of the important rights declared by the United Nations for aboriginal /native communities. Right of Self-determination is also elementary and indispensable from international law perspective. It is associated with predominant uniformity, regional cohesion and non-intercession. It develops a kind of self-independence and creates aspirations as a matter of collective right with decision-making power which can be efficiently recognised among tribal societies. In this way, it may help them to bring back societal customary governance and resolve their divergent interest and conflicts among numerous communities in a local area. In a way, the ABS mechanism can function smoothly without any hurdle. Biodiversity Management Committee (BMC) has a sincere responsibility to secure and enhance the quality of people biodiversity register (PBR). BMC has a substantial right to claim technical and financial assistance from the State Biodiversity Board for maintenance and close supervision of PBRs (Coombe, 2001).

There is always a certain level of vulnerabilities around the ambit of BMC controlled by local representatives or Gram Panchayat against possible intervention or misappropriation of natural resources by transnational entities with the support of socio-political pressure (Richards, 2004). Enforcement of such right can bring a certain level of transparency, endurance and perseverance among tribal societies and numerous indigenous communities. Right of development has also been construed as one of the fundamental collective rights of tribal societies and indigenous communities. In the context of biopiracy and bioprospecting agreement, this right will encourage development-friendly trade prospect without any hegemony and exploitation.

The idea of inclusive growth is closely associated with the social and economic development of the indigenous territories. A holistic approach should be adopted to address the serious concerns related to food insecurity, poverty and the adverse impact of biodiversity degradation. A biodiversity management fund can be created, which can channelise fund money for indigenous innovation of natural resources and providing enrichment to agricultural research practices that serve the interest of tribal societies and indigenous communities. This commercial facility can help in creating necessary modalities for local indigenous resources network where it can be recognised appropriately for maintenance (Houck, 1997).

Progressive human right aspirations need to be recognised against the illegitimate commodification by TNCs with pecuniary interest only. A typical deliberation may arise whether patentability of already discovered indigenous resource compromise with right of development of indigenous communities. The idea of distributive justice in the ABS mechanism can resolve the conflicting relationship between patentability rights and human rights. It is expected that the State should ensure transparency in the application aspect of ABS mechanism and possibly reduce bureaucratic barrier, which creates an obstacle. There must not be any interface between benefit claimant as state and economic rights of indigenous communities.

REFERENCES

Abraham & Afreen. (2008). Bioprospecting: Promoting and Regulating Access to Genetic Resources and Benefit Sharing. *Indian Institute of Management Calcutta.* Retrieved from https://www.iimcal.ac.in/sites/all/files/pdfs/wps-631_1.pdf

Belsare, D. K. (2007). *Introduction to Biodiversity*. New Delhi: APH Publishing House.

Bhutani, S., & Kohli, K. (2016). *ABS and the Ayurveda Industry, Cases related to Access and Benefit Sharing, Litigating India's Biological Diversity Act: A Study of Legal Cases.* Foundation for Ecological Security and Kalpvriksh Environmental Action Group.

Blakeney. (2004). Bioprospecting and Biopiracy, in Intellectual Property and Biological Resources. *Marshall Cavendish*, 393-424.

Bonito Boats, Inc. v. Thunder Craft Boats, Inc., 489 U.S. 141, 150 (1989)

Bordwin, H. J. (1985). The Legal and Political Implications of the International Undertaking on Plant Genetic Resources. *Ecology Law Quarterly*, *12*(1053), 1053–1064.

Chen, J. (2006). There is No Such Thing as Biopiracy … And it's a Good Thing Too. *McGeorge Law Review*, *37*(1), 3.

Ciftci, S., & Howard-Wagner, D. (2012). Integrating indigenous justice into alternative dispute resolution practices: A case study of the aboriginal care circle pilot program in nowra. *Australian Indigenous Law Review*, *16*(2), 81–98.

Coombe, R. (2001). The Recognition of Indigenous Peoples' and Community Traditional Knowledge in International Law. *St. Thomas Law Review*, 14.

Dutfield, G. (2004). *Intellectual Property, Biogenetic Resources & Traditional Knowledge*. London: Earthscan Publication.

Dutfield, G. (2006), Protecting Traditional Knowledge: Pathways to the Future. *ICTSD Programme on IPRs and Sustainable Development*. Retrieved from http://www.iprsonline.org/unctadictsd/docs/Graham%20final.pdf

Dutfield, G., & Suthersanen, U. (2005). Harmonisation or differentiation in intellectual property protection? The lessons of history. *Prometheus*, *23*(2), 131–147. doi:10.1080/08109020500085528

Gayler v. Wilder 51 U.S. 477 (1850)

Gubarev, M. V. (2012). Misappropriation and patenting of traditional ethnobotanical knowledge and genetic resources. *Journal of Food Law & Policy*, 72.

Hayden, C. (2003). When Nature Goes Public: The Making and Unmaking of Bioprospecting in Mexico. Princeton University Press.

Houck, O. (1997). On the Law of Biodiversity and Ecosystem Management. *Minnesota Law Review*, 869.

Krishnamurthy, K. V. (2003). *Textbook of Biodiversity*. Science Publishers. doi:10.1201/9781482280180

Liang, B. A. (2011). Global governance: Promoting Biodiversity and Protecting Indigenous Communities against Biopiracy. *Journal of Commercial Biotechnology*, *17*(3), 249. doi:10.1057/jcb.2011.16

Mgbeoji, I. (2003). Beyond Rhetoric: State Sovereignty, Common Concern, and the Inapplicability of the Common Heritage Concept to Plant Genetic Resources. *Leiden Journal of International Law*, *16*(4), 821–837. doi:10.1017/S092215650300147X

Mgbeoji, I. (2006). *Global Biopiracy: Patents, Plants, and Indigenous Knowledge*. New York: Cornell University Press.

Mooney, P. R. (2002). Why We Call it Biopiracy. In Bioprospecting: From Biodiversity in the South to Medicines in the North. Spartacus Forlag AS Publication.

Narasaiah, M. L. (2005). *Biodiversity and Sustainable Development*. New Delhi: Discovery Publishing House.

Nwabueze, R. (2003). Ethnopharmacology, Patents and the Politics of Plant Genetic Resources. *New Europe Law Review*, *11*, 585.

Pritchard, D. (2005). International biodiversity-related treaties and impact assessment-how can they help each other? Biodiversity-related Treaties. *Impact Assessment and Project Appraisal*, *23*(1), 8. doi:10.3152/147154605781765706

RAFI. (1998). *RAFI Report Exposes Global Biopiracy, Institute for Agriculture and Trade Policy*. Retrieved from https://www.iatp.org/news/rafi-report-exposes-global-biopiracy

Raghvan. (2001). Protection of Traditional Knowledge. *Minn. Intell. Prop. Rev., 2*(1).

Richards, D. (2004). *Intellectual Property Rights and Global Capitalism: The Political Economy of the TRIPs Agreement*. M.E. Sharpe.

Robinson, D. (2010). *Confronting Biopiracy Challenges, Cases and International Debates*. London: Earthscan Publication. doi:10.4324/9781849774710

Shiva, V. (2001). *Protect or Plunder? Understanding Intellectual Property Rights*. London: Zed Books Publication.

Singh, J. (2008). *Biodiversity, Environment & Sustainability*. New Delhi: MD Publications Ltd.

Swanson, T. M. (1998). *Intellectual Property Rights & Biodiversity Conservation: An Interdisciplinary Analysis of the Values of Medicinal Plants*. Cambridge University Press.

Tejera, V. (1999). Tripping over Property Rights: Is it possible to reconcile the Convention on Biological Diversity with article 27 of the TRIPS Agreement? *New England Law Review*, *33*, 971.

Tinker. (1994). Introduction to Biological Diversity: Law, Institutions, and Science. *Buffalo Journal of International Law*, 1.

Verma, S.K. (2004). Protecting Traditional Knowledge: Is a Sui Generis System an Answer? *JWIP, 7*(765).

Woods, M. (2002). Food for Thought: The Biopiracy of Jasmine and Basmati Rice. *Albany Law Journal of Science & Technology*, *13*, 126.

Wynberg, R. (2004). Rhetoric, Realism and Benefit Sharing: Use of Traditional Knowledge of Hoodia Species in the Development of an Appetite Suppressant. *The Journal of World Intellectual Property*, *7*(6), 851–876. doi:10.1111/j.1747-1796.2004.tb00231.x

Chapter 7
Biopiracy:
Challenges Before India

Anindya Bhukta
Netaji Mahavidyalaya, India

Sebak Kumar Jana
https://orcid.org/0000-0002-3532-4350
Vidyasagar University, India

ABSTRACT

Bio-piracy indicates unauthorized use of bio-resources of a country either by the individuals or institutions or companies of other countries. The countries with enormous bio-resources, like India, become the victims of biopiracy. The paper highlights different issues relating to biopiracy in the context of food security of India. It has been argued that the distress of farmers has increased a lot after the emergence of GM seeds. First of all, GM seeds raise the cost of cultivation by monopolizing the seed business in the hands of a few. Secondly, taking monopoly control over the market by the MNCs became easier because technology allowed them to develop seeds which can be used once-for-all. The farmers, therefore, have to give up their traditional practice of saving and sharing of seeds. The paper cites various instances of biopiracy in India and explains how biopiracy jeopardizes the food security and health security of the people in India. Events of piracy of plants with medicinal values and medicinal knowledge of traditional healers are also on increase at a rapid pace in India. This trend also poses challenges health security of India. More initiatives need to be taken at different levels including government and NGOs need to be taken in documenting codified and non-codified traditional knowledge (TK).

DOI: 10.4018/978-1-7998-1835-9.ch007

INTRODUCTION

The events of biopiracy are occurring more frequently than before all over the world, especially in the southern hemisphere. The victims, in most of the cases, are the developing world, especially the countries in Southern hemisphere like India, South Africa, among others, which are rich in biodiversity. Developing and underdeveloped of Southern hemisphere is the source of 90 per cent of the world's biological wealth. India, for example, has 81,000 species of fauna and 47,000 of flora, including 15,000 plant varieties unique to the country. In spite of this richness, these countries hold only 3 per cent of patent worldwide. Industrial countries, on the other hand, hold 97 per cent of all patents and are driving the rush to patent plant genetic resources (Baxter, 1999).

Bio-piracy indicates unauthorized use of bio-resources of a country either by the individuals or institutions or companies of other countries. It refers to "appropriation, generally by means of patents, of legal rights over indigenous biomedical knowledge without compensation to indigenous groups who originally developed such knowledge" (Sudha, 2014). Naturally, the countries with enormous bio-resources, like India, became the victims of biopiracy. It is a mere coincidence that the major share of global bio-resources was possessed by the poor underdeveloped or developing countries. These poor countries are being the victims of biopiracy practised by the rich countries.

The indigenous communities of bio-resource rich countries, by their intense search for food and medicine, discovered various parts of plants and animals useful for the purpose. The entire human race then got benefitted from their discoveries, but none of them claimed anything in return. But the invention of biotechnology in the 1970s changed the scenario a lot. The multi-national companies of the developed countries, like DuPont, Syngenta, Pharmacia, Dow an Aventis, certainly discovered immense profit prospect from the use of this knowledge of indigenous communities. The plundering of this traditional knowledge along with the bio-resources of the underdeveloped countries started with immediate effect. These multi-national companies, thereafter, started patenting the products they developed by using this knowledge and bio-resources in their own name. For example, the farmers in the north-west of Mexico have long been producing a bean which is an important staple and also an important source of income of them. In 1994 Larry Proctor, a US citizen collected this seed. He then developed a new variety of this bean from the mother seed. The new variety was different from the original one only in colour. The new variety had a yellow coat. Mr Proctor called the variety 'Enola' and applied for a patent. He was granted a patent in 1999 by the US Patent and Trademark Office (USPTO). The patent was later assigned to his seed company POD-NERS.

It is against this malpractice of developed countries a Canadian activist Pat Mooney first coined the term bio-piracy (Mgbeoji, 2006). After obtaining the patent right, the MNCs started accusing underdeveloped countries of pirating or unlawfully appropriating their intellectual property rights. It is at this juncture the Third World Countries started counteracting First World Countries of misappropriating the knowledge of their indigenous people. This allegation of misappropriation was then termed bio-piracy. Bio-piracy is thus meant for an unauthorized appropriation of bio-resources and associated knowledge regarding their uses without making proper compensation to the indigenous people who originally possess this knowledge, and to the countries as well who owns the biological resources.

Biopiracy, therefore, stands on the way to the development of these bio resource-rich countries. These countries fail to exploit their resources because they lack technical knowledge of using these resources in industrial processes. The developed countries, rich in technology but poor in resources, are taking advantage of this slackness of the developing world. They are continuously using these bio-resources for their own. In return, developing countries have been paid only an infinitesimal fraction of the value for the raw materials and knowledge they contribute (ETC, 2002). Nevertheless, the United Nations Development Program claimed in 2001 that two per cent royalty charge levied by developing countries on genetic materials developed by local communities in the southern hemisphere that has been patented in the industrialized North would generate more than $5 billion from medicinal plants alone (UNDP, 2001). Therefore, it is not difficult to understand the detrimental effects of this bio-piracy on the socio-economic life of people of the poor, but resource-rich countries.

Development of social entrepreneurship (Gauthier et al. 2016) can be a useful tool to prevent biopiracy. The present paper mainly focuses on how biopiracy endangers our food and health security.

TRADITIONAL KNOWLEDGE ON AGRICULTURAL KNOW-HOW

Traditional knowledge (TK), also known as indigenous knowledge (IK) or local knowledge (LK) generally refers to the matured long-standing traditions and practices of certain regional, indigenous, or local communities. It also encompasses the wisdom, knowledge, and teachings of these communities. Indigenous knowledge (IK) has also been referred to as the unique, traditional, local knowledge existing within and developed around the specific conditions of women and men indigenous to a particular geographic area. Some examples may be mentioned in this regard.

Table 1. Importance of genetic resources

Sector	Size of the total market in 2006	Importance of genetic resources
Pharmaceutical	US$ 640 billion	US$ 640 billion
Biotechnology	US$ 70 billion from public companies alone	US$ 70 billion from public companies alone
Agricultural seeds	US$ 30 billion	US$ 30 billion
Personal care, botanical, and food and beverage industries	US$ 22 billion for herbal supplements US$ 12 billion for personal care US$ 31 billion for food products	US$ 22 billion for herbal supplements US$ 12 billion for personal care US$ 31 billion for food products
Note: The value of the market size is converted to Indian Rupee by the authors on the basis of the average exchange rate of INR vis-à-vis US$ as per data published by the RBI on September 16, 2013.		

Source: Bhukta (2019)

1. A legume such as Flemingiavestiita, which fixes up to 250 kg of nitrogen per hectare per year is cultivated by north-east Indian tribal communities to cope up with the problem of the declining length of shifting agricultural follow cycles, managed under infertile mountain soil conditions.
2. Under the declining soil fertility and site degradation, as in Charrapunji in north-east India, the shift from shifting agriculture to home garden-based traditional plantation systems could be viewed as a human response based on TK.
3. Traditional societies maintain a variety of complex multispecies agroecosystems, operated under varied levels of intensification, ranging from casually managed shifting agricultural systems, through a whole variety of rotational fallows, agroforestry systems, compound farms, traditional cash cropping systems, crop rotating system etc. maintained at the middle-intensity levels, leading to the modern high energy input agriculture, we are dealing with over a hundred typologies. The complexity of these agroecosystems is due to TK-based biodiversity (sub-specific and species level – crop and associated biodiversity) management, both in space and time.

FOOD SECURITY UNDER THREAT

The most important threat that these countries are facing is the threat to their food security. Food security in different parts of the world is now endangered. One of the reasons behind such a situation is the unabated piracy of bio-resources and associated traditional knowledge. Giant MNCs of the world, backed by the present IPR system, especially which was introduced by the TRIPS agreement, are now challenging the food security of different countries. Shiva (1993), in an article, opines that, by making seed-saving and seed-sharing criminal acts "The Agreement on Agriculture legalizes the dumping of genetically engineered foods on countries and criminalizes actions to protect the biological and cultural diversity on which diverse food systems are based" (Shiva, 1993).

"Food security", as defined by 1996 World Food Summit (WFS) "exists when all people, at all times, have physical, social and economic access to sufficient, safe and nutritious food which meets their dietary needs and food preferences for an active and healthy life". Food insecurity, on the other hand, refers to the non-availability of food. The FAO defines food insecurity as: "A situation that exists when people lack secure access to sufficient amounts of safe and nutritious food for normal growth and development and an active and healthy life." Any analysis of food security will examine whether a change from security to insecurity or insecurity to security actually takes place and also the probability of such a change happening. Factors that may lead to a situation of food insecurity include non-availability of food, lack of access, improper utilization and instability over a certain time period (Muro, 2010).

In this regard, however, we must also mention, in brief, the threat to our food sovereignty caused by biopiracy. Food sovereignty is quite a new concept, which emphasizes on the preservation and protection of food traditions based on ecologically sustainable management of land, soils, water, seas, seeds, livestock and other bio-resources. The novelty of this concept is that it includes, as compared to food security, the security of livelihoods, gender equity, environmental objectives, land and property rights and agrarian reform policies, local autonomy and democratic system of governance. It urges resistance to corporate control of the food system (Karmakar & Jana, 2014). It is of no doubt that food sovereignty can only be fulfilled by extending protection to bio-resources and associated traditional knowledge.

During the 1960s, the green revolution took place in different countries of the world, including India. Thereafter, excessive dependency on high-yielding varieties (HYV) seeds and accompanying inputs has resulted in the slow disappearance of traditional crop varieties. For example, 'in the Indian state of Andhra Pradesh, one study found that the incursion of the Green Revolution led to a loss of 95 per cent of traditional rice varieties without their collection or documentation' (Grain, 2001).

The Case of Basmati

On September 2, 1997, the US patent office granted a patent to an American company RiceTec Inc a patent on Basmati" rice. However, this particular variety of rice owes its origin in India. In its patent application, Rice Tec mentioned that this particular variety of rice is mainly grown in the Tarai region of the Himalayan range, but the company had derived an improved version of Basmati. The patent was, therefore, given on the process of breeding RiceTec's novel rice lines and the method to determine the cooking properties and starch content of the rice grains (Jamil, 1998). The Government of India submitted scientific evidence of 50,000 pages to oppose this patent to the US Patents and Trademarks Office, claiming that high-quality basmati varieties of India already possess these characteristics (The Gurdian, 2000). In 1998, India exported nearly 0.6 million tonnes of basmati rice to the US only. The battle of India was, therefore thought to be the first-ever attempt by any developing country to fight against a US company over the control of the world's food supplies. India finally won this battle in 2001.

The Case of Brinjal (Egg Plant)

During 2005-06, Monsanto, a US-based multinational company, with the help of its Indian subsidiary Mahyco and a few agricultural universities in India, developed a genetically modified version of indigenous brinjal genome of India by inserting a bacterial gene into the indigenous variety. However, Monsanto did not take prior permission from India's National Biodiversity Authority for their experiment over India's bio-resource. The Indian National Biodiversity Authority (NBA) filed legal action against Monsanto (and their collaborators) for accessing local brinjal varieties for development of their genetically engineered version of brinjal without taking any prior consent of the competent authorities, which is considered an act of biopiracy. The law mandates that "when biodiversity is to be accessed in any manner for commercial, research and other uses, local communities who have protected local varieties and cultivars for generations, must be consulted and if they consent benefits must accrue to them as per the internationally applicable Access and Benefit Sharing Protocol." (Sharma et al., 2018).

The green revolution introduced a mono-cropping culture. Mono-cropping means planting one variety of a plant. The most obvious danger of mono-cropping is that the practice can be catastrophic if the crop is afflicted by the disease. The chance of being affected by diseases is also very high in case of HYV seeds. The new rice varieties introduced by the Philippines-based International Rice Research Institute (IRRI) in the late 1960s proved vulnerable to pests and diseases. In the Indian state of Punjab, insects and pests which, prior to the Green Revolution had proven to be insignificant, became major problems with the onset of new rice varieties. By 1991, rice cultivation in Punjab had become vulnerable to 'about 40 insects and 12 diseases' (Shiva, 1993).

Before the introduction of HYV seeds, new varieties of seeds were either discovered or bred by the traditional farmers. The farmers, all over the world, from time immemorial, made them engaged in search of plants with nutritional and medicinal values from a vast pool of wild plant varieties. In this process, they discovered varieties of edible and medicinal plant resource. Their endeavour, however, did not end here. They, thereafter, tried to breed new plant varieties from the varieties available to them by cross-breeding, the process which they learnt from the natural pollinators. The plant varieties either discovered or bred in this way proved to be tolerant to local climatic conditions and hence were little prone to diseases, except the attack of new bacteria.

However, this is not the case for HYV seeds or recently introduced GM crops, because they are never tested OK to be suitable for cultivation in different climatic conditions. As a result, these seeds are prone to diseases. Green Revolution, in this way, by introducing mono-cropping culture, not only increases the cost of cultivation but also pushed a large number of farmers to a high-risk zone. Cost of cultivation increase because along with seeds, the farmers have to purchase chemical fertilizers, pesticides and insecticides to get a good harvest. But even then, sometimes, they are facing situations of crop-failure due to the attack of unknown bacteria.

Multinational companies entered into seed business with HYV seeds. Now they are trying to shift their business to GM seeds. We must take note of the fact that all these seeds, which are developed in laboratories, would not at all come into existence if the mother seeds were primarily developed by the traditional farmers. The practice of mono-cropping culture introduced with the launching of HYV seeds, in a sense, therefore, was the outcome of misappropriation of the knowledge, as well as seed resource of traditional farmers.

The distress of farmers has increased a lot after the emergence of GM seeds. First of all, GM seeds raise the cost of cultivation by monopolizing the seed business in the hands of a few. These big seed-multinationals were originally engaged in the business of pesticides and insecticides. Advancement in biotechnology in the 1980s opened up new opportunities of business to them. Using biotechnology when scientists became able to insert insecticide-resistant genes to the seeds, these companies discovered a new profit prospect to be added to their existing business. The laboratories of these insecticide-companies started giving birth to seeds which are resistant to various insects except the particular insect against which the company is producing its own. What happened as a result was that the farmers who were purchasing the seed of a particular company were also compelled to purchase the insecticide of the same company. The consolidation of seed and insecticide business in this way gave birth to five so-called ‘Gene Giants’, namely DuPont, Pharmacia, Syngenta, Dow and Aventis – laying claim to a global market share of 60 per cent of the pesticide industry, 25 per cent of the world’s seed market and almost 100 per cent of genetically modified crops (Meek, 2000). In the ultimate course, the monopoly control over the seed business by these firms leads to increasing cost of cultivation. Moreover, to tighten their grip over the market, these companies often form an illegal cartel. A consortium of farmers in the United States and other countries once alleged that

Table 2. Market concentration of global agricultural input industries: Share of the global market (per cent)

	Year	Four-firm concentration ratio	Eight-firm concentration ratio
Crop seed and biotechnology	1994	21.1	29.0
	2000	32.5	43.1
	2009	53.9	63.4
Agricultural chemicals	1994	28.5	50.1
	2000	41.0	62.6
	2009	53.0	74.8

Source: Fuglie et al. (2012)

from 1996 onwards corporations like Monsanto, Du Pont, Dow Chemical, Novartis, Astra Zeneca and some other entered into a licensing arrangement to create a cartel in which Monsanto would be the "hub" of the GM industry, and the co-conspirators the "spokes" (Downes, 2003).

Secondly, taking monopoly control over the market by the MNCs became easier because technology allowed them to develop seeds which can be used once-for-all. The farmers, therefore, have to give up their traditional practice of saving and sharing of seeds. In addition to this technological help, the MNCs are also taking the help of law in order to prevent this age-old culture altogether. For example, the proposed Seed Bill (Seed Bill 2004, which was revised and renamed thereafter as Seed Bill 2010) of our country prohibited saving and sharing of seeds by the farmers.

Thirdly, herbicide-resistant plants kill weeds which are an essential part of the food supply in South Asia and Africa. In India, for example, women use up to 150 species of plants as medicine, food or fodder, which would ordinarily be described by the biotechnology industry as weeds. In West Bengal, 124 of so-called 'weed' species collected from rice fields are of economic importance to local farmers.

Last but not least, herbicide-resistant plants systematically destroy the food security of the countries, particularly of developing countries, by establishing the monocropping culture deep-rooted. In the traditional form of agriculture, farmers depend on rotational and mixed-cropping culture in order to keep the soil healthy and make the field disease-free. But the new GM plants engage the farmers, by luring them with huge profit-promise, in mono-cropping. To get rid of the problem of soil infertility and pest-attack chemical fertilizers and pesticides are used. This cropping culture imposes huge debt-burden on the farmers. Thus whenever a crop failure occurs, the farmers commit suicide. According to Shiva (1993), the use of hybrid cotton seeds by the farmers can directly be made responsible for the epidemic of farmers' suicide in the Warangal area of Andhra Pradesh. These farmers, who had traditionally grown pulses, millets and paddy, were lured by the seed companies to buy the seeds, described by them as "white gold", which were supposed to make them millionaires. The farmers were instead pauperised, Shiva concluded.

TRADITIONAL KNOWLEDGE ON HERBAL MEDICINE

In ancient times people used herbal medicines. Herbal medicines are medicines made of biomaterials, of plants and animals. Members of aboriginal communities, through their keen observation, discovered these medicines. Thereafter, this knowledge of them passed over generation after generation. Even today, in rural Bengal, we find some families who are known as Kabiraj family. In other provinces of India, as well as in other countries, we find such families, although in the different designation. These are the families who inherit the traditional knowledge of herbal medicine.

It is, in fact, in the context of herbal medicine that the issue of biodiversity and biopiracy has gained so much importance in today's world. Today modern medicines are mostly based on this traditional knowledge of medicine. However, the problem is that the aboriginal communities which possessed this knowledge cannot make any profit from it. This is so because the drug companies, especially, multi-national companies, who actually use their knowledge do not get ready to share at least a part of their profit with these communities.

HEALTH SECURITY UNDER THREAT

The importance of traditional medicines, popularly known as 'alternative medicine' is continuously increasing all over the world. In one of the studies by the World Health Organisation, it is estimated that 80 per cent of the population of developing countries relies on traditional plant-based medicines for their health requirements (WHO, 1991).

With this increasing importance, events of piracy of plants with medicinal values and medicinal knowledge of traditional healers are also on the increase at a rapid pace. This trend, on the one hand, seriously challenges health security of the concerned country, and, on the other, dampens their prospect of foreign exchange earnings from the export of plants and parts of plants thereof with medicinal values. India, being a mega-diversity hotspot[1] of the world, is one among the worst sufferers.

The Case of Turmeric

In 1995, Suman K Das and Harihar P Cohy, on behalf of the University of Mississippi Medical Centre, USA, obtained a patent on the ' use of turmeric in wound healing ' from the US patent office. When this event came to the knowledge of the Government of India, a complaint petition was filed by the Council of Scientific Research (CSIR), an autonomous institution under the Department of Science and Technology, Government of India, to the US patent office, challenging the novelty of the said invention. In support of their challenge, the CSIR submitted documents of authenticated translation of some texts written originally in Sanskrit, Urdu and Hindi along with a paper published in the journal of the Indian Medical Association in 1953. After examining all the documents, the US patent office in 1997 upheld India's petition and thereby revoked the patent on the anti-inflationary applications of turmeric on the ground of absence of novelty.

The Case of Neem

The neem (scientifically known as Azadirachta Indica) has its native in Africa and South and South-east Asia, especially in India. Indians described the tree as 'azad darakht-i-Hindi', which literally means 'the free tree of India' (Lukose, 2009). In some Sanskrit texts, the tree is described as the 'curer of all ailments'. In fact, almost every part of this tree is used either as insect and pest repellent in agriculture, or as human and veterinary medicine, or as toiletries and cosmetics. Such uses of the tree are mentioned in different Indian texts since the ages of Rig-Veda written nearly 3000 to 4000 years ago.

In the year 1992, the European Patent Office (EPO) granted a patent to a US-based multinational company W R Grace on a neem-based product. Thereafter, a number of patents were granted to W R Grace and several other companies on different neem-based products. In 1995, legal opposition to these patents was filed jointly by the Research Foundation for Science, Technology and Ecology based in Delhi, the International Federation of Organic Agriculture Movements based in Germany and the Green Party in the European Parliament, Brussels. Their claim was that the fungicidal effect of hydrophobic extracts of neem seeds was known and used for centuries on a broad scale in India, both in Ayurvedic medicine to cure dermatological diseases and in traditional Indian agricultural practice to protect crops from being destroyed by fungal infections. This argument by the plaintiffs clarified that the patents were granted violating at least two statutory requirements of granting a patent, namely novelty and inventive steps.

In defence, the opponent party argued that since this traditional knowledge regarding the use of neem was never published in any academic journal, such

Table 3. Medicinal plants: Availability and use

Region	Medicinal Plants available so far	Medicinal Plants used so far
World	250000	35000-70000
China	35000	10000-11250
India	45000	7500-8000

Source: Compiled from different sources

knowledge cannot enjoy the privilege of the prior art. However, this argument did not make any sense to the judiciary, and finally, in 2005, the four-member panel of the Technical Board of Appeals of the EPO revoked the patents on neem products.

India is considered to be the treasure house of medicinal plant species and also of traditional medicinal knowledge. Although it is very difficult to specify the number of such plant species, rough estimates are always available. The Ministry of Environment and Forest, Government of India, has identified and documented over 9,500 species of medicinal plants that are significant for the pharmaceutical industry. Of these, 2000 to 2300 species are used in traditional medicines, while at least 150 species are used commercially on a large scale (EXIM Bank, 1997). According to another estimate, there are about 45,000 medicinal plant species in India, with concentrated spots in the region of Eastern Himalayas, Western Ghats and Andaman & Nicobar Island. The officially documented plants with medicinal potential are 3000, but traditional practitioners use more than 6000 (Patro, 2016). In another project report, The All India Coordinated Research Project on Ethno-botany has revealed that the tribal communities have knowledge of the use of over 9,000 plant species. For healing alone, they use over 7,500 species of plants. This figure does not include the number of animals, insects, lichens, fungi, minerals, soils, and so forth that are also used for human and veterinary health care (Sahai, 2004).

Owing to this richness in biodiversity[2] and also to her richness in the traditional knowledge base of indigenous people, India could be the major exporter of alternative medicines. But the plundering and patenting of medicinal plants and associated knowledge of using the resources by the large MNCs prevent India to be the leader of alternative medicine. The absence of appropriate legal protection mechanism is making India incapable of exploiting this golden opportunity.

Trading of medicinal plants, both in the national and international market, both in terms of value and volume, is increasing at a rapid pace. A study conducted by the National Medicinal Plants Board (NMPB) in collaboration with the Foundation for Revitalization of Local Health Tradition (FRLHT), Bangalore estimated that total traded quantity of medicinal plants in India was about 0.319 million metric tonnes for the year 2005-06. In a recent study by NMPB in collaboration with ICFRE,

Dehradun estimated that consolidated commercial demand for herbal raw drugs for the year 2014-15 stood at 0.512 million metric tonnes.

World market of herbal medicine is also increasing rapidly. The last three decades have seen substantial growth in herb and herbal product markets across the world. For example, according to an FAO estimate total traded value of herbal medicine in the world market in 1994, was12.4 billion US dollar. The value increased to 19.5 US dollar in1999 and 22.4 US dollar in 2002 (FAO, -). The rapid growth of trade in medicinal plants can be attributed to worldwide interest in herbal products as well as in traditional health systems. At present, 80 per cent of the population in developing countries rely largely on plant-based drugs for their health care needs and the WHO has estimated that in coming decades a similar percentage of the world population may well rely on plant-based medicines (FAO, opcit). On the other hand, the percentage of people using traditional medicines in developed countries hovers around 50 per cent of the total population, e.g., 42 per cent in the USA, 48 per cent in Australia and 49 per cent in France relies on traditional medicine. The major exporters of herbal medicines are some developing countries like China, the Republic of Korea, Chile, India, Brazil and Thailand. Except for China, all of these countries suffer huge trade deficit every year, and thereby always remain in need of foreign exchange. If piracy of medicinal plants and associated knowledge of their use cannot be prevented, economies of these countries will definitely suffer a lot.

INDIA'S FIGHT AGAINST BIOPIRACY

Several attempts were made by the MNCs, especially those with the US origin, to misappropriate Indian bio-resources and associated traditional knowledge. They were able to obtain patent rights too from the respective patent authorities. How did India fight against these patent rights and how was she able to revoke them are described in Boxes 1 and 2. In order to prevent the repetition of such events, documentation of traditional knowledge also started taking place in the new Millennium on behalf of both government and non-governmental organizations. A traditional knowledge digital repository, known as Traditional Knowledge Digital Library (TKDL) was built up by the Council of Scientific and Industrial Research (CSIR) and the Department of Ayurveda, Yoga and Naturopathy, Unani and Siddha and Homeopathy (AYUSH).

Besides this government level initiative, several other initiatives have been taken by some leading NGOs in India, who play important roles in documenting codified and non-codified TK. To name some of them are Gene Campaign, Society for Research and Initiatives for Sustainable Technologies and Institutions (SRISTI), Kerala Shastra Sahitya Parishad (KSSP), Research Foundation of Science, Technology and Ecology (RFSTE), Navdanya, Kalpavriksha, Beej Bachao Andolan etc.

Table 4. Indian export and import of botanical raw drugs

Year	Export			Import		
	Quantity (in metric ton)	Value (in Rs. millions)	Value (in US$ million	Quantity (in metric ton)	Value (in Rs. millions)	Value (in US$ million)
2005-06	56014.17	5792.05	256414.05	36143.68	1916.57	84846.60
2006-07	55854.62	7199.91	326012.06	39311.68	2615.69	118438.22
2007-08	60379.24	7414.39	298355.05	38675.35	2864.99	115287.28
2008-09	69822.45	10310.75	473469.82	42310.85	3545.77	162821.62
2009-10	74611.74	9718.63	460857.48	51987.63	3780.85	179287.95
2010-11	104115.13	11700.06	533288.83	58076.93	4910.76	223832.26
2011-12	97244.43	16364.26	784175.48	53753.29	5943.81	284827.14
2012-13	128247.37	24374.86	1325992.49	54798.97	6757.74	367621.00
2013-14	122374.91	27730.04	1677720.11	68209.25	9687.26	586097.64
2014-15	134436.52	32113.34	1963525.22	64545.34	10757.21	657734.55

Source: DGCIS, 2015

With these initiatives, India has become successful, at least to some extent, to check the pace of events of misappropriation of Indian bio-resources. But the introduction of genetically modified seeds by the MNCs and the revision of the Indian Patent Act in the line of WTO provisions both the food security and medicinal security of India still remain at stake. A list of the brief description of biopiracy cases relating to India and how these cases were fought by the Indian government is given in this respect in Table 6.

CONCLUSION

It is clearly evident from the above discussion that biopiracy may have a huge impact on the food and health security of developing countries like India. First of all, it will ultimately destroy the locally adapted, traditional crop varieties of India, which are cheaper alternatives (Bhattacharya *et al.*, 2013). It is a common practice of Indian farmers to segregate a fraction of their harvest for planting in the next growing season (Sharma 2018, Bhattacharya 2014). They use this saved seed for their own use as well as for selling it to other farmers of the locality. Succumbing to the pressure of giant MNCs India has already been compelled to forbid some such practices of farmers in the proposed Seed Bill. Although the bill exempts a farmer from registration of their seed varieties, it makes it mandatory that any seed sold by a farmer must conform to the minimum limits of germination, and physical

Table 5. Export and import structure in India of herbal and medicinal plants

Year	Export				Import			
	Quantity (Tonnes)	Value (Rs. millions)	Value (US$ millions)	Growth increasing/ decreasing	Quantity (Tons)	Value (Rs. millions)	Value (US$. millions)	Growth increasing/ decreasing
1991-92	387444.43	1948.57	47688.62	-	3566.97	142.62	3490.34	-
1992-93	37405.18	2003.08	61392.06	2.72	2887.97	162.90	4992.75	12.45
1993-94	32948.78	2219.10	69603.27	9.73	4341.92	134.64	4222.93	-20.99
1994-95	35953.07	2828.07	88797.53	21.53	4467.34	166.21	5218.86	19.00
1995-96	35493.85	3130.15	104702.89	9.65	2623.70	203.25	6798.50	18.22
1996-97	42592.97	4081.40	144889.29	23.31	5977.38	442.81	15719.68	54.10
1997-98	40754.97	4167.16	154871.78	2.06	5116.01	374.09	13903.13	-18.37
1998-99	42047.03	4585.86	192929.84	9.13	5441.29	421.34	17725.98	11.21
1999-00	43339.10	5004.55	216860.84	8.37	5766.56	468.58	20305.01	10.08
2000-01	41991.18	3395.36	155115.17	-47.39	6134.39	235.09	10739.85	-99.32
2001-02	47352.81	3616.05	172456.06	6.10	5378.15	255.10	12166.11	7.84
2002-03	40168.42	3164.51	153147.56	-14.27	6673.46	385.784	18670.13	33.88

Source: Kumar & Janagam (2011)

and genetic purity that are applicable to sell them commercially (Parliamentary Research Service, 2006). But considering the level of literacy of Indian farmers on an average, it seems to be impossible for them to maintain this quality. Moreover, it is estimated that above 80 per cent of seeds planted in India comes from seeds saved and exchanged by farmers. It is, therefore, very much difficult to implement this provision. Secondly, the farmers in developing countries like India would face the challenges more because the poor farmers of these countries cannot afford to buy seed each year.

Events of piracy of plants with medicinal values and medicinal knowledge of traditional healers are also on the increase at a rapid pace in India. This trend also poses challenges to the health security of India along with the interest of the intellectual property rights of the traditional healers. Therefore, more initiatives need to be taken at different levels, including government and NGOs in documenting codified and non-codified TK, which are to be noticed.

Table 6. List of biopiracy cases of India

Sl. No.	Common name	Indigenous use	Patentee	Action by the Indian Government
1	*Haldi*/ turmeric (*Curcuma longa*)	Treatment for sprains, inflammatory conditions and wounds	Two scientists from the University of Mississippi were granted US patent 5,401,504on the use of turmeric in1995	The US Patent and Trademark Office rejected all patent claims related to turmeric after the Indian government challenged the patent.
2	Neem (*Azadirachta Indica)*	effective medicine for many types of human and animal diseases	A US timber importer began importing neem seeds to his company headquartered in Wisconsin since 1971. In 1985, the bio-pesticide derived from neem tree received clearance from the US Environmental Protection Agency (EPA).	In May 2000, a coalition of groups successfully overturned the patent held by the US company, WR Grace and the US Department of Agriculture over the Indian neem tree.
3	Rice (Basmati)	Unique Aroma and Flavour	On 2 September 1997, Texas-based RiceTec Inc. was granted patent number 5663484 for a new plant variety that is a cross between American long-grain rice and Basmati rice.	By mid-2000, the Indian government challenged some of the claims of the RiceTec patent and the world's largest importer of Basmati rice, Saudi Arabia
4	Ginger (*Zingiber officinale)*	Treatment against cough and cold	Patent granted by US patent office on eight ginger formulation, Nicholas John Larkins	In 2011, the Department of Ayush and Council of Scientific Industrial Research (CSIR) intervened with evidence with age-old Ayurveda and Unani books dating back to 18thcentury.
5	Indian Wheat variety, Nap Hal		Monsanto, the biggest seed corporation, was assigned the patent (No. EP 0445929 B1) on wheat on May 21st, 2003 by the EPO under the simple title, "plants."	On January 27th, 2004. The Research Foundation for Science, Technology and Ecology along with Greenpeace and Bharat Krishak Samaha filed a petition at the EPO challenging the patent rights given to Monsanto, leading to the patent being revoked. (Shiva, 2012).

Source: Sharma et al. (2018)

REFERENCES

Argumedo, A., & Pimbert, M. (2006). *Protecting indigenous knowledge against biopiracy in the Andes*. IIED.

Baxter, B., Mayer, S., & Wijeratna, A. (1999). *Crops and Robbers: Biopiracy and the Patenting of Staple Food Crops. A Preliminary Findings of an Action Aid Investigation*. London: Action Aid; Available at http://www.actionaid.org

Bhattacharya, S. (2014). Bioprospecting, biopiracy and food security in India: The emerging sides of neoliberalism. *International Letters of Social and Humanistic Sciences*, (23), 49-56.

Bhukta, A. (2019). *Projecting Traditional Knowledge: A Search for an Effective IPR Law for India* (Ph. D Thesis). Vidyasagar University.

Browne, A. (2000, June 25). India fights US basmati rice patent. *The Guardian*.

Choudhary, B. (2002). The new international seed treaty: Promises and prospects for food security. *Current Science*, *83*(4), 366–369.

Cullet, P. (2004). Intellectual property rights and food security in the south. *The Journal of World Intellectual Property*, *7*(3), 261–286. doi:10.1111/j.1747-1796.2004.tb00209.x

De Muro, P., & Mazziotta, M. (2010). *Towards a Food Insecurity Multidimensional Index*. Available at nitropdf.com/professional

DGCIS. (2015). *Foreign Trade (Export and Import) of Herbal Raw Drugs*. Author.

Downes, G. (2003). *Implications of Trips for Food Security in the Majority World*. www.comhlamh.org

ETC Group. (2002). *DuPont and Monsanto – Living in Synergy?* Available at http://www.etcgroup.org/article.asp?newsid=315

EXIM Bank. (1997). *Study on Export Potential of Ayurveda and Siddha Products and Services*. Author.

FAO. (2009). *A Global Treaty For Food Security And Sustainable Agriculture: International treaty on plant genetic resources for food and agriculture*. FAO.

Fuglie, K. O., King, J. L., Heisey, P. W., & Schimmelpfennig, D. E. (2012). Rising concentration in agricultural input industries influences new farm technologies. *Amber Waves*, *10*(4).

Gauthier, J., Meyer, C., & Cohen, D. (2016). Framing Sustainable Practices: Middle Managers and Social Intrapreneurial Championing. *International Journal of Sustainable Entrepreneurship and Corporate Social Responsibility*, *1*(2), 21–39. doi:10.4018/IJSECSR.2016070102

Grain. (2001). *Intellectual Property Rights: Ultimate Control of Agricultural R and D in Asia*. Available at www.grain .org/publications/asiaipr-en.cfm

Haider, A. (2016). Reconciling patent law and traditional knowledge: Strategies for countries with traditional knowledge to successfully protect their knowledge from abuse. *Case W. Res. J. Int'l L.*, *48*, 347.

Jamil, U. (1998). *Biopiracy: The Patenting of Basmati by Ricetec*. Working Paper Series # 37. Commission on Environmental, Economic and Social Policy – South Asia and Sustainable Development Policy Institute.

Karmakar, A. K., & Jana, S. K. (2014). Policies and Strategies for Achieving Food and Nutrition Security in India: Myths and Realities. In *Dynamics of Food Security in India*. New Delhi: Kumud Publications.

Kumar, M. R., & Janagam, D. (2011). Export and import pattern of medicinal plants in India. *Indian Journal of Science and Technology*, *4*(3), 245–248.

Meek, J. (2000, Nov. 15). Beginners guide to gene patents. *Guardian*.

Mgbeoji, I. (2001). Patents and Traditional Knowledge of the Uses of Plants: Is a Communal Patent Regime Part of the Solution to the Scourge of Bio Piracy. *Indiana Journal of Global Legal Studies*, *9*(1), 9. Available at http://www.repository.law.indiana.edu/ijgls/vol9/iss1/9

Parliamentary Research Service. (2006). *Legislative Brief: The Seeds Bill, 2004*. Available at www. prsindia.org

Patro, L. (2016). Medicinal Plants of India: With special reference to Odisha. IJARIIE, 2(5).

Sahai, S. (2004). Commercialization of Traditional Knowledge and Benefit Sharing. In *Protecting and Promoting Traditional Knowledge: Systems, National Experiences and International Dimensions*. UNCTAD.

UNDP. (2001). *Human Development Report*. New York: UNDP.

KEY TERMS AND DEFINITIONS

Biopiracy: Biopiracy indicates unauthorized use of bio-resources of a country either by the individuals or institutions or companies of other countries.

Food Security: All people, at all times, have physical, social and economic access to sufficient, safe and nutritious food which meets their dietary needs and food preferences for an active and healthy life.

GM Crops: Genetically modified crops (GM crops) are plants used in agriculture, the DNA of which has been modified using genetic engineering methods.

MNC: A multinational corporation (MNC) which has facilities and other assets in at least one country other than its home country.

Neem: Is a natural herb that comes from the neem tree. It is known for its pesticidal and insecticidal properties.

Traditional knowledge (TK): Generally refers to the matured long-standing traditions and practices of certain regional, indigenous, or local communities.

Chapter 8
Protection of Indian Traditional Rice Varieties:
Role of PPV and FRA

Moghanraj Yadhav G.
VAANGHAI, Nagapattinam, India

Balaguru Balakrishnan
Jamal Mohamed College, Tiruchirappalli, India

Nagamurugan N.
Government Arts College, Madurai, Tamilnadu, India

ABSTRACT

The crop genetic diversity has been sustainably maintained by the farmers of different regions for generations through cross-breeding. Competition among commercial ventures has placed these traditional varieties under severe exploitation and pilferage. The Indian government, to preserve these traditional varieties, has established PPV and FRA (Protection of Plant Varieties and Farmers Rights Act), which are on par with Intellectual Patent Rights (IPR). This gives the rights and ownership of the crop breed and its characterization to the traditional farmers who developed it. The researchers along with VAANGHAI, an NGO, have represented the traditional farmers, who are growing and maintaining traditional crops in Cauvery River's coastal delta region in Tamil Nadu to characterize and register their varieties under PPV and FRA. This study has identified around 69 rice varieties and characterized them based on their uniqueness, distinctiveness, stability, uniformity, test trials, and adaptability potential. Most potential rice varieties were registered under this act.

DOI: 10.4018/978-1-7998-1835-9.ch008

INTRODUCTION

Traditional Knowledge (TK) or Indigenous Knowledge (IK) is generally referred to as traditional and cultural practices of native people in a specific geographic area, wherein their knowledge is orally passed on from generation to generation. The knowledge pertains to their culture, environment and innovative remedies, as solutions for problems identified at local levels (Warren, 1992). It is normally associated with folk nomenclatures and herbal medicine (Farnsworth 1988), taxonomies of plants (Berlin, 1992), the environment (Ellen et al. 2000), disease aetiology (Berlin and Berlin 1996), and agricultural practices (Brush 1992). It also comprises utilisation of natural resources for agriculture, health and management by developing innovative technologies and passing on the information through cultural transmission, by native tribes/people in a territory, and most important is constantly evolving in response to the changing environment (Mafongoya and Ajayi, 2017). This deep and long-established relationship with the natural environment has taught these indigenous people to adapt well to the dynamic environment and respond to the impacts of climate change (Ihenacho et al., 2019).

This traditional knowledge is depleting at an alarming rate due to the adaptation of commercially viable modern technologies and the negligence of traditional farming practices. The Intergovernmental Panel on Climate Change (IPCC, 2009) has indicated that rising temperature, drought, flood, desertification and weather extremes will severely affect agriculture. Agricultural researchers worldwide are working towards minimising such calamities and other effects of climate change to increase productivity within a finite natural resource basis. Finally, they have concluded that traditional agro-ecosystem is one of the best alternatives to mitigate the ensuing climate, because these systems are less vulnerable to catastrophic loss, and they have the option to grow a wide range of crops and varieties in various spatial and temporal arrangements. Preservation of these traditional varieties will help in sustaining valuable crop varieties in future especially for their unique characteristics and cultural identities. This chapter identifies such crop varieties, characterises and assists in registering them under the aegis of PPV & FRA (Protection of Plant Varieties and Farmers' Rights Act) on behalf of rural traditional farmers in Tamil Nadu, India.

BACKGROUND

Crop Diversity

Crop genetic diversity contributes significantly to the stability and sustainability of farming systems and is valued for proving important attributes, including, *inter alia*, agronomic characteristics, biotic and abiotic stresses and other factors of cultural and socio-economic importance. Genes from wild crop relatives have been particularly important in providing resistance to pests and diseases. They are concentrated on the specific geographical regions, which are referred to as their '*centres of origin of diversity*'. These centres provide a convenient focus for assessing the conservation status of crop genetic diversity (Stolton et al., 2006). Crop diversification increases resilience and brings higher spatial and temporal biodiversity on the farm (Joshi, 2005). According to Lin (2011), crop diversification improves soil fertility, controls pests and diseases, and brings about yield stability, nutrition diversity and health. It can also serve as a superior substitute for chemicals to maintain soil fertility. Truscott et al., (2009) considers crop diversification, an environmentally sound alternative to the control of parasites and in the maintenance of soil fertility in agriculture. Diversified cropping systems, in general, tend to be agronomically more stable and resilient. This resilience is mainly because they are usually associated with reduced weed and insect pressures, reduced need for nitrogen fertilizers (especially if the crop mix include leguminous crops), reduced erosion (because of cover crops inclusion), increased soil fertility and increased yield per unit area (Lin, 2011). Moreover, diversified cropping systems can also provide habitats for beneficial insects, and this can help reduce the number of pests by rendering host crops less apparent for colonisation by parasites.

India is characterised by the complex agro-ecosystem differentiated by its climate, soil, vegetation and other features. National Bureau of Soil Survey and Land use planning has classified 20 broad-based agro-ecological zones (Sehgal, 1992) and the National Bureau of Plant Genetic Resources (NBPGR) has listed more than 320 species of Crop Wild Relatives (CWR) native to India. Among them, the major cultivated plants comprise rice, wheat, maize, cotton, Kodo millet, aubergine, mango, black pepper, sugarcane, brassica, groundnut, garlic/onion, cassava and cowpea. These crop species have as many varieties, which has been developed for centuries. For example, Rice has 50,000 varieties, Mango with 1000 varieties, and Sorghum with 5000 varieties (WCMC, 1992; FAO, 1997) etc.

Traditional Knowledge and Crop Diversity

The traditional systems of crop production have emerged over centuries of cultural and biological evolution and represent the accumulated experiences of indigenous farmers. The farmers produce indigenous crops through the knowledge of environmental conditions and seasonal changes, with no influences from external inputs like capital or modern scientific knowledge (Maroyi, 2012). The genes from such crop wild relatives have been particularly important in providing resistance to pests and diseases (Maxted, 2003). Genetic resources of crops are invaluable assets that are being conserved for generations by the farmers to increase productivity (Hasan et al., 2015). Indigenous farmers developed traditional varieties or landraces, which are more genetically diverse than modern varieties (CBD Secretariat, 2010). International Treaty on Plant Genetic Resources for Food and Agriculture (ITPGRFA), which came into force in 2004, addresses issues on the significance of crop diversity. UN sustainable development target 2.5 has pointed out, that by 2020, we have to maintain the genetic diversity of seeds, cultivated plants through seed banks at a regional and national level and promote access to fair and equitable sharing of benefits arising from the utilisation of genetic resources and associated traditional knowledge.

Genetic Erosion

Food and Agriculture Organisation (FAO) estimates that about 75 per cent of the genetic diversity of agricultural crops has been lost in the last century (FAO, 1998). This loss is clearly illustrated by a survey of 75 US crop species, carried out by the Rural Advancement Fund International (RAFI), which report that 97% of the varieties listed in old United States Department of Agriculture (USDA) catalogues are now extinct (Fowler and Mooney, 1990). Equally, dramatic losses have also been recorded in Europe. In Germany, about 90% of historical diversity of crops has been lost, and in South Italy, about 75% of the crop varieties have disappeared (Hammer, 2002).

Developing countries like India have the richest reservoirs of biodiversity. Agriculture is often a major component and it provides jobs, ensuring food security, and maintaining social structure. The introduction of modern high-yielding crop varieties, changes in crop rotation and pest management strategy, and greater dependence on agrochemicals have seriously threatened the biodiversity of both forest ecosystem and agroecosystem (Jana, 1999). Complete abandonment or long term fallowing of agricultural land, use of chemical fertilisers and plantation of multipurpose trees on farmland are the common threats to farming systems, as seen in the Himalayan region (Gilmour & Nurse, 1991; Rao & Saxena, 1996; Nautiyal et al., 1998), which led to the loss of over 40 crop species and hundreds of varieties of cereals, millets, pseudo-cereals, pulses, oilseeds, tubers, bulbs and spices in the Garhwal Himalaya of Uttar Pradesh (Maikhuri et al., 1997).

Particularly the crop genotypes like rice are being gradually eroded from their respective places of origin and are on the verge of becoming extinct due to competition from high yielding varieties, difficulties of cultural practices and improper means of storage (Ram et al., 2007; Maxted & Kell, 2009). The developmental activities and exploitive land-use pattern have destroyed the natural habitats, and modern varieties (high yielding varieties in rice) have replaced indigenous cultivars and landraces, resulting in a substantial reduction of genetic diversity (Sajib et al., 2012). However, growing commercial use of these resources beyond the traditional context means they are increasingly vulnerable to misappropriation and misuse by third parties. That is why holders of traditional knowledge and many international policymakers are calling for new policies and laws in this area.

The seeds of wild relatives and landraces are the basis of productive, social and cultural processes that can give some autonomy to farmers, to save and reuse them for food production. Hence, all farming communities know how to save, store and wisely share their precious seeds. Due to the development of agribusiness, there would be an increase in the risks of misappropriation. Hence, IPRs are important to the developing countries, whose primary source livelihood is based on agriculture (Anja et al., 2015). For avoiding such misappropriations and misuse by the third parties, many policymakers are developing better resilient policies in this area (Ouma, 2017).

Protection of TK under IPR System – Indian Context

TK provides rich research clues in the field of drug development and crop breed development having resistance to pests, diseases and climate changes. Misappropriation of TK in order to legitimise the exclusive ownership and control over biological resources and biological products and processes i.e. bio-piracy is prevalent over centuries in most of the developing countries. TK is considered a casualty to bio-piracy due to encroachment of knowledge and lack of appropriate legal systems or awareness. In the recent past, several cases of bio-piracy of TK from India have been reported, and prominent among them are the cases pertaining to patenting of a healing compound in Turmeric, a compound extracted from Neem for its fungicidal properties and a Basmati rice variety by multinational companies, which had been traditionally used in India for centuries. India had to fiercely fight for its rights by quoting its ancient literature and fortunately won (Mukherjee, 2008; Balasubramanian, 2017). It will not be possible for all similar cases in future as entities may find ways to circumvent the legal processes. The situation calls for reinforced protection by registration of our valuable traditional resources and practices as early as possible to avoid such situations in future. Therefore, after the successful efforts of India's revocation of patents on Turmeric, Neem and Basmati, India focused on protection of TK of Indian origin, especially Ayurvedic, Siddha and farmers varieties and developed its own Traditional Knowledge Digital Library (TKDL) under PPV & FRA based on TRIPS agreement and Convention of Biological Diversity.

The Ministry of AYUSH had established Traditional Knowledge Digital Library (TKDL) in collaboration with Council for Scientific & Industrial Research (CSIR), which includes about 290, the Indian system of medicine in five international languages namely English, Japanese, French, German and Spanish. Access of TKDL has been provided to International Patent offices (IPOs) under the International Agreement. In addition, pre-grant oppositions on patent applications along with prior art search evidence from TKDL are submitted on a regular basis. TKDL provides open access to patent offices in different countries, so the herbal formulation-based patent filed in India patent office can be evaluated through Prior Art Search in TKDL and patents revoked if necessary. This foolproof system has successfully established India's authority in its TK.

In continuation with TRIPS sui generis system and according to PPV and FR act 2001, the Indian government established Protection of Plant Varieties and Farmer's Rights Authority (PPV & FRA) in 2005 under the Ministry of Agriculture, exclusively for registration of traditional crops and varieties. The act envisages registration and transfer of benefits to the rightful owner of the crop variety or practices.

This chapter is based on the relevant conventions and treaties for developing the PPV & FRA in India and is discussed.

Conventions, Treaties Plant Varieties Protection and Farmers Rights

Convention on Biological Diversity

Conservation of biological diversity was raised by the Convention on Biological Diversity (CBD), which came into force in 1993. The conservation and sustainable utilisation and access to biological diversity were considered as national sovereignty by CBD. Consequently, many issues regarding the rights of the conservers, users, breeders, farmers and intellectual property have emerged.

The CBD plays a key role in defining who gains access to information about genetic resources, protection, conservation and the sustainable use of genetic resources and related knowledge, how the benefits are shared (including traditional communities), and what technologies are developed and transferred with implications for conservation and sustainable use of biological diversity.

Article 5 and 6 of the International treaty – CBD-Target 2010 is based on plant genetic resources for food agriculture and has given the highest priority to conservation, collection, characterisation, evaluation and sustainable use of crop genetic resources (Ref: Convention on Biological Diversity).

This treaty is mainly focused on the following agendas.

1. Promote or support, as appropriate, farmers and local community's efforts to manage and conserve on-farm their plant genetic resources for food and agriculture.
2. Promote in situ conservation of wild crop relatives and wild plants for food production, including plants in protected areas, by supporting, inter alia, the efforts of indigenous and local communities.
3. Cooperate to promote the development of an efficient and sustainable system of ex situ conservation, giving due attention to the need for adequate documentation, characterisation, regeneration and evaluation, and promote the development and transfer of appropriate technologies for this purpose with a view to improving the sustainable use of plant genetic resources for food and agriculture.
4. Promoting, as appropriate, plant breeding efforts, which, with the participation of farmers, particularly in developing countries, strengthen the capacity to develop varieties particularly adapted to social, economic and ecological conditions, including in marginal areas.
5. Promoting, as appropriate, the expanded use of local and locally adapted crops, varieties and underutilised species.
6. Supporting, as appropriate, the wider use of the diversity of varieties and species in on-farm management, conservation and sustainable use of crops and creating strong links to plant breeding and agricultural development in order to reduce crop vulnerability and genetic erosion, and promote increased world food production compatible with sustainable development.

The articles 15, 16 and 19 are of special relevance to IPR and are described below.

Article 15 concerns access to genetic resources. Part 15.1 recognises the *sovereign rights of States over their natural resources* a notion that challenges the major international agreements on IPR protection of plants, animals and microorganisms. Furthermore, part 15.7 states that *each Contracting Party shall take legislative, administrative and policy measures with the aim of sharing in a fair and equitable way, the results of research and development and the benefits arising from the commercial and other utilisation of genetic resources with the Contracting Party providing such resources. Such sharing shall be upon mutually agreed terms.*

Article 16 concerns access to and transfer of technology. Part 16.1 recognises that the transfer of technology, including biotechnology is an essential element to the *attainment of the objectives of this Convention*, viz. *the conservation of biological diversity, the sustainable use of its components and the fair and equitable sharing of the benefits arising out of the utilisation of genetic resources* Part 16.3, like 15.7, has implications for IPRs: Each Contracting Party shall take legislative, administrative or policy measures, as appropriate, with the aim that Contracting Parties, in particular those that are developing countries, which provide genetic resources are provided access to and transfer of technology which makes use of those resources on mutually agreed terms, including technology protected by patents and other intellectual property rights.

Article 19 handles Biotechnology and distribution of its benefits - part 1 stipulates that each party shall take similar institutional measures to *provide for the effective participation in biotechnological research activities by those contracting parties, especially developing countries, which provide the genetic resources for such research and where feasible in such contracting parties*. Part 19.3 calls upon parties to consider a binding protocol to the convention on the safe transfer, handling and use of biotechnological products.

(Source: CBD, 2018)

Apart from protecting innovations, access to genetic resources is another basic aspect including biotechnology as a new tool for the conservation and sustainable use of plant genetic resources for food and agriculture. In 1983, Southern regional members of the United Nations Food and Agriculture Organisation (FAO) initiated the International Undertaking on Plant Genetic Resources (IUPGR). This agreement promotes the proper conservation and use of all plant genetic resources, including those produced by modern techniques, and ensuring access to them without undue restrictions. Moreover, it seeks to enable "all countries to make full use of their plant genetic resources for the benefit of their agricultural development"

1. **Conservation of Germplasm:** The seeds can be conserved in seed banks (*ex situ*) and also continue cultivation and management of a diverse set of crop populations by farmers in on-farm (*in situ*) as required in order to allow the process of evolution and adaptation to continue with the crop plant, ensuring that new germplasm is generated over time.
2. **Community Seed Bank Establishment:** The stakeholders should collect the seeds of traditional varieties from the farmer's land and segregate them based on their duration. The seeds are then multiplied and stored in the seed banks. For the development of pure lines (uniform and stable), they have to select the seeds with uniformity and multiply them in the field. The final crop

is harvested and the seeds collected and stored separately for the benefit for farmers and researchers.

3. **Registration of Plant Varieties:** Registration under the IPR system is required to restore the traditional farmer's inherent right to save, use, and exchange the seeds among themselves. The farmer is permitted to freely exchange the seed material with other farmers of the region.

Union for the Protection of New Varieties of Plants (UPOV)

The first multilateral system for the protection of Plant Breeder's Rights' (PBRs) was created through the convention establishing the International Union for the Protection of New Varieties of (UPOV) 1961 (Biswajit, 2002), which was first revised in 1978. The convention recognises the breeder of the new plant variety. There were 42 articles dealt in this convention on the protection of new varieties of plants. Under the 1978 Act, not all plant varieties were protected, but were limited to a number of genera and species. According to article 2(1) of the 1978 act, member states shall grant either any one of the types of protection and the same botanical genera and species. Article 5 (1) focused on the following rights i.e., prior authentication from the breeder is required for i) the production for purposes of commercial marketing ii) the offering for sale (iii) the marketing of the reproductive or vegetative propagating material. Article 6 dealt with the conditions required for protection, which includes

1. **Novelty**: Avoid plant varieties already existing
2. **Distinctness:** Clearly distinguishable by one or more important characteristics
3. **Homogeneity:** The variety must be sufficiently homogeneous, having regard to the particular features of its sexual reproduction or vegetative propagation
4. **Stability:** The variety must be stable in its essential characteristics, that is to say, it must remain true to its description after repeated reproduction or propagation.

Article 7 of the 1978 Act emphasises the protection of plant varieties granted after the examination of the variety which falls in the criteria as defined in article 6, for this breeder of the concerned plant variety, provided they/he furnish all the necessary information and propagating materials. The period of protection was less than 15 years for vines, forest, fruit and ornamental trees and for the rootstocks, which was less than 8 years (UPOV, 1978). The 1978 Act was strengthened in 1991. It recognised the right of breeders to use protected varieties to create new varieties and provide a detailed definition of plant varieties he introduces.

Plant Varieties

The plant kingdom has been classified based ranks i.e. Kingdom, Division, Class, Order, Family, Genus and Species respectively. It is also known that there are varieties within a species or subspecies. The breeders grow the same plant species in different environmental conditions and as a result these plants after getting adapted to the new environmental conditions, change their characteristics and show variation from the parent's species, and they may or may not carry the parental characters, which is then called as plant variety.

To be more specific UPOV Convention 1991 (Article 1(vi)) defines it as a plant grouping within a single botanical taxon of the lowest known rank, which grouping, irrespective of whether the conditions for the grant of a breeder's right are fully met, can be

1. Defined by the expression of the characteristics resulting from a given genotype or combination of genotypes,
2. Distinguished from any other plant grouping by the expression of at least one of the said characteristics and
3. Considered as a unit with regard to its suitability for being propagated unchanged;"

The terms mentioned in the 1978 acts pertaining to the condition of protection clearly defined in the 1991 act. Novelty (article 6), Distinctness (article 7), Uniformity (article 8) and Stability (article 9). Scope of the Breeder's Right in article 14 and Exceptions to the Breeder's Right (article 15) (UPOV, 1991).

Trade-Related Aspects of Intellectual Property Rights (TRIPS)

Agreement by WTO and UPOV is the two major treaty systems that regulate the IPRs of plant varieties. Agreement on TRIPS by WTO member countries provided some form of Intellectual property Protection on Plant varieties (Carlos et al., 2015). Article 27.3(a) of TRIPS Article exclude the characteristics from patentability i.e., (a) diagnostic, therapeutic and surgical methods for the treatment of humans or animals and 27.3(b) of the TRIPS Agreement states protection of plant varieties either by patents or by an effective sui generis protection or both.

At present, all over the world, plant varieties are protected by different countries by giving protection in three ways: i) by granting patents or; ii) by providing effective *sui generis* system or; iii) by any combination of patents and *sui generis* system (Patil, 2005). With the signing of the TRIPs Agreement of the World Trade Organisation (WTO), India has agreed to provide protection to plant varieties adopted *sui generis* system (one's own system of protection of plant varieties) as an alternative or addition to a patent system for protecting plants. Indian Parliament passed the PPV & FRA in 2001 and the regulations for implementing the act were formulated in 2003. The ministry of agriculture, Government of India, has been identified as a nodal agency for implementing the act under the authority of PPV & FRA.

PPV and FRA

India is the first country, which adopted the *sui generis* system and setup PPV and FRA under the Ministry of Agriculture during the year 2005. PPV and FRA Act legislation granting rights to both breeders and farmers simultaneously (Dewan, 2011) and covers all plants except microbes i.e., food crops, oilseeds, fibre and fodder crops, species, aromatic and medicinal plants, vegetables, fruits, ornamental, plantation, biofuel plants, mulberry, forest trees, urban trees, mangroves under traditional cultivation and conservation. The act fulfils the DUS (Distinctiveness, Uniformity and Stability) guidelines. Guidelines for DUS were developed for several crop varieties including trees. DUS guidelines for cereals, pulses, oilseeds, fibres, spices, fruits, orchids, vegetables, flowers, sugarcane, medicinal & aromatic plant, plantation crops are specified and developed by PPV and FRA in its manuals (Appendix I). According to PPV & FRA around 1,935 crop varieties including traditional and farmer's varieties of India are successfully registered so far.

Objectives of PPV and FRA

1. To recognize and protect the rights of farmers for their contribution made at any time in conserving, improving and making available plant genetic resources for the development of new plant varieties.
2. To encourage the development of new varieties of plants for accelerated agricultural development
3. To accelerate agricultural development in the country and protect Plant Breeder's Rights (PBR) and to stimulate investment in research and development (R& D) both in public and private sector, for breeding new plant varieties
4. To facilitate the growth of the seed industry as this will ensure the availability of good quality seed and plant material to the farmers.

According to PPV & FRA, Essentially Derived Varieties (EDV), means a variety which has been essentially derived from existing variety by any of the following a) Genetic Engineering derived, b) Develop through mutation, c) Propagated through tissue culture, d) Derived by genetic back cross, e) Change the Ploidy conditions, but EDV is clearly distinguishable from initial varieties in the expression of the essential characteristics of genotypes or combination of parental genotype.

The farmer's variety has been traditionally cultivated in their fields as a wild relative of landrace. The pure lines have to be characterised according to DUS test guidelines and passport data must include distinct characteristics of candidate variety, which is published in the Plant Variety Journal of India (PVJI) for inviting opposition within 90 days. If there is no opposition filed, the certificate of registration is granted to the applicant and its details are published in the PVJI. Farmers are exempted from every kind of fee other than annual fees (PPV & FRA).

Based on the above as envisaged in PPV and FRA act, the study envisages documentation of some Traditional Rice Varieties (TRVs) and characterisation of TRV and identifies their Distinctiveness, Uniqueness and Stability for registration under PPV & FRA act. The authors have focused on the collection, cultivation and characterisation of traditional farmers' rice varieties from Kaveri delta and coastal belt of Tamil Nadu. Pure line of potential TRVs was registered at PPV & FRA, Ministry of Agriculture, Government of India.

METHODOLOGY

Study Area

Kaveri delta and Coastal belt region (Figure 1) comprising Tiruchirappalli, Tanjore, Pudukottai, Perambalur, Ariyalur, Nagapattinam, Cuddalore, Ramanathapuram, Tuticorin and Tiruvarur districts in Tamil Nadu was taken up for the assessment. These regions were chosen as these come under rice cultivation as their major crop with many traditional varieties still under cultivation. In recent years, rice cultivation in these regions has suffered great losses due to water scarcity and rapid climate changes. In addition, the intrusion of seawater into the coastal belt during the Tsunami in the year 2004 has increased the salinity of the soil thus affecting rice cultivation. However, TRVs cultivated in these regions have well adapted to the changing climatic conditions and have developed physiological mechanisms to withstand salt stress. The farmers are encouraged to grow these traditional varieties for their ability to sustain in adverse climate conditions. Similarly, farmers already practicing traditional farming methods are identified and their seeds are collected for DUS assessment.

Location Map

Figure 1. Location map of the study area

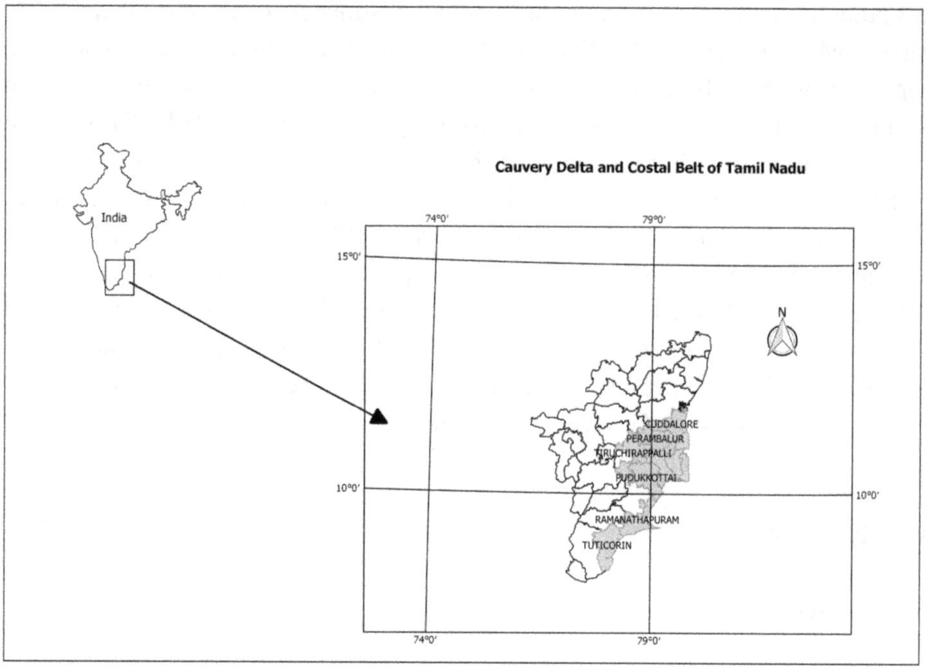

Experimental Design

1. **Documentation:** Potential farmers who cultivated TRVs were identified and their farms visited and information on their farming practices, seed selection, seed sowing methods, season, irrigation, fertiliser, Crop protection, post-harvest methods, seed storage methods, farm tools and uniqueness were documented. On confirmation of the TRVs based on the standard Questionnaire, the seeds were obtained from the practicing farmers and their consent collected via Prior Inform Consent (PIC) by explaining the purpose of the collection of their seeds.
2. **Field preparation**: Dry soil ploughing was carried out twice before sowing. This method ensures better gas exchange, increase immunity to pest and diseases. Puddling and levelling operations were done before the transplantation. The process involves flooding the land with water up to 0.5 cm above the soil level after levelling for transplantation, thereby saving roots and foliage of young seedlings.

3. **Manuring:** FYM (Farm Yard Manure) were applied in the field a week before puddling. Bio-fertilisers were thoroughly mixed with FYM and the mixture put in a wet jute sack and allowed to incubate to facilitate the multiplication of microbes).
4. **Seed Bank establishment:** 69 rice crop varieties were collected, stored and labelled properly in VAANGHAI seed banks and classified them based on its growth duration.
   a. 1. Short duration (66-110 days) - 15 nos.
   b. 2. Medium duration (120-135 days) - 25 nos.
   c. 3. Long duration (140-180 days) - 29 nos.
5. **Nursery preparation:** Nursery bed (2400 sq. ft.) was prepared containing highly enriched organic manure like FYM, rice mill ash and earthworm castings. The rice seeds were soaked in water for 18 hours, followed by treating with cow's urine in order to enhance the germination. Precautions were taken to avoid pests and diseases. Wet seeds were kept in jute sacks for 18 hours. The seeds begin to sprout at this stage and later these seeds were spread on the nursery bed. 12 to 15-centimetre-long seedlings were observed within a week. Neem extract was sprayed (as a foliar spray) to the young seedling, which acted as a growth promoter and improved pest and disease resistance.
6. **Transplantation:** Seedlings of the rice varieties were transplanted to the main field (i.e., into 300 Square feet patches, each with 30 feet length x 10 feet breadth) in a straight file with 10-inch-wide spaces. The emerging young seedlings were transferred to the field again in a single file as specified above. The seed kernels were collected from the field on 14th, 28th, 42nd and 55th day from the date of planting and observed for proposed characteristics.
7. **Harvest:** The grains were harvested after attaining maturity. After the harvest, the panicles were removed manually from the straw and sun-dried for storage. After 60 days of harvest, the paddy seeds were packed in 500 gm x 3 packets (1.5 kg / variety) and stored in the VAANGHAI Gene bank and the same submitted to National Bureau for Plant Genetic Resources (NBPGR), New Delhi.
8. **Farmers Network and Seed Distribution:** The pure lines of seeds were distributed among the farmers through the *Ulavar Mugaam* for Multi-Location Trials (MLT) and to identify the geographic adaptability of the seeds. The unique and potential varieties were identified based on the following characteristics.
9. **Selection of Varieties:** The target TRVs were selected based on a) Adaptability to different geographical region b) Yield potential c) Turnout of rice d) Cooking quality e) Uniqueness (*Medicinal importance, table quality*).
10. **Characterisation and Registration:** Characterisations were carried out for the selected varieties. The characterisation included Coleoptiles Colour, Early

plant Vigour, Basal leaf sheath Colour, Leaf Blade Colour, Leaf pubescence, Flag leaf, Ligule Colour, Ligule shape, Collar Colour, Auricle Colour, Internode Colour, Panicle exertion, Panicle type, Stigma Colour, Apicule Colour, Awning, Hull Colour, Sterile lemma, Days to maturity, Seed coat Colour, Aroma, Thresh ability, Leaf length, Leaf width, Days to 50% flooring, Plant Height, Total number of tillers, Effective tillers, Panicle length, No of grains panicle, Number of filled grains panicle, Grains length to width ratio, weight of 100 grains, Grains yield/packet (grams) and Biotic stress susceptibility.

RESULTS AND DISCUSSION

Based on the characters specified above, the promising rice candidates i.e., six varieties were selected for registration. Each variety was neatly packed as per PPV & FRA specification, i.e. 500 gm x 3 packets (1.5 kg/variety) and submitted for registration at PPV & FRA in New Delhi.

The registration of the Rice crop (*Oryza sativa* L.) varieties as specified below were granted by PPV & FRA in recognition of concerned breeders in the geographic territory.

Table 1.

Registered Crop varieties	PPV & FRA Registration Details *(with certificate number and date)*
Kudai Vazhai	REG/2011/1338; 131 of 2016 issued on 22 April 2016
Kavuni	REG/2011/1341; 132 of 2016 issued on 22 April 2016
Karung Kuruvai	REG/2011/1336; 133 of 2016 issued on 22 April 2016
Jeeraga Samba	REG/2011/1337; 134 of 2016 issued on 22 April 2016
Kattuyanam	REG/2011/1340; 065 of 2016 issued on 10 February 2016
Kallundai	REG/2011/1339; 066 of 2016 issued on 10 February 2016

India had been a victim of severe loss of its traditional practices and varieties, due to modern development in agriculture. Coupled with it, India is also facing pilferage of its traditional varieties to interested entities, who had been denying the rights and benefits to the original breeders of the crop varieties, based on which the new varieties are produced. It is the sole right of a country to protect its traditions and rights of its farmers. Similarly, Sinthupundaja & Kohda (2017) have studied in detail the role of corporate social responsibility (CSR) in creating shared value

(CSV) among the industry and farmers. It is a good initiative wherein the farmers are included as shareholders. The traditional crops especially the crop varieties cultivated in Tamil Nadu is based on natural farming, wherein chemical fertilizer's usage is totally avoided, as these plants are highly sensitive. The initiative of the Indian government in providing Intellectual Property (IP) protection for these traditional crop varieties would sustain the farmers' rights and at the same time generate income for their future security. According to the PPV & FR Act, the registration granted for unique varieties can also be extended to include Geographic Indicators (GI) to protect the region itself under the aegis of IPR. To cite some examples, the rice variety Kavuni is an excellent food for diabetics as it has a very low glycaemic index, secondly Kallundai, another rice variety improves muscle strength, etc. The IP certified with quality of the crop products increases the green purchase intention, which is the intentional purchase of products and services with an idea of minimal harm to the health and environment (Tullani et al., 2018).

FUTURE RESEARCH DIRECTIONS

Traditional farmers are excellent plant breeders, with rich knowledge on crop varieties, cultivation practices and maintenance in different climatic conditions, which has been developed for centuries. The farmers have also developed crop varieties that can sustain even in the current climatic scenario i.e., mitigate the hurdles due to climate change. Hence, the traditional knowledge of developing the crop varieties has to be encouraged and the DUS guidelines developed according to more and newer emerging crops. Characterisation and registration of pure lines of cultivated crops with its Geographical Indication (GI) tag by the PPV & FRA will be an added advantage in fortifying its initiatives under IPR.

CONCLUSION

Traditional knowledge is a rich repository of knowledge that is developed, sustained and passed on from generation to generation within a community, often forming part of its cultural or spiritual identity for centuries. It gives identity to the cultural expressions, the ecology, agricultural practices, contribution to medicine, innovative technologies, and environmental management of an area under human care. The traditional knowledge has undergone a notable erosion in recent decades due to development and its mismanagement. There are also cases of crop failures due to overexploitation of resources and rampant chemical alternatives coupled with climate changes. The traditional knowledge also faces a greater threat in misappropriation and exploitation for commercial profit, wherein the grass root farmers are denied their rights and neither recognised nor benefited for their shared knowledge. Intellectual Property Protection of Traditional Knowledge is essential for protection, sustained exploitation and benefit-sharing. Traditional agro-ecosystem and farmers varieties are the right alternative solution to improve the food production as these systems include a wide range of crops and varieties in various spatial and temporal arrangements that are less vulnerable to catastrophic environmental changes. Based on the UPOV acts, TRIPs agreements and CBD conventions, the Indian government has taken initiatives to protect and promote the traditional knowledge and carefully formulated the TKDL for Indian traditional medicine and PPV & FRA for protecting traditional crops and farmer's varieties. PPV & FRA has also developed guidelines for different crop varieties to register under Intellectual Property (IP). In this study, there were 69 Traditional Rice Varieties (TRVs) collected from farmers in the Kaveri delta and coastal belt region in Tamil Nadu, India. Most of the TRVs are found to be drought and flood stress-tolerant. Characterisations of these TRVs were done based on PPV & FRA guidelines. The germplasm of the TRVs was deposited at the National Bureau of Plant Genetic Resources (NBPGR), New Delhi. Potential crop varieties (TRVs) were selected based on their uniqueness and table quality, assessed following DUS guidelines of PPV & FRA, and characterised. Genetic resources of TRVs were deposited at NBPGR, New Delhi. Among them, six varieties, which had higher DUS characteristics, were registered in the name of the society, which the farmers represented under the PPV & FRA act in 2016. In the future, the farmers will enjoy the rights and relevant benefits of the knowledge shared in a secure environment of PPV & FRA. The methodology adopted for characterisation of rice varieties in this study can be replicated in future similar assessments.

ACKNOWLEDGEMENT

We are grateful to the Ministry of Agriculture and its Protection of Plant Varieties and Farmers' Rights Authority for providing funding support for the project "Characterisation and Registration of Traditionally Cultivated rice varieties along Coastal Belt and Kaveri Delta of Tamil Nadu". We especially thank Dr. Gautham (former Chairman PPV & FRA, Ministry of Agriculture), Mr. R. K. Trivedi (Former register PPV & FRA), Dr. Baijnath Singh (Birsa Agriculture University Kanke, Ranchi, Jharkhand), Dr. Tejbir Singh (Registrar, PPV & FRA), Dr. S. R. Dhua (Principal Scientist, CRRI, Cuttack), Dr. L. V. Subba Rao (Principal Scientist, DRR, Hyderabad), Mr. Dipal Roy Choudhury, (Joint Registrar PPV & FRA) for their regular monitoring and valuable suggestions. Our sincerest and heartfelt thanks to Late Dr. S. Nagarajan (former Chairman, PPV & FRA), Late Dr. Robin (Professor and Head, Department of Rice, TNAU, Tamil Nadu), Honoured professors (KVK, Sikkal, Tamil Nadu and Indian Rice Institute, Aduthurai, Tamil Nadu), for their support. We also acknowledge the contribution of the dedicated farmers from the study region in Tamil Nadu for their contribution in characterisation and registration of Traditional Rice Varieties and the Staff members of VAANGHAI for their support. We thank the reviewer for the careful and insightful *review* of our manuscript.

REFERENCES

Anja, C., & Morten, W. (2015). *The UPOV Convention, Farmers Rights and Human Rights, an integrated assessment ofpotentially conflicting legalframework.* Deutsche Gesellschaft fur Internationale Zusammenarbeit (GIZ).

Balasubramanian, S. (2017). *India: Traditional Knowledge And Patent Issues: An Overview Of Turmeric, Basmati, Neem Case.* Retrieved on 13/10/2019 from http:// www. mondaq. com/india/ x/ 586384/Patent

Berlin, B. (1992). *Ethnobiological classification: Principles of categorisation of plants and animals in traditional societies.* Princeton, NJ: Princeton University Press. doi:10.1515/9781400862597

Berlin, E. A., & Berlin, B. (1996). *Medical ethnobiology of the Highland Maya of Chiapas, Mexico: the gastrointestinal diseases.* Princeton, NJ: Princeton University Press.

Biswajit, D. (2002). *Sui Generis Systems for Plant Variety Protection, Options under Trips.* Discussion Paper. Quaker United Nations Office.

Brush, S. B. (1992). Ethnoecology, biodiversity, and modernisation in Andean potato agriculture. *Journal of Ethnobiology, 12*, 161–185.

Carlos, M. (2015). *Plant Variety Protection in Developing Countries: A Tool for Designing a Sui-Generis Plant Variety Protection System: An Alternative to UPOV 1991.* Working paper. Association for Plant Breeding for the Benefit of Society (APBREBES).

Dewan, M. (2011). IPR Protection in Agriculture: An Overview IPR Protection in Agriculture: An Overview. *Journal of Intellectual Property Rights, 16*, 131–138.

Ellen, R., Parkes, P., & Bicker, A. (Eds.). (2000). *Indigenous Environmental Knowledge and its Transformations.* Amsterdam, The Netherlands: Harwood Academic Publishers.

Farnsworth, J. D. (1988). Screening plants for new medicines. In E. O. Wilson (Ed.), *Biodiversity* (pp. 83–97). Washington, DC: National Academy Press.

Food and Agriculture Organisation (FAO). (n.d.). Retrieved on 15.08.2019 from http://www.fao.org/3/y5714e/y5714e03.htm

Hasan, M., & Abdullah, H.M. (2015). *Plant Genetic Resources and Traditional Knowledge: Emerging Needs for Conservation.* doi:10.1007/978-981-10-0060-7_6

Ihenacho, R.A., Orusha, J.O., & Onogu, B. (2019). Rural Farmers Use of Indigenous Knowledge Systems in Agriculture for Climate Change Adaptation and Mitigation in Southeast Nigeria. *Annals of Ecology and Environmental Science, 3*(1), 1-11.

ITPGRFA Secretariat. (2017). Retrieved on 26 July 2018 from; http://www.fao.org/plant-treaty/areas-of-work/farmers-rights

Joshi, P. (2005). *Crop diversification in India: nature, pattern and drivers.* New Delhi, India: Asian Development Bank.

Lin, B. B. (2011). Resilience in agriculture through crop diversification: Adaptive management for environmental change. *Bioscience, 61*(3), 183–193. doi:10.1525/bio.2011.61.3.4

Mafongoya, P. L., & Ajayi, O. C. (Eds.). (2017). *Indigenous Knowledge Systems and Climate Change Management in Africa.* Wageningen, The Netherlands: CTA.

Maroyi, A. (2012). Enhancing food security through cultivation of traditional food crops in Nhema communal area. Midlands Province, Zimbabwe. *African Journal of Agricultural Research, 7*, 5412–5420.

Maxted, N. (2003). Conserving the genetic resources of crop wild relatives in European protected areas. *Biological Conservation, 113*(3), 411–417. doi:10.1016/S0006-3207(03)00123-X

Mukherjee. (2008). *A Study of the Basmati Case (India-US Basmati Rice Dispute): The Geographical Indication Perspective.* Available at SSRN: https:// ssrn.com/abstract=1143209

Ouma, M. (2017). Traditional knowledge: the challenges facing international lawmakers. *WIPO Magazine.* Retrieved on 18/10/2019 from https://www.wipo.int/wipo_magazine

Patil, C. R. S. (2005). Plant Breeders Rights. *Kare Law Journal*, 53. Retrieved on 26 July 2018) from http://plantauthority.gov.in

Secretariat, C. B. D. (2005). Handbook of the Convention on Biological Diversity Including its Cartagena Protocol on Biosafety (3rd ed.). Academic Press.

CBD Secretariat. (2010). *Linking biodiversity conservation and poverty alleviation: A state of knowledge review*. CBD Technical Series no. 55.

Sinthupundaja, J., & Kohda, Y. (2017). *Effects of Corporate Social Responsibility and Creating Shared Value on Sustainability. International Journal of Sustainable Entrepreneurship and Corporate Social Responsibility*, *2*(1), 27–38.

Stolton, S., Maxted, N., Lloyd, B. F., Kell, S., & Dudley, N. (2006). *Food Stores: Using Protected Areas to Secure Crop Genetic Diversity*. WWF.

Tullani, H., Raiswa, S., & Richa, D. (2018). Green Innovation and Ethical Responsibility: Do They Improve Customer's Green Purchase Intentions? *International Journal of Sustainable Entrepreneurship and Corporate Social Responsibility*, *3*(1), 35–52. doi:10.4018/IJSECSR.2018010103

UPOV. (1978). *UPOV, Act of 1978, International Convention for the Protection of New Varieties of Plants*. Retrieved on 03.11.2019 from https://www.upov.int/ export /sites/upov /upovlex/ en/conventions /1978/ pdf/act1978.pdf

UPOV. (1991). *UPOV, Act of 1991. International Convention for The Protection of New Varieties of Plants*. Retrieved on 03.11.2019 from https://www.upov.int/export/ sites/ upov/ upovlex /en/conventions /1991/ pdf/ act1991.pdf

Warren, D. M. (1992). *Indigenous Knowledge, Biodiversity Conservation and Development*. Paper Presented in International Conference on Conservation of Biodiversity in Africa: Local Initiatives and Institutional Role, Nairobi, Kenya.

WIPO Lawmakers Magazine. (2019). https://www.wipo.int /wipo_magazine/en/ 2017/01/article_0003. html

APPENDIX

1. Acid lime (*Citrus aurantifolia* Swingle)
2. Almond (*Prunus dulcis*)
3. Amaranth (*Amaranthus tricolor* L.)
4. *Amaranthus caudatus, A. edulis* and *A. cruentus*
5. Apple (*Malus domestica* Borkh)
6. Apricot (*Prunus armeniaca* L.)
7. Arecanut (*Areca catechu* L.)
8. Bael (*Aegle marmelos* Correa)
9. Banana (*Musa* spp.)
10. Barley (*Hordeum vulgare* L.)
11. Barnyard millet (*Echinocloa frumentaceae* (Roxb.) Link)
12. Bell Pepper and Paprika (*Capsicum annuum* L.)
13. Betelvine (*Piper betle* L.)
14. Bitter Gourd (*Momordica charantia* L.)
15. Black pepper (*Piper nigrum* L.)
16. Bottle Gourd (*Lagenaria siceraria* (Mol.) Landl.)
17. Bougainvillea (Bougainvillea Comm. ex Juss.)
18. Brahmi (*Bacopa monnieri* L.)
19. Brinjal/Eggplant (*Solanum melanogena* L.)
20. Buckwheat (*Fagopyrum* sp.; *F. esculentum* and F. tataricum)
21. *C. assamica* & *C. assamica* ssp lasiocalyx.)
22. Cabbage (*Brassica oleracea* L.var. captitata)
23. Canna (*Canna* L.)
24. Carnation (*Dianthus caryophyllus* L.)
25. Cashew (*Anacardium occidentale* L.)
26. Cassava (*Manihot esculenta* Crantz.)
27. Castor (*Ricinus communis* L.)
28. Casuarina (*Casuarina equisetifolia* L. and *Casuarina junghuhniana* Miq)
29. Cauliflower (*Brassica oleracea* L.var. botrytis)
30. Cherry (*Prunus avium* L.)
31. Chilli
32. China Aster (*Callistephus chinensis* (L.)Nees.)
33. Chir pine (*Pinus roxburghii*) Sargent
34. Chironji (*Buchanania lanzan* Sperng.)
35. Chrysanthemum (*Chrysanthemum*)
36. *Cicer arietinum* L.
37. Coconut (*Cocos nucifera* L.)

38. *Colocasia esculenta* var. *stoloniferum*
39. *Colocasia esculenta* var.*antiquorum*
40. Coriander (*Coriandrum sativum* L.)
41. Cucumber (*Cucumis sativus* L.)
42. Custard apple / Sugar apple (*Annona squamosa* L.)
43. *Cyrtosperma chamissonis* /*C. merkusii*)
44. Damask Rose (*Rosa damascene* Mill)
45. Date Palm (*Phoenix dactylifera* L.)
46. Deodar (*Cedrus deodara* (Roxb.) G.Don)
47. Dicoccum wheat and other Triticum species (*Triticum curum* Desf.)
48. Durum wheat
49. Elephant Foot Yam (*Amorphophallus Paeoniffolius*)
50. Eucalypts (*Eucalyptus camaldulensis* Dehnh. and *E. tereticornis* Sm.)
51. Faba bean (*Vicia faba* L.)
52. Fenugreek (*Trigonella foenum graecum* L.)
53. Finger Millet (*Eleusine coracana* (L.) Gaertn.)
54. Foxtail Millet (Setaria italica (L.) Beauv.)
55. Garlic (*Allium sativum* L.)
56. Ginger (*Zingiber officinale* Rosc.)
57. Gladiolus (Gladiolus L.)
58. *Gossypium arboretum* L. and *G. herbaceum* L.
59. *Gossypium hirsutum* L. and *G. barbadense* L.
60. Grain Amaranth (*Amaranthus hypocondricus)*
61. Grapes (*Vitis* spp.)
62. Groundnut (*Arachis hypogaea* L.)
63. Guava (*Psidium guajava* L.)
64. Indian gooseberry (*Emblica officinalis* Gaertn.)
65. Indian Jujube (Ber) (*Ziziphus mauritiana* Lamk.)
66. Indian Mustard & KaranRai (*Brassica juncea* L.Czern & Coss & *Brassica carinata* A Braun)
67. Isabgol (*Plantago ovate* Forsk.)
68. Jamun (*Syzygium cuminii* Skeels)
69. Japanese Plum (*Prunus salicina* L.)
70. Jasmine (*Jasminum auriculatum* L.)
71. Jasmine (*Jasminum multiflorum* L.)
72. Jasmine (*Jasminum sambac* L.)
73. Jatropha (*Jatropha curcas* L.)
74. Jute (*Corchorus olitorius* L. and *Corchorus capsularis* L.)
75. Kalmegh (*Andrographis paniculata* ((Burm.f.) Wall. ex Nees))
76. Karanj (*Pongamia pinnata* (L.) Pierre)

77. Kidney bean (*Phaseolus vulgaris* L.)
78. Kodo millet (*Paspalum scorbiculatum* L.)
79. Lentil (*Lens culinaris* Medik)
80. Litchi (*Litchi chinensis* Sonn.)
81. Little millet (*Panicum sumatrense* Roth. Ex Roemer and Schultes)
82. Maize (*Zeamays* L.)
83. Mandarin (*Citrus reticulata* Blanco)
84. Mango (*Mangifera indica* L.)
85. Marigold (*Tagetes spp*. L.)
86. Melia *(Melia dubia* Cav.)
87. Menthol mint (*Metha arvensis* L.)
88. Moringa (Drumstick) (*Moringa oleifera* Lam.)
89. Mulberry (*Morus* spp.)
90. Muskmelon (*Cucumis melo* L.)
91. Neem (*Azadirachta indica* A. Juss.)
92. Noni (*Morinda citrifolia* L.)
93. Nutmeg (*Myristica fragrans* Houtt.)
94. Oat (*Avena sativa* L.)
95. Okra/Lady's finger (*Abelmoschus esculentus* (L.) Moench.)
96. Onion (*Allium cepa* L.)
97. Orchid (*Cattleya* Lindl.)
98. Orchid (*Cymbidium* Sw.)
99. Orchid (*Dendrobium* Sw.)
100. Orchid (*Oncidium* Sw.)
101. Orchid (*Paphiopedilum* Pfitz.)
102. Orchid (*Phalaenopsis* Blume)
103. Orchid (Vanda jones ex R. Br.)
104. Palak/Spinach beet (*Beta vulgaris* var. bengalensis Roxb.)
105. Papaya (*Carica papaya* L.)
106. Peach (*Prunus persica* L.Batsch.)
107. Pear (*Pyrus communis*)
108. Pearlmillet (*Pennisetum glaucum* (L.) R.Br.)
109. Periwinkle (*Catharanthus roseus* L.G.Don.)
110. Pigeon pea (*Cajanus cajan* (L.)Millsp.)
111. *Pisum sativum* L.
112. Pomegranate (*Punica granatum* L.)
113. Poplar (*Populus deltoides* L.)
114. Potato (*Solanum tuberosum* L.)
115. Proso millet (*Panicum miliaceum* L.)
116. Pumpkin (*Cucurbita moschata* Duch. ex Poir.)

117. Rapeseed (*Brassica rapa* L.)
118. Rice (*Oryza sativa* L.)
119. Ridge gourd (*Luffa acutangula* (L.) Roxb.)
120. Rose (*Rosa* spp. Other than *R. damascene*)
121. Safflower (*Carthamus tinctorius* L.)
122. Salix acmophylla
123. Salix alba
124. Salix jessoensis
125. Salix matsudana
126. Salix nigra
127. Salix rubens
128. Small Cardamom (*Elettaria cardamomum* Maton)
129. Sorghum (*Sorghum bicolor* (L.) Moench)
130. Soybean (*Glycine max* (L.) Merrill)
131. Strawberry (*Fragaria x ananasan* Duch.)
132. Sugarcane (*Saccharum* L.)
133. Sun flower (*Helianthus annus* L.)
134. Sweet orange (*Citrus sinensis* (L.) Sbeck)
135. Sweet Potato (*Ipomoea batatas* L. Lam)
136. Tamarind (Tamarindus indica L.)
137. Taro (*Colocasia esculenta* var. *esculenta)*
138. Tea (*Camellia sinensis*)
139. Tomato (*Lycopersicon lycopersicum* (L.) Karsten ex. Farw.
140. *Triticum aestivum* L.
141. Triticum dicoccum L. & *Triticum* species.
142. Tuberose (Polianthes tuberosa L.)
143. Turmeric (*Curcuma longa* L.)
144. *Vigna mungo* (L.) Hepper
145. *Vigna radiata* (L.)Wilczek.
146. Walnut (*Juglans regia* L.)
147. Watermelon (*Citrullus lanatus* (Thunb.) Mansf.)
148. Willow (*Salix tetrasperma*)

Chapter 9
Women Custodians of Tradition

Sudha Jha Pathak
Bennett University, India

ABSTRACT

Hidden in the obscure spirals of rural subconscious of Bihar are vast memories of history, culture, and tradition. These memories are invoked and brought forth by the subtle nuances of folklore, song, and painting by women. A sub-stratum of women memories of power and energy has existed since the ancient past where women were the repositories and sustainers of heritage. Madhubani painting can be said to be a creation of communal spiritual experience. It can be comprehended not just as an aesthetic wonder but also as a representation of collective mind, expressing millennia of traditional knowledge of the women artists and a form of transmitting a series of ancestral motifs. The uniqueness of this beautiful art form along with its specific geographical location has led to it being conferred its own geographical identification or GI tag by the government. The region has evoked the interest and appreciation of art connoisseurs, scholars, and tourists from all over the world, thus creating a niche for itself in the world of art.

INTRODUCTION

"History is to be seen displayed in full detail in the villages of India-provided one has the vision and insight required to read that history"(Kosambi, 1997).

History has witnessed the growth of rural centres of socio-cultural, religious life of great antiquity. These pockets of cultural resurgence were spread out all over the country. Besides the existence of numerous outstanding urban centres of art and

DOI: 10.4018/978-1-7998-1835-9.ch009

culture, the hinterlands and the rural expanses also witnessed a healthy and major proliferation of various art forms of brilliance and ingenuity. It steadfastly made possible the emergence and expression of beautiful practices of art and culture and witnessed remarkable achievements in the domain of art, language and music which have transformed the villages and provided life and sustenance to culture and tradition.

India has the distinction of having its historical elements being conspicuously visible and manifest in the arts and culture of the villages. History is richly portrayed in the rural arts of India which are the visual expression of the common folk of rural India. It represents the art of the people tuned to the rhythm and various manifestations of nature along with a central concern for the earth as the basis and cornerstone of the human life. The Mithila or Madhubani painting can be said to be a creation of the community's spiritual experience. This art of the rural people is imbued with the moorings and memories of their culture and tradition, as it also represents an art manifesting the social rituals, fertility, rites to invoke the gods, and the kernel of energy and power within the community. These rural arts thus incorporate within its wider domain the artefacts of history and of the living present as well as their relationship to the past.

The woman artist enjoys a pivotal and unique position in the Mithila tradition of art as she symbolized the artistic creative process inherent in this tradition. She is the channel by means of which this inherited tradition of art flows, made more auspicious and relevant in the context of the present. This river of tradition and knowledge flows in the subconscious and the heart of the women who have acted as the repositories and nurturers of heritage and culture. These memories are invoked and brought forth by them through the subtle nuances of folklore and art forms.

Mithila has had a rich intellectual, cultural legacy and its art expressions has a distinct identity of its own. Art plays a pertinent role in the sustenance and support of cultural traditions besides providing a voice to the creativity of the women artists of the region. This chapter focusses on women of Mithila who have acted as custodians of the tradition of Madhubani paintings which are not just an aesthetic wonder but also a medium of expression of the traditional knowledge of the artists acquired and refined along the timeline of a millennium. This chapter focuses on how the woman artist is the channel by means of which this inherited tradition of art flows and blossoms, increasingly becoming more celebrated and popular in the context of the present.

There is a need to preserve this ancient ethnic art form which is intrinsically embedded in Mithila's culture and tradition. Unfortunately, this great art heritage is getting lost in the process of commercialization and mass production. Using art as a tool and means for commodification leads to a loss of tradition as the artisans have to alter their work in terms of themes, designs keeping in mind the demands of the market. This chapter focuses on the need to address the issues involved in the preservation of this art form which is getting lost in the quagmire of cheap imitations and blatant profit motives.

Traditional Art and History

Madhubani paintings, like other folk-arts is largely community oriented. "Mithila painting is a product of communal spiritual experience....a manifestation of a collective mind, embodying millenia of traditional knowledge" (Vequaud, 1977).

The villages emerged as the sanctuaries of art, religion, literature and culture since the earliest times where the religious preachers, poets, musicians, painters took refuge or found sustenance. These villages thus served as custodians of local history, tradition, mythology, folk-tales and folk-lore. Hidden in the intricate spirals of rural subconscious are vast memories of history, culture and tradition. Located deep in this sub-consciousness of India is the knowledge of a lost river which is instrumental in nurturing the soil of this country, which is the river of creation, art and cultural traditions and is, therefore, sacred. These memories are summoned, conceptualized and given a shape, form and definite characteristics by the rural people, especially the women folks, through the mediums of folklore and the various art forms like music, song, dance and painting.

The rural arts of India are the visual expression of people, manifesting their cultural, religious and sociological moorings. It is the art tuned to the rhythm of nature and its cyclic laws with a central focus on the earth, which sustains life in its various facets and concomitantly their roots and traditions, and hence looms large as a broader paradigm. It is the art invoked with culture, traditions and fertility rituals, rites and art that invoke the gods and other mythological figures as well as the various forces and forms of nature.

Madhubani paintings are ancestral in their derivation since they have been inherited from traditions (*parampara*) rooted in the culturally enriched past of the Maithil women and has evolved since time immemorial .A sub-stratum of feminine memories of power and energy has existed since the ancient past where women are the repositories of heritage as also the ones sustaining and enriching it. The woman artist creating Madhubani paintings provided the link with the forms of the great ancient cultural and artistic tradition.

Equally remarkable is the transmission of folklore, rites and rituals and the traditions and various forms of culture, flowing from mother to daughter, through the medium of art, poetry, rituals, songs, dance, music and the skills allied to the same. When questioned about her skill and her understanding of art and the mastery over its forms, a woman from rural India stated, "it is from a *parampara*, a time without beginning. We hold this knowing in our wombs" (Jayakar, 1989).

Indeed, the unique feature of Madhubani paintings is that women are the masters of this beautiful art form which is a novel feature in the world of art. Women artists who could create such beautiful works of art for decades must be aesthetically and culturally refined. According to Coomaraswamy, "Indian women, at the present day, in so far as they have not been brought up to date, are our best conservators of Indian culture" (as cited by Thakur, 1981). This is apt and absolutely correct in the context of the women painters of Mithila who are generally not so literate and up-to-date but are the best custodians of this art form. Thus, the women of Mithila have acted as custodians of the tradition of Madhubani paintings, creating splendid pieces of art and giving shape to their artistic ingenuity through a series of traditionally remarkable motifs and symbols rooted in the local rural cultural heritage and history.

The cardinal role played by women in preserving this tradition has highlighted by the scholars and connoisseurs of art. "For about three thousand of years, the women and only the women of Mithila have been making devotional paintings of the gods and goddesses of the Hindu pantheon. It is, no exaggeration, then, to say that this art is the expression of a most genuine aspect of Indian civilization" (Vequaud, 1977).

The region of Mithila located in North Bihar is famous all over the world for the beautiful Madhubani paintings. Mithila, also known as ancient Videha, was the birth-place of Sita. The term Madhubani literally means "forests of honey". The region of Mithila broadly encompasses the districts of Madhubani, Darbhanga, Muzaffarpur, Saharsa, parts of Monghyr, Purnea. In 1972, the district of Madhubani was created out of the former district of Darbhanga following the reorganization of districts in the state of Bihar.

Mithila has had a rich intellectual, cultural legacy and its art expressions have a distinct identity of their own. Madhubani paintings have had a long history and can be traced back to the Vedic times. Madhubani has also been the centre of the intellectual and cultural pursuits of Mithila. The region is home to the lyrics of Vidyapati, who sang his poetry in the 14th century; the songs of Krishna-Radha, the worship of *Shakti* in the form of Gauri. Mithila was also the stronghold of Sanskrit learning which existed along with the vernacular language, literature, and paintings. The Karnataka dynasty that ruled over Mithila from the 12th-14th centuries provided patronage to the art and culture of the region. Later the Oinavara dynasty also extended their patronage and the ancient *samskara* rites and the associated rituals were enforced.

Madhubani has the distinction of having several eminent celebrity women artists like Sita Devi, Jagdamba Devi, Baua Devi, and Mahasundari Devi. Jitwarpur village in Madhubani district has the distinction of having three women artists who were awarded the *Padma-Shri* -Jagdamba Devi, Sita Devi, and Baua Devi. Prime Minister Narendra Modi had gifted Hannover Mayor Stefan Schostok a painting made by

Baua Devi during his visit to Germany. Jitwarpur and Ranti villages in Madhubani district have played a key role in the evolution and success of Madhubani paintings.

The art of Mithila painting has been carried on as a part of the local tradition and culture. The women of Madhubani have been expressing the social, cultural and ritualistic world around them through the medium of the paintings. In the backdrop of hardly any contact with the outside world, the women artists of Mithila could preserve their traditions, their art and style of painting over a long period of time stretching for centuries. However, most of these artists remained shrouded in anonymity and continued making the paintings as a part of their daily ritual. Most of the literary texts of Mithila did not refer to the contributions of women in the socio-cultural life of Mithila. Indirect references to the paintings have appeared in some regional texts from 14th century onwards. However, most of these artists remained anonymous making these paintings only as part of their day-to-day rituals.

One of the first outsiders to draw attention to the mural paintings of Mithila was W. G. Archer, a British civil servant who had an opportunity to work in the Mithila region. He was posted at Purnea as Collector of the district in 1937-38, and subsequently in 1940 he visited Darbhanga and Purnea districts again as Provincial Census Superintendent. This provided him with an opportunity to study the paintings and collect some aide-memories from the women. It was W.G. Archer who looked upon these paintings as art pieces for the first time. The result of his researches was published in the form of an article 'Maithil Painting' in the journal *Marg* in the year 1949.Some of the works that Archer collected were sent to the India Records Office in London (presently a part of the British Library).

The drought in 1960-61 in Bihar helped unleash the potential and creativity of the local rural artistic talent lying embedded in their subconscious as the drought accentuated the economic crisis of the people there which led to the Mithila women making the paintings for commercial sale. In the wake of this development, some eminent women artists were discovered such as Sita Devi, Jagdamba Devi, Mahasundari Devi, Baua Devi (Thakur1981).

The drought also served as a catalyst which provided an opportunity to outsiders to visit the state and enabled them to see and study the visual tradition of Madhubani paintings which was hitherto virtually unknown to the outside world. Mrs. Pupul Jayakar played an instrumental role in initiating relief projects in Ranthi and Jitwarpur villages of Madhubani (Rekha, 2010). Notable efforts were made by Shri Upendra Maharathi of Patna and B.M. Kulkarni, a young artist, in the relief measures initiated for the women artists (Thakur1981). The women were also encouraged to paint on hand made paper using poster paints and replicate the traditional designs on paper rather than walls. The paintings were then sent to New Delhi and sold to provide funds for famine relief by the All India Handicrafts Boards. The Government of

India, the state government of Bihar as well as the Regional Craft Guilds played a notable role in aiding the women artists in art production as well as marketing.

Subject- Matter of Paintings

The paintings blossomed in the region of Mithila as an integral part of rural life. The village community life is sustained, enriched and reinforced by the social gatherings, singing, ceremonies and festivities, rituals, traditional story-telling. There exists a conglomeration of beliefs and ideas from the past ranging from religion to popular folk-tales. The paintings on the mud-walls are in fact like a visual picture-book from which one can comprehend the stories and episodes of the epics, the common prevalent rituals, myths and legends.

The main theme of the paintings is the celebration and exaltation of nature, flora, fauna, love and fertility. There is an attempt to evoke the mood and spirit for this celebration by means of the paintings. The distinctive features of these paintings include the use of bright colours along with unreal shapes and figures usually portraying mythological themes or scenes from household rituals.

Intricately associated with the rituals as well as the cultural and domestic traditions of the area, the Madhubani paintings are as natural and essential as the performance of household chores. The paintings were originally done by ladies as an ordinary domestic art intricately related to their social life. Since ancient times women made traditional paintings on the floors and walls called *aipanas* and *bhittichitras*. The artists surpass the field of practical utility to create an exquisite work of art. The source of inspiration for the women artists is mostly religious and the beauty of nature. Certain social and religious ceremonies like marriage, *kohbar* (paintings made in the nuptial chamber), thread ceremony *(upanayana* or *yagnopavit)*, birth, *Madhusravani* (celebrating the arrival of the monsoon season), *Chhath* (a festival dedicated to Sun God, which is celebrated on the sixth day of *Chaitra*; *Chhath* means sixth day) required paintings and the women artists made them as integral parts of the ritual. After the ceremony was over, art would lapse, the women would resume their household chores. Indeed, the paintings were the proof of the vivid sensibility in the region. Later, when another ritual recurred, the paintings were made again as the ordinary woman would transform into an artist and the walls would bloom once again with the paintings (Archer, 1949).

The paintings are modelled and created on clay walls as their canvas. The mud wall would be plastered with cow-dung and the colours would be applied directly to this wall or a coat of whitewash would first be applied to the wall prior to drawing the paintings on it. Traditionally, when the occasion for painting a wall arose, the women of the house would gather together. The most skilled woman of them all would take the lead in making the painting and draw out the shapes. Once the main lines had been drawn out, the other women would fill in the shapes with colour (Archer, 1977).

The traditional patterns and designs are adhered to as the art is handed down the generations. The younger girls are trained gradually. Sometimes they filled in the details, thus progressively absorbing the style and became minor artists by the time they were of marriageable age. By participating in the painting from an early age, the young girls of the family could grasp and memorise the designs by heart.

Madhubani paintings are primarily wall paintings and it is the wall in the house which traditionally acted as a canvas to project their art. The use of the wall as a canvas explains why the paintings were regarded as temporary which contrasts with the western notion of regarding art as eternal to some degree. We must keep in mind the notion that the idea of permanence of art is a relatively recent notion.

Gradually, the tradition of painting and drawing on paper was adopted by the women of this region. They were usually made in pen-and-ink and water colour. These include paintings of the deities like Krishna, Rama besides others. Some families maintained a collection of aide-memories or paper patterns on which the family's designs were recorded in a miniature form. Paper paintings were made and utilised as aide-memories by the women to teach their daughters the basics of *alankara*, the traditional ornamental designs and forms which were unique to each family. Often when a bride left her home after marriage, she would take these designs with her as models. She would be able to continue her family's tradition of painting as well add on to the ritual of her husband's family. These aide-memories constitute a specialized category of traditional artefacts and designs, which were idealized and preserved for posterity. Many of these designs are in the possession of the India Office Library, London (Archer, 1977).

The Maithils are worshippers of *Shakti* and Bhagvati Gauri is regarded as their *kuladevi* (goddess for the family). The *Ramayana* is popular in Mithila as the birth-place of Sita. The *Bhagavata Purana* is also familiar to the people there. All these provide the themes for the making of paintings of Siva-Sakti, Rama-Sita and Krishna-Radha, along with the social and wedding scenes, flora and fauna. Goddess Durga, regarded as an embodiment of Power (*Shakti*) is highly venerated in the region. She is often depicted in the paintings as riding a lion- a divine form assumed by her in order to destroy the evil forces and demons (Figure 1).

Floral, geometrical, animal and bird motifs are mostly used to fill up the gaps. The symbols and deities depicted in the paintings are meant to protect the family members from all evil. The creative expression of the women artists is manifest by means of the sun, moon, lotus, bamboo grove, snakes (illustrated in Figure 2 by Baua Devi), fishes, birds which all symbolise fertility and proliferation of life. Animals and other living beings like the fish, elephant, tortoise, and the colourful floral

Figure 1. Painting of Goddess Durga riding on tiger by Jagdamba Devi

Figure 2. Painting of a god and snakes by Padma Shri Baua Devi

forms are very popular amongst the Madhubani painters and these are beautifully designed and painted by them.

An urban artist would portray an elephant, snake or lotus for its own sake, but in the context of Madhubani paintings, the animal or flower would have specific association with a legend or ritual. This sort of symbolism is not very easy to explain, as the meaning of a subject in a specific context would differ from one occasion to another. Further, for a ceremony a design or representation will have a religious sanctity and importance which might not hold good once the ceremony is over.

Kohbar Paintings

The wedding paintings are referred to as *kohbar* and are made on the walls of the *kohbar-ghar* (nuptial chamber). The *kohbar-* paintings (Figure 3) represent centuries of tradition and ritual which have shaped the artistic expression of these paintings portraying love and fertility in marriage.

For the *kohbar- ghar* two types of paintings were the favourites, i.e. of gods and goddesses and auspicious symbols. The main objective was to invoke the deities like Rama-Sita, Krishna-Radha, Shiva-Parvati, Durga to obtain their blessings for

Figure 3. Kohbar Painting by Baua Devi

the newly-weds. The paintings made in the *kohbar-ghar* also act as a setting to the worship of goddess Gauri.

The *kohbar- ghar* is decorated and made auspicious with fresh plaster, and painted with images of deities, the symbols of love and fertility like the flowering bamboo and lotus, flowers, serpents. The painting incorporates a central large *mandala*, surrounded by six smaller *mandalas* along with other symbols and designs to highlight the couple's fertility and longevity (Figure 4 *Kohbar* painting made by Ganga Devi). Other popular themes in the *kohbar* include the parrots symbolizing the lovebirds, turtles symbolizing longevity, serpents and fishes regarded as symbols of fertility, the sun and moon as they are regarded to be eternal and having life-giving qualities. Human beings are regarded as an integral part of nature in these paintings and there exists the representation of man or gods co-existent with nature in complete harmony.

Naina Jogin, a goddess of the *Jogin* sect is also invoked by the women during marriage rituals. She is depicted in the paintings in the four corners of the wall in the *kohbar -ghar*. Elaborate rituals were laid down to ward off the evil forces. The

Figure 4. Kohbar by Ganga Devi

multifarious traditions of paintings, folk-songs and rituals highlight the miraculous powers of *Naina Jogin*.

Traditional Art: Distinctive Features

Madhubani paintings, like other folk-arts is largely communal. The women artists developed the art that was meaningful to them and retained the themes and patterns which were repeated with very slight variations.

Colour has a distinctive role to play in a painting as it creates its mood, rhythm and pulse. It is also instrumental in providing a background to the themes and subject matter e.g. deities, human beings, flora and fauna in the painting. For instance, the use of deep red in plenitude to define and enclose space is a device used to draw attention to the central figures, concentrate energy and bind the diverse elements together. The profuse use of red also enhances the sense of life and vitality.

Before the use of artificial colours, the colours were prepared from natural products. The tradition of extracting colours from plants has continued since the writing of the *Sarada Tilaka* in the 11th century. Black was prepared from *kajal* or soot, yellow from turmeric, red from *kusum* flower, orange from *palasa* flower, green from *bilva* leaf. White was procured by powdering rice and mixing with water. The brush was made by the women artists by attaching cotton at the tip of a twig. The main lines of the painting are outlined in black, while different twigs are used for different colours (Jayakar, 1980).

There are some characteristic features in the paintings created by the Madhubani artists; for example, the nose of the figure is pointed and often merges into the forehead. Though most of the figures are in profile, the eyes are made in a frontal presentation. The eyes are regarded as the source of *Sakti*, the cardinal point of power, like in all rural art representations. After the painting is complete, the pupil is drawn within the eye, which in fact helps to create a sense of direct communication with the beholder (Jayakar, 1980).

The stylisation of form, drawing the nose and the eye in a characteristic manner as indicated above, use of the flower, bird, serpent to fill up the vacant spaces are some of the features which display the sophisticated understanding of the artist regarding the nuances of painting and provide an insight into the origin of early miniature paintings. In some of the paintings, vertical and horizontal arrangements were utilised to highlight occasions and draw demarcations between them. The strategies used in miniature paintings to convey the impression of vastness by placing minute figures of man, animal or birds juxtaposed with towering figures to create scale and convey immensity of nature is also apparent in the Mithila paintings.

There are different styles of Madhubani painting which can be categorised as *Bharni, Kachni, Geru, Gobar* and *Godana*. Prominent among them are the *Bharni* and *Kachni* styles. The *Bharni* style is produced by brahmins while the *Kachni* style is produced by the kayasthas. The *Bharni* style is characterized by bright, vibrant colours and nominal use of lines while in the *Kachni* style beautiful motifs are created by the elaborate use of lines. A style very close to the tradition of folk-art is the *Geru* style which is characterized by the lack of ornamentation and a very prominent black line. The paintings made by the lower sections of the society can be categorised into two categories - *Gobar* or cowdung painting and *Godana* or tattoo painting.

The Mithila paintings are made by women belonging to all sections of the society and can be distinguished by their distinctive designs, styles, use of colour and themes. The higher castes women leading a restricted lifestyle adhered to themes and styles which were ritualistic. Their paintings became more intricate in their designs which led to the growth of the *bharni* and *kachni* styles.

In the kayastha paintings, there is more use of ochres and earth colours whereas in the brahmin paintings there is use of rich, vibrant colours like red, orange, turmeric yellow along with shades of pink and green. Passion and energy are expressed using red and yellow. Another difference between the two styles is that the brahmin painting makes use of lines only to give a border to the coloured areas and mostly aims to achieve brilliant colourful images, kayastha paintings on the other hand deliberately makes minimal use of colour and rather achieves intensity through the use of lines. In brahmin paintings, the lines are thin and wavering while in kayastha paintings the lines are firm and dynamic. The most important aspect and dominant feature of kayastha paintings is their remarkable rhythm, while in brahmin paintings it is inadvertent and casual.

The third school of painting belongs to the lower castes which can be characterized by elongated horses and elephants in black and stark paintings made on mud-walls. These paintings are simpler and less sophisticated with less emphasis on ornamentation. These paintings have a diverse vision and perception. They narrate on the exploits of a mythical ruler Raja Sailesa along with other legends. The theme, lines, colour and narration of these paintings convey elements of confidence and assertion.

The brahmins and kayasthas concentrated on religious themes whereas the lower caste artists took recourse to greater freedom of expression by portraying themes of everyday life. Due to the initiative and efforts of a few artists, paintings made by lower castes gradually carved out a distinct identity for itself with a diverse perspective from that of the upper caste paintings. The eminent artist, Jamuna Devi's painting of a dalit disposing of the carcass of a cow is a famous illustration of this genre of painting since she herself was from this community. These paintings have been described as "expressionist and passionate" (Anand, 1984).

While comparing the Maithil paintings with western counterparts, Archer has stated that "If we are to find an analogy in European art we might say that the colours of brahmin paintings are parallel to those in paintings by Miro while those of kayastha paintings resemble the black and terracotta colours of Greek vases" (Archer, 1949).

It is also pertinent to note that the ability to transform, adapt and recreate the archaic myths, rituals and the cultural traditions in keeping with the ethos and the characteristic trends and features of the present is a distinguishing feature of Indian culture and tradition. This remarkable trend is discernible in the Madhubani paintings as well as the same, while retaining the basic traits and general features traditionally associated with them, has evolved over a period of time in keeping with the historical and cultural developments and the contemporary themes.

Appreciation of Paintings

A considerable portion of Maithil history remains unrecorded and obscured as the voices of women remain marginalized by the male writers and find expression only in the folk-songs sung by women, rituals and little traditions. This marginalization of women has continued even regarding the history of Maithil art and paintings.

Some women artists, however, have emerged as masters of their art. They have received appreciation from the Government for their notable contribution in the promotion of this art. The elevation of the ritualistic actions of women to the status of an art provided them with social status and prestige. This also provided them with an opportunity to bargain for a better position in society as well as recognition and name in the world outside. A new perspective was put forth raising the status of Maithil art to high art or *kulin* art. It has aptly been stated regarding the success and popularity achieved by women that it is a mild irony in Mithila that the fame of women has surpassed that of the men, for Mithila art is now known throughout the world (Brown, 1997).She has stressed on the importance of women for painting and portraying a feminine art-form from their perspective (Brown, 1997).

Our former Prime Minister Mrs. Indira Gandhi was one of the first to admire and appreciate this art form and even invited a woman artist to paint her house. Other women artists have also been commissioned to make these paintings in big hotels, railway compartments and stations, public offices. Some of them like Sita Devi, Mahasundari Devi, Jagdamba Devi, Baua Devi, whose paintings, characterized by their distinctive style and appeal, have also been awarded the prestigious *Padma Shri* by the Government. One of the earliest and most famous amongst the women artists was Sita Devi (Figures 5 and 6), who was conferred the *Padma Shri*, the award being inscribed as:" for superior art, this national award of 1975 has been given to Srimati Sita Devi for keeping the ancient culture alive through her art."

This painting (Figure 5) portrays the *Ardhanarisvara* (half-male, half-female) concept embodied in the images of Siva and Parvati painted by the eminent artist Sita Devi. The female aspect represents beauty and fertility while the male aspect represents Mahesa assuming all forms of Trinity-as the Destroyer, Preserver and Creator. He is guarded by serpents, mostly cobras. In this form they represent the complementarity and interdependence of the male and female aspects.

In due course of time, the uniqueness of this beautiful art form along with its association with a specific geographical region has led to it being conferred its own Geographical Identification or GI tag by the Government. The Madhubani painting has evoked the interest and appreciation of art connoisseurs, scholars and tourists from all over the world, thereby creating a niche for itself in the world of art.

Figure 5. Ardhanarisvara Painting by Sita Devi

Figure 6. Painting by Sita Devi

Challenges and Problems

Now economic compulsions along with the inevitable intrusion of the dialectics of modern contemporary world into this traditional domain of art have resulted in the proliferation and mass-production of these paintings. In contemporary times, the originality and uniqueness of this art form has been grossly undermined by the mass production of the paintings for the markets as these are often sold to ignorant customers who are not connoisseurs of art.

While this has, on the one hand, led to an erosion in the authenticity and artistic value of this art form, simultaneously the women artists are being deprived of their due price. There exists a threat that such mass-production would in fact stifle the authenticity, spontaneity and pristine beauty of this art which had not emerged originally with any commercial motive of making profit.

The work of art has increasingly become a commodity which was originally intended to ensure the happiness of the bride, forge identities with the gods and goddesses, or bring about protection from evil forces. The Madhubani paper art became a commodity to be bought and sold in the international art market. The noted Mithila artist Lalita Devi stated," The traditional themes of Mithila are now broken up into fragments to make it more sellable. Those pieces don't make any sense, no stories in them, meanings are lost, but they still sell" (Ray, 2012).

Many of the old and traditional styles of Madhubani paintings have become extinct, as the lack of support and encouragement has forced many artists to leave their profession. Geru painters as Bhagwati Devi have stopped painting as there were no takers for their art.

In fact, a distinct erosion in the purity of this art ensued once it was transferred on paper as the paper was not the ritual space assigned to the painting, and there was no sacredness involved in the painting once it was removed from its natural ground and traditional ambience. The spontaneity of art was lost and it fell prey to regulation and regimentation by the external forces.

Accordingly, the scale and size of the painting was fixed and decided by the external forces; the size was not to cover the entire wall but was to be 22'' by 30'' and such standard dimensions of the paper were specified. The artist had no option but to meet these specifications while making the painting on paper.

The originality in terms of the themes is also often compromised keeping in mind the requirements of the market - for if it remotely resembles Madhubani art, it sells. Thus, even the traditional themes are now characterised and determined by the new buzzwords like "More novelty and contemporary themes", 'No more *kohbars*!" or "to reduce the intricacies" or there were commands like "This is a good painting. Make more paintings like this." They were also asked to "paint the self", portraying their lives; keeping in mind such stipulations, the women artists depicted their own lives which became objects for their paintings. Women artists had to adhere to these demands and specifications which corroded the authenticity of this art. Along with this, the use of artificial colours as well as pencils has become quite common in place of the traditional materials. Also, in contrast to the original traditional art, which was basically drawing in free-hand, some artisans nowadays often take recourse to the use of blocks, scales etc. which is also a challenge to the purity and authenticity of this art.

Along with the objectification of women in their works, a new perspective, having a distinct positive aspect other than its role in strengthening the process of commodification and commercialization of art, has opened in the increasing trend of signing of the paintings by the women artists. Most of the paintings made previously were unsigned by the women artists and the works did not carry their names. The only exception was perhaps Ganga Devi who signed her name in the front. Women have traditionally been excluded from the books of genealogy, but in the domain of the paintings we are now witnessing the naming of the women artists like Jagdamba Devi, Sita Devi, and Mahasundari Devi along with others (Jayakar, 1980).

It has been highlighted that using art as a tool and means for commodification leads to a loss of tradition as the artisans have to alter their work in terms of themes, designs keeping in mind the demands of the international market. As a result, barring a few eminent artists who have gained recognition at the national and international level, the plight of the vast multitude of ordinary artists is quite pathetic. They are not able to get a decent price for their work and find it difficult to continue with painting as a primary source of livelihood. Often, they take recourse to compromising on the authenticity and purity of their painting to cater to the demands of the market. The problem is aggravated by the presence of middlemen on whom the women artists have to depend upon for the sale of their work. Several artists in fact prefer to become middlemen rather than produce these art works as they earn better by selling the art works of others on a commission basis rather than investing their time and energy in making paintings. The middlemen exploit the artists by not giving them a fair price, while at the same time selling their work at a higher price and pocketing the profit for themselves.

Most of the women artists are either illiterate or semi-literate and are not capable or comfortable in marketing their work, dealing with banks for loans, commuting alone to towns, cities to participate in exhibitions, fairs for the promotion of their paintings which in turn makes them dependant on the local middlemen.

RECOMMENDATIONS

In view of the debilitating factors affecting the stature and soul of the Madhubani painting, as discussed above, a great art heritage is being lost in the ongoing process of commercialization. As such, there is a need for more support and encouragement from the Government, art -lovers as well as NGOs to provide a fresh impetus to this art form. There is the need for the initiation of a dialogue between scholars, promoters and artists.

According to Gauri Mishra, the founder of Sewa Mithila," Preserving the traditional themes is the next big challenge for today's era." It was in 1983 that Gauri Mishra established Sewa, Mithila, a branch of the Self-Employed Women's Association (SEWA). Sewa-Mithila undertook several measures to highlight the relevant issues affecting the women artists and facilitate resolution of the problems faced by them. Other measures like anti-dowry campaigns, literacy, and nutrition was also undertaken by Sewa Mithila.

In 2010, an organization dedicated to the traditional art forms of Mithila named Mithilasmita was founded to rekindle and preserve the authentic folk art and heritage. Ihitashsri Mishra decided to focus on the problems confronting the women of rural Madhubani practising the art of painting which was getting lost in the quagmire of cheap imitations and huge profit motives of the middlemen.

Organizations like Sewa Mithila have put in a lot of effort in the preservation of this beautiful art form, its heritage as well as providing a means of livelihood for these women. It has taken special efforts to see that the artists get a decent price for their work, as well as an improvement in their living standards. This organization has also carried forward the message of preservation of this art form at the international level with blogs, websites and social media pages. The need of the hour is more organizations like it in order to address the problems faced by the women artists.

While there is doubtlessly a need to popularise Madhubani art, it is also necessary to locate and discover the art in its local context which would also take into consideration the voices and perspectives of the women artists. A balance needs to be maintained between traditional autonomy of art as well as design and content of traditional art forms. Further, the challenge to the art lies in accepting the modern values and norms of today's technological cultures and consumer-oriented societies and thus in the way losing communion with nature. At the same time, there is a pressing need to safeguard and nurture the needs and economic interests of the artists. This can be ensured by providing the Government's as well as non-governmental support (such as NGOs, associations and art bodies and concerned citizens in key positions), extending marketing support to the artists so as curb their exploitation, formation of the artists' cooperatives.

CONCLUSION

Stella Kramrisch has stated that there are two kinds of folk-art (i) time-bound and (ii) the timeless. In the first type, there are variations of form which appear during the course of its history while in the second type there are forms that repeats itself with little or no variation (Thakur, 1981). Madhubani paintings belongs to this category, the chief features of which are its bold, simple forms. The strong shapes, along with the bright colours contribute to its vigour and beauty. Some of the distinguishing features of this art form include use of simple outlines, simplification of colours and volumes so that shading is ruled out, some exaggeration for better expression, as well as the use of relative size, stylization of designs. We must appreciate the distinct features of Madhubani art like its rhythmic paintings, the bold and bright colours and a feeling of directness in the paintings.

The art of Mithila is unique for it represents an amalgamation of the culture and tradition of the region. All the motifs mingle together to provide ornament, to provide texture, to fill the entire canvas and create an ambience of profusion. Madhubani paintings are masterpieces of rural art and tradition and are an expression of the celebration of nature, love and life which is manifest in the beautiful blooming flowers, lush foliage, fishes and birds as well as the deities.

On comparing the Madhubani painting with other modern folk-arts, we find that there are deep variations between them. Madhubani paintings is the result of collective social effort of the women and their aesthetic consciousness whereas modern art is non-traditional and individualistic and is a manifestation of an individual artist. However, due to its ritualistic nature Madhubani paintings are often repeated so that there is limited originality "whereas the modern artist even when he borrows from the folk is concerned with the new." (Thakur, 1981).

The Madhubani paintings though rooted in tradition and is "popular" in character, has made significant contributions to modern art in India. However, the survival and sustenance of this traditional knowledge is under threat as a result of the commercialisation of art and the threat of shift from the traditional motifs and themes, thereby eroding its pristine values and qualities. The folk-arts like the Madhubani painting would survive today in their aesthetic forms which are of great artistic interest provided they do not get corrupted by the forces of modernisation.

There is still a lot to be depicted and portrayed about this traditional art and finally the women will express it by their talent and creativity. Art traditions and sensibilities that took years to mature need to be preserved for posterity in its authentic form. The priceless art heritage of Madhubani must be preserved by maintaining the dignity and glory of this art without losing its soul and primary traits, including its communion with nature and tradition.

REFERENCES

Anand, M. R. (1984). Madhubani Paintings. New Delhi: Publications Division, Ministry of Information and Broadcasting, Govt. of India.

Archer, M. (1977). *Indian Popular Painting in the India Office Library*. London: H. M. Stationery Office.

Archer, W. G. (1949). Maithil Painting. *Marg*, *3*(3), 32.

Brown, C. H. (1982). Folk Art and The Art Books: Who Speaks for The Traditional Artists? *Modern Asian Studies*, *16*(3), 519–522. doi:10.1017/S0026749X00015298

Brown, C. H. (1996). Contested Meanings: Tantra and the Poetics of Mithila Art. *American Ethnologist*, *23*(4), 717–737. doi:10.1525/ae.1996.23.4.02a00030

Chavda, J. (1990). The Narrative Paintings of India's Jitwarpuri Women, *Woman's. Art Journal*, *11*(1), 26–28.

Heinz, C.H. (2006). Documenting the Image in Mithila Art. *Visual Anthropology Review*, *22*(2), 31.

Jain, D. (1980). *Women's Quest For Power: Five Indian Case Studies*. Delhi: Vikas Publishing House.

Jain, J. (1997). *Ganga Devi: Tradition and Expression in Mithila Painting*. Ahmedabad: Mapin Publishing.

Jayakar, P. (1971). Paintings of Mithila. *The Times of India*, 29.

Jayakar, P. (1980). *The Earthen Drum: An Introduction to the Ritual Arts of India*. New Delhi: National Museum.

Jayakar, P. (1989). *The Earth Mother*. New Delhi: Penguin Books.

Kosambi, D. D. (1997). *The Culture and Civilization of Ancient India in Historical Outline*. Delhi: Vikas Publishing House.

Mathur, J. C. (1966). The Domestic Arts of Mithila. *Marg*, *20*(1), 43–55.

Mishra, V. (1979). *The Cultural Heritage of Mithila*. Allahabad: Mithila Prakasana.

Ray, R. (2012). *Bonding with Roots to Revive Madhubani Folk Art*. New Global Indian.

Rekha, N. (2003). Harijan Paintings of Mithila. *Marg*, *54*(3), 64–77.

Rekha, N. (2010). From folk art to fine art: changing paradigms in the historiography of Maithil Painting. *Journal of Art Historiography*, 2.

Rekha, N. (2011). Maithil Paintings: An Enquiry into its Historiographical Trajectory (1947-1997). Folklore and Folkloristics, 4(2).

Sinha, N. N. (2010). Madhubani: A Contemporary History (1971-2011). *Proceedings of Indian History Congress, 71st Session.*

Szanton, D. (2004). *Folk Art No Longer: The Transformations of Mithila Painting.* New Delhi: Academic Press.

Szanton, D., & Bakshi, M. (2007). Mithila Painting: The Evolution of an Art Form. Berkeley, CA: Ethnic Arts Foundation.

Thakur, U. (1981). *Madhubani Painting*. New Delhi: Abhinav Publications.

Vequaud, Y. (1977). *The Women Painters of Mithila; Ceremonial Paintings from an Ancient Kingdom*. London: Thames and Hudson.

Chapter 10
Intellectual Property Management by Innovative Firms:
Evidence From Tunisia

Chiraz Touil
IHEC, University of Sfax, Tunisia

Souhaila Kammoun
IHEC, CODECI, University of Sfax, Tunisia

ABSTRACT

The aim of this chapter is to show that innovation can only produce value once it is legally protected. Indeed, the law is involved throughout the entire life cycle of innovation. Thus, legal protection helps to transform innovation into an intangible asset for the company (patent, trademark, designs and models, databases, etc.). The chapter presents the different legal choices that allow the firm to develop innovation internally or externally. The authors explain that the firm, as a taxpayer, must optimize its accounting and tax choices in relation to innovative activities. Moreover, legal management implies an optimization of the legal and tax structure of the corporate structure in the sense that it is important to choose the most suitable form for an innovative activity. They also show that protecting innovation helps to exploit it through several legal techniques of different natures, such as contractual assignment or concession tools (licenses) or other judicial tools. The legal management of innovation appears as one of the key factors for the success of the innovative firm.

DOI: 10.4018/978-1-7998-1835-9.ch010

INTRODUCTION

The term legal management of the company and especially the innovative company refers to the mobilization of legal or judicial mechanisms in order to achieve a generally extra-legal objective. The law is not an objective; it is a means to the success of the company (Amann and Lethelleux, 2005). Legal know-how, often marginalized and neglected by managers, is becoming a fundamental pillar of any strategic construction. Involved throughout the company's life cycle and accompanying its choices, it can be a determining factor for success or a direct or indirect cause of ephemeral or definitive failure.

In this case, a legal strategy is considered effective if the means used make it possible to achieve the expected results despite any change in the expected or unexpected context. The legal strategy, integrated into the company's overall strategy, is also oriented towards the most advantageous or, at the very least, the least expensive result. The legal strategy is then considered efficient. Nevertheless, is the law that is presented as "public good" supposed to create a competitive advantage?

The rule of law is presumed to be known to all as soon as it comes into force. Moreover, nothing prevents a competitor from imitating the legal resources used or from reproducing the oriented choices. Clearly, legal strategies can hardly lead to sustainable competitive results.

In reality, what is public is only legal knowledge (Amann and Lethelleux, 2005). Legal know-how is rather a skill that develops according to the lawyer's experience and transforms throughout his professional career, thus transforming into real value for the benefit of some companies and at the expense of others. Intellectual property law, managed by a specialised and experienced lawyer, is no longer a simple static legal framework that is imposed by the company as a constraint. It becomes a real capital of wealth by being both a defensive protection body and a source of offensive value creation (Aliouat, 2010). The law is no longer an obstacle, it is now an opportunity.

Undoubtedly, the theory of law increasingly incorporates managerial metaphors. The use of new concepts such as legal management (Barthelemy, 1993), legal strategy (Barney, 1991; Barney, 2001), legal performance (Collard and Roquilly, 2010), legal intelligence or engineering (Berthelemy, 1993; Aliouat and Roquilly, 1996; Champaud, 2006 and Danet, 2006) contributes to the generation of a new legal framework that is normative and inventive, factual and strategic (Aliouat, 2010). Some authors dare to use more audacious concepts such as "legal tricks" (Bagley, 2008), "legal cunning" (Aliouat, 2010) or even "legal game" (Ost and Van de Kerchove, 1994). According to Aliouat and Roquilly (1996), the law is "*a formidable instrument for skillfully capturing value, no longer necessarily based on the conventional norm, but more on trickery or cunning (tactical or strategic)*".

In fact, the real asset of the lawyer of an innovative company is to apply the law to the concrete case that depends on the company's internal and external environment and its financial and human resources. The same legal rule may lead to different qualifications, interpretations and solutions when applied effectively. The argument of strategic choices in relation to intellectual property assets may end up advising different solutions for two innovations produced by the same company or by the same inventor and suitable for industry. It is possible to propose to patent the first one and to keep the second one secret. Between the virtual and the real, between law and reality, there is a great distance to travel.

In order to fulfil this role effectively, the company's lawyer must master several branches of law such as commercial law, company law, tax law, social law and above all intellectual property law. The latter discipline constitutes the set of exclusive rights granted to the author of a work of the mind with regard to intellectual creations. It includes literary and artistic property law and industrial property law. The law of literary and artistic property is governed in Tunisia by Law No. 1994-36 of February 24, 1994[1], while industrial property law is regulated by several texts such as Law No. 2000-84[2] on patents, Law No. 2001-36 of April 17, 2001 on the protection of trademarks, trade and service[3] and Law No. 2001-21 on the protection of industrial designs[4].

This legal protection is far from static. The strategist or manager of an innovative company must be open-minded and attentive to all internal and external stakeholders. The company's legal expert must assume, in this context, a very delicate function; listening, understanding, qualifying legally, protecting innovation and advising on the best strategy to transform the idea into a real asset. In concrete terms, the lawyer of the innovative company seeks to deliver, with his team and external consultants, a service with the best quality/price ratio, whose objective is to create value. To achieve this objective, he must set up an efficient organisation and processes, manage the relationship with his external consultants as well as possible and act as a multidisciplinary project manager in all the company's major operations.

In concrete terms, the lawyer of the innovative company seeks to deliver, with his team and external consultants, a service with the best quality/price ratio, whose objective is to create value. To achieve this objective, he must set up an efficient organisation and processes, manage the relationship with his external consultants as well as possible and act as a multidisciplinary project manager in all the company's major operations.

Supposed to be a true organizational science (Paillusseau, 1989), law accompanies, supervises and guides several disciplines such as finance, marketing and human resources management. It equates science and technology.

The lawyer of an innovative company is no longer just an expert in the law, especially intellectual property (IP) law, but a man of communication, leadership, synthesis, focused on the operational, the concrete, and the quantifiable: he is a manager.

This shows the importance of our research theme. For us, it is a question of explaining how the legal instrument has contributed to changing the simplistic vision of wealth, leading to a reconsideration of the notion of heritage through the diversification of its sources. Intangible elements are becoming more valuable and can even constitute the most expensive substance of wealth. The idea, and precisely the inventive idea, long conceived as an extra-patrimonial value, can be capitalized under certain legal conditions. The notion of legal management of innovation, which continues to disrupt the world of business and enterprise, especially in the most developed countries, has therefore emerged. Development is now measured on the basis of indicators relating to the production of innovation. The world is currently divided into two main poles: countries that produce innovation and countries that consume innovation.

The question raised in this chapter is to know to what extent the optimization of legal protection choices for innovation makes it possible to enhance it by transforming it into real wealth in the same way as the company's material assets. In order to achieve such an objective, the manager must first prepare the innovation incubator, i.e. the company to host it and develop it under the best possible conditions. A company may be poorly adapted to innovation. The legal, human and financial package chosen can slow down or at least disrupt any innovative activity.

The chapter is set out as follows: the first section underlines the necessity to start with the legal management of an IP-producing firm. The second section is focused on the legal management of innovation. The chapter terminates with a discussion and conclusion.

THE LEGAL MANAGEMENT OF AN IP-PRODUCING FIRM

The legal framework available in Tunisia offers several possible latitudes to protect the idea and especially innovation. Without legal protection, it is no longer possible to talk about the management of the firm's intangible assets. Moreover, for innovation to be recognized as the property of the firm or in another term a property, it must first be legally protected. This is an essential preliminary.

Law converts to a managerial approach, intervening throughout the entire life cycle of the firm and innovation. From the creation of the firm, through the design of the innovation and its exploitation to the end of the cycle, the firm's lawyer must ensure that the most efficient and effective choices are applied. The manager, assisted by the firm's qualified legal expert, must therefore choose the most relevant choices in terms of legal arrangements relating to the firm in general and to the ownership of the innovation in particular.

Legal management involves optimizing the legal and tax structure of the company's corporate structure. When creating the company, it is important to choose the status best suited to an innovative activity (1). Depending on the option chosen, the entry of an investor to finance the innovation or to help exploit or commercialize it will be more or less facilitated. In addition, as a taxpayer, the company must optimize its accounting and tax choices in relation to innovative products and services (2). As an employer, an IP-producing firm i.e. an innovative firm must ensure that it attracts a high-quality wage bill. The employee can be the source of innovation. It is then necessary to prepare employment contracts including specific clauses (3).

Optimization of the Legal Status of an IP-Producing Firm

You have to think about management from the very beginning of the firm. In this respect, the legal strategies of the founder of the innovative firm must be oriented either to the preservation of value or to the creation of value. The development of a good legal status makes it possible, among other things, to achieve this objective.

By choosing the most appropriate legal form, the firm is allowed to operate within a legal framework setting out the powers and penalties in order to avoid any abuse of powers and corporate assets. The objective is to preserve the value of the firm.

Through the design of an exhaustive and precise legal status, the entrepreneur ensures that the ground is prepared for the firm's development. Choosing the right legal status for an innovative firm is crucial. The firm's growth, its ability to finance, its ability to attract economic partners and qualified employees depend on it. Legal strategies then create value.

This Law and Management approach (Masson and Bouthinon-Dumas, 2011), although still unknown in Tunisia, is gaining new momentum, especially in innovation-producing countries. The law is no longer only a source of constraint and risk but also a mechanism integrated into real large-scale strategies. Legal management or legal strategy aims, through the mobilisation of legal or judicial instruments, to increase the chances of success of the innovative firm. As an organizational science, the law governs the other dimensions of the firm: economics, marketing, media, coordination and proposing solutions.

When setting up a firm, it is essential to choose the most appropriate legal form (Caprioli, 2007). An inappropriate form can have negative consequences on several levels (Guyon, 2002). The Tunisian Commercial Companies Code (CCC) offers a wide range of choices. Whether the activity is industrial, artisanal, or agricultural, the entrepreneur has the choice between two totally different categories: the sole proprietorship, a natural person and the legal person business also called a firm. Several social, accounting and tax criteria guide the choice.

In many cases, the entrepreneur guides his choice according to the tax impact only what can be a serious error for the company affecting its growth potential (Chaerels, 2012). In order to optimise the choice of legal form, it is important to answer the following questions:

- Do you need almost all of your net income taxable at the PIT (Personal Income Tax) to live?
- Would you like to partner with one or more people?
- Does your activity generate risks?
- Do you need to hire staff?
- Do you need to use bank loans or other external sources of financing?
- Would you like your children or others to take over your business?
- Do you want to make your activities sustainable?
- Would you like to receive rent from your company?
- Would you like to benefit from the tax advantages related to the nature of the activity or the location?

An innovator who chooses to create his own start-up has the choice between a sole proprietorship and a single-member limited liability company (single-member LLC). The individual firm has the advantage of a flexible legal framework without major legal constraints. Taxation is elementary, allowing you to borrow the lump sum scheme. In fact, it is the easiest way to start a business. It does not require the drafting of statutes or capital contributions. The administrative formalities are much reduced. The cost of incorporation is low and the entrepreneur is the sole owner of his business. He is free to make decisions and adopt strategies (Marchand, 2012).

However, the firm is totally confused with the entrepreneur. Considered a natural person, it does not allow the assignment of an autonomous patrimony to the firm. In the event of failure or potential bankruptcy, the entrepreneur risks the ruin of all his personal assets since the liability is unlimited. This form thus presents a huge risk for the creator of an innovative society.

The entrepreneur can also opt for the Single-member LLC form (Dahdaouch and Dahdouch, 2007; Mellouli and Frikha, 2013), which is more complicated in terms of management, taxation and accounting, but more secure in terms of risk management. This form requires the creation of a legal personality through the registration of the firm in the recently created national firm register[5], which illustrates the birth of a legal person independent of the entrepreneur's natural person. The sole shareholder benefits from a legal regime allowing part of his assets to be allocated to the share capital. In the event of difficulties, liability is limited; the firm's creditor can only have recourse against the share capital. The personal assets are then preserved, which makes it easier to manage the risk of difficulty and bankruptcy.

An innovative entrepreneur, who chooses to create his own Startup by leading this adventure alone, must ensure that the choice of social form is optimized. The form of sole proprietorship, although advantageous in terms of start-up and management methods, does not offer any real prospect of growth, especially in terms of financing. The chances of obtaining significant credit to finance innovation, which is expensive, are reduced if one opts for the form of sole proprietorship. This form only allows actions of limited importance (Guyon, 2002). The form of Single-member LLC allows both to reduce social risk and to maximize economic growth opportunities. An innovative entrepreneur who prefers not to partner to monopolize his innovation must make the right choice according to his needs, financial means and ambitions.

For companies with more than one shareholder, the CCC provides for six types of company, namely General Partnership (GP), Limited Partnership Company (LPC), Joint Venture Company (JVC), Limited Liability Company (LLC), Public Limited Company (PLC) and Limited Partnership by Share (LP), representing three main families of legal entities: partnerships (GP, LPC and JVC), limited liability companies (PLC and LP) and the hybrid company, namely LLC[6]. In practice, 3 types of companies are actually chosen by entrepreneurs. These are JVC, LLC and PLC. The other forms are only dead letters. For an innovative company, the choice of the most appropriate form depends on the number of shareholders, the value of the capital allocated, the powers of the directors and the extent of their legal responsibility as well as the company's development prospects (Chaerels, 20012). As pointed out by Carbonnier (1979), "*to each his own society, to each his own right*".

The form of a joint venture is equivalent to micro-enterprises. When you own innovation and have modest capital and are an adventurer, you can try JVC. To this end, it is necessary to choose an apparent manager who registers the company in his personal name in the national register of companies as a sole proprietorship. It is the apparent manager who assumes all accounting, social and tax obligations. The management of the company is very flexible; it is even possible to provide for a limitation of liability between partners. With regard to the public, it is the apparent manager who is considered to be the company manager. It is inexpensive compared to other forms of companies. The only legal requirement for JVC is its occult nature. The company must be kept secret by its partners. Any disclosure to the third party transforms it into a de facto General Partnership, pending its regularization. It is therefore a very fragile form of society.

Nevertheless, this company has the merit of limiting the risk of failure. Once the business succeeds, the entrepreneur always has the opportunity to change to a more open form of company that allows for greater opportunities for economic development.

The Limited Liability Company (LLC), considered the standard company in Tunisia, is the most suitable form for SMEs (Small and Medium-sized Enterprises). This entity has a minimum of two partners and a maximum of 50. No minimum capital requirement is required and industrial input is now possible since the 2007 reform[7]. Although subject to a more rigid regime of creation, management and operation than the above-mentioned companies, this entity has the advantage of allowing the limitation of social risk through the limitation of liability. In short, it is the most suitable form for an innovative company of medium economic size. Through appropriate drafting of the articles of association, the mechanisms for the transfer of shares and access by third parties to share capital can be made more flexible.

The Public Limited Company (PLC), the most rigid legal form, has, like all other forms of enterprise, advantages and disadvantages for an innovative company. This society is more complicated in terms of the mechanisms of creation and management. It is also more burdensome in terms of accounting, tax and social obligations. However, it presents the most appropriate legal framework for good governance standards. Thanks to very detailed regulations, this company is subject to a set of rules imposing management, decision-making and control bodies. The law converted to the managerial spirit finds in the PLC the most fertile ground. This form is equivalent to innovative companies that are more economically important than LLCs. The company must have at least 7 shareholders and a minimum capital of 5,000 TD. It also allows a wide latitude of development by transforming a closed PLC into a PLC with a public offering.

The following table summarizes the possible choices for the social form of an IP-producing firm.

In addition to choosing the most appropriate legal form, appropriate drafting of the articles of association is able to prepare the right ground for an innovative activity within the company. Several legal mechanisms make it possible, as part of a managerial process, to plan the risks arising from an innovative activity and prepare for effective and efficient management.

The company's legal expert begins his legal watch by carefully choosing the company's purpose to be included in the articles of association. Innovative companies generally offer various legal advantages at several levels. Law n°2016-71 of 30 September 2016, on the investment law and law n°2017-8 of 14 February 2017, on the reform of the tax benefits system, provides several tax advantages for innovative companies. A good drafting of the statutes can generate a gain even before any activity begins. An inappropriate reaction can be a direct cause of a one-time or permanent loss.

Still concerning the drafting of the statutes, it is essential to delimit the powers and responsibilities of the managers of innovative companies, especially with regard to the legal exploitation of innovation. Control bodies such as general meetings,

Table 1. Social forms of an IP-producing firm

	Sole proprietorship	Single-member Limited Liability Company (Single-member LLC)	Joint Venture Company (JVC)	Limited Liability Company (LLC)	Public Limited Company (PLC)
Number of partners	Single contractor	Sole shareholder	2 partners at least	2 shareholders at least and 50 at most (art 93)	At least 7 shareholders (Art. 160 CCC)
Share capital	No notion of capital	No minimum required	Freely fixed	No minimum required	5,000DT for the Public Limited Company without Public Offering and 50,000DT for the Public Limited Company Making a Public Offering for Savings (art 161 CCC) divided into shares with a minimum value of 1DT
Management	Entrepreneur	Managing partner, natural person art (149 CCC)	Apparent manager declared as a sole proprietorship	The manager(s), physical person, partner or not art 112 CCC)	CEO or CEO for day-to-day management and a board of directors
Decision-making process	Entrepreneur	manager	Apparent manager	The manager (s) for day-to-day management	Or a Management Board of up to 5 members (188 CCCs)
Responsibility	Liability for debts on personal property	Limited to contributions except for civil or criminal liability	Freely determined in the articles of association	Limited to contributions	General Manager or Executive Board
Tax regime	Personal Income Tax (PIT)	Corporate Income Tax (CIT)	Personal Income Tax (PIT)	Corporate Income Tax (CIT)	Corporate Income Tax (CIT)
Interpretation	Attractive for its simplicity	Allows you to create solo while benefiting from the advantage of the corporate form	Equivalent to micro-enterprises. Attractive for its simplicity and risk limitation	Standard company or anywhere adapted to many projects that require a certain rigor in management.	Reserved for companies with very high potential that are targeting the stock exchange or international markets

Source: Authors' development

boards of directors or management boards may be used for any operation affecting the commercialization of innovation in order to limit the risk of abuse. Non-compliance is in fact a legitimate cause for dismissal by the partners or through judicial channels.

In addition, the drafter of the articles of association can protect innovation through the mechanism of shareholders (Guyon, 2002) and partners' agreements (Maeterlinck, 2012) by means of specific clauses. Confidentiality clauses may be inserted that impose an obligation on shareholders to keep the innovation produced by the company secret until it is legally protected. Clauses relating to the transferability of securities and shares may also be included in order to facilitate the transfer or increase control (Guyon, 2002). It is also possible to provide for clauses of inalienability limited in time (Guyon, 2002).

Obviously, the legal management of innovation begins with the drafting of the statutes of an innovative company, which then influences its accounting and tax arrangements.

Tax Optimization of an IP-Producing Firm

Taxation is and will remain "*a necessary parameter for the management of any organization*" (Rossignol, 2010). This financial constraint is a source of risk for the company. The optimization of this risk (Yaich, 2007; Hentati, 2008; Omri and El Aissi, 2012 and Omri and Menchaoui, 2012) begins by making the right choice that can provide either a reduction in the tax rate, a tax exemption or a benefit of any other nature. The innovative company must therefore ensure that it has a clear understanding of the company's tax environment in order to achieve this (Baccouche, 2009). A wrong choice of tax structure is an unavoidable loss factor.

Act No. 2017-08 of 14 February 2017 reforming the tax benefits system and Act No. 2016-71 of 30 September 2016, on the investment law, introduced a new system repealing the investment incentive code. The new regulations can be summarized in the following five points:

1. Tax benefits for exploitation, for companies working in regional development areas and in agriculture and fisheries, for exporting companies, for companies working in the context of support and pollution control activities, and for newly created companies.
2. Tax benefits for reinvestment outside the company in initial capital or its increase, in companies working in regional development areas and in agriculture and fisheries, fully exporting companies, innovative companies, companies created by young entrepreneurs, and venture capital investment companies and venture capital funds.
3. The reduction of the minimum tax.
4. The elimination of physical reinvestment.
5. Tax and customs provisions relating to fully exporting companies, with a redefinition of the notion of export.

The manager of a newly created or existing company must take this new consideration into consideration in order to reduce costs and enjoy the benefits. As already mentioned, the drafting of the statutes remains an unavoidable condition to be able to benefit from them. The new law mentions innovative companies as entities that inherently benefit from certain tax advantages.

Article 74 of Act No. 2017-08 provides that"(...), *any income or profits reinvested in the subscription to or increase in the initial capital shall be fully deductible and within the limit of the income or profit subject to tax: - companies making investments that enable the development of technology or its mastery and innovation investments in all economic sectors, with the exception of investments in the financial and energy sectors, other than renewable energies, mining, real estate development, local consumption, trade and telecommunications operators*".

The law provides that approval of the nature of this investment is granted by the decision of the minister in charge of finance. This tax advantage is subject to several conditions provided for in Article 75 of the same law, including in particular the keeping of accounts in accordance with the accounting legislation of companies for persons exercising an industrial or commercial activity or a non-commercial profession as defined by the Personal Income Tax and Corporate Income Tax Code. In addition, the company's legal manager can, through a precise arrangement of the articles of association and administrative declarations, provide the company with other benefits that may reduce expenses.

The reading of the texts leads to the conclusion that the legal manager of an innovative company can optimize the assembly thanks to a double structural and spatial choice.

At the structural level, some activities provide the company with mainly tax advantages. The drafting of the statutes is then very important. Choosing the wrong term can deprive you of a lower rate and even a tax exemption. The tax code provides for several rates that depend on the chosen activity. The Finance Act for 2019 also provided for an exemption from tax for newly created companies until 2020 on condition that they declare investment projects for a period of four years from the effective date of commencement of the activity. The company's food must also take care to ensure that the civil or commercial nature of the activity is properly addressed. This has very significant legal consequences for the ownership of a business and the right to renew a commercial lease.

At the spatial level, the company manager can optimize the choice of the location area. Depending on the company's potential, it can choose either the national or external environment. Internally, some areas provide tax benefits (regional development areas). Other criteria may motivate the choice of the environment (infrastructure, population needs, missing activities, etc.). The choice of environment can be a factor of success or a cause of failure. The entrepreneur may also choose to produce for the local market or export depending on his financial potential and the weight of his company. The search for external markets requires a more or less pronounced knowledge of legal systems in order to avoid chance and unpredictability.

Optimization of the Social Structure of an IP-Producing Firm

As an employer, an IP-producing firm i.e. the innovative company has an interest in attracting a quality wage bill. The employee can be the source of innovation. She actually has a special need for recruitment. The employee is not always a dependent who carries out the orders of his superiors. It can generate wealth once it produces innovation. This raises the problem of ownership of innovation. The company is required to plan this problem and avoid potential future conflicts over the right to exploit innovation through the optimization of employment contracts.

A priori, the law has reserved a solution in case of production of an innovation by an employee. Article 43 of Act No. 1994-36 of 24 February 1994 on literary and artistic property provides that "*Unless otherwise stipulated, software created by one or more employees of an organization in the performance of their duties belongs to the employing organization, to which all the rights granted to authors are vested*" (Mezghani, 2000). The provisions of the first paragraph of this Article shall also apply to employees of the State, local authorities and public institutions.

The legislator's intervention is even more precise regarding the ownership of the patent. According to Article 10 of Law No. 2000-84 on Patents for Inventions, "an invention made in the course of an employment relationship by an employee who is required by virtue of his actual duties to carry out an inventive step, studies and research expressly entrusted to him, shall belong to the employer". The same article adds that "*an invention made in the field of activity of the employer by an employee not required by his work to perform an inventive step, and through the use of data or means accessible to him by reason of his employment, belongs to the employee, unless the employer notifies him of his interest in the invention in accordance with the provisions of Article 16 of this Law*" (Safi, 2006).

Once the employer has made the declaration of interest in accordance with the provisions of the law, the right to the patent is considered to have belonged to it from the outset. The inventor employee shall then be entitled to fair compensation, taking into account the economic value of the invention and any benefit arising from the exploitation of the invention for the benefit of the employer. In the absence of agreement between the parties on the amount, this compensation shall be fixed by the competent court.

Contractual engineering makes it possible to further organize the relationship between innovative companies and employees. The insertion of various clauses in the employment contract allows the innovative company to opt for certain tools to protect its innovation, provided that it complies with mandatory standards. These contractual clauses generally have as their purpose either the imposition of ancillary obligations on employees or the recognition of additional rights for them (Mzid, 2012).

The validity of employee-friendly clauses is easier to accept. This is the case, for example, of the employment stability clause, used to attract certain employees with a particular qualification generally required by innovative companies. They may also, through the same clause, seek to strengthen the professional loyalty of an innovative employee (Mzid, 2012; Petit, 2000 and Savatier, 1991).

But more often than not, the clauses included in the employment contract aim to protect the innovative company. These clauses raise more difficulties both in terms of their legality and in terms of their implementation. The most frequent clauses in this respect include the exclusivity clause, the non-competition and confidentiality clause and the clause transferring ownership of the innovation to the company. The same clauses may be reproduced in subcontracts and internship agreements.

The exclusivity clause makes it possible to prohibit the employee from any activity, even if it is not in competition with the employer, outside the company. This clause must be justified by a legitimate interest of the company.

The exclusivity clause differs from the non-competition clause (Serra, 1998; Serra, 2002; Vatinet, 2002; Blan-Jouvan, 2007; Mechri, 2009 and Bouaziz, 2012) regulating post-contractual relations by prohibiting the employee from carrying on a competing activity or from working for a competing company after the termination of the employment contract. Although challenged by a well-established doctrine (Pellisier, 1990), the Tunisian judge admitted its validity while demanding certain conditions. In a judgment of the Tunis Court of First Instance No. 39131 of 13 January 2005, it was considered that this clause should not totally prevent employees from exercising their right to work, which is recognised as a fundamental human right. For it to be valid, it must be limited in time and space. Another judgment adds, in addition, that it must be essential to the protection of a legitimate and serious interest of the company concerned (Lahmar, 2006).

When it comes to an innovative company, one or other of these clauses is, in principle, appropriate and justified by the legitimate interest of the company which needs to protect its innovation from any unauthorised exploitation or disclosure. In other words, these clauses are intended either to ensure the exclusive exploitation of an innovation that is already protected, or to keep it secret if it is not yet protected.

The confidentiality clause is often included in an employment contract to complement a non-competition clause. As Professor Vivant notes, the secrecy to be kept is an element of the non-competition due (Vivant, 1990). This type of clause is customary in employment contracts involving innovative activity. The employee undertakes by a specific clause not to disclose any information that he may have become aware of during the provision of his service. It is a negative obligation not to qualify by Nammour (1992) as an obligation of result. Undisclosed information may include research conducted by the company, an unprotected patent, design or model or a trade secret kept secret by the company (Vincent, 2001).

The clause transferring ownership of the innovation to the company is inserted once ownership of the innovation reverts to the employee as provided for in Article 10 of Law No. 2000-84 on patents. A question arises in this respect: does this type of clause exempt from the obligation of the declaration of interest required by law? In other words, does this clause amount to a declaration of interest provided for by any inventive activity of the employee?

A careful reading of the text leads to the conclusion that this type of clause does not automatically transfer ownership of the innovation from the employee to the company. The latter remains bound by the declaration of interest to benefit from the property.

Freedom of contract continues to produce other forms of clauses designed to protect the innovative company. The combination of legal and contractual tools makes it possible to preserve this structural framework conducive to the invention. This will then make it possible to stimulate innovation, which in turn will benefit from a very effective legal framework for protection. The legal management of the innovative company and therefore generally followed by legal management of the innovation as intangible value.

THE LEGAL MANAGEMENT OF INNOVATION

Today, the company's legal expert must put on many costumes: the traditional "guardian", the newest "business partner", the unexpected "communicator" and the original manager. As such, he may do or have done. Sometimes it is up to him to act like a professional by carrying out the technical procedures for the legal protection of innovation. Once protected, innovation offers the company significant potential for commercialization. The company's lawyer changes the nature of his intervention, assists, accompanies and advises. The action now belongs to the company, which can choose either an internal or an external valorisation of its protected innovation. Clearly, the protection of innovation is an essential prerequisite for its valorisation.

From the Protection of Innovation

A company can only benefit from its innovation once it acquires ownership. Once ownership is acquired, the company is able to optimize the legal consequences.

Conditions for Acquiring Ownership of the Invention

The invention can be legally translated into several forms such as patents, trademarks, designs and models (Bouchoux, 2007 and Azema and Galloux, 2012). The legal manager, involved downstream in the design of the innovation, is faced with several possible options. Each choice to be made can generate wealth or cause possible failure. The decision taken is based on several indicators such as consistency with the firm's overall strategy, its internal and external environment, especially with regard to the industrial property (IP) policies of its competitors.

The first decision to be taken concerns about legal protection. You can choose to protect the invention or not. Legal protection does not always produce value. A patent, trademark, design or model may not have a serious chance of competing or being marketable. It is therefore necessary to start with a feasibility study to study the freedom of exploitation, its desirability and to assess the risks arising from it.

Concerning the patentable invention, Article 2 of Law No. 2000-84 on Patents for Inventions provides that "*the patent shall be granted for new inventions involving an inventive step and capable of industrial application*". Three substantive conditions are therefore required for filing a patent. These are novelty, inventiveness or inventive step and industrial application.

The invention is new if it is not included in state of the art constituted by everything that has been made available to the public before the filing date of the patent application. You don't invent what's already known.

The activity is inventive if it is not obvious to a skilled person. Article 5 of Law No. 2000-84 considers an invention to involve an inventive step if, "*for a skilled person, it is not obvious, in comparison with state of the art at the date of filing of the patent application or, where applicable, at the date of the priority validly claimed for it*". This criterion makes it possible to distinguish the invention from the simple innovation that can be carried out by a skilled person in the context of a simple execution operation. The inventive step is therefore a qualitative leap from state of the art to patent teaching[8].

Finally, the invention must be susceptible to industrial application, i.e. it must be of a technical nature. Article 6 of Law No. 2000-84 specifies that "*the invention is susceptible of industrial application if its object can be manufactured or used in any kind of industry or in agriculture*".

The firm also has an interest in protecting its ornamental creations that accompany the technical or practical aspect of an industrial or craft object (Aouachria, 2019). The design that constitutes its substance may be quarterly (the shape or texture of the object) or bi-weekly (patterns, lines or colours). This form of invention helps to make the product more aesthetically pleasing. Aesthetics or design are currently a major factor motivating consumer choice. "*Industrial innovation is nowadays enshrined in the form of products, as it is in the case of patents. The designer is involved in the same way as the engineer in the development of the product*" (De Passemar, 1997). They say that form sells.

However, creators often find themselves in delicate situations either because they are unaware of the texts governing the subject or because they have consulted their legal advisors late. Opting for a managerial strategy of innovation thus imposes a referral of the conditions of access to protection.

According to Law No. 2001-21 of February 6, 2001 on the Protection of Industrial Designs, it is necessary to start by meeting substantive conditions to acquire this property.

On the one hand, in order to be able to file a design, it is necessary that the form is inspired by a purely ornamental and non-functional concern. "*The right on drawings seeks to reward free aesthetics, patents, useful technology*" (Cohen, 2002). As such, Article 2(2) of the Law provides that "*if the same object has been considered both as a new industrial design and as a patentable invention and if the elements constituting the novelty of the design are inseparable from those of the invention, such object may be protected only in accordance with the provisions of the Patent Law*". It is thus clear that the creation of a design or patent does not pursue the same objective.

On the other hand, Article 2 of Law No. 2001-21 requires the novelty of the design by providing that "*the provisions of this Law shall apply to any new design, any new plastic form, any industrial product which differs from its similar, either by a distinct and recognizable configuration conferring a character of novelty on it, or by one or more external effects giving it its own and new physiognomy*".

The legislator maintains in this respect an objective condition driven by the requirement for a new contribution from the creator different from what already exists[9]. The term novelty is to be distinguished from originality, which has a rather subjective aspect. Originality is the author's personal imprint on his work. The original is not necessarily new. To acquire ownership of a design, it is therefore necessary to rely on a prior art search by designating it. To cite only two examples, trial judges considered that a cheese model for the first case and a glass model for the second case are not new and cannot claim filing as a protected model since they are known internally and internationally. This right is granted only to those who enrich the sector with a new creation. The novelty may be total or partial. In a judgment handed down on 30 May 2005, the Grombalia Court of First Instance recognised a new model of street lamp inspired by the cage of Sidi Bousaid (Fathi Annabi case, cited by Aouachria, 2019). It is therefore not required that the novelty be absolute, unlike what is provided for patents. Anyone who disputes the novelty must provide proof of the existence of prior art.

The brand, another form of innovation, is now reaching a spectacular high point (Hadrich, 2007). According to Article 2 n°2001-36 of 17 April 2001, the trademark or service mark is a visible sign making it possible to distinguish the products offered for sale or the services rendered by a natural or legal person. Thus, may constitute a trademark:

- Names in all forms, such as words, word assemblies, patronymic names, geographical names, pseudonyms, letters, numbers and acronyms;
- Figurative signs, such as drawings, reliefs, logos, slogans, forms, in particular those of the product or its packaging or those characterising services, arrangements, combinations or shades of colour;
- Sound signs, such as sounds and musical phrases.

Brands are increasingly becoming an important part of the firm's strategy. Marking products is a choice that generally indicates the effective and efficient triggering of the production process. Marking serves a triple purpose: identifying the product, supporting the firm's advertising and commercial strategy and encouraging investment. The decision to mark is based on the fulfilment of certain substantive conditions.

The brand must be:

- A distinctive sign: the mark identifies the product and makes it possible not to mislead the consumer.
- A lawful sign: the trademark must not be contrary to the law and public order.
- An available sign: the trademark must not infringe prior rights.

A strategic decision to label must be optimized according to certain indicators that allow you to choose the best option for the firm. It is necessary to start by verifying the existence of the different legal conditions, ensuring that the trademark is sufficiently distinctive and easy to use in an advertising context and verifying that the name of the corresponding domain is available. Choosing the right brand can attract or retain customers, which is inevitably a likely source of income. A simple logo can turn into silver. In this respect, several strategic choices are available. The corporate name can be used as a brand name. What Delattre (2001) calls an "umbrella brand" allows significant savings. The firm may also choose to separate its corporate name from its brands. The firm name registered in the Commercial Register is accompanied by the registration of trademarks at INNORPI (National Institute of Standardization and Industrial Property).

For all the above-mentioned types of industrial property, compliance with the substantive conditions is a prerequisite for the transition to the formal conditions illustrating the acquisition of industrial property. In fact, it is the filing with INNORPI that allows the legal protection of innovation. This formality is accompanied by an obligation to pay certain fees set in advance by INNORPI. Any decision to file must take into account the profitability of the innovation. It is sometimes more interesting to stop the payment of royalties and give up industrial property.

The finalization of the filing procedures allows ownership of the innovation, which has several legal consequences for the author of the agreement and for third parties.

The Legal Consequences of Protecting Innovation

The innovation embodied in the acquisition of industrial property for the firm is based in practice on a trade-off between the need to stimulate research for the innovator through the recognition of an exclusive right of exploitation and the need to slow down the research of others by recognizing the inventor's right to prevent another from pushing his creation further without his permission. Ownership of the invention is therefore not only dependent on law. It is also privative of right against third parties and precisely against competitors. In short, the ownership of innovation is both exclusive and private.

Exclusive Ownership of the Innovation

The filing of a patent, trademark, design and model is equivalent to a birth certificate for a natural or legal person. The invention, which is legally recognized and protected from the moment the application is filed, offers the inventor a right of ownership. In concrete terms, the deposit allows its author to benefit from a presumption of ownership. This is a simple presumption which allows any contestant to provide evidence to the contrary.

This full real right confers all the prerogatives over the invention. You can use, exploit or transfer. The owner can monopolize everything, concede the operation or transfer ownership by assignment. The firm's manager, better placed to judge the firm's human and financial potential and its competitive abilities, is empowered to choose the most effective and efficient strategy.

Intellectual property law, converted to a managerial approach, makes it possible to deal with possible choices and make an informed decision while planning for possible risks.

This exclusive right of exploitation is rather temporary. The duration of the exploitation of the patent is 20 years as provided for in Article 36 of Law No. 2000-84 on patents. The duration of exploitation of a design depends on the will of the creator. It can be 5 years, 10 years or 15 years maximum. For the brand, the operating period is more open. It can be used for 10 years and can be renewed indefinitely. The operating period begins from the filing date of the application. Duration is also a decision-making factor for economic exploitation.

In order to exploit the ownership of the innovation economically, the owner has a very varied contractual system. The in-house lawyer must have, in this context, a rational, systematic and pre-established approach to any legal operation; he will use standard contracts and checklists (manager contracts). It can propose operating or consultation contracts.

Operating agreements can take several forms such as assignment, licensing or concession, distribution, sponsorship, franchise agreements, R&D agreements, collaboration and technology transfer, etc. (Demolin and Rigo, 2012). The legal manager, the legal advisor or the entrepreneur himself chooses the most appropriate contractual technique that maximizes wealth, limits losses while avoiding economic and legal risks.

Each act has its own legal consequences. The contract for the transfer of the patent, design or trademark entails a transfer of ownership of the innovation with all the related prerogatives. Other acts involve a transfer of use and exploitation, the property remains the property of the inventor's breading, who retains only paternity.

Licenses or licensing is a specific form of concession of the exploitation of the invention. The license allows a patent, trademark, and copyright, know-how to be exploited under specific conditions and for specific purposes, most often in return for financial considerations. This is a permission given by a firm to use the intellectual property in exchange for a compensation called royalties.

Implicitly, licensing is a form of partnership between two parties (sometimes more) bound by a contract of a duration chosen by them. The licensor is commonly referred to as the licensor, while the purchaser of the same license is referred to as the licensee. Any licensing transaction is based on the existence of intellectual property rights, often underutilized, that could have significant market value for another firm.

The franchise agreement, a brand-specific technique, is a system that offers brands potential for development without investing heavily (Leloup, 2000; Demolin and Rigo, 2012; Demolin and Demolin, 2012). It can be said more abruptly that this contract makes it possible to develop with other people's money. Franchising allows you to create a firm with better performance and a lower failure rate compared to an isolated firm by taking advantage of the reputation of a well-known brand and its assistance. In Tunisia, the legal framework for this act is relatively recent. The legal conditions for its development were put in place with Act No. 69-2009 of 12 August 2009 on the modernization of the distribution trade, in particular the provisions of articles 14 to 17 on franchising. Franchising is a contract but also a business strategy that can enable it to further exploit its success by creating an operating network.

The consultation contracts are also varied. They are intended to offer agreements for sharing the exploitation of the invention. Examples include patent pool contracts, subcontracting or joint ventures.

Contractual engineering, which is very active and inventive in the intellectual property sector, has not finished providing other models for the intrinsic or extrinsic exploitation of innovation. The rise of the Internet has contributed to the dematerialization of contractual processes by giving rise to electronic distribution and exploitation contracts. This has made it more difficult to prove the contractual relationship and manage the resulting risks

In any case, these contractual tools for the protection of innovation allow inventors to control and repress any unauthorized exploitation. This gives rise to the private aspect of ownership of the innovation.

Private Aspect of Ownership of the Innovation

The owner of the innovation, with an exclusive right of exploitation, may deprive others of any unauthorized exploitation. With regard to patents, Le Bas (2002) states that they are becoming "*less and less a tool to protect innovation and more and more a tool to block innovation by rival firms*". In the event of abuse of power, the texts have developed a whole coercive legal arsenal designed to punish by judicial or extrajudicial means.

Enforcement and retention legal actions may take the form of counterfeiting or seizure for counterfeiting. Any infringement of the inventor's property rights constitutes a forgery incurring the author's civil and criminal liability. Infringement seizure is a means of proof of counterfeiting and, more generally, of any infringement of an intellectual property right. This procedure makes it possible, with the authorization of a judge, for the holder of the industrial property right who considers himself to be the victim of an infringement of this right, to have it recorded by a bailiff authorised to enter any place where the infringement can be recorded and to seize the evidence of the infringement.

Extrajudicial actions are generally administrative in nature, specifically customs. These are border measures. The owner of an industrial property right and his successors in title may, if he has serious grounds for suspecting that counterfeit products are being imported, submit a written request to the customs authorities requesting that customs clearance of such products be suspended. Similarly, customs authorities may on their own initiative suspend the customs clearance of suspected counterfeit goods. It is up to the court to decide what action to take on counterfeit products either by destroying them under the control of the customs services or by excluding them from the commercial circuit.

Clearly, all these mechanisms share the same objective: to protect the product from counterfeiting.

Tunisian case law further pushes the protection of the invention of counterfeiting by revealing flexibility in the initiation of the action or its proof. Thus, it considered that the infringement action is not subject to prejudice. According to the Tunisian Court of Cassation, the mere risk of confusion in the minds of the public justifies the appeal for infringement. It is sufficient for the judge to consider that confusion may recur for him to accept the action.

Also, case law undermines protection by assessing infringement by similarities and not by differences. It is sufficient for him to reproduce significant elements of the product for counterfeiting purposes. In a case dated February 13, 2017 relating to the trademark ESPRIM/ESPRIT, the Tunis Court of Appeal (CA) stated that there is no infringement since there are no similarities (Decision of the Monastir Court of Appeal, No. 6124 of 13 February 2017, cited by Aouachria, 2019).

In the same context, Tunisian case law affirms in an almost static way the indifference of good faith to counterfeiting, which significantly extends the sphere of legal protection (Rajhi, 2008). Ultimately, legal knowledge converted to legal engineering or legal intelligence is essential when it comes to an innovative firm. This legal know-how is based on multidisciplinary management. It is important for a legal advisor or legal director to understand the firm's internal and external environment with its various technical, financial, human and other aspects. This then makes it possible to identify the needs and risks specific to the means of protecting innovation available through legislation or case law.

The legal aspects then become strategic and must be understood as far in advance as possible. The lawyer assisting or practicing in the context of an innovative firm is no longer just an expert, he is above all a manager who will enable the firm, through the expected means of protection, to transform the invention into wealth. Protecting helps to enhance value.

Towards the Promotion of Innovation

If protection results in money being spent, recovery is the way to recover the money spent. Whether it is an internal or external valorisation, the legal management of innovation eventually transforms the idea into money.

Internal Valorisation of Innovation

The internal valorisation of innovation is reflected in the monopoly decision, which can be both the most successful and the most risk-bearing. According to Peteraf (1993), the company can develop sustainable rent-generating capacities on the basis of scarcity or monopoly, non-substitution, inimitability, or market imperfections concerning a patent, database, software, designs or models. Intellectual property is then a source of value through an internal valorisation strategy. IP law offers a wide range of techniques to enhance this strategy. Some companies do not know or cannot make this choice. Others, on the contrary, excel in this exercise. For example, until 2010, Microsoft has obtained more than 90% of its margins by exploiting its copyright against unauthorized copies of its products (Aliouat, 2010). The case of Apple, with the introduction of the iPhone on the smartphone market, is just as revealing of this legal capacity that proactive firms succeed in developing (Roquilly, 2009).

Like any valorisation decision, this monopoly strategy is named on a triptych: the company's overall strategy, the company's internal resources and the competitors' intellectual property policies. Undoubtedly, intellectual property strategy is only one component of the company's overall strategy. It must be consistent with its projects and must be communicated to all staff.

The firm's overall strategy can take several forms as outlined by Le Loarne and Blanco (2009):

- Aggressive strategy: adapted to a growth objective and which allows you to oppose your rights to anyone who claims to encroach on your territory.
- Dominant strategy: to file numerous IP rights to constitute a "minefield" and thus strengthen the leadership position.
- Preventive strategy: Avoid litigation and use IP rights as a bargaining chip in the event of a dispute with an aggressive competitor
- Partnership strategy: use IP to build relationships with partners in the form of cross-licensing or participation in a patent pool that makes a "common pot". This is the case in the field of electronics and telecommunications.

It can be deduced that the monopoly strategy of the invention is generally integrated within the framework of an aggressive or dominant strategy generally accessible to leading market firms with significant competitive weight. Opting for a monopoly through a Start-up or an SME is an adventure without clear outcomes (Ollivier and Simon, 2013).

This extreme strategy imposes the benefit of colossal internal capacity in terms of the firm's human and financial resources. The firm must have qualified, well-trained personnel who are constantly aware of the importance of the entity's intangible assets. The firm must also ensure that it plans additional expenses to manage the risks of more likely legal conflicts in these circumstances. The monopoly strategy also depends on technological and competitive monitoring. The decision to monopolize depends on the competitive weight of others and their inventive dynamics.

The monopoly places the owner of the invention in a privileged position to prohibit its customers and competitors from marketing similar products. This property makes it possible to benefit from an annuity situation that compensates for the efforts made. The monopoly can be achieved through several legal protection mechanisms. The entrepreneur may choose to file the patent, design or trademark without assigning its exploitation. It may also opt for industrial secrecy. Companies in the catering industry generally choose to keep recipes secret and not patent them. The entrepreneur can make another legal arrangement; Bring innovation into the public domain. It simply publishes the innovation to benefit from it. When an organization does not want to patent an invention that is difficult to keep secret, it has an interest in disclosing it, which prevents any subsequent filing. Another choice is possible in case the patent risks forfeiture. You can bounce from a patent to brand protection. To anticipate the consequences of the loss of the patent's exploitation rights following its expiry and transfer to the public domain, the firm may choose to take greater advantage of its product by registering it as a trademark. The examples of the Teflon and Lycra brands are significant.

On an international scale, several firms have opted for the internal valorisation of industrial and intellectual property. The economic face spreads several success stories. As an example, we can mention AT&T, the American historical operator founded in 1885, which started its activities with Graham BELL's patent monopoly. Currently, AT&T is the largest provider of local and long-distance telephone services and XDSL in the United States and the 2nd largest mobile service operator. At the same time, the famous French industrial group "Air Liquide" monopolized George CLAUDE's (1902) patent on gas liquefaction.

Despite the temptation of this strategy, it remains a high-risk legal and economic choice.

From a legal point of view, the monopoly strategy is likely to raise a situation of abuse of dominant position. In fact, the monopoly favours abusive practices that abnormally restrict competition, which is contrary to domestic and international standards. The example of the Microsoft case is illustrative. Between 2004 and 2013[10], the European Commission had repeatedly condemned Microsoft for abuse of dominant position and breach of competition rules and had mainly forced the company to disclose to its competitors certain technical information relating to its Windows operating system[11]. In addition, the monopoly strategy multiplies the risks of legal disputes. The monopoly forces competitors to try by any means to force a breach in this monopolistic situation. This results in considerable costs to prosecute counterfeiters[12].

Also at the economic level, the market does not appreciate monopolistic situations. The consumer does not appreciate having a single supplier. Competition remains an essential factor in reducing prices.

The firm's lawyer must seek, in adopting such a strategy, to plan these legal and economic risks. Sometimes it is more obvious to start a conflict. Sometimes it is wiser to avoid conflict. The lawyer is then called upon to prepare manager contracts intended to negotiate compromises in order to avoid a conflict or initiate infringement proceedings against competitors.

The monopoly strategy is certainly attractive but remains high-risk. External valorisation through the sharing of the invention reduces the risk of conflict and minimizes operating costs.

The External Valorisation of Innovation

The external valorisation of IP is based on a desire to share the exploitation of IP. IP sharing can result from either an IP commercialization policy or an IP entrepreneurship policy (Binctin, 2015; Breese, 2002). The strategy for commercializing innovation is also known as the licensing strategy (Breese, 2002; Corbel, 2007; Verges, 2019; Doyen and Pierre, 2019). The drafting of operating contracts allows the firm to grant the exploitation of patents, designs, models and trademarks while retaining ownership. The legal protection techniques, which have already been analysed, such as licenses and franchising, allow the firm to enhance the value of innovation.

Some firms, especially multinational ones, use what is known as technology standardization to impose their licenses on their competitors. A firm that applies a policy of standardizing its product offers a single version of a product on all its foreign markets. In its quest for profitability (which depends jointly on costs and sales), the firm that chooses to standardize its offer favours a strategy of cost minimization. The standardization of the product can be done on several of its components: for example, in the design of the product or its packaging.

Android appears in this context as the most symptomatic example. It is the most widely used mobile operating system in the world, ahead of Apple's iOS, with more than 80% market share in smartphones for all its versions and adaptations[13].

Launched in June 2007 following Google's 2005 acquisition of the start-up of the same name, the system was first designed for Smartphones and touch-pads, then diversified into connected objects and computers such as televisions (Android), cars (Android Auto), Chrome books (Chrome OS that uses Android applications) and smart-watch (Wear OS). Several companies use this technology through licensing agreements such as Motorola, Samsung, Acer, Asus, Toshiba and Sony, which has made Google the undisputed market leader.

This Android operating system, which is a top-notch example, was the direct cause of the European Commission's opening of an investigation. In July 2018, the Commission fined Google (€4.3 billion) for abuse of a dominant position[14]. This system is precisely criticized for allowing Google to put its services in a monopoly position by offering them by default, regardless of the brand of the device or the type of personalization of the operating system by the manufacturers. According to Brussels, this has a direct impact on the consumer who is limited compared to the many third-party applications and services that could be offered by competitors[15].

Another strategy of commercialization through licenses can be advanced. The firm can carry out licensing instead of counterfeiting actions. Threatening to engage in conflicts is then used as a bargaining chip to impose the conclusion of licenses on favourable terms on the innovative firm. The latter makes a double profit, by limiting the costs resulting from conflicts and by benefiting from the royalties resulting from licenses.

The external valorisation of innovation can be the subject of a real partnership action. The objective of this strategy is to share the costs and risks of know-how. The partners must ensure that each partner's IP rights are organised by contractual means. Cooperation between partners may aim at innovation or the commercial exploitation of the innovation. The effectiveness of IP entrepreneurship depends essentially on two factors:

-Choice of the appropriate form of partnership:

Partners can opt for the patent pool mechanism, which is a technique for combining patents for collective exploitation (Lampe and Moser, 2010). This is a form of partnership by patenting. In fact, it happens that several organizations work independently on technology, and each holds patents. Rather than fighting each other, they have an interest in pooling their patents for collective exploitation while avoiding sterile competition. The partnership contract determines the reciprocal obligations and rights of each party.

The legal technique of subcontracting is another possible form of partnership. It is a question of entrusting a partner with the manufacture of a product protected by IP law.

Also, the joint venture reflects another category of closer partnership. In this context, it is not enough to conclude a classic contract. Instead, a new firm is being created in which each partner has an interest. This common structure may be limited to one project. It may also consist of the creation of a common research and development organisation.

- Take precautions to avoid conflicts with partners:

Care must be taken to anticipate potential conflicts in the partnership contract precisely with regard to the ownership of IP results. Consideration may be given to including a clause in the contracts providing for a possible transaction in the event of a conflict. We can even plan the distribution of the right to exploit and commercialize intellectual property rights and the distribution of financing.

CONCLUSION AND RECOMMENDATIONS

Innovation that is legally protected by IP is increasingly being debated at the micro and macro levels.

At the microeconomic level, innovation allows the company to survive and develop through the marketing of inventive products that can sometimes transform consumer habits. The chapter emphasizes that the company's strategic choices are determined according to its capacities and economic weight. It can then opt for a strategy of monopoly or sharing of innovation. In any case, the planning of choices and their optimization make it possible to enhance the value of legally protected innovation by transforming the idea into a real asset for the company.

At the macroeconomic level, innovation is becoming a real growth driver, enabling producing countries to maintain their lead over emerging countries. It is an institutional concern that is increasingly driving political, economic, social and environmental discourse. One only has to look at the parallelism of the curves of patents filed, the growth rate and the wealth of nations.

However, Tunisia remains a country that consumes innovation. The management of innovation transformed into IP is a recent dialect that some companies have tried but remains unknown to others, usually in the form of family and closed SMEs. The Tunisian manager may choose to mark, register a design or even a patent, but it is rare for him to undertake a real IP strategy within his company. The available legal framework is far from being an obstacle. There is no shortage of legal texts. What is really lacking is an effective long-term economic development program that integrates innovation as an engine of growth. Innovation management could be a possible low-cost solution to revive the Tunisian economy.

REFERENCES

Amann, B., & Lethielleux, L. (2005). *Le droit, outil de gestion*. Pearson Education.

Aliouat, B., & Roquilly, Ch. (1996). L'ingénierie juridique, Les dix outils clés du management. édition du GO, Presses du management.

Aliouat, B. (2010). Les stratégies de propriété intellectuelle et leur ingénierie juridique: Une nouvelle approche managériale du droit fondée sur le recours à la ruse. *Revue des Sciences de Gestion*, 21-23.

Aouachria, F. (2019). *La protection des dessins et modèles industriel en droit tunisien, mélange en l'honneur de Nabila MAZGHANI*. Maison du livre.

Azema, J., & Galloux, J.-C. (2012). *Droit de la propriété industrielle*. Dalloz.

Baccouche, N. (2009). Environnement fiscal de l'entreprise en Tunisie. 24ème édition des journées de l'entreprise. Institut Arabe des Chefs d'Entreprises.

Bagley, C. E. (2008, July 17). Look for the silver lining. Piracy is a bad thing. But sometimes companies can turn it to their advantage. *The Economist*.

Barney, J. B. (2001). Resource-based theories of competitive advantage: A ten year retrospective on the resource-based view. *Journal of Management*, *27*(6), 643–650. doi:10.1177/014920630102700602

Barney, J. B. (1991). Firm resources and sustained competitive advantage. *Journal of Management*, *17*(1), 99–120. doi:10.1177/014920639101700108

Barthelemy, J. (1993). *L'ingénierie juridique: un concept, Cahiers de droit de l'entreprise*. JCP.

Binctin, N. (2015). Stratégie d'entreprise et propriété intellectuelle, LGDJ. In *Les stratégies de l'entreprise fondées sur la propriété intellectuelle*. Available at: https://www.iptrust.fr/wp-content/uploads/2016/03/Strate%CC%81gie_breese_masson.pdf

Bouaziz, H. (2012). La clause de non concurrence en droit de travail. *Actes de la journée d'études sur les clauses du contrat de travail.*

Bouchoux, D. (2007). *La propriété intellectuelle: le droit des marques, le droit d'auteur, le droit des brevets d'invention et des secrets commerciaux*. Nouveaux horizons.

Bouthion-Dumas, H., & Masson, A. (2012). Le rôle du droit dans les stratégies des acteurs économiques. In *Stratégies juridiques des acteurs économiques. Editeur: Larcier*. Collection Droit, Management et Stratégies.

Breese, P. (2002). *Stratégies de propriété industrielle*. Dunod.

Caprioli, E. A. (2007). Introduction au management juridique de l'innovation. *Journal des Sociétés*, *45*. Available at: https://www.caprioli-avocats.com

Carbonnier, J. (1979). *Essai sur les lois*. Rep Défrénois.

Chaerels, A. (2012). *Le choix de la forme juridique la mieux adaptée: approche transversale, in ouvrage collectif intitulé la création d'une société innovante*. Anthemis.

Champaud, C. (2006). *Les stratégies juridiques des entreprises*. Dalloz.

Cohen, D. (2002). Le nouveau droit des dessins et modèles. ECONOMICA.

Collard, C., & Roquilly, Ch. (2010). *La performance juridique: pour une vision stratégique du droit dans l'entreprise*. LGDJ.

Corbel, P. (2007). *Management stratégique des droits de la propriété intellectuelle*. Gualino.

Dahdouch, C. & Dahdouch, H. (2007). *Entreprises sociétaires et groupement privés*. IHE.

Danet, D. (2006). Au croisement du management stratégique des entreprises, *Journée de recherche « stratégie et transversalité »*. Université de Nice Sophia Antipolis.

Delattre, E. (2001). Le changement de nom des entreprises: évolution quantitative et typologie. *Revue Française de Marketing, 181*.

Demolin, P., & Demolin, V. (2012). *Le contrat de franchise, analyse et commentaires de 15 années de jurisprudence, 1995-2010*. Retrieved from: http://www.dbblaw.eu/fr/news/pierre-et-vronique-demolin-publient-le-contrat-de-franchise

Demolin, P., & Rigo, M. (2012). Protéger la propriété intellectuelle de l'entreprise innovante en mettant en place des contrats de distribution efficaces pour ses produits et services. In La création d'une société innovante, aspects juridiques et fiscaux particuliers. Athémis.

De Passemar. (1997). La protection des brevets, des marques, des indications géographiques et des dessins et modèles industriels. Séminaire de l'OMPI sur la propriété intellectuelle et les accords sur les ADPIC. Organisé par l'OPMI.

Doyen, D. & Pierre, P. (2019). *Guide de management de la PI pour les business managers*. INPI.

Guyon, Y. (2002). *Les sociétés, Aménagement statutaires et conventions entre associés*. Ed. LGDJ.

Hentati, A. (2008). L'optimisation fiscale en matière d'impôt sur les sociétés, rôle de l'expert-comptable. *Mémoire pour l'obtention du diplôme d'expertise comptable*.

Lahmar, I. (2006). *Commentaire du jugement du tribunal de première instance de Tunis n° 39131 précité*. RJL.

Lampe, R., & Moser, P. (2010). *Do Patent Pools Encourage Innovation? Evidence from the 19th-Century Sewing Machine Industry*. NBER Working Paper n°15061.

Le Bas, C. (2002). Fonctionnement, transformation et tension du système de brevet. *Revue d'Economie Industrielle, 99*.

Le Loarne, S., & Blanco, S. (2009). *Management de l'innovation*. Pearson.

Leloup, J.-M. (2000). La franchise, Droit et pratique (3rd ed.). Paris: Encyclopédie Delmas.

Maeterlinck, A. (2012). *La répartition des pouvoirs dans les statuts et les conventions d'actionnaires, ouvrage collectif intitulé. La création d'une société innovante, aspects juridiques et fiscaux particuliers*. Anthémis.

Marchand, B. (2012). *Les démarches liées à la création d'une entreprise, ouvrage collectif intitulé la création d'une société innovante*. Anthémis.

Mellouli, S., & Frikha, S. (2013). Les sociétés commerciales. Maison du livre.

Masson, A., & Bouthion-Dumas, H. (2011). L'approche Law and mangement. *Revue Trimestrielle de Droit Commercial et de Droit Economique*, *2*, 233-254.

Mechri, F. (2009). *Le droit du travail en Tunisie*. Sud Edition Tunis.

Mezghani, N. (2000). La protection du logiciel par la loi n°94-36. RTD..

Mzid, N. (2012). Observations préliminaires sur les clauses du contrat de travail. *Actes de la journée d'études sur les clauses du contrat de travail.*

Nammour, F. (1992). Les clauses de secret. In Droit des sociétés commerciales. LATRACH.

Ost, F., & Van De Kerchove, M. (1994). Le jeu: un paradigme pour le droit. *Revue internationale de droit comparé*, *46*(1), 303-305.

Paillusseau, J. (1989). *Le droit est aussi une science d'organisation*. RTD.Com.

Peteraf, M. A. (1993). The cornerstones of competitive advantage: A Resource based view. *Strategic Management Journal*, *14*(3), 179–191. doi:10.1002mj.4250140303

Petit, F. (2000). *Sur les clauses de garantie d'emploi*. Dr.Soc.2000.

Roquilly, Ch. (2009). Le cas de l'Iphone en tant qu'illustration du rôle des ressources juridiques et de la capacité juridique dans le management de l'innovation. *Management*, *§§§*, 142–175.

Safi, Z. (2006). *Le droit du travail, le contrat du travail. Centre de publication universitaire.*

Savatier, J. (1991). *Les garanties contractuelles de stabilité de l'emploi*. Dr.Soc.1991.

Serra, Y. (2002). *Tsunami sur la clause de non concurrence*. D.2002.

Serra, Y. (1998). *Les fondements et le régime de l'obligation de non concurrence.* RTD.Com.

Vincent, M. (2001). La protection du secret en propriété industrielle, Université Lille II. *Mémoire, DEA, année universitaire 2000-2001.*

Vatinet, R. (2002). *Les conditions de validité des clauses de non concurrence: l'imbroglio.* Dr.Soc.2002, n°1.

Verges, E. (2019). *Contrats sur la recherche et l'innovation - Nouveauté: Techniques contractuelles. Valorisation de la recherche. Transferts de technologies.* Dalloz.

Vivant, M. (1990). *Les clauses de secret, in les principales clauses entre professionnel.* PUAM.

Yaich, R. (2007). La maîtrise des risques fiscaux. In L'impôt sur les sociétés. Les éditions Raouf Yaïch.

ADDITIONAL READING

Al-Dmour, R. H., Mohammed, T., & Al-dmour, H. H. (2019). Factors Influencing Students' Intentions Towards Entrepreneurship: Comparative Study. *International Journal of Sustainable Entrepreneurship and Corporate Social Responsibility*, *4*(1), 1–26. doi:10.4018/IJSECSR.2019010101

Bernardino, S., Santos, J. F., & Ribeiro, J. C. (2019). Social Entrepreneur's Networks and Institutional Environment: Ties That Bind. *International Journal of Sustainable Entrepreneurship and Corporate Social Responsibility*, *4*(2), 1–22. doi:10.4018/IJSECSR.2019070101

Gay, C., & Szostak, B. (2017). Management de l'innovation. Nouveaux enjeux et défis, Méthodes faciles à appliquer, Illustrations et témoignages récents. Management Sup, Dunod.

Kammoun, S. (2015). *Innovation et compétences pour innover des firmes: modélisation du comportement innovant dans l'industrie française.* Editions Universitaires Européennes.

Kialo, S. M. (2018). Processus d'innovation et propriété industrielle: Intégration des brevets dans les bureaux d'études d'une entreprise industrielle. *Revue Congolaise de Gestion*, *2*(26), 11–42. doi:10.3917/rcg.026.0011

Maher, C. (2019). Public Policy and the Sustainability of Third Sector Social Enterprises. *International Journal of Sustainable Entrepreneurship and Corporate Social Responsibility*, *4*(1), 42–56. doi:10.4018/IJSECSR.2019010103

Olivier, P., & Simon, Ph. (2013). *La gestion et l'usage de la propriété intellectuelle par le entreprises françaises, Étude pour le Commissariat général à la stratégie et à la prospective*. WINNOVE.

KEY TERMS AND DEFINITIONS

Industrial Design: A two-dimensional element such as the ornamentation, patterns, lines or colours of a product. A Title to protect the aesthetic aspect of a finished product.

Industrial Model: A three-dimensional element. More precisely, it is the shape of a product.

Innovation: The process by which new ideas or inventions are generated and converted into a new product, a new service or a new process that creates value. These new ideas must be economically feasible, applied by the firm and converted into a new offer in order to further satisfy a specific need of customers and for which customers will pay.

Invention: The conversion of new ideas into a new product, service or new process. To be considered as an invention, a new idea needs to be proven as workable.

Management: The process of administering, coordinating and controlling the activities of the organization in order to achieve defined objectives, irrespective of its nature, type, structure, and size.

Optimization: Finding an alternative way to achieve the highest performance or the most effective cost under the given constraints, by minimizing undesired factors and maximizing desired ones.

Patent: New inventions involving an inventive step and capable of industrial application. A patent aims to protect the functional and technical aspects of the product.

Strategy: Set of decisions or course of actions which assist the entrepreneurs in achieving specific business objectives efficiently and effectively.

Trademark: The trademark or service mark is a visible sign making it possible to distinguish the goods offered for sale or the services rendered by a natural or legal person.

ENDNOTES

1 Law No. 1994-36 of 24 February 1994 on literary and artistic property, JORT.1994, No. 17, p. 361.

2 Law No. 2000-84 of the Law on Patents for Inventions, JORT.2000, No. 68, p. 1983.

3 Law No. 2001-36 of 17 April 2001 on the protection of trademarks, JORT.2001, No. 31, p. 834.

4 Law No. 2001-21 of 6 February 2001 on the protection of industrial designs, JORT.2001, No. 12, p. 257.

5 Article 7 of Law No. 2018-52 of 29 October 2018 on the National Company Register, which replaced Law No. 95-44 of 2 May 1995 on the Commercial Register.

6 See in this regard concerning Tunisian law, in particular: Dahdouch, and Dahdouch, (2007); Mellouli and Frikha (2013) et Khrroubi (2016).

7 Last paragraph of article 97 of the CSC as amended by article 16 of law n°2007-69 of 27 December 2007.

8 According to Article 5, three criteria are used to define inventiveness: a) Tradesman: a skilled person, a specialist with an average qualification in his field; b) the state of the art and c) non-obviousness: the invention must not be obvious to the skilled person.

9 See in this regard, CFI.Sfax, Judgment No. 1519, 4/06:2002, unreported: "novelty is a condition for the acquisition of protection by industrial design law in accordance with Article 7 of the 2001 Law".

10 -Commission decision of 24 March 2004 confirmed by the decision of the Court of First Instance of the European Communities of 17 September 2007. - Decision of the European Commission of 27 February 2008. - Decision of the European Commission of 6 March 2013. These various decisions are published in the Official Journal of the European Union, see: eur-lex.europa.eu

11 In 2004, Microsoft was ordered to pay €500 million for abuse of a dominant position. In 2008, the European Commission increased the financial penalty against Microsoft to €860 million for not changing its anti-competitive practices despite its first conviction in 2004. In 2013, the Commission again fines Microsoft €561 million for using Internet Explorer, its browser, to the detriment

of its competitors. See in this respect: COMBIER (E), Abuse of a dominant position: the European Commission's largest fines, article published on 24 January 2014 on the website https://www.lesechos.fr/2018/01/abus-de-position-dominante-les-plus-grosses-amendes-de-la-commission-europeenne-982719

12 DALET (A-S), About the Microsoft case: monopolisation and abuse of a dominant position, article published on 16 April 2009 on this website: https://blogs.parisnanterre.fr/content/propos-de-l%E2%80%99affaire-microsoft-monopolisation-et-abus-de-position-dominante-par-anne-sophie-d

13 Auffray, Ch. (2019). Chiffres clés: les OS pour Smartphones, 15 juillet 2019, article publié sur le site: https://www.zdnet.fr/actualites/chiffres-cles-les-os-pour-smartphones-39790245.htm

14 On 17 July 2018, the European Commission imposed a record fine of €4.34 billion on Google for its abuse of a dominant position in the mobile manufacturers' market through its proprietary Android system. On 9 October 2018, Google chose to challenge this decision before the European Union Court: it is a new arms deal between the European Union and one of the GAFAMs in the regulation of the single market, or even this site: http://www.iredic.fr/2019/02/12/affaire-google-android-alphabet-refuse-de-ceder-devant-la-commission-europeenne/

15 Margrethe Vestager, Commissioner for Competition Policy, made the following statement: Today, mobile Internet represents more than half of the world's Internet traffic. It has changed the lives of millions of Europeans. This case involves three types of restrictions imposed by Google on Android device manufacturers and network operators to ensure that traffic on Android devices is directed to Google's search engine. In this way, Google uses Android as a vehicle to consolidate the dominant position of its search engine. These practices have deprived its competitors of the opportunity to innovate and compete on their merits. They have deprived European consumers of the benefits of effective competition in the important market for mobile devices. This practice is illegal under EU rules on anti-competitive practices", see the European Commission's Official Journal https://ec.europa.eu/commission/presscorner/detail/fr/IP_18_4581

APPENDIX 1: Laws consulted in the Official Journal of the Republic of Tunisia (JORT)

- Personal and corporate income tax code. - Law No. 2001-36 of 17 April 2001 on the protection of trademarks, JORT.2001, No. 31, p. 834. - Law n°2016-71 of 30 September 2016, on the investment law, JORT n°82 of 7 October 2016)
- The Commercial Companies Code
- The Commercial Code
- The Labour Code
- Law No. 1994-36 of 24 February 1994 on literary and artistic property, JORT.1994, No. 17, p. 361.
- Law No. 2000-84 of August 24, 2000, on patents for inventions, JORT.2000, No. 68, p. 1983.
- Law No. 2001-21 of 6 February 2001 on the Protection of Industrial Designs, JORT.2001, No. 12, p. 257.
- Law n°2009-69 of 12 July 2009 on distribution trade, JORT n° 65 of 14 August 2009, p.2349.
- Law n°2017-8 of 14 February 2017, recasting the tax benefits system, JORT n°15 of 21 February 2017.
- Law n°2018-52 of 29 October 2018 on the national business register, JORT n°89 of 6 November 2018.

APPENDIX 2: CASE LAWs

- Judgment of the Tunis Court of First Instance No. 39131 of 13 January 2005, RJL, February 2006, p. 129, in Arabic.
- Judgment of the Court of First Instance of Sfax, No. 1519, rendered on 4-06-2002, unpublished.
- Judgment of the Ariana Court of First Instance, delivered on 03/05/1993, unpublished.
- Judgment of the Tunis Court of Appeal n°13211, rendered on 02/03/1994, unpublished.
- Judgment of the Grombalia Court of First Instance, delivered on 30 May 2005, Fathi Annabi case, unpublished.
- Sfax Court of First Instance, judgment No. 2452, delivered on 1 June 2004, unpublished.

- Sfax Court of First Instance, judgment n°2122 delivered on 02/12/2003, unpublished.
- Judgment of the Tunisian Court of Cassation, No. 47075 of 9 July 2011, unpublished.
- Decision of the Monastir Court of Appeal, No. 6124 of 13 February 2017, unpublished.

These unpublished judgments are cited by Aouachria (2019).

Chapter 11
Traditional Knowledge and State Compliance:
A Case Study From New Zealand

Claudia Masoni
Independent Researcher, Italy

ABSTRACT

The chapter analyses Indigenous traditional knowledge and traditional ecologic knowledge in the context of international intellectual property instruments (IP). In so doing, the chapter studies the major international intellectual property law regimes such as the Agreement on Trade Related Aspects of Intellectual Property Rights and the Convention on Biological Diversity to prove that such instruments are ill suited to protect Indigenous peoples' knowledge and the biological resources in their custody. The New Zealand case Wai 262 shows in detail how international economic pressures often trump any aim to create national sui generis IP instruments to safeguard Indigenous knowledge.

INTRODUCTION

It is today widely known that the General Agreement on Tariffs and Trade's (GATT) negotiations did not formally include any discourse on Indigenous traditional knowledge (TK) and traditional cultural expressions (TCE). Consequently, Indigenous TK was not included in any debate that took place during the establishment of the World Trade Organisation (WTO) and the creation of the TRIPS Agreement (Trade-Related Aspects of Intellectual Property Rights) as multilateral treaty regulating trade and commerce among member states. As an international agreement, TRIPS was

DOI: 10.4018/978-1-7998-1835-9.ch011

mainly negotiated by developed countries at the expense of developing countries and particularly the least developed nations. Thus, back in the 1990s TRIPS reflected aggressive trade politics of developed countries led by the USA and European Union (EU) in partnership with key international business players (Drahos, 2004).

Today, after 20 years, TRIPS is considered by many as an international instrument that promotes asymmetric economic unfairness. In this scenario, developing countries and Indigenous peoples are currently seeking equality and fair treatment. This chapter will, therefore, analyse the logic of the TRIPS Agreement to illustrate how today it uncomfortably sits in a changed world. Since its creation, many things have substantially changed; the world scenario has changed and the logic that brought to the creation and wording of such an Agreement today fails to include and protect categories of rising interest and concern such as traditional knowledge and traditional ecologic knowledge (TEK). Additionally, today more than yesterday, developing as well as the least developed countries struggle to accept the advice of the USA and the EU on how TRIPS provisions should be interpreted and applied, in total disregard to Indigenous peoples' needs and expectations. The logic of commerce resides in trade harmonisation; but a harmonisation dictated by states with more economic and political power. Thus, today TRIPS fails to protect Indigenous TK and TEK and the discontentment of developing countries and least developing countries is increasingly influencing the general compliance with TRIPS. While there is consensus within WIPO (World Intellectual Property Organisation) and in the TRIPS Council to revise the Agreement to include those categories that were initially left out, such a revision seems currently unrealizable. This chapter analyses Aotearoa-New Zealand *Wai 262* as a case study. The issues presented by *Wai 262* are not only common to most of all Indigenous societies of the world, but the claim is clear and well presented, and the response of the Crown clearly shows how a state, instead of protecting the traditions of Indigenous peoples related to biodiversity and genetic resources, uses the TRIPS international treaty system as argumentation to justify the refutation to create national legislation (*sui generis* or not) which would effectively protect Indigenous TK and TEK.

Indigenous Traditional Knowledge and Traditional Ecologic Knowledge Within Trips and CBD

Economic exploitation of Indigenous TK and TEK has, over the years, called for a better protection of Indigenous tangible and intangible property. Today, all over the world Indigenous heritage is exploited at an unprecedented pace. In some cases, Indigenous knowledge, art and materials of spiritual significance are used without the knowledge or the permission of the group. This cultural heritage includes unique information, practices and knowledge (biological, medicinal and sacred) that often, once taken away from the community, lose its cultural relevance.

Over the past decades, biotechnology, pharmaceutical and human health care industries have raised their interests in natural traditional remedies as sources of new biochemical compounds for pharmaceutical drugs. New trends in health care have called for more nature-based remedies to cure illnesses, transforming the natural environment into a huge reservoir of remedies to be exploited. In so doing, TK and TEK have become leading sources of new product development (Mugabe, 1998).

In this scenario, it is fair to say that, in the last thirty years, developing countries and Indigenous peoples have contributed considerably to the global drugs industry. As original keepers of most of the ecologic knowledge of the world, Indigenous peoples have been exploited of their knowledge, and their cultures have been eroded (Mugabe, 1998).

Today, while Indigenous issues are globally well documented, the international fora still struggles to address the claims that have historically characterised Indigenous populations. Much of the problems depend on the lack of internationally accepted legal definitions, which clearly define the scope of the rights allocated to Indigenous peoples and holders of TK and TEK.

Not only is there no completely accepted existing definition of who Indigenous peoples are (Dutfield and Sutherland, 2018), but the international legal system currently struggles to define and address Indigenous heritage, culture, TK and TEK. In 2002 the report filed by experts at the World Intellectual Property Organisation (WIPO) considered the importance of having a clear definition of Indigenous TK and, under the pressure of developed countries, in its place, they restated a non omni-comprehensive list of what might constitute TK (WIPO, 2002). In so doing, WIPO failed to provide a clear and globally accepted international-level definition of TK. Again, in 2018 WIPO specified several categories of TK, including secret TK, sacred TK, narrowly diffused TK and widely diffused TK (WIPO, 2018). And yet, it failed to come up with a globally accepted definition. The consequences of this are comprehensible. The failure to come up with an international legal definition of TK slows down the advancement of the debate on the protection of Indigenous knowledge. When questioned about this, WIPO responded that while there is not a global consensus on a formal designation of TK, working concepts do exist. They may not be as precise as a scientific or restrictive legal definition, but they provide nonetheless the essential elements for the understanding of the nature and scope of TK as a legal subject matter (WIPO, 2002).

Indigenous Traditional Knowledge: A Problem of Definition

It is today widely accepted that Indigenous TK (in its narrower connotation) involves the study and usage of plants for medical and other useful properties Indigenous peoples have obtained from the biological diversity of their soils as well as the knowledge of combinations of plants having therapeutic properties for the community (Meyer, 2001).

In the 1990s Dutfield and Posey identified several types of TEK, including:

- Uses, preparation, processing and formulations of useful species/varieties;
- Planting methods, care, selection criteria, or storage of species;
- Ecosystem conservation and cultural landscapes (eg sacred sites)
- Biological resources that originate in Indigenous lands and territories; and
- Systems of knowledge classification such as traditional plant taxonomies (Posey and Dutfield, 1996).

Whereas, according to Martha Johnson, TK and TEK:

- is recorded and transmitted through oral tradition;
- is learned through observation and hands-on experience;
- is based on the understanding that the elements of matter have a life force. (All parts of the natural world are therefore infused with spirit);
- does not view human life as superior to other animate and inanimate elements: all life-forms have kinship and are interdependent;
- is holistic (whereas western science is reductionist) - and is intuitive in its mode of thinking (whereas western science is analytical);
- is mainly qualitative (whereas western science is mainly quantitative);
- is based on data generated by resource users. (As such it is more inclusive than western science, which is collected by a specialized group of researchers who tend to be more selective and deliberate in the accumulation of facts);
- is based on diachronic data (whereas western science is largely based on synchronic data);
- is rooted in a social context that sees the world in terms of social and spiritual relations between all life-forms. (In contrast, western science is hierarchically organized and vertically compartmentalized); and
- derives its explanations of environmental phenomena from cumulative, collective and often spiritual experiences. Such explanations are checked, validated, and revised daily and seasonally through the annual cycle of activities (Johnson, 1992).

Johnson clarifies that a great deal of TK and TEK is empirical and systematic, and can be correctly considered scientific. Maybe not scientific *stricto sensu* (as for the Western idea of science), but verifiable by observation or experience, and methodologically acquired by Indigenous peoples.

It is true that the term TK is notoriously problematic. According to Dutfield, in fact, TK is not static and it evolves in unexpected ways. Often the same knowledge is hybridized with associated knowledge that comes from other places. In other cases, it is impossible to fix in time and space such knowledge or ascertain with certainty that it is pure and unadulterated. Geography and history have proven that seeds, plants and know-hows tend to move and change; to be influenced by contacts with other cultures, or by sudden unexpected natural upheavals (Dutfield and Sutherland, 2018). As such, TK is part of the heritage of both Indigenous and local communities.

Much of the knowledge that Indigenous peoples claim today is the result of lengthy contact (forced or not) with other civilisations. And yet, though this is often the case, it is also true that most of the biodiversity richness of the world still belongs to developing countries inhabited by traditional peoples, Indigenous and local communities. These communities often live traditionally and respect the resources they use. Often alien to the concept of private intellectual property and economic exploitation, Indigenous peoples use the resources for the community. Since the use of the resource is local, most Indigenous communities are unaware of the privatization of natural community resources and associated knowledge.

On the other hand, conscious of the richness of their natural ecosystems, governments of developing countries in which Indigenous peoples live might give to the word 'community resources' an economic connotation that has nothing to do with any holistic Indigenous tradition while, at the same time, accepting and encouraging an exploitation of Indigenous resources that will not bring any benefit to the keepers of the knowledge. In this case the exploitation becomes both national and international. Biopiracy (Mooney, 2000), as a new form of Western imperialism, is expropriating Indigenous genetic resources and TK. Corporations and multinationals take TK and, using science, alter these 'discoveries' and patent them to 'resell the derived products or processes at exorbitant rates to the very people from whom they stole them in the first place' (Maskus, 2004). This *Biocolonialism* (another term related to biopiracy) is jeopardizing Indigenous traditional practices whilst stealing from them the economic profits gained from the patented knowledge (Curci, 2010). Therefore, since biotechnologies have become a significant component of the national wealth of developed countries, most of the resistance to create and implement regulations safeguarding indigenous TK is rooted in the 'economic profits' that TK generates (Mgbeoji, 2006). Dutfield stresses how, persistently, developing countries have been complaining that 'foreign corporations acquire resources and TK from their countries, use them in their research and development programs, and acquire patents and other Intellectual Property Rights (IPR) – all without compensating the provider countries and communities' (Dutfield, 2001). Much depends on the fact that TK and TEK are often considered (erroneously) to be in the public domain; in other cases, under a neo-colonialist spell, Indigenous knowledge is simply considered common heritage of humankind of which anyone can freely dispose. While this is not the proper avenue to give these issues the appropriate attention, it is important to stress that such assumptions have, over the years, greatly harmed Indigenous peoples and their cultures by privatising knowledge that was not supposed to enter the general market.

TK and TEK in the Modern World

While it is true that TK comprises complex, unfixed, stratified and orally transmitted information whose provenance and belonging is often uncertain, a good part of TK and TEK present characteristics and traditional boundaries that can be fixed in time and space and are sufficient for claims of exclusivity. The origins of these TK and TEK date back to traditions of specific communities, ethnic groups or nation states, that could be mapped with respect to more widespread available knowledge commonly referred as being in the 'public domain' (Dutfield and Sutherland, 2018). Traditionally, Indigenous societies and local communities are responsible for the discovery, development and preservation of a broad range of TK and TEK (medicinal plants, herbal formulations, agricultural and forest products) which, once traded outside its original setting, and traded internationally, may acquire considerable economic value (Dutfield, 2006). Hence, every Indigenous society manages its own resources in a way that is traditional to the laws of the community. And these laws can vary greatly from one community to another and much of it depends on the stratification and complexity of the specific Indigenous society concerned. While such resources are still used 'traditionally' within the Indigenous context, biological, genetic and related TK are used outside their natural setting, for the production of different profitable products. In this case, patents and breeder's rights conferring exclusive monopoly rights can be easily obtained on the resulting products. In most cases, the original holders of the knowledge do not receive any recognition or economic compensation for their contribution in maintaining and/or developing the knowledge (Posey and Dutfield, 1996).

TK and TEK In the International IP System

Today, the continuously rising economic value of Indigenous TK has magnified the exploitation of their TK and TEK. Copyrights, patents, trademarks and trade secrets have become keys to grant prosperity in an era where the control of any prototype is as profitable as its reproduction (Brown, 2005). Intellectual Property Rights protection systems, such as patents, are today considered unsuitable for the protection of TK because Indigenous knowledge generally does not satisfy the basic requirements of 'novelty' and 'inventiveness' demanded by patent law. Moreover, natural products in their embryonic form cannot be patented; under the 'Doctrine of Nature', they are of communal usage and cannot be the property of individuals, corporations or States (Nair, 2005). Additionally, IP rights are limited in time (20 years for patents and 50/70 years for copyright) and do not grant retroactive protection for knowledge that is of old lineage.

TRIPS and CBD

Realistically, within states (both developed and developing), the greatest threats to Indigenous knowledge come from the extension of government controls, unjust land policies, cultural modification policies and inappropriate conservation management. Internationally, the biggest threat is represented by bilateral and multilateral agreements like TRIPS, which have been ratified by biodiversity-rich developing countries and less biodiversity-rich developed countries (Swiderska, 2004). TRIPS is an international agreement between all the member states of the World Trade Organisation. It came into force in 1995 with the purpose being to establish *inter alia* for all WTO Member Countries a 'detailed set of substantive minimum standards governing the availability, scope and use of intellectual property rights'. It imposes high international minimum standards governing copyright, rights related to copyright law, patents, trademarks, geographical indications of origin, trade secrets, industrial designs, integrated circuits rights and unfair competition (Reichman, 2000). The international minimum standards of intellectual property protection set out in TRIPS determine the level of competition for knowledge goods that are sold or licensed on the global market. At the time of TRIPS' creation, no discourse on Indigenous TK had reached international status as an important issue to be dealt with both nationally and internationally. Built on the Paris and Berne Conventions, therefore, TRIPS does not contain any related clauses on TK and TEK (Goldstein, 2001).

Article 27.1 regulates patentable subject matter, where patents are available for any invention provided that they are new, involve an inventive step and are capable of industrial application; whereas Article 27.2 states that: 'Members may exclude from patentability inventions, the prevention within their territory of the commercial exploitation of which is necessary to protect *ordre public* or morality, including to protect human, animal or plant life or health or to avoid serious prejudice to the environment, provided that such exclusion is not made merely because the exploitation is prohibited by their law'. Though TRIPS does not define the notion of *ordre public* and morality, it appears clear that all the inventions which might cause harm to human, animal, plant life and the environment may be excluded. States are given flexibility to assess the level of harm or if there ever was any harm to human, animal and plant life. It implicates that inventions that cause harm to the above categories might actually be accepted. Additionally, under such provision, genetic-engineered organisms, life forms, TK and TEK (Mugabe, 1998), and modified genes or whole organisms which meet TRIPS requirements can be patented. Article 27.3 in fact narrows the scope of exclusion from patentability and suggests that states are free to provide additional national protection to plant varieties through patents and/or *sui generis* systems. In so doing, TRIPS allows national governments to exclude from patentability some invention involving plants, animals and biological processes, denying such a protection to micro-organisms, non-biological and microbiological processes. According to the UN Conference on Trade and Development's (UNCTAD) Report of 2014, 'it was at this time that developing countries argued for the need to re-examine the implications of allowing the so-called 'patenting of life', including examining the impact of patenting genes and other living organisms'. In fact, Article 27.3 underlines that plant varieties are eligible to only some form of protection (patent protection or *sui generis* provisions).

To counterbalance the many existing gaps within TRIPS, the Convention on Biological Diversity (CBD), which entered into force in 1993, represents the main legally binding instrument allowing Indigenous peoples and local communities to manifest their interest and demands for a better protection of their TK. According to Article 1, the main objectives of the Convention are the conservation of the world's 'biological diversity, the sustainable use of its components and the fair and equitable sharing of the benefits arising out of the utilization of genetic resources'. Articles 15.1, 15.4 and 15.5 of the CBD, establish the principles of fair and equitable sharing of benefits derived from the use of genetic resources, and provides that 'specific measures to facilitate benefit sharing have to be formulated at the national level.' Article 15 also recognises the sovereignty of States over their natural resources and their authority to determine access to genetic resources, which must be granted on mutually agreed terms and subject to prior informed consent of the provider party (Maskus, 2004) However, Article 15 recognises only States as sovereign of their national genetic resources and ignores the propriety rights of Indigenous peoples and local communities in the same territories while, at the same time, ignoring their right holders' status. And yet, Article 15 demonstrates that there is now broad international acceptance for the creation of national legislation for the protection of national genetic resources and the relationship of Indigenous peoples with such resources. The United Nations Declaration on the Rights of Indigenous Peoples (UNDRIP) not only recognises 'the right to maintain, control, protect and develop their intellectual property over such cultural heritage, traditional knowledge, and traditional cultural expressions' but it encourages States to 'take effective measures to recognize and protect the exercise of these rights' (Article 31). This means that the protection of Indigenous TK is not only a matter of IP law, but it is also a matter of human rights law.

Article 8(j) of the CBD is perhaps the most authoritative provision dealing with TK. Broad in scope, Article 8(j) nonetheless presents limitations which prevent it from being an effective instrument for the protection of Indigenous TK. The Convention, in fact, leaves open to States whether or not to protect TK, and to decide which kind of protection can be granted to Indigenous TK holders. The language 'as far as possible and as appropriate' was, for example, negotiated during the drafting process by those governments that did not intend to commit themselves to protect Indigenous peoples and their rights. Besides, Article 8(j) does not talk of 'protection' of TK, but its provision is limited to 'respect, preserve and maintain' TK. As such, CBD does not guarantee Indigenous peoples and local communities any right over their knowledge (Mugabe, 1998); but it rather guarantees minimum protection to TK, by putting in a central position the condition of 'prior informed consent' and 'equitable sharing of benefits' in the process of promoting the wider usage of genetic resources.

Article 8(j) stresses the importance 'to respect, preserve and maintain knowledge, innovations and practices of Indigenous and local communities embodying traditional lifestyles relevant for the conservation and sustainable use of biological diversity and promote their wider application with the approval and involvement of the holders of such knowledge, innovations and practices and encourage the equitable sharing of the benefits arising from the utilization of such knowledge, innovations and practices'. And yet, as seen above, the Article subjects such a provision to national legislation and the willingness of countries to provide such level of protection to Indigenous TK and guaranteeing the benefit sharing arising from the commercialisation of TK and TEK. Additionally, CBD does not provide any clear definition of 'Indigenous knowledge' 'local communities' knowledge' or 'innovations' and practices' leaving to states the task to define such categories as they wish.

The Convention was created with the precise intent to regulate access to genetic resources while guaranteeing the sharing of benefits of biotechnological research. However, this new protection of genetic information and knowledge is left to 'private or state contracts between bio prospecting firms and public authorities or private research entities', and the sharing of benefits is merely 'encouraged' (Cottier, 1998). In 2010, CBD member states adopted the Nagoya Protocol on Access to Genetic Resources and the Fair and Equitable Sharing of Benefits Arising from their Utilization to the Convention on Biological Diversity with the objective to encourage 'the fair and equitable sharing of benefits arising from the utilization of genetic resources, thereby contributing to the conservation and sustainable use of biodiversity'. Article 12(1) states that 'Parties shall in accordance with domestic law take into consideration indigenous and local communities' customary laws, community protocols and procedures, as applicable, with respect to traditional knowledge associated with genetic resources'. Although well written and fairly inclusive, as pointed out by Dutfield and Sutherland, the words 'take into consideration' seem to leave states too much flexibility for an effective engagement in the protection of Indigenous TK and TEK. Additionally, while the Protocol places 'customary laws' firmly at the center of national and global governance of TK and associated genetic resources, it does not provide 'well-defined and legally certain obligations onto corporations to observe customary law' (Dutfield and Sutherland, 2018).

Is a Revision of TRIPS Possible?

In recent years, the Conference of the Parties (COP) to the CBD and the World Intellectual Property Organisation (WIPO) and its Inter-Governmental Committee on Intellectual Property and Genetic Resources, Traditional Knowledge and Folklore have called for a revision of TRIPS that would take into account the CBD's objectives to protect the rights and knowledge of Indigenous and local communities. Many developing countries (Latin America, Caribbean Group and South Africa) have jointly submitted several proposals to the TRIPS Council calling for an amendment (WIPO, 2015). They asked that during the patents application process involving biological material and TK, disclosure of origin of the biological resources and TK used for the invention should be made mandatory; and should include evidence of prior informed consent being granted along with fair and equitable benefit-sharing under the national legislation of the country of origin (Swiderska, 2004).

Under such an amendment, TRIPS would require authorisation for access to genetic resources and benefit sharing within the borders of a WTO member state while, at the same time, ensuring prior informed consent (Laxman and Ansari, 2012). However, several developed countries, lead by the USA, replied that compulsory disclosure of origin is incompatible with TRIPS because it establishes a substantive condition (Dutfield, 2005; Maskus and Reichman (eds), 2006). Additionally, most of the developed countries considered TK as fundamentally and intrinsically inconsistent with the IPR system that supports private ownership of information. Intellectual property law, in fact, assigns exclusive rights to 'the use of information for economic gain in order to solve problems of appriopriability and to avoid market failure' (Cottier and Panizzon, 2006). TRIPS is also incompatible with TK because it promotes a time limited exclusive right to genetic resources and is supported by an IPR system that does not accommodate holistic practices and traditional ways of ownership (such as community rights and farmers' rights) (Laxman and Ansari, 2012). Strict state compliance with CBD gives countries the right to nationally control access to genetic resources, whereas enforcing access and benefit sharing would create a discriminatory precedent between those WTO member states which adhere to CBD and those which do not, in violation of the TRIPS' building principles of national treatment and most favoured nation treatment (Harper, 1997) according to which advantages accorded by a WTO member to the nationals of any other country must be accorded to the nationals of all WTO members. In this case, states could in theory be 'pursued for redress under the WTO dispute settlement mechanism' (Jungcurt, 2012). The threat of economic sanctions against the genetic resources supplier would therefore convince most states to give priority to TRIPS over CBD, even in those cases where it is more in their interest to implement the mechanisms of CBD instead.

From a political and economic perspective, it is natural and convenient for developed countries to consider TRIPS fundamentally incompatible with CBD and to justify it by the fact that the agreements deal with different subject matters and were created for different purposes (Jungcurt, 2012). Additionally they differ in the allocation of property rights in genetic resources. While CBD is based on general notions of equity and fair treatment, TRIPS is considered by many developing countries as the product of aggressive trade politics to the advantage of the USA in partnership with other developed countries (Drahos, 2004). This is why developing countries (especially Latin America, Asia and African states) are currently pushing for a revision of TRIPS to include fairer conditions for less developed countries, or a harmonisation between TRIPS and CBD. Some governments indeed believe that TRIPS and CBD are mutually compatible and a harmonisation on matters relating to the use of genetic resources and the protection of TK is not only essential but also feasible. However, Drahos points out that such harmonisation might never happen because certain states, like the USA and other leading developed countries, do not see any conflict between TRIPS and CBD, on the basis that the provisions of the two treaties are not 'generally related and where there is a relationship there is sufficient flexibility allowing states to fulfil their obligations under both' (Drahos, 2004). While this might be true, on the other hand, the economic pressures faced by developing countries remain strong. Born under a bargain narrative where TRIPS was considered a compromise between developed and developing countries, with the promise of technical assistance and foreign investments that never arrived, the Agreement required developing countries to strengthen IPR nationally (Yu, 2006). Considered the result of a coercive narrative, while TRIPS is today considered an unfair trade document that developed countries imposed on developing countries, it is incorrect to say that developing countries were not aware of the consequences that a strong IPR regime would bring upon them (Yu, 2006).

Developing Countries and TRIPS

Realistically, it is true that the current IPR system became universal only because it was pushed forward by powerful economic interests and 'imposed' upon developing countries, most of which, had a long history of subjection to colonial rule (Yu, 2006). However, the Agreement contains many ambiguities that provide member states 'wiggle room' and 'policy space' in choosing how to implement it (Yu, 2006). Article 27.2, for example, is vague enough to allow strategic interpretative confusion. Three bodies of international law (patent, trade and environment) merge into a single article without 'graceful' organisation (Harper, 1997). Additionally, the morality criterion expressed in the article is not clarified by TRIPS, thereby leaving states free to broaden the concept. The same happens for the word 'invention,' which remains undefined so is open to interpretation. Encouraged by this vagueness, the Andean Community, for example, has made a list of things that, for them, do not constitute 'invention'. The list contains: discoveries, scientific theories and mathematical methods; the entirety or part of living beings as encountered in nature, natural biological processes, biological material existing in nature or which may be isolated, including the genome or germ plasm of any natural living being. Other countries, like the USA, allow patents for genes and gene fragments. So, while Article 27 seems clear about what can and cannot be patented, in its last part (3(b)), it calls upon member States to grant protection for plant varieties either by patents or by the creation of an "effective *sui generis*" system. At present, no international consensus whatsoever exists on what a '*sui generis*' system needs to include and what should be excluded (Maskus, 2004). This leaves countries enough space and liberty to create or amend national laws, which do not protect Indigenous TK. What is necessary is the desire to do so. In fact, history has proven that while developing countries push for the elaboration of sustainable development and biodiversity friendly model laws, or the amendment and harmonisation of existing laws, on the other hand, they are not unfamiliar to the utilitarian logic that moves the world economy. They have often used the general IPR lack of TK protection to obtain concessions from developed countries (Dutfield, 2001). Thus, while developed countries were required to implement the TRIPS Agreement by 1996, developing countries, for example, managed to negotiate additional time (by 2000); or, under the Doha Declaration (2002), those developing countries that had not granted products patents for an area of technology could have the deadline extended to 2016 (India and Brazil for example) (Wong and Dutfield (eds), 2011). In addition to that, the authority to establish national *sui generis* legislation (TRIPS Article 27.3 (b)) could be created by developing countries and rich diverse biodiversity countries that wished to develop counter regime norms setting up maximum standards for national TK and TEK. The vagueness of TRIPS language and the presence of CBD as counterbalancing legal forces can work in favour of those nations – developing and less-developed ones – that need to be aligned with an economic liberalised and competitive economic environment. What is still lacking internationally could, therefore, be achieved nationally by creating *sui generis* legislation to protect national biodiversity, community resources, TK holders' rights, customary laws and Indigenous practices. In the end, it comes down to the will and capacity of countries to fill the gaps that the international legal system still possesses. And yet, many developed and developing countries have failed to protect TK, TEK and Indigenous people's interests within their own borders. Allured by financial gains in a ruthless global economy, many countries have used their compliance with international treaties as an excuse to refuse the creation of any national *sui generis* legislation. This has allowed national economic exploitation of TK, TEK and biodiversity resources, thereby strengthening the economic position of these states within the global economy. On this matter, Article 15 of the CBD justifies such national policies by 'recognizing the sovereign rights of States over their natural resources, the authority to determine access to genetic resources rests with the national governments and is subject to national legislation'.

In this complex scenario, the Aotearoa-New Zealand *WAI 262* case (which stands for *Waitangi Tribunal case no 262 – The Flora and Fauna and Cultural Intellectual Property Claim*) clearly shows how states can manipulate politics and economic agendas to deny intellectual property rights to Indigenous peoples. Although New Zealand is a developed country, and does not share many of the economic and political threats of developing countries, this case is emblematic in its own right. It clearly describes the negotiative struggles between government and Indigenous peoples and the economic considerations that, in most cases, win over other more reasonable moral and ethical considerations. It addition to that, *Wai 262* also represents one of the most complete and thorough studies of Indigenous knowledge associated to guardianship, culture, flora and fauna.

Wai 262

Wai 262 is a very important claim of extreme complexity brought by Māori against the New Zealand Crown before the Waitangi Tribunal (Williams, 2001). Not only has it been investigated for 20 years, leaving behind a huge quantity of literature, but the Final Report represented an all-encompassing study on Indigenous customs and traditions. Though *Wai 262* is generally known as the 'flora and fauna claim', its scope is significantly wider. It combines a wide range of elements, 'including traditional practices of Māori, spiritual values, and other aspects which are perhaps more recognizable as cultural features rather than intellectual property' (Sumpter, 2006). Essentially, the claimants argued that 'their rights to control, manage, and utilize Indigenous flora and fauna, and the genetic resources they contain, arise from Article 2 of the Treaty of Waitangi and … the Crown had an active duty to protect these interests and that the Crown has breached the Treaty by denying Māori proprietary interests in indigenous flora and fauna, including through some intellectual property laws and agreements'. The claim thus challenged the constitutional position of the Treaty of Waitangi, its historical significance and its legal authority. It challenged most of New Zealand environmental legislation developed since 1840 and the policies and practices of the Crown. Most importantly, it claimed Māori sovereignty over taonga species (native birds, plants and animals of special cultural significance and importance). Claimants also stressed that the kaitiaki relationship (guardianship) with taonga species should be recognized in the New Zealand IP system and should take priority over commercial interests. Such commercial interests should not be allowed without the approval of Māori kaitiaki (Kaitiakitanga means guardianship and protection. It is a way of managing the environment, based on the Māori worldview) (Waitangi Tribunal, 2011). Guardianship confers authority to Indigenous peoples. It implies custodianship of spiritual and traditional practices, which can be managed only after guardians' authorisation is sought and conferred. It does not confer proprietary rights as intended by the Western IP legal system, but it gives rights that depend on the kaitiaki responsibility to 'safeguard and protect the integrity of taonga across generations' (Waitangi Tribunal, 2011). Since kaitiakitanga (guardianship and conservation) does not confer Western proprietary rights, the New Zealand IP system is not focused on the kaitiaki obligation to safeguard and protect the integrity of mātauranga (knowledge, wisdom, understanding, skill) of taonga works and taonga species. Rather, according to the claimants, the focus of IP law is 'on facilitating commercial exploitation' (Waitangi Tribunal, 2011). Like many other Indigenous guardians around the world, Māori claimants stated that they should be considered as key players in commercial development of natural healing remedies and have a say in how and when such remedies could be used (Waitangi Tribunal, 2011). Basically the claimants contested:

- unauthorised use of mātauranga Māori in research based on bioprospecting, and the resulting unauthorised scientific or commercial use of genetic and biological resources of taonga species;
- offensive interference with whakapapa (genealogy) for taonga species when they are subjected to genetic modification; and
- use of IP regime to exploit rights in the genetic and biological resources of taonga species in ways that exclude kaitiaki and undermine the relationship between kaitiaki and taonga species (Waitangi Tribunal, 2011).

While the claimants focused on the need to protect and ensure the katiaki relationship with taonga (as an all-encompassing and special relationship), the

Crown seemed more focused on ensuring the protection of proper incentives for innovation and economic development as well as the assurance of New Zealand participation in world trade economy (Waitangi Tribunal, 2011). Regarding the 'special relationship' that kaitiaki have with taonga species, the Crown rejected any general claim that such an all-encompassing relationship could equal ownership of genetic resources, and reconfirmed that the New Zealand IP system protected Māori interests over natural and genetic resources 'sufficiently'. In so doing, the Crown made clear that it preferred instead a system that encouraged exploitation of New Zealand biodiversity, 'with the maximum sustainable access to biological resources and minimum compliance and transaction costs possible' (Waitangi Tribunal, 2011). Consequently the Crown asserted its opposition to the creation of a national *sui generis* system that would require the prior-informed consent of kaitiaki.

Aotearoa-New Zealand and TRIPS

While such a *sui generis* system would be in accordance with the TRIPS Agreement's high minimum standards, it would, nonetheless, 'unreasonably hamper innovation and economic development in the growing biotechnology field' (Waitangi Tribunal, 2011). Additionally, the Crown rejected a general claim to Māori ownership over taonga species or any other right over New Zealand genetic resources, including a general claim to IP rights. Again the Crown denied Māori rights to protect New Zealand national resources from any national and international negative effect on the research and innovation process that would ultimately affect national economy and economic standing in the international fora. On this subject, the claimants replied that New Zealand compliance with TRIPS would not justify a national refusal to provide effective mechanisms to protect Māori TK and TEK. Being signatories of the CBD Convention and its following instruments (Bonn Guidelines and Nagoya Protocol), New Zealand is aware that commercial research on genetic resources and TK should not be undertaken without the prior-informed consent of Māori people and TK holders. It follows that New Zealand should create legislation that would require participation of kaitiaki in those matters where mātauranga Māori is used for bioprospecting (Waitangi Tribunal, 2011). However, such right would be allowed where Indigenous peoples have 'relevant' rights over genetic resources under national laws. In other words, in those cases where national laws refuse to acknowledge Indigenous rights over TK and TEK, Indigenous peoples would effectively be denied participatory rights in national decisions over biological resources. After all, Article 15 of the CBD (which is today the most Indigenous-friendly international Instrument) clearly states that 'in recognizing the sovereign rights of States over their natural resources, the authority to determine access to genetic resources rests with the national governments and is subject to national legislation'. This is reconfirmed in Article 6 of the Nagoya Protocol which states that 'in accordance with domestic law, each Party shall take measures, as appropriate, with the aim of ensuring that the prior informed consent or approval and involvement of indigenous and local communities is obtained for access to genetic resources where they have the established right to grant access to such resources'. In addition to that, as seen above, in matters regarding genetic resources, the IP high minimum standards set out in the TRIPS Agreement will always take priority over any discourse on access-benefit sharing and prior-informed consent, unless it is widely proven that those standards can cause serious damage or threat to the biological diversity of a member country. Given that benefit-sharing and prior-informed consent are currently unenforceable, there is nothing in TRIPS that requires patent applicants to disclose in their application whether TK or genetic resources have contributed to the invention. True, as seen above, at the international level EU and developing countries such as Brazil and India have sent out proposals to include within TRIPS a mandatory requirement for the 'disclosure of the country providing/source of genetic resources and/or associated traditional knowledge for which a definition will be agreed in patent application', but no modification of TRIPS is currently underway.

Wai 262 and National IP Revision

During the hearings, the claimants often stressed that the kaitiaki relationship, being all-encompassing, amounts to ownership of the genetic resources of a given specie. As such, the protection of such a relationship should be included within national legislation. In addition to that, and in respect of TRIPS Article 27.2 on morality and *ordre public*, national legislation should be amended or created to exclude or modify patentability in those cases where national beliefs and values are contrary to national standards of morality. In this regard, the Waitangi Tribunal recommended a revision of the national IP to include formal measures to protect kaitiaki relationship and the creation of a new Patent Act which would provide for the establishment of a Māori Advisory Committee to advise the Commissioner of Patents on 'whether an invention seeking patent protection is derived from Māori traditional knowledge or from Indigenous plants or animals, and whether commercial exploitation of the invention is likely to be contrary to Māori values' (Waitangi Tribunal, 2011). On this matter the Crown stated that, while it is possible to recognise the kaitiaki relationships with taonga species, however, there is no justification for recognising any direct right of kaitiaki over the resources. In other words, Māori 'might have created the knowledge, but they did not create the species' (Waitangi Tribunal, 2011). The Crown recognised the importance to recognise the role played by kaitiaki in protecting taonga species and their biological and genetic material and that such a relationship needed a 'reasonable degree of protection' (Waitangi Tribunal, 2011).

Thus, the Crown was forced to admit that the national and international IP systems were never designed to accommodate Indigenous issues over their TK and TEK and is ill suited to such a task. It followed that, in 2013, under section 225 of the Patents Act the Commissioner of Patents appointed Members of the Patents Māori Advisory Committee (Patents MAC). In so doing, the Crown seemed to implement the Waitangi Tribunal recommendations that specifically requested the creation of such a Committee. However, the Committee 'can only act on the Commissioner's request'. In other words, it cannot act independently. Additionally, while it can advise the Commissioner of Patents whether an invention is derived from Māori TK, Indigenous plants and animals, or if it is contrary to Māori values, it cannot stop patents to be allocated.

While the new Patent Act reconfirms TRIPS morality and *order public* requirements and stresses that the Commissioner is able to refuse patents that are contrary to *ordre public,* it can give an arbitrary interpretation to what *ordre public* is without requesting the intervention of the MAC. Whereas, under the old Patents Act (1953), the ground of rejection was limited to those cases in which the use of the invention was contrary to morality.

The Waitangi Tribunal considered that issues relating to Māori relationship with *taonga* species could be considered more of an issue of social policy as opposed to morality *per se* and thus suggested that *ordre public* should instead become a ground to reject the grant of a patent. And yet, while the refusal on such grounds is possible, it is limited to 'where the commercial exploitation of the invention is contrary to *ordre public*. This does not cover the situation where the patenting itself is the act which would be offensive to Māori' (Henry Hughes).

The Tribunal also recommended the creation of a disclosure requirement under which 'patent applicants be required to disclose whether any matauranga Maori or taonga species have contributed to the research of the invention'; and yet there is nothing in the new Patent Act that suggests that such a requirement was introduced (Henry Hughes). The same happened to the Plant Varieties Act. The Tribunal recommended an amendment of the Act to include the kaitiaki relationship, but no significant amendments were ever made. This seems to suggest that, while the Crown was somehow forced to accept Māori claims over taonga species and genetic resources as legislative challenges that needed to be dealt with, on the other hand, it preferred to limit Māori and kaitiaki rights over taonga species and TK significantly, under the justification that such *sui generis* rights, would compromise New Zealand economic participation in the global economic market and would prevent foreigners from investing in a country that puts so many obstacles to national economic development. By limiting or undermining Māori participation in the research and development associated with national biologic resources, not only would New Zealand's international economic participation be non affected, but national and international investors in genetic resources would not be discouraged in investing in a country that would otherwise leave too much decision-making space to its Indigenous population. In the end, the fear of future international pressures won over any national *sui generis* consideration.

Solutions and Recommendations

From a close look at *Wai 262*, it becomes clear that international instruments, moved by a positivist approach, left states legislative space for the creation of *sui generis* laws that could integrate and complete the regulations set out by international agreements. The logic of this is straightforward: only states are in the best position to know what they need nationally and can draft laws that are comprehensive and reflective of the internal needs and expectations of Indigenous peoples and local communities. However, *Wai 262* and state practice also proved that such a positivist consideration for state sovereignty has not produced the expected results. Until now, most of existing national *sui generis* regimes ‘have tended to focus on commercial and benefit-sharing objectives’ while drawing ‘on existing IPR concepts, rather than fully reflecting Indigenous peoples’ needs and aspirations’ (Swiderska, 2004). Additionally, many developed and less-developed countries have not yet taken any positive steps to implement effective laws incorporating protection for Indigenous peoples’ rights and/or customary laws. In those cases when, like in New Zealand, governments ‘seem’ to have created *sui generis* legislation inclusive of prior-informed consent and access and benefit-sharing, those provisions do not always address Indigenous claims in ways reflective of the ‘collective’ ownership of TK and TEK that might instead require collective decision-making by communities or by an Indigenous group as a whole entity (Swiderska, 2004).

Like a dog who bites its tail, states blame international laws for limiting their national legislative freedom, and international instruments blame countries for failing in the creation of laws for the protection of Indigenous TK and biological resources. In this scenario, proposals for the amendment and/or harmonisation of TRIPS and CBD seem currently to be one possible solution, but not the best one. Winning over the USA and multinationals’ resistance to amending TRIPS to include a mandatory disclosure of origin requirement would resolve part of the problem. IPRs, when conferred, grant time-limited rights over knowledge. Indigenous peoples might instead require the allocation of perpetual rights over TK and biological resources. To do this, capitalistic monopolies need to shift from a utilitarian logic that does not question who makes the goods, or whether the goods are fairly and equitably distributed to one concentrating upon who needs the goods and who benefits from their distribution. The global economy needs a more equitable regime and the very notion of development should be holistic and comprehensive of all the different realities of the world.

How to Solve the Problem: Possible Scenarios

Over the years, several developing countries' delegations have repeatedly brought forward proposals for an international legally binding *sui generis* regime to protect Indigenous TK and to prevent unfair exploitation both nationally and in user countries. To do this, countries could agree on the establishment of common standards for the protection of TK and TEK; such norms or legal frameworks could be used to monitor the international use of TK and provide working global definitions of TK. Bonding under agreed norms, developing countries could create a regional mapping of TK while, at the same time, convincing reluctant developed countries to join. A regional framework would probably succeed in creating enough pressure on developed countries to convince them that a revision of national laws is necessary and, at the same time, might make them more enthusiastic about an international harmonisation (Swiderska, 2004). Any legal regime at a national and international level should guarantee the full participation of Indigenous communities or TK holders in all the policy and legal practices involving Indigenous TK and TEK and should ensure that their participation is not merely advisory. Drahos agrees that an international regime 'of some kind' is today desired and necessary. He agrees that a framework treaty that contains some general principles is advisable. It would provide guidelines, codes of conduct and protocols that, over time, could evolve into something more concrete. Such a treaty would offer member states the means of cooperation and coordination on the enforcement of TK and would coordinate the creation of an international enforcement pyramid. By concentrating on coordinating and enforcing existing norms, the treaty would harmonise the international legal system on TK and genetic resources. The interaction of national standards among member states would be based on reciprocity, national treatment, most-favoured nation status and mutual recognition (Drahos, 2004). It would also include best practice declaration requirements for those patents based on TK and include best practice guidelines for the declaration of the origin of genetic resources and the use of TK (Drahos, 2004). A Global Bio Collective Society acting as an international agency could control that Treaty provisions are internationally respected, and could provide advisory information for the implementation of such norms nationally (Drahos, 2004).

It is true that a single all-encompassing *sui generis* system for the protection of TK may be too specific and not flexible enough to accommodate local needs. It is also true that allocating exclusive rights to Indigenous peoples is today unfeasible and would certainly be resisted by most of the countries. However, it is also true that the system that was conceived in the 1990s, today is mostly unsuitable. Indigenous issues are now global and national legislation must include, in one way or another, Indigenous rights. The protection of genetic resources and TK cannot be dealt with at the point of commercialisation, but it must instead be regulated at the point of access.

Pre-existing International Regulations for the Protection of Indigenous Peoples

While today in many parts of the world Indigenous peoples are the victims of national governments, new conditions for an harmonious and cooperative relationship between Indigenous groups and governments should be requested, protected and guaranteed. There is no need for the creation of brand new laws. Indigenous issues have been circulating for a long time. Today, Article 31 of the UNDRIP clearly states that the protection of Indigenous 'cultural heritage, traditional knowledge and traditional cultural expressions, as well as the manifestations of their sciences, technologies and cultures, including human and genetic resources, seeds, medicines, knowledge of the properties of fauna and flora, oral traditions…' is not only a human right but also an intellectual property one. Thus, Indigenous peoples have the right to maintain, control, protect and develop their intellectual property over such cultural heritage, traditional knowledge, and traditional cultural expressions. The Article also states that, in conjunction with Indigenous peoples, States shall take effective measures to recognize and protect the exercise of these rights. True, the Declaration remains vague on what 'effective measures' might be, and yet it represents an important working instrument that reflects most of international customary laws and state practice on Indigenous peoples. Additionally, Article 29 and Articles 1(1)(b), 2(2) and 13(1) of the ILO Convention No. 169 directly refer to Indigenous peoples, while reconfirming that Indigenous peoples have the right to be granted 'special measures' to control, develop and protect their culture, values and traditional practices. Again, the Convention is silent on which 'special measures' can be effectively and successfully used.

Agenda 21 was adopted at the United Nations Conference on Environment and Development in Rio (also known as the 'Earth Summit') as the programme of action for environment and development (Meyer, 2001). Although the Agenda has no legally binding capacity, it sets goals, activities and models for implementation considered vital for the preservation and achievement of sustainable development (Meyer, 2001). Both Indigenous communities and local farmers are specifically mentioned in Chapter 26 of the Agenda as holders of important information for the preservation of the world ecosystems. Some of the provisions of the Agenda refer to other international instruments that share the same concerns and goals for the protection of Indigenous knowledge. Chapter 26(2) refers to those goals as already contained in such international legal instruments as ILO 169, which have most recently been incorporated into the UNDRIP. Likewise, apart from the Rio Declaration, some interest in Indigenous TK is formally expressed in the 'Forest Principles' (Principle 12(d)) and in the UN Convention to Combat Desertification (Article 16(g)). Both recognise the importance to protect TK and to grant recognition to Indigenous intellectual property. While both instruments are, like Agenda 21, not binding on member States, they show a rising global consensus on the importance of protecting Indigenous TK.

Possible Solutions

On a general note, solutions for the protection of Indigenous TK and TEK could include *inter alia*:

- the creation and development of a legal framework on intellectual collective rights to TK;
- the creation of an international system of TK certification to be used by Indigenous peoples to market their products;
- the establishment of a system that facilitates the procedures of registration of TK and also provides economic assistance;
- the development of a contractual structure for any use of TK and TEK;
- the creation of an information system on how TK can be managed for the safeguarding of biodiversity and sustainable development;
- the active participation of Indigenous representatives to the implementation of Article 8(j);
- the right to veto when the acquisition and use of TK may have a negative impact on the life of the community;
- the acknowledgement of Indigenous customary laws and traditional practices;
- the promotion of social justice and equity; and
- the recognition and reinforcement of customary laws and practices and traditional resources management system with proven efficacy in protecting biodiversity (Drahos, 2004).

CONCLUSION

In considering the protection of Indigenous knowledge, in theory all branches of intellectual property law can play a part, as long as the applicable criteria of intellectual property regulations are met. So far, IPR has failed effectively to protect Indigenous TK and TEK. Rights conferred by IP are, in fact, limited. Patents and Copyrights, for example, have finite term protection; once expired, the knowledge enters the public domain, where it can be freely used by anyone even if it is secret or sacred.

Traditionally, Indigenous peoples share a communal view of property, and they generally support collective efforts (Long and D'Amato, 2000). Indigenous communities are structured around complex kingship systems, with different responsibilities and rights assigned to different members of the tribe (Roy, 2009). Community customary laws govern the permissions to use TK and genetic resources. While TK can be used for commercial purposes, this is only after extensive consultations among the keepers of such knowledge have been carried out and they consent (Roy, 2009).

This rich Indigenous knowledge system is today getting increasing attention from the non-Indigenous world. Environmentalists and researchers praise Indigenous knowledge as a model of harmony with nature, human ecology and sustainable development. Indeed, Indigenous knowledge is the result of centuries of interaction with nature and its resources; as such it represents not only a potential source of income, but also a valuable cultural heritage and a tool for survival that needs to be respected and safeguarded. Most recently, biotechnology, pharmaceutical and human health care industries have increasingly grown in interest in natural products and the research of new possible compounds for drugs, chemical and agro-products development (Mugabe, 1998). Consequently, TK has acquired a commercial value it did not possess before, and the risk of misappropriation, exploitation and biopiracy has grown accordingly. Since most of indigenous TK is in the form of unwritten information preserved within oral traditions, once exploited it becomes difficult, if not impossible, to ascertain the initial ownership of the knowledge and to give Indigenous communities a fair share of the economic value of the remedy sold in the market (Mugabe, 1998). If that was not enough, the loss of indigenous biodiversity, can lead indigenous communities to lose the knowledge of this diversity, thereby degrading their ability to preserve the diversity and resulting in the destruction of their holistic ways of life and cultural unity (Meyer, 2001). In this scenario, IPR is today considered unfit to accommodate Indigenous rights. Since its creation, IPR's main function has been to play as an instrument 'fashioned through a particular kind of colonial politics that facilitated the historical exclusion of indigenous interests from broader policy developments in this field to start with' (Anderson, 2009). Therefore, though recent decades have questioned extensively the meaning of Indigenous TK and how it could be effectively protected, at present it proves close to impossible to use the Western legal intellectual property framework to guarantee any effective protection of Indigenous knowledge (Riley, 2004). Given the obviously diverse understandings of nature and knowledge and the economic profit gained from its exploitation, IPR has suspiciously tried to stay away from Indigenous peoples' TK and holism for as long as possible, while always disagreeing on the creation of *sui generis* legislation for ensuring the protection of Indigenous knowledge. Consequently, and irrespective of Indigenous peoples and developing countries' influence over international legal instruments today, if a state decides to exploit the TK of an Indigenous community, there is no global legal agreement that can prevent it from happening. In light of this, a reform of current IPR regimes becomes essential. The more this issue is highlighted and discussed in the international arena and in academia, the more states and international organizations will feel under pressure to create new laws and enforceable mechanisms for protecting TK.

To this end, the chapter has tried to shed light on the legal obstacles that today undermine any effective protection of Indigenous TK. It has presented proposals, provisions and solutions that are currently being discussed to address the 'issue' nationally and globally. Legal policies and existing legal provisions have been investigated from a legal and ethical/moral perspective, in the attempt to prove that most of the failures in safeguarding TK are imputable to a deeply rooted and widely spread states' resistance to protect Indigenous TK effectively. So far, international organizations, such as WIPO and UNESCO, have tried to accommodate TK holders' rights within the existing IPR systems. Discussions have been taking place within the TRIPS Council and the CBD-COP for an amendment of TRIPS and/or an harmonisation of TRIPS with CBD's provisions. Such attempts have so far been unsuccessful. As seen above, while international law guarantees state sovereignity over natural resources and TK, in so doing, it often encourages unethical, exploitative state practice. On the other hand, those countries that want to protect Indigenous TK, often get stuck in the procedural unfairness of international IPR instruments. By trumping developed countries' resistance, an international regulatory system harmonious of existing laws protecting Indigenous TK is today necessary and advisable. Today more than ever, any asymmetric economic and political power needs to be rebalanced and a more holistic approach to development needs to be, not only considered, but encouraged.

REFERENCES

Andean Community. (n.d.). *Decision No. 486 Establishing the Common Industrial Property Regime*. Retrieved from https://wipolex.wipo.int/en/text/223718

Brown, M. F. (2005). Heritage Trouble: Recent Work on the Protection of Intangible Cultural Property. *International Journal of Cultural Property*, *12*(01), 40–61. doi:10.1017/S0940739105050010

Cottier, T. (1998). The Protection of Genetic Resources and Traditional Knowledge: Towards More Specific Rights and Obligations in World Trade Law. *Journal of International Economic Law*, *1*(4), 555–584. doi:10.1093/jiel/1.4.555

Cottier, T., & Panizzon, M. (2006). Legal Perspectives on Traditional Knowledge: the Case for Intellectual Property Protection. In International Public Goods and Transfer of Technology Under a Globalized Intellectual Property Regime. Cambridge: Cambridge University Press.

Curci, J. (2010). *The Protection of Biodiversity and Traditional Knowledge in International Law of Intellectual Property*. Cambridge: Cambridge University Press.

Drahos, P. (2004). Towards an International Framework for the protection of Traditional Group Knowledge and Practice. In *UNCTAD-Commonwealth Secretariat Workshop on Elements of National Sui Generis Systems for the Preservation, Protection and Promotion of Traditional Knowledge, Innovations and Practices and Options for an International Framework*. UNCTAD.

Dutfield, G. (2001). TRIPS-Related Aspects of Traditional Knowledge. *Case Western Reserve Journal of International Law*, *2*(33), 233–275.

Dutfield, G. (2006). Legal and Economic Aspects of Traditional Knowledge. In International Public Goods and Transfer of Technology Under a Globalized Intellectual Property Regime. Cambridge: Cambridge University Press.

Dutfield, G., & Sutherland, U. (2018). *Traditional Knowledge and Genetic Resources: Observing Legal Protection Through the Lens of Historical Geography and Human Rights*. Queen Mary University of London. Legal Studies Research Paper No. 286/2018.

Goldstein, P. (2001). *International Intellectual Property Law*. New York: Foundation Press.

Harper, M. B. (1997). TRIPS Article 27.2: An Argument for Caution. *William and Mary Environmental Law and Policy Review*, *21*, 381. Retrieved from https://scholarship.law.wm.edu/wmelpr/vol21/iss2/4

Henry Hughes Intellectual Property Australia and New Zealand. (n.d.). Retrieved from www.henryhughes.com/site/news/wai-262-patents-and-plant-variety-rights- revisted.aspx?fbclid=IwAR0xjqkXpA9et3XWozgvp7jzvETB8ZzHQZZTVL6bdp7Q13wsbQAtCj8hWBY

Johnson, M. (1992). Research on Traditional Environmental Knowledge: Its Development and Its Role. In *Lore: Capturing Traditional Environmental Knowledge*. International Development Research Centre.

Jungcurt, S. (2012). *Institutional Interplay in Regime Complex on Plant Genetic Resources Conflict and Learning*. Academic Press.

Law Library of Congress. (2010). New Zealand – Maori Culture and Intellectual Property Law. Global Legal Research Center.

Laxman, L., & Ansari, A. H. (2012). The Interface Between TRIPS and CBD: Efforts Towards Harmonisation. *Journal of International Trade Law & Policy, 11*(2), 108–132. doi:10.1108/14770021211239640

Leaflet, No. 12: WIPO and Indigenous Peoples. (n.d.). Retrieved from https://www.ohchr.org/Documents/Publications/GuideIPleaflet12en.pdf

Long, D. E., & D'Amato, A. (2000). *A Coursebook in International Intellectual Property*. St. Paul: West Group.

Maskus, K. E. (Ed.). (2004). *The WTO, Intellectual Property Rights and the Knowledge Economy*. Cheltenham: Edward Elgar Publishing.

Matauranga Maori and Taonga. (n.d.). Wellington: Waitangi Tribunal Publications.

Meyer, A. (2001). International Environmental Law and Human Rights: Toward an Explicit Recognition of Traditional Knowledge. *Review of European Community & International Environmental Law, 10*(1), 37–46. doi:10.1111/1467-9388.00259

Mgbeoji, I. (2006). *Global Biopiracy*. Vancouver: UBC Press.

Mooney, P. R. (2000). Why We Call it Biopiracy. In Responding to Bioprospecting: From Biodiversity in the South to Medicines in the North. Spartacus.

Mugabe, J. (n.d.). *Intellectual Property Protection and Traditional Knowledge*. Retrieved from https://www.wipo.int/edocs/pubdocs/en/intproperty/762/wipo_pub_762.pdf#page=104

Nair, M. D. (2005). Traditional Medicines and Medical Plants, and their Protection Modalities from an Intellectual Property Perspective. *Plant Genetic Resources, 3*(2), 314–319. doi:10.1079/PGR200580

Posey, D., & Dutfield, G. (1996). *Beyond Intellectual Property Rights: Toward Traditional Resource Rights for Indigenous Peoples and Local Communities*. Ottawa: IDRC.

Reichman, J. H. (2000). The TRIPS Agreement Comes of Age: Conflict or Cooperation With the Developing Countries? *Case Western Reserve Journal of International Law*, 32.

Riley, M. (Ed.). (2004). *Indigenous Intellectual Property Rights*. Walnut Creek: Altamira Press.

Roy, A. (2009). Recent Developments in Law Reform and Indigenous Cultural and Intellectual Property in Australia. *European Intellectual Property Review*, *31*(1).

Sumpter, P. (2006). *Intellectual Property Law: Principles and Practices*. New Zealand: CCH.

Swiderska, K. (2004). *Traditional Knowledge protection and Customary Law: Policy Issues and Challenges*. Background Paper prepared (IIED) for the Planning Workshop on Protecting community rights over traditional knowledge: Implications of customary laws and practices. Retrieved from https://pubs.iied.org/pdfs/G01252.pdf

TeAra Encyclopedia of New Zealand. (n.d.). Retrieved from https://teara.govt.nz/en/kaitiakitanga-guardianship-and-conservation/page-1

The Nagoya Protocol on Access and Benefit-Sharing. (n.d.). Retrieved from www.cbd.int/abs/about/default.shtml

UNCTAD. (2014). The Convention on Biological Diversity and the Nagoya Protocol: Intellectual Property Implications. The International Framework for Access and Benefit Sharing. UNCTAD.

Waitangi Tribunal. (2011). *Ko Aotearoa Tēnei: A Report into Claims Concerning New Zealand Law and Policy Affecting Māori Culture and Identity*. Retrieved from https://forms.justice.govt.nz/search/Documents/WT/wt_DOC_ 68356054/KoAotearoaTeneiTT1W.pdf

WIPO Model Law Needs Revision. (2015). *Developing Countries Say; Developed Countries Reluctant*. Retrieved from https://www.ip-watch.org/2015/07/30/wipo-model-law-needs-revision-developing-countries-say-developed-countries-reluctant/

Wong, T., & Dutfield, G. (Eds.). (2011). *Intellectual Property and Human Development*. Cambridge: Cambridge University Press.

Yu, P. K. (2006). TRIPS and Its Discontents. *Journal of Intellectual Property Law Review*, 369.

Compilation of References

Abraham & Afreen. (2008). Bioprospecting: Promoting and Regulating Access to Genetic Resources and Benefit Sharing. *Indian Institute of Management Calcutta*. Retrieved from https://www.iimcal.ac.in/sites/all/files/pdfs/wps-631_1.pdf

Abraxis Bioscience LLC v. Union of India and Ors. M.P.NO.57/2010 IN OA/3/2010/PT/DEL; OA/3/2010/PT/DEL.

Aggarwal, A. (2006). Strategic Approach to Strengthening the International Competitiveness in Knowledge Based Industries: The Indian. *Die Pharmazeutische Industrie*.

Ahuja, V. K. (2009). *Intellectual Property Rights in India*. LexisNexis Butterworths Wadhwa Nagpur.

Ajanta Pharma v. Allergan Inc. and Controller of Patents and Designs, Order No. 172 of 2013.

Alberta (Education) v. Canadian Copyright Licensing Agency (Access Copyright), 2012 SCC 37

Albert, K. M. (2006). Open access: Implications for scholarly publishing and medical libraries. *Journal of the Medical Library Association: JMLA*, *94*(3), 253. PMID:16888657

Aliouat, B. (2010). Les stratégies de propriété intellectuelle et leur ingénierie juridique: Une nouvelle approche managériale du droit fondée sur le recours à la ruse. *Revue des Sciences de Gestion*, 21-23.

Aliouat, B., & Roquilly, Ch. (1996). L'ingénierie juridique, Les dix outils clés du management. édition du GO, Presses du management.

Amann, B., & Lethielleux, L. (2005). *Le droit, outil de gestion*. Pearson Education.

American Arbitration Association, Patent Arbitration Rules, revised rules and fees for cases filed on or after May 1, 1992 4 (1992).

American Arbitration Association. (2006). *Resolution of Patent Disputes Supplementary Rules*. Retrieved from http://www.adr.org/sp.asp?id=27417

American Geophysical Union v. Texaco Inc., 60 F.3d 913 (2nd Cir. 1994).

Anand, M. R. (1984). Madhubani Paintings. New Delhi: Publications Division, Ministry of Information and Broadcasting, Govt. of India.

Andean Community. (n.d.). *Decision No. 486 Establishing the Common Industrial Property Regime*. Retrieved from https://wipolex.wipo.int/en/text/223718

Anderson, J. (2012). On Resolution, Intellectual Property and Indigenous Knowledge Disputes Prologue. *Landscapes of Violence*, *2*(1), 1–14.

Anja, C., & Morten, W. (2015). *The UPOV Convention, Farmers Rights and Human Rights, an integrated assessment of potentially conflicting legal framework*. Deutsche Gesellschaft fur Internationale Zusammenarbeit (GIZ).

Aouachria, F. (2019). *La protection des dessins et modèles industriel en droit tunisien, mélange en l'honneur de Nabila MAZGHANI*. Maison du livre.

Archer, M. (1977). *Indian Popular Painting in the India Office Library*. London: H. M. Stationery Office.

Archer, W. G. (1949). Maithil Painting. *Marg*, *3*(3), 32.

Argumedo, A., & Pimbert, M. (2006). *Protecting indigenous knowledge against biopiracy in the Andes*. IIED.

Arnold, T. & Schuruman, G. W. (1991). *Alternative Dispute Resolution in Intellectual Property Cases*. Academic Press.

Arnold, T. (1993). Fundamentals of Alternative Dispute Resolution: Why Prefer ADR in Patent Litigation. *Practising L. Inst: Patents, Copyrights, Trademarks, and Literary Property Course Handbook*, 655-657.

Article 20, International Chamber of Commerce Rules of Arbitration, 1998.

Article 22, International Dispute Resolution Procedures, 2008.

Article 24(3), UNCITRAL Arbitration Rules as revised in 2010.

Article 27, UNCITRAL Model Law on International Commercial Arbitration, 2006.

Article 3.4-5, 9.4, IBA Rules on the Taking of Evidence in International Commercial Arbitration, 1999.

Article 50(b), WIPO Arbitration Rules.

Article 65, WIPO Arbitration Rules, 2014

Article 9 (4), IBA Rules on the Taking of Evidence in International Commercial Arbitration, 1999.

Article V(1)(b) New York Convention, 1958.

Australian Government: Australian Research Council-Open Access Policy. (n.d.). Retrieved from https://www.arc.gov.au/pdf/Open_Access/ARC_Open_Access_Policy_Version_2015.1.pdf

Authors Guild, Inc. v. Hathi Trust, 755 F.3d 87 (2d Cir. 2014).

Ayyangar, N. R. (1959). *Report on the Revision of the Patents Law*. Manager of Publications.

Azema, J., & Galloux, J.-C. (2012). *Droit de la propriété industrielle*. Dalloz.

Baccouche, N. (2009). Environnement fiscal de l'entreprise en Tunisie. 24ème édition des journées de l'entreprise. Institut Arabe des Chefs d'Entreprises.

Bagley, C. E. (2008, July 17). Look for the silver lining. Piracy is a bad thing. But sometimes companies can turn it to their advantage. *The Economist*.

Baker, H. W. (2009). Arbitrating Patent Infringement Disputes. *Convergence*, *5*(90), 93.

Balasubramanian, S. (2017). *India: Traditional Knowledge And Patent Issues: An Overview Of Turmeric, Basmati, Neem Case*. Retrieved on 13/10/2019 from http://www. mondaq. com/india/ x/ 586384/Patent

Balmer, L. N. (1995). Alternative Dispute Resolution in Patent Controversies. *Risk (Concord, NH)*, *6*(145), 1–52.

Bandhua Mukti Morcha v. Union of India, (1984) 2 S.C.R, 67.

Barney, J. B. (1991). Firm resources and sustained competitive advantage. *Journal of Management*, *17*(1), 99–120. doi:10.1177/014920639101700108

Barney, J. B. (2001). Resource-based theories of competitive advantage: A ten year retrospective on the resource-based view. *Journal of Management*, *27*(6), 643–650. doi:10.1177/014920630102700602

Barthelemy, J. (1993). *L'ingénierie juridique: un concept, Cahiers de droit de l'entreprise*. JCP.

Basheer, S. (2017). *A Fair Education in a Copyright World?* Retrieved from https://spicyip. com/2012/09/a-fair-education-in-copyright-world.html

Baxter, B., Mayer, S., & Wijeratna, A. (1999). *Crops and Robbers: Biopiracy and the Patenting of Staple Food Crops. A Preliminary Findings of an Action Aid Investigation*. London: Action Aid; Available at http://www.actionaid.org

Beckman Instruments, Inc. v. Technical Development Corp. (1970) 433 F.2d 55, 167 USPQ 10 (7th Cir.)

Beiter. (2019). *The Protection of the Right to Education by International Law 19*. Academic Press.

Beiter, K. D. (2005). *The protection of the right to education by international law: Including a systematic analysis of article 13 of the International Covenant on Economic, Social and Cultural Rights*. BRILL.

Bell, C., & Kahane, D. (2004). *Intercultural Dispute Resolution in Aboriginal Contexts*. Vancouver: University of British Columbia Press.

Belsare, D. K. (2007). *Introduction to Biodiversity*. New Delhi: APH Publishing House.

Berlin, B. (1992). *Ethnobiological classification: Principles of categorisation of plants and animals in traditional societies*. Princeton, NJ: Princeton University Press. doi:10.1515/9781400862597

Berlin, E. A., & Berlin, B. (1996). *Medical ethnobiology of the Highland Maya of Chiapas, Mexico: the gastrointestinal diseases*. Princeton, NJ: Princeton University Press.

Berne Convention, 1886

Bhattacharya, S. (2014). Bioprospecting, biopiracy and food security in India: The emerging sides of neoliberalism. *International Letters of Social and Humanistic Sciences*, (23), 49-56.

Bhukta, A. (2019). *Projecting Traditional Knowledge: A Search for an Effective IPR Law for India* (Ph. D Thesis). Vidyasagar University.

Bhutani, S., & Kohli, K. (2016). *ABS and the Ayurveda Industry, Cases related to Access and Benefit Sharing, Litigating India's Biological Diversity Act: A Study of Legal Cases*. Foundation for Ecological Security and Kalpvriksh Environmental Action Group.

Binctin, N. (2015). Stratégie d'entreprise et propriété intellectuelle, LGDJ. In *Les stratégies de l'entreprise fondées sur la propriété intellectuelle*. Available at: https://www.iptrust.fr/wp-content/uploads/2016/03/Strate%CC%81gie_breese_masson.pdf

Biswajit, D. (2002). *Sui Generis Systems for Plant Variety Protection, Options under Trips*. Discussion Paper. Quaker United Nations Office.

Blackman, S. H., & McNeill, R. M. (1998). Alternative Dispute Resolution in Commercial Property Disputes. *The American University Law Review*, *47*, 709–1734.

Blakeney. (2004). Bioprospecting and Biopiracy, in Intellectual Property and Biological Resources. *Marshall Cavendish*, 393-424.

Bonito Boats, Inc. v. Thunder Craft Boats, Inc., 489 U.S. 141, 150 (1989)

Bordwin, H. J. (1985). The Legal and Political Implications of the International Undertaking on Plant Genetic Resources. *Ecology Law Quarterly*, *12*(1053), 1053–1064.

Born, B. G. (2006). International arbitration and forum selection agreements: drafting and enforcing. *Kluwer Law International*, 11.

Born, B.G. (2014). Article. *International Commercial Arbitration, 2*(86).

Born, G. (2015). BITS, BATS and Buts: Reflections on International Dispute Resolution. *ESIL Lectures*. Retrieved from http://www.globalarbitrationreview.com/cdn/files/gar/articles/BITs_BATs_and_Buts2.pdf

Bouaziz, H. (2012). La clause de non concurrence en droit de travail. *Actes de la journée d'études sur les clauses du contrat de travail*.

Bouchoux, D. (2007). *La propriété intellectuelle: le droit des marques, le droit d'auteur, le droit des brevets d'invention et des secrets commerciaux*. Nouveaux horizons.

Bouthion-Dumas, H., & Masson, A. (2012). Le rôle du droit dans les stratégies des acteurs économiques. In *Stratégies juridiques des acteurs économiques. Editeur: Larcier*. Collection Droit, Management et Stratégies.

Breese, P. (2002). *Stratégies de propriété industrielle*. Dunod.

Briner, R. (1994). *The Arbitrability of Intellectual Property Disputes with Particular Emphasis on the Situation in Switzerland.* Worldwide Forum on the Arbitration of Intellectual Property Disputes, Geneva, Switzerland. Retrieved from http://www.wipo.int/amc/en/events/conferences/1994/briner.html

Brown v. Board of Education of Topeka, 347 U.S. 483 (1954)

Brown, C. H. (1982). Folk Art and The Art Books: Who Speaks for The Traditional Artists? *Modern Asian Studies*, *16*(3), 519–522. doi:10.1017/S0026749X00015298

Brown, C. H. (1996). Contested Meanings: Tantra and the Poetics of Mithila Art. *American Ethnologist*, *23*(4), 717–737. doi:10.1525/ae.1996.23.4.02a00030

Browne, A. (2000, June 25). India fights US basmati rice patent. *The Guardian.*

Brown, M. F. (2005). Heritage Trouble: Recent Work on the Protection of Intangible Cultural Property. *International Journal of Cultural Property*, *12*(01), 40–61. doi:10.1017/S0940739105050010

Brriner, R. (1994). *The arbitrability of Intellectual Property Disputes with particular emphasis on the situation in Switzerland.* Worldwide Forum on the Arbitration of Intellectual Property Disputes, Geneva, Switzerland. Retrieved from https://www.wipo.int/amc/en/events/conferences/1994/briner.html

Brunda, B. B. (1987). Resolution of Patent Disputes By Non-Litigation Proce-dures. *AIPLA Quarterly Journal*, *15*(73), 82–83.

Brush, S. B. (1992). Ethnoecology, biodiversity, and modernisation in Andean potato agriculture. *Journal of Ethnobiology*, *12*, 161–185.

Cambridge University Press et al. v. Patton et al.,769 F.3d 1232 (11th Cir. Ga. 2014).

Cambridge University Press v. Becker, 863. F.Supp.2d 1190 (N.D.Ga., 2012).

Campbell v. Acuff-Rose Music, 510 U.S. 569 (1994).

Caprioli, E. A. (2007). Introduction au management juridique de l'innovation. *Journal des Sociétés*, *45*. Available at: https://www.caprioli-avocats.com

Carboni, A., Humphreys, G., Margellos, T., Bonne, S., Crupi, M, Strümann, S., Müller, P., & Player, J. (2018). Chapter 1: Mediation as a Resolution Method in IP Disputes. In Mediation: Creating Value in International Intellectual Property Disputes. Kluwer Law International.

Carbonnier, J. (1979). *Essai sur les lois*. Rep Défrénois.

Carlos, M. (2015). *Plant Variety Protection in Developing Countries: A Tool for Designing a Sui-Generis Plant Variety Protection System: An Alternative to UPOV 1991*. Working paper. Association for Plant Breeding for the Benefit of Society (APBREBES).

Carmichael. (1983). The Arbitration of Patent Disputes. *ARB. J*, 38.

CBD Secretariat. (2010). *Linking biodiversity conservation and poverty alleviation: A state of knowledge review*. CBD Technical Series no. 55.

Chaerels, A. (2012). *Le choix de la forme juridique la mieux adaptée: approche transversale, in ouvrage collectif intitulé la création d'une société innovante*. Anthemis.

Champaud, C. (2006). *Les stratégies juridiques des entreprises*. Dalloz.

Chaudhuri, S. (2005). *The WTO and India's pharmaceuticals industry: Patent protection, TRIPS, and developing countries*. Oxford University Press.

Chavda, J. (1990). The Narrative Paintings of India's Jitwarpuri Women, *Woman's. Art Journal, 11*(1), 26–28.

Chen, J. (2006). There is No Such Thing as Biopiracy … And it's a Good Thing Too. *McGeorge Law Review, 37*(1), 3.

Chon, M. (2006). Intellectual property from below: Copyright and capability for education. *UC DAViS l. reV., 40*, 803.

Choudhary, B. (2002). The new international seed treaty: Promises and prospects for food security. *Current Science, 83*(4), 366–369.

Christoph, A. (2009). *Traditional Knowledge, Traditional Cultural Expressions*. New York: Kluwer Law International.

Ciftci, S., & Howard-Wagner, D. (2012). Integrating indigenous justice into alternative dispute resolution practices: A case study of the aboriginal care circle pilot program in nowra. *Australian Indigenous Law Review, 16*(2), 81–98.

Claude, R. P., & Weston, B. H. (Eds.). (1992). *Human rights in the world community: issues and action*. University of Pennsylvania Press.

Cohen, D. (2002). Le nouveau droit des dessins et modèles. ECONOMICA.

Collard, C., & Roquilly, Ch. (2010). *La performance juridique: pour une vision stratégique du droit dans l'entreprise*. LGDJ.

Company 1 vs. Company 2 & Anr. (2017) EWHC 2319 (QB).

Coombe, R. (2001). The Recognition of Indigenous Peoples' and Community Traditional Knowledge in International Law. *St. Thomas Law Review*, 14.

Cooper, C. J., & Madigan, K. (1989, May 8). The Economy must keep its speed Down to Swerve Away From Inflation Bus. *Business Outlook,* p. 31.

Copyright Act, 1709, 1710, 8 Ann., c. 19 (Eng.).

Corbel, P. (2007). *Management stratégique des droits de la propriété intellectuelle*. Gualino.

Cottier, T., & Panizzon, M. (2006). Legal Perspectives on Traditional Knowledge: the Case for Intellectual Property Protection. In International Public Goods and Transfer of Technology Under a Globalized Intellectual Property Regime. Cambridge: Cambridge University Press.

Cottier, T. (1998). The Protection of Genetic Resources and Traditional Knowledge: Towards More Specific Rights and Obligations in World Trade Law. *Journal of International Economic Law, 1*(4), 555–584. doi:10.1093/jiel/1.4.555

Creative Commons. (n.d.). *About*. Retrieved from https://creativecommons.org/about

Cullet, P. (2004). Intellectual property rights and food security in the south. *The Journal of World Intellectual Property, 7*(3), 261–286. doi:10.1111/j.1747-1796.2004.tb00209.x

Curci, J. (2010). *The Protection of Biodiversity and Traditional Knowledge in International Law of Intellectual Property*. Cambridge: Cambridge University Press.

Curley, A. J. (1976). Arbitration of Patent-Antitrust Disputes: Business Expediency vs. Public Interest. *The PTC Journal of Research & Education, 18*(107), 107–108.

Dahdouch, C. & Dahdouch, H. (2007). *Entreprises sociétaires et groupement privés*. IHE.

Danet, D. (2006). Au croisement du management stratégique des entreprises, *Journée de recherche « stratégie et transversalité »*. Université de Nice Sophia Antipolis.

David, G. M. (2012). *Indigenous Knowledge and the Environment in Africa and North America*. Ohio University Press Athens.

De Muro, P., & Mazziotta, M. (2010). *Towards a Food Insecurity Multidimensional Index*. Available at nitropdf.com/professional

De Passemar. (1997). La protection des brevets, des marques, des indications géographiques et des dessins et modèles industriels. Séminaire de l'OMPI sur la propriété intellectuelle et les accords sur les ADPIC. Organisé par l'OPMI.

Delattre, E. (2001). Le changement de nom des entreprises: évolution quantitative et typologie. *Revue Française de Marketing, 181*.

Demolin, P., & Demolin, V. (2012). *Le contrat de franchise, analyse et commentaires de 15 années de jurisprudence, 1995-2010*. Retrieved from: http://www.dbblaw.eu/fr/news/pierre-et-vronique-demolin-publient-le-contrat-de-franchise

Demolin, P., & Rigo, M. (2012). Protéger la propriété intellectuelle de l'entreprise innovante en mettant en place des contrats de distribution efficaces pour ses produits et services. In La création d'une société innovante, aspects juridiques et fiscaux particuliers. Athémis.

Dewan, M. (2011). IPR Protection in Agriculture: An Overview IPR Protection in Agriculture: An Overview. *Journal of Intellectual Property Rights*, *16*, 131–138.

DGCIS. (2015). *Foreign Trade (Export and Import) of Herbal Raw Drugs.* Author.

Dinesh, B. (2013, February 14). *India's Patent Office Revokes Sutent cancer drug patent.* Retrieved from http://www.worldipreview.com/news/india-s-patent-office-revokes-suten-cancer-drug-patent.

Downes, G. (2003). *Implications of Trips for Food Security in the Majority World.* www.comhlamh.org

Doyen, D. & Pierre, P. (2019). *Guide de management de la PI pour les business managers.* INPI.

Drahos, P. (2004). Towards an International Framework for the protection of Traditional Group Knowledge and Practice. In *UNCTAD-Commonwealth Secretariat Workshop on Elements of National Sui Generis Systems for the Preservation, Protection and Promotion of Traditional Knowledge, Innovations and Practices and Options for an International Framework.* UNCTAD.

Duggan, M., Garthwaite, C., & Goyal, A. (2016). The market impacts of pharmaceutical product patents in developing countries: Evidence from India. *The American Economic Review*, *106*(1), 99–135. doi:10.1257/aer.20141301 PMID:31178595

Dutfield, G. (2006), Protecting Traditional Knowledge: Pathways to the Future. *ICTSD Programme on IPRs and Sustainable Development.* Retrieved from http://www.iprsonline.org/unctadictsd/docs/Graham%20final.pdf

Dutfield, G. (2006). Legal and Economic Aspects of Traditional Knowledge. In International Public Goods and Transfer of Technology Under a Globalized Intellectual Property Regime. Cambridge: Cambridge University Press.

Dutfield, G., & Sutherland, U. (2018). *Traditional Knowledge and Genetic Resources: Observing Legal Protection Through the Lens of Historical Geography and Human Rights.* Queen Mary University of London. Legal Studies Research Paper No. 286/2018.

Dutfield, G. (1999). *Project on the Convention on Biological Diversity and the International Trade Regime.* Oxford University Press.

Dutfield, G. (2000). *IPRs and Biodiversity: Conflict or Synergy?* Oxford University Press.

Dutfield, G. (2001). TRIPS-Related Aspects of Traditional Knowledge. *Case Western Reserve Journal of International Law*, *2*(33), 233–275.

Dutfield, G. (2004). *Intellectual Property, Biogenetic Resources & Traditional Knowledge.* London: Earthscan Publication.

Dutfield, G., & Suthersanen, U. (2005). Harmonisation or differentiation in intellectual property protection? The lessons of history. *Prometheus*, *23*(2), 131–147. doi:10.1080/08109020500085528

Edwards, O. (1992). Technology Meets the Today. *Forbes*, 130.

Eide, A., Krause, C., & Rosas, A. (1995). *Economic, social and cultural rights. In Economic Social and Cultural Rights A Textbook*. Kluwer Academic Publishers.

Eiland, L. M. (2009). The Institutional Role in Arbitrating Patent Disputes. *Pepp. Disp. Resol. Law Journal*, *9*(283), 283.

Eisenberg, S. R. (1989). Patents and the Progress of Science: Exclusive Rights and Experimental Use. *The University of Chicago Law Review. University of Chicago. Law School*, *56*(3), 1017–1019. doi:10.2307/1599761

Ellen. (2000). *Indigenous Environmental Knowledge and its transformation: Critical Anthropological Perspectives*. Amsterdam: Alan Psychology Press.

Ellen, R., Parkes, P., & Bicker, A. (Eds.). (2000). *Indigenous Environmental Knowledge and its Transformations*. Amsterdam, The Netherlands: Harwood Academic Publishers.

ETC Group. (2002). *DuPont and Monsanto – Living in Synergy?* Available at http://www.etcgroup.org/article.asp?newsid=315

EXIM Bank. (1997). *Study on Export Potential of Ayurveda and Siddha Products and Services*. Author.

FAO. (2009). *A Global Treaty For Food Security And Sustainable Agriculture: International treaty on plant genetic resources for food and agriculture*. FAO.

Farley, A. M. (1986). The Role of Arbitration in the Resolution of Patent Disputes. *Touro Law Review*, *3*(47), 49.

Farnsworth, J. D. (1988). Screening plants for new medicines. In E. O. Wilson (Ed.), *Biodiversity* (pp. 83–97). Washington, DC: National Academy Press.

Farrell, J. P., & Heyneman, S. P. (1989). *Textbooks in the Developing World: Economic and Educational Choices*. EDI Seminar Series. Publications Sales Unit, The World Bank.

Feist Publications, Inc. v. Rural Telephone Services Co., 499 U.S. 340 (1991).

Food and Agriculture Organisation (FAO). (n.d.). Retrieved on 15.08.2019 from http://www.fao.org/3/y5714e/y5714e03.htm

Foster, S. E. (2008). Prelude to compatibility between human rights and intellectual property. *Chi. J. Int'l L.*, *9*, 171.

Fuglie, K. O., King, J. L., Heisey, P. W., & Schimmelpfennig, D. E. (2012). Rising concentration in agricultural input industries influences new farm technologies. *Amber Waves*, *10*(4).

Fuller, L. L., & Winston, K. I. (1978). The Forms and Limits of Adjudication. *Harvard Law Review*, *92*(2), 353–409. doi:10.2307/1340368

Gauthier, J., Meyer, C., & Cohen, D. (2016). Framing Sustainable Practices: Middle Managers and Social Intrapreneurial Championing. *International Journal of Sustainable Entrepreneurship and Corporate Social Responsibility*, *1*(2), 21–39. doi:10.4018/IJSECSR.2016070102

Gayler v. Wilder 51 U.S. 477 (1850)

Geingos, V., & Ngakaeaja, M. (2003). *WIPO, PCT Notable Inventions: "Hoodia" appetite suppressant.* Retrieved from http://www.wipo.int/ pct/en/inventions/hoodia

Gilead Pharmasset, LLC v. Union of India and Anr., WP(C) 687/2015 and CM No.1222/2015.

Ginsburg, S. J. (2006). *International Copyright and Related Rights: The Berne Convention and Beyond.* Academic Press.

Global Monitoring Report, E. F. A. (2009). *Overcoming Inequality: Why Governance Matters.* Retrieved from https://unesdoc.unesco.org/images/0017/001776/177683E.pdf

Goldsmith, H. (1971). Patent, Trademark and Copyright Arbitration guide. *Journal of the Patent Office Society*, *53*(224), 226.

Goldsmith, H. (1976). Addendum: Patent, Trademark and Copyright Arbitration Guide. *Idea: The PTC Journal of Research & Education*, *18*(29), 31.

Goldstein, P. (2001). *International Intellectual Property Law*. New York: Foundation Press.

Gopalkrishnan, N.S, (1998). Impact of Patent System on Traditional Knowledge. *Cochin University Law Review,* (1), 219.

Grain. (2001). *Intellectual Property Rights: Ultimate Control of Agricultural R and D in Asia.* Available at www.grain .org/publications/asiaipr-en.cfm

Green, C. (2013, December 18). *UNESCO Launches Open Access Repository Under Creative Commons*. Retrieved from https://creativecommons.org/weblog/entry/41265

Gregg, A., & Paradise, G. A. (1995). Arbitration of patent infringement disputes: Encouraging the use of Arbitration through Evidence Rules Reform. *Fordham Law Review*, *64*, 247.

Gubarev, M. V. (2012). Misappropriation and patenting of traditional ethnobotanical knowledge and genetic resources. *Journal of Food Law & Policy*, 72.

Gupta, A. (2001). WIPO-UNEP Study on the Role of Intellectual Property Rights in the sharing of benefits arising from the use of Biological Resources and Associated Traditional Knowledge. Kaula Lampur: WIPO-UNEP.

Gupta, A. (1996). Patent on Neem: Will it deprive Indian farmers of right to use it? *Biotechnology Law Report*, *15*(1), 6–14. doi:10.1089/blr.1996.15.6

Guyon, Y. (2002). *Les sociétés, Aménagement statutaires et conventions entre associés*. Ed. LGDJ.

Haider, A. (2016). Reconciling patent law and traditional knowledge: Strategies for countries with traditional knowledge to successfully protect their knowledge from abuse. *Case W. Res. J. Int'l L., 48*, 347.

Harper, M. B. (1997). TRIPS Article 27.2: An Argument for Caution. *William and Mary Environmental Law and Policy Review, 21*, 381. Retrieved from https://scholarship.law.wm.edu/wmelpr/vol21/iss2/4

Hasan, M., & Abdullah, H.M. (2015). *Plant Genetic Resources and Traditional Knowledge: Emerging Needs for Conservation*. doi:10.1007/978-981-10-0060-7_6

Hayden, C. (2003). When Nature Goes Public: The Making and Unmaking of Bioprospecting in Mexico. Princeton University Press.

Heinz, C.H. (2006). Documenting the Image in Mithila Art. *Visual Anthropology Review, 22*(2), 31.

Helfer, L. R., & Austin, G. W. (2011). *Human rights and intellectual property: Mapping the global interface*. Cambridge University Press. doi:10.1017/CBO9780511976032

Henry Hughes Intellectual Property Australia and New Zealand. (n.d.). Retrieved from www.henryhughes.com/site/news/wai-262-patents-and-plant-variety-rights- revisted.aspx?fbclid=IwAR0xjqkXpA9et3XWozgvp7jzvETB8ZzHQZZT VL6bdp7Q13wsbQAtCj8hWBY

Hentati, A. (2008). L'optimisation fiscale en matière d'impôt sur les sociétés, rôle de l'expert-comptable. *Mémoire pour l'obtention du diplôme d'expertise comptable*.

Heyneman, S. (2006). *The role of textbooks in a modern system of education: Towards high-quality education for all*. Academic Press.

Higgins, C., Lavin, T., & Metcalfe, O. (2008). *Health impacts of education: A review*. Institute of Public Health in Ireland.

Houck, O. (1997). On the Law of Biodiversity and Ecosystem Management. *Minnesota Law Review*, 869.

Houston, S. (2008). Beyond homo economicus: Recognition, self-realization and social work. *British Journal of Social Work, 40*(3), 841–857. doi:10.1093/bjsw/bcn132

ICC Arbitration Rules, 2017

Ihenacho, R.A., Orusha, J.O., & Onogu, B. (2019). Rural Farmers Use of Indigenous Knowledge Systems in Agriculture for Climate Change Adaptation and Mitigation in Southeast Nigeria. *Annals of Ecology and Environmental Science, 3*(1), 1-11.

Indian Arbitration & Conciliation Act, 1996.

Indian Council of Medical Research. (2009). Retrieved from: https://www.icmr.nic.in/

ITPGRFA Secretariat. (2017). Retrieved on 26 July 2018 from; http://www.fao.org/plant-treaty/areas-of-work/farmers-rights

Jain, D. (1980). *Women's Quest For Power: Five Indian Case Studies*. Delhi: Vikas Publishing House.

Jain, J. (1997). *Ganga Devi: Tradition and Expression in Mithila Painting*. Ahmedabad: Mapin Publishing.

Jamil, U. (1998). *Biopiracy: The Patenting of Basmati by Ricetec*. Working Paper Series # 37. Commission on Environmental, Economic and Social Policy – South Asia and Sustainable Development Policy Institute.

Jaszi, P. (1991). Toward a theory of copyright: The metamorphoses of authorship. *Duke LJ*, 455.

Jayakar, P. (1971). Paintings of Mithila. *The Times of India*, 29.

Jayakar, P. (1980). *The Earthen Drum: An Introduction to the Ritual Arts of India*. New Delhi: National Museum.

Jayakar, P. (1989). *The Earth Mother*. New Delhi: Penguin Books.

Jha, A. (2011). *Traditional Indian Medicine with Specific Reference to Buddhist and Tribal Medicine*. Research India Press Publisher.

Johnson, M. (1992). Research on Traditional Environmental Knowledge: Its Development and Its Role. In *Lore: Capturing Traditional Environmental Knowledge*. International Development Research Centre.

Joshi, P. (2005). *Crop diversification in India: nature, pattern and drivers*. New Delhi, India: Asian Development Bank.

Judiciary and Judicial Procedure, 28 U.S.C. § 1338, 2000.

Jungcurt, S. (2012). *Institutional Interplay in Regime Complex on Plant Genetic Resources Conflict and Learning*. Academic Press.

Kapczynski, A. (2009). Harmonisation and its discontents: A case study of TRIPS implementation in India's pharmaceutical sector. *California Law Review*, *97*, 1571.

Karmakar, A. K., & Jana, S. K. (2014). Policies and Strategies for Achieving Food and Nutrition Security in India: Myths and Realities. In *Dynamics of Food Security in India*. New Delhi: Kumud Publications.

Kilb, P. K. (1993). Arbitration of Patent Disputes: An important option in the age of information technology. *Fordham Intell. Prop. Media & Ent. L.J.*, *4*(599), 613.

Kim, Y. K., & Khalil, U. (2016). The Procedural Benefits of Arbitrating Patent Disputes. *J. Arb. Stud*, *26*(51), 52.

Kingsbury, B. (2005). The Emergence of Global Administrative Law. *Law and Contemporary Problems*, (68), 15–62. Retrieved from https://scholarship.law.duke.edu/lcp/vol68/iss3/2

Kosambi, D. D. (1997). *The Culture and Civilization of Ancient India in Historical Outline*. Delhi: Vikas Publishing House.

Krishnamurthy, K. V. (2003). *Textbook of Biodiversity*. Science Publishers. doi:10.1201/9781482280180

Kumar, M. R., & Janagam, D. (2011). Export and import pattern of medicinal plants in India. *Indian Journal of Science and Technology*, *4*(3), 245–248.

La Viña, A. G., Hoff, G., & DeRose, A. M. (2003). The outcomes of Johannesburg: Assessing the world summit on sustainable development. *SAIS Review (Paul H. Nitze School of Advanced International Studies)*, *23*(1), 53–70. doi:10.1353ais.2003.0022

Lahmar, I. (2006). *Commentaire du jugement du tribunal de première instance de Tunis n° 39131 précité*. RJL.

Lampe, R., & Moser, P. (2010). *Do Patent Pools Encourage Innovation? Evidence from the 19th-Century Sewing Machine Industry*. NBER Working Paper n°15061.

Lanjouw, J. O. (1998). *The Introduction of Pharmaceutical Product Patents in India: Heartless Exploitation of the Poor and Suffering? (No. w6366)*. National Bureau of Economic Research.

Law Library of Congress. (2010). New Zealand – Maori Culture and Intellectual Property Law. Global Legal Research Center.

Laxman, L., & Ansari, A. H. (2012). The Interface Between TRIPS and CBD: Efforts Towards Harmonisation. *Journal of International Trade Law & Policy*, *11*(2), 108–132. doi:10.1108/14770021211239640

Le Bas, C. (2002). Fonctionnement, transformation et tension du système de brevet. *Revue d'Economie Industrielle*, *99*.

Le Loarne, S., & Blanco, S. (2009). *Management de l'innovation*. Pearson.

Leaflet, No. 12: WIPO and Indigenous Peoples. (n.d.). Retrieved from https://www.ohchr.org/Documents/Publications/GuideIPleaflet12en.pdf

Lear, Inc. v. Adkins, (1969) 395 U.S. 653.

Leloup, J.-M. (2000). La franchise, Droit et pratique (3rd ed.). Paris: Encyclopédie Delmas.

Lew, J. (1994). *The Arbitration of Intellectual Property Disputes*. Retrieved from https://www.wipo.int/amc/en/events/conferences/1994/lew.html

Lew, M. D. J., Mistelis, A. L., & Kröll, S. (2003). *Comparative International Commercial Arbitration*. Kluwer International Law.

Liang, L. (2016). *Oxford and Cambridge University Publishers v. Students of India*. Retrieved from https://kafila.org/2012/08/27/oxford-and-cambridge-university-publishers-v-students-of-india/

Liang, B. A. (2011). Global governance: Promoting Biodiversity and Protecting Indigenous Communities against Biopiracy. *Journal of Commercial Biotechnology*, *17*(3), 249. doi:10.1057/jcb.2011.16

Lin, B. B. (2011). Resilience in agriculture through crop diversification: Adaptive management for environmental change. *Bioscience*, *61*(3), 183–193. doi:10.1525/bio.2011.61.3.4

Long, D. E., & D'Amato, A. (2000). *A Coursebook in International Intellectual Property*. St. Paul: West Group.

M/s. BDR Pharmaceuticals International Pvt. Ltd. v. *M/s. Bristol Myers Squibb Co.*, CLA No. 1 of 2013.

Maeterlinck, A. (2012). *La répartition des pouvoirs dans les statuts et les conventions d'actionnaires, ouvrage collectif intitulé. La création d'une société innovante, aspects juridiques et fiscaux particuliers*. Anthémis.

Mafongoya, P. L., & Ajayi, O. C. (Eds.). (2017). *Indigenous Knowledge Systems and Climate Change Management in Africa*. Wageningen, The Netherlands: CTA.

Malhan. (2001). Protecting Traditional Knowledge Systems. *Indian Journal of Environmental Law*, *2*(1), 85–91. Retrieved from https://www.ecolex.org/details/literature/protecting-traditional-knowledge-systems-ana-067982/

Marchand, B. (2012). *Les démarches liées à la création d'une entreprise, ouvrage collectif intitulé la création d'une société innovante*. Anthémis.

Marcus v. Rowley, 695 F.2d 1171. Princeton University Press v. Michigan Document Services Inc., 99 F.3d 1381 (6th Cir. 1996).

Maroyi, A. (2012). Enhancing food security through cultivation of traditional food crops in Nhema communal area. Midlands Province, Zimbabwe. *African Journal of Agricultural Research*, *7*, 5412–5420.

Marzetti, M. (2016, December 13). *Argentina Passes Open Access Act for Publicly Funded Research*. Retrieved from http://www.ip-watch.org/20

Maskus, K. E. (2000). *Intellectual property rights in the global economy*. Peterson Institute.

Maskus, K. E. (Ed.). (2004). *The WTO, Intellectual Property Rights and the Knowledge Economy*. Cheltenham: Edward Elgar Publishing.

Masson, A., & Bouthion-Dumas, H. (2011). L'approche Law and mangement. *Revue Trimestrielle de Droit Commercial et de Droit Economique*, *2*, 233-254.

Masson, D. J. (1995). Fixation on Fixation: Why Imposing Old Copyright Law on New Technology Will Not Work. *Industrial Law Journal*, *71*, 1049.

Matauranga Maori and Taonga. (n.d.). Wellington: Waitangi Tribunal Publications.

Mathur, J. C. (1966). The Domestic Arts of Mithila. *Marg*, *20*(1), 43–55.

Maxted, N. (2003). Conserving the genetic resources of crop wild relatives in European protected areas. *Biological Conservation*, *113*(3), 411–417. doi:10.1016/S0006-3207(03)00123-X

Mayor. (1994). The D.G of UNES and Cultural Organization.

Mechri, F. (2009). *Le droit du travail en Tunisie*. Sud Edition Tunis.

Meek, J. (2000, Nov. 15). Beginners guide to gene patents. *Guardian*.

Mellouli, S., & Frikha, S. (2013). Les sociétés commerciales. Maison du livre.

Merck Sharp and Dohme Corporation and Anr. v. Glenmark Pharmaceuticals, 201 126 DLT (2013).

Meyer, A. (2001). International Environmental Law and Human Rights: Toward an Explicit Recognition of Traditional Knowledge. *Review of European Community & International Environmental Law*, *10*(1), 37–46. doi:10.1111/1467-9388.00259

Mezghani, N. (2000). La protection du logiciel par la loi n°94-36. RTD..

Mgbeoji, I. (2001). Patents and Traditional Knowledge of the Uses of Plants: Is a Communal Patent Regime Part of the Solution to the Scourge of Bio Piracy. *Indiana Journal of Global Legal Studies*, *9*(1), 9. Available at http://www.repository.law.indiana.edu/ijgls/vol9/iss1/9

Mgbeoji, I. (2003). Beyond Rhetoric: State Sovereignty, Common Concern, and the Inapplicability of the Common Heritage Concept to Plant Genetic Resources. *Leiden Journal of International Law*, *16*(4), 821–837. doi:10.1017/S092215650300147X

Mgbeoji, I. (2006). *Global Biopiracy*. Vancouver: UBC Press.

Mgbeoji, I. (2006). *Global Biopiracy: Patents, Plants, and Indigenous Knowledge*. New York: Cornell University Press.

Mishra, V. (1979). *The Cultural Heritage of Mithila*. Allahabad: Mithila Prakasana.

Mohanty, A. (2014, June 4). *Analysing the Delhi University v. Publishers Photocopying Case*. Retrieved from https://spicyip.com/2012/09/analysing-delhi-university-v-publishers.html

Mooney, P. R. (2000). Why We Call it Biopiracy. In Responding to Bioprospecting: From Biodiversity in the South to Medicines in the North. Spartacus.

Mooney, P. R. (2002). Why We Call it Biopiracy. In Bioprospecting: From Biodiversity in the South to Medicines in the North. Spartacus Forlag AS Publication.

Moore, W. C. (2003). *The Mediation Process: Practical Strategies For Resolving Conflicts*. San Francisco: Jossey-Bass Publishers.

Morgera, E., & Tsioumani, E. (2010). The Evolution of Benefit Sharing: Linking Biodiversity and Community Livelihoods. *Review of European Community & International Environmental Law*, *19*(2), 150–173. doi:10.1111/j.1467-9388.2010.00674.x

Mueller, J. M. (2006). The tiger awakens: The tumultuous transformation of India's patent system and the rise of Indian pharmaceutical innovation. *U. Pitt. l. Rev.*, *68*, 491.

Mugabe, J. (n.d.). *Intellectual Property Protection and Traditional Knowledge*. Retrieved from https://www.wipo.int/edocs/pubdocs/en/intproperty/762/wipo_pub_762.pdf#page=104

Mukherjee. (2008). *A Study of the Basmati Case (India-US Basmati Rice Dispute): The Geographical Indication Perspective*. Available at SSRN: https:// ssrn.com/abstract=1143209

Mzid, N. (2012). Observations préliminaires sur les clauses du contrat de travail. *Actes de la journée d'études sur les clauses du contrat de travail.*

Nagel, T. (2005). *The Problem of Global Justice, Philosophy and Public Affairs*. Oxford: Blackwell Publishing Inc.

Nair, M. D. (2005). Traditional Medicines and Medical Plants, and their Protection Modalities from an Intellectual Property Perspective. *Plant Genetic Resources*, *3*(2), 314–319. doi:10.1079/PGR200580

Nammour, F. (1992). Les clauses de secret. In Droit des sociétés commerciales. LATRACH.

Narasaiah, M. L. (2005). *Biodiversity and Sustainable Development*. New Delhi: Discovery Publishing House.

Natco Pharma Ltd. v. Bayer Corp., C.L.A.No.1 of 2011 (ICPD 2012)

Natco Pharma Ltd. v. UoI & Ors.; *M/S Cancer Patients Aid Association v. UoI & Ors*., Civil Appeal No. 2706-2716 of 2013

National Agricultural Library. (2016). Retrieved from: https://data.nal.usda.gov/dataset/holobee-database-v20161

Niblett, B. (1995). Intellectual Property Disputes: Arbitrating the Creative. *Dispute Resolution Journal*, *64*, 65.

Novartis AG & Ors v. *Wockhardt Ltd.* CS (OS) 646/2014.

Novartis AG And Ors. v. Ranbaxy Laboratories Ltd., I.A. No. 17139/2014 in CS.

Novartis AG v. Union of India (UOI) and Ors.

Nwabueze, R. (2003). Ethnopharmacology, Patents and the Politics of Plant Genetic Resources. *New Europe Law Review*, *11*, 585.

Okediji, R. L. (2006). *The international copyright system: limitations, exceptions and public interest considerations for developing countries*. Academic Press.

Osi, C. (2008). Understanding Indigenous Dispute Resolution Processes and Western Alternative Dispute Resolution: Cultivating Culturally Appropriated Methods in Lieu of Litigation. *Cardozo Journal of Conflict Resolution*, *10*, 163.

Ost, F., & Van De Kerchove, M. (1994). Le jeu: un paradigme pour le droit. *Revue internationale de droit comparé*, *46*(1), 303-305.

Ouma, M. (2017). Traditional knowledge: the challenges facing international lawmakers. *WIPO Magazine*. Retrieved on 18/10/2019 from https://www.wipo.int/wipo_magazine

Paillusseau, J. (1989). *Le droit est aussi une science d'organisation*. RTD.Com.

Pandey, A. (2016). *Delhi University vs. Publishers: A Critical Appraisal on Doctrine of Fair Dealing Vis a Vis Fair Use*. Retrieved from http://ijlljs.in/delhi-university-vs-publishers-aniket-pandey-b-b-a-ll-b-corporate-law-hons-5th-yr-university-of-petroleum-energy-studies-dehradun-and-apoorv-pandey-b-b-a-ll-b-hons-3rd-yr-itm-universi/

Parliamentary Research Service. (2006). *Legislative Brief: The Seeds Bill, 2004*. Available at www. prsindia.org

Patent Arbitration Rules § 28, 2005.

Patents (Amendment) Act, 1999.

Patents (Amendment) Act, 2005.

Patents Act of 1952, 35 U.S.Code. §294(d) (1952).

Patil, C. R. S. (2005). Plant Breeders Rights. *Kare Law Journal*, 53. Retrieved on 26 July 2018) from http://plantauthority.gov.in

Patro, L. (2016). Medicinal Plants of India: With special reference to Odisha. IJARIIE, 2(5).

Pecoul, B., Chirac, P., Trouiller, P., & Pinel, J. (1999). Access to essential drugs in poor countries: A lost battle? *Journal of the American Medical Association*, *281*(4), 361–367. doi:10.1001/jama.281.4.361 PMID:9929090

People's Biodiversity Registers. (2019). Retrieved from: http://nbaindia.org/uploaded/pdf/PPT_PBRs_Guidelines.pdf

Peppard, F.T. (2000). New International Evidence Rules Advance Arbitration Process. *Wis. Law*, *73*, 18.

Peteraf, M. A. (1993). The cornerstones of competitive advantage: A Resource based view. *Strategic Management Journal*, *14*(3), 179–191. doi:10.1002mj.4250140303

Petit, F. (2000). *Sur les clauses de garantie d'emploi*. Dr.Soc.2000.

Pharmaceuticals Ltd. v. Symead Labs Limited, I.A. No. 5908/ 2013 (Order XXXIX Rules 1 and 2 CPC) and I.A. No. 5417/ 2013 (Order VII Rules 10 and 11 CPC) in CS (OS) No. 678/ 2013.

Pinel, S. L., & Evans, M. J. (1994). *Tribal Sovereignty and the Control of Knowledge, Intellectual Property Right for Indigenous Peoples*. Kluwer Law International.

Posey, D., & Dutfield, G. (1996). *Beyond Intellectual Property Rights: Toward Traditional Resource Rights for Indigenous Peoples and Local Communities*. Ottawa: IDRC.

Pritchard, D. (2005). International biodiversity-related treaties and impact assessment-how can they help each other? Biodiversity-related Treaties. *Impact Assessment and Project Appraisal*, *23*(1), 8. doi:10.3152/147154605781765706

Priyadarshini, S. (2014, December 24). *India Unveils New Open Access Policy*. Retrieved from blogs.nature.com/indigenus/2014/12/india-unveils-new-open-access-policy.html

Protection of Traditional Knowledge. (2019). *Traditional Cultural Expression*. Retrieved from: https://www.bananaip.com/ip-news-center/round-table-on-protection-of_25/

RAFI. (1998). *RAFI Report Exposes Global Biopiracy, Institute for Agriculture and Trade Policy*. Retrieved from https://www.iatp.org/news/rafi-report-exposes-global-biopiracy

Raghvan. (2001). Protection of Traditional Knowledge. *Minn. Intell. Prop. Rev.*, *2*(1).

Ray, R. (2012). *Bonding with Roots to Revive Madhubani Folk Art*. New Global Indian.

Redfern, A., Hunter, M., Blackaby, N., & Partsides, C. (2004). *Law and Practice of International Commercial Arbitration*. Thomson/Sweet & Maxwell.

Reichman, J. H. (2000). The TRIPS Agreement Comes of Age: Conflict or Cooperation With the Developing Countries? *Case Western Reserve Journal of International Law*, 32.

Rekha, N. (2010). From folk art to fine art: changing paradigms in the historiography of Maithil Painting. *Journal of Art Historiography*, 2.

Rekha, N. (2011). Maithil Paintings: An Enquiry into its Historiographical Trajectory (1947-1997). Folklore and Folkloristics, 4(2).

Rekha, N. (2003). Harijan Paintings of Mithila. *Marg*, *54*(3), 64–77.

Richards, D. (2004). *Intellectual Property Rights and Global Capitalism: The Political Economy of the TRIPs Agreement*. M.E. Sharpe.

Right to Education. (n.d.). Retrieved from https://mhrd.gov.in/rte

Rijksoctrooiwet 1995 [Patent Act 1995], art. 80, Stb. 1995, 51 (Neth.)

Riley, M. (Ed.). (2004). *Indigenous Intellectual Property Rights*. Walnut Creek: Altamira Press.

Robinson Daniel, F. (2017). *Protecting Traditional Knowledge*. Abingdon: Routledge. doi:10.4324/9781315666358

Robinson, D. (2010). *Confronting Biopiracy Challenges, Cases and International Debates*. London: Earthscan Publication. doi:10.4324/9781849774710

Roquilly, Ch. (2009). Le cas de l'Iphone en tant qu'illustration du rôle des ressources juridiques et de la capacité juridique dans le management de l'innovation. *Management*, *§§§*, 142–175.

Rosendal. (2000). *The Convention on Biological Diversity and Developing Countries*. Springer.

Roy, A. (2009). Recent Developments in Law Reform and Indigenous Cultural and Intellectual Property in Australia. *European Intellectual Property Review, 31*(1).

Rule 15, the *AAA Patent Arbitration Rules*,1992.

Rule 32, *SIAC Rules*, 2016

Safi, Z. (2006). *Le droit du travail, le contrat du travail. Centre de publication universitaire.*

Sahai, S. (2004). Commercialization of Traditional Knowledge and Benefit Sharing. In *Protecting and Promoting Traditional Knowledge: Systems, National Experiences and International Dimensions*. UNCTAD.

Sajko, K. (2009). Intellectual Property Rights and Arbitration: Miscellaneous. In *Patents and Technological Progress in a Globalized World.* Springer. doi:10.1007/978-3-540-88743-0_32

Sarfaty, A. G. (2007). International Norm Diffusion in the Pimicikamak Cree Nation: A Model of Legal Mediation. *Harvard International Law Journal, 48*(2), 441.

Saturday *Evening Post Corp. v. Rumbleseat Press Inc.* (1987) 816 F.2d 1191, 1197 (7th Cir. 1987) (Judge Posner).

Savatier, J. (1991). *Les garanties contractuelles de stabilité de l'emploi.* Dr.Soc.1991.

Scheinin, M. (2003). *UN Human Rights Committee: Protecting Indigenous Livelihoods and Cultural Rights*. Geneva, Switzerland: Centre on Housing Rights and EvictionsPublishers.

Scott, C. (1999). Reaching beyond (without abandoning) the category of economic, social and cultural rights. *Hum. Rts. Q., 21*(3), 633–660. doi:10.1353/hrq.1999.0043

Secretariat of CBD. (2001). *Handbook of the Convention on Biological Diversity*. Rio: Earthscan Publications Ltd.

Secretariat, C. B. D. (2005). Handbook of the Convention on Biological Diversity Including its Cartagena Protocol on Biosafety (3rd ed.). Academic Press.

Section 2(2) r.w. Section 9 of the India Arbitration and Conciliation Act, 1996.

Sekolec, J., & Getty, B. M. (2003). An Emerging Consensus on Mediation and Conciliation. *Journal of Dispute Resolution, 1*, 175-181.

SenGupta, N. (2019). *Traditional Knowledge in Modern India*. Shimla: Springer. doi:10.1007/978-81-322-3922-2

Serra, Y. (1998). *Les fondements et le régime de l'obligation de non concurrence.* RTD.Com.

Serra, Y. (2002). *Tsunami sur la clause de non concurrence*. D.2002.

Sheikh, D. (n.d.). Fair Use and Course Packs: A Comparative Perspective. Retrieved from https://kafila.org/2012/08/27/fair-use-and-course-packs-a-comparative-perspective-danish-sheikh/

Shiv Shai Singh. (2000). *The law of Intellectual Property Rights*. New Delhi: Deep and Deep.

Shiva, V. (2001). *Protect or Plunder? Understanding Intellectual Property Rights*. London: Zed Books Publication.

Simon, S. B. (2005). Intellectual Property and Traditional Knowledge: A Psychological Approach to Conflicting Claims of Creativity in International Law. *Berkley Law Journal*, *20*(4), 1613–1616.

Simpson, S. W., & Omer Kesikli, O. (2006). The Countours of Arbitration Discovery. *ALA. Law*, *67*(280), 280–282.

Singh, D. V., & Kumar, P. (2005). *Photocopying of Copyrighted Works for Educational Purposes: Does it Constitute Fair Use?* Academic Press.

Singh, J. (2008). *Biodiversity, Environment & Sustainability*. New Delhi: MD Publications Ltd.

Sinha, N. N. (2010). Madhubani: A Contemporary History (1971-2011). *Proceedings of Indian History Congress, 71st Session.*

Sinthupundaja, J., & Kohda, Y. (2017). *Effects of Corporate Social Responsibility and Creating Shared Value on Sustainability. International Journal of Sustainable Entrepreneurship and Corporate Social Responsibility*, *2*(1), 27–38.

Smith, A. M., Cousté, M., Hield, T., Jarvis, R., Kochupillai, M., Leon, B., ... Branch, J. (2006). Arbitration of Patent Infringement and validity issues worldwide. *Harvard Journal of Law & Technology*, *2*(19), 333.

Sonowal, R., & Goswami, A. (2015). Opportunistic Infections in HIV Seropositive Patients: A Study in a Tertiary Hospital in Assam, Northeast India. *Tuberculosis (Edinburgh, Scotland)*, *53*, 65–43.

South African Patents Act, 1978, Act 57 of 1978.

Sreedharan, T.P. (2004). *Biological Diversity of Kerala: A survey of Kalliasseri Panchayat*. Kannur District: Deep and Deep.

Stolton, S., Maxted, N., Lloyd, B. F., Kell, S., & Dudley, N. (2006). *Food Stores: Using Protected Areas to Secure Crop Genetic Diversity*. WWF.

Sumpter, P. (2006). *Intellectual Property Law: Principles and Practices*. New Zealand: CCH.

Supplementary Rules for the Resolution of Patent Disputes (c)(l 2)-(13).

Swanson, T. M. (1998). *Intellectual Property Rights & Biodiversity Conservation: An Interdisciplinary Analysis of the Values of Medicinal Plants*. Cambridge University Press.

Swiderska, K. (2004). *Traditional Knowledge protection and Customary Law: Policy Issues and Challenges.* Background Paper prepared (IIED) for the Planning Workshop on Protecting community rights over traditional knowledge: Implications of customary laws and practices. Retrieved from https://pubs.iied.org/pdfs/G01252.pdf

Szanton, D., & Bakshi, M. (2007). Mithila Painting: The Evolution of an Art Form. Berkeley, CA: Ethnic Arts Foundation.

Szanton, D. (2004). *Folk Art No Longer: The Transformations of Mithila Painting*. New Delhi: Academic Press.

Tania & Gold. (2012). *Genetic Resources and Traditional Knowledge: Case Studies and Conflicting interests*. Edward Elgar Publishing Limited.

Taubman, A., Wager, H., & Watal, J. (2012). *A Handbook on the WIPO Trips Agreement*. Cambridge University Press.

TeAra Encyclopedia of New Zealand. (n.d.). Retrieved from https://teara.govt.nz/en/kaitiakitanga-guardianship-and-conservation/page-1

Tejera, V. (1999). Tripping over Property Rights: Is it possible to reconcile the Convention on Biological Diversity with article 27 of the TRIPS Agreement? *New England Law Review*, *33*, 971.

Tellez, M. V. (2006). Recognising the Traditional Knowledge of the San People: The Hoodia Case of Benefit-Sharing. Carol Bonnett Publisher.

Thakur, U. (1981). *Madhubani Painting*. New Delhi: Abhinav Publications.

The Australian Copyright Act, 1968

The Biotechnology Regulatory Authority of India Bill. (2013). Retrieved from https://www.prsindia.org/billtrack/the-biotechnology-regulatory-authority-of-india-bill-2013- 2709/

The Chancellor, Masters & Scholars of University of Oxford & Ors v. Rameshwari Photocopy Services &Anr., I.A. No. 14632/2012 in CS (OS) No. 2439/ 2012.

The Chancellors, Masters and Scholars of the University of Oxford and Others v. Rameshwari Photocopy Services, CS(OS) 2439/2012, I.As. No. 14632/2012 (of the plaintiffs u/O 39 R-1&2 CPC), 430/2013 (of D-2 u/O 39 R-4 CPC) & 3455/2013 (of D-3 u/O 39 R-4 CPC).

The Constitution of India The Constitution of the USA Universal Copyright Convention U.N. Comm. on Rights of the Child The Federal Research Public Access Act (FRPAA), 2012

The Copyright Act of Canada, 1921 Indian copyright act, 1957

The Indian Patents Act, 1970, Act 39 of 1970

The Nagoya Protocol on Access and Benefit-Sharing. (n.d.). Retrieved from www.cbd.int/abs/about/default.shtml

The Newzealand Copyright Act 1994

The Patents Act, 1970.

The UK Copyright, Designs and Patents Act 1988 Right to Education Act, 2009

The UNCITRAL Model Law. (1985). Retrieved from https://www.uncitral.org/pdf/english/texts/arbitration/ml-arb/07-86998_Ebook.pdf

The United States Copyright Act of 1976 (17 U.S.C. §107)

The Universal Declaration of Human Rights (UDHR), 1948

Theurich, S. (2009). *Art and Cultural Heritage Dispute Resolution*, Retrieved from https://www.wipo.int/wipo_magazine/en/2009/04/article_0007.html

t. Hoen, E. (2002). TRIPS, pharmaceutical patents, and access to essential medicines: A long way from Seattle to Doha. *Chi. J. Int'l L.*, *3*, 27. PMID:15709298

Tinker. (1994). Introduction to Biological Diversity: Law, Institutions, and Science. *Buffalo Journal of International Law*, 1.

Tomaševski. (n.d.). *Removing Obstacles in the Way of the Right to Education: Right to Education Primers No. 1,* 5. Tomaševski: Primers.

Traditional Knowledge Digital Library. (n.d.). Retrieved from https://www.wipo.int/meetings/en/2011/wipo_tkdl_del_11/about_tkdl.html

Tripathi, S. K. (2003). Traditional Knowledge Significance and Implication. *Indian Journal of Traditional Knowledge*, *2*(2), 102.

Tullani, H., Raiswa, S., & Richa, D. (2018). Green Innovation and Ethical Responsibility: Do They Improve Customer's Green Purchase Intentions? *International Journal of Sustainable Entrepreneurship and Corporate Social Responsibility*, *3*(1), 35–52. doi:10.4018/IJSECSR.2018010103

U.S. *Patents Act*, 35 U.S. Code §294.

UNAIDS. (n.d.). *UNAIDS: Reports on the Global HIV/AIDS Epidemic*. Retrieved from www.unaids.org/epidemic_update/report/Epi_report.pdf

UNCTAD. (2014). The Convention on Biological Diversity and the Nagoya Protocol: Intellectual Property Implications. The International Framework for Access and Benefit Sharing. UNCTAD.

UNDP. (2001). *Human Development Report*. New York: UNDP.

Unni Krishnan, J.P. v. State of Andhra Pradesh, (1993) 1 SC.R. 594.

UPOV. (1978). *UPOV, Act of 1978, International Convention for the Protection of New Varieties of Plants*. Retrieved on 03.11.2019 from https://www.upov.int/ export /sites/upov /upovlex/ en/ conventions /1978/ pdf/act1978.pdf

UPOV. (1991). *UPOV, Act of 1991. International Convention for The Protection of New Varieties of Plants*. Retrieved on 03.11.2019 from https://www.upov.int/export/sites/ upov/ upovlex /en/ conventions /1991/ pdf/ act1991.pdf

Van Noorden, V. R. (2015). *Chinese Agencies Announce Open Access Policies*. Retrieved from http://www.nature.com/news/chinese-agencies-announce-open-access-policies-1.15255

Vatinet, R. (2002). *Les conditions de validité des clauses de non concurrence: l'imbroglio*. Dr.Soc.2002, n°1.

Vequaud, Y. (1977). *The Women Painters of Mithila; Ceremonial Paintings from an Ancient Kingdom*. London: Thames and Hudson.

Verges, E. (2019). *Contrats sur la recherche et l'innovation - Nouveauté: Techniques contractuelles. Valorisation de la recherche. Transferts de technologies*. Dalloz.

Verkey, E. (2005). *Law of Patents*. Eastern Book Company.

Verma, S.K. (2004). Protecting Traditional Knowledge: Is a Sui Generis System an Answer? *JWIP, 7*(765).

Vincent, M. (2001). La protection du secret en propriété industrielle, Université Lille II. *Mémoire, DEA, année universitaire 2000-2001*.

Vishwanathan, M. (2013, June 8). *The Sunitinib Saga Continues: Third Time's the Charm?* Retrieved from http://spicyip.com/2013/06/the-sunitinib-saga-continues-third.html

Vivant, M. (1990). *Les clauses de secret, in les principales clauses entre professionnel*. PUAM.

Waitangi Tribunal. (2011). *Ko Aotearoa Tēnei: A Report into Claims Concerning New Zealand Law and Policy Affecting Māori Culture and Identity*. Retrieved from https://forms.justice.govt.nz/search/Documents/WT/wt_DOC_ 68356054/KoAotearoaTeneiTT1W.pdf

Warren, D. M. (1992). *Indigenous Knowledge, Biodiversity Conservation and Development*. Paper Presented in International Conference on Conservation of Biodiversity in Africa: Local Initiatives and Institutional Role, Nairobi, Kenya.

Wichard, J. C., & Wendland, W. B. (2006). *Mediation as an Option foe Resolving Disputes between Indigenous/ Traditional Communities and Industry Concerning Traditional Knowledge*. Cambridge, UK: Cambridge University Press.

WIPO Lawmakers Magazine. (2019). https://www.wipo.int /wipo_magazine/en/ 2017/01/ article_0003. html

WIPO Model Law Needs Revision. (2015). *Developing Countries Say; Developed Countries Reluctant*. Retrieved from https://www.ip-watch.org/2015/07/30/wipo-model-law-needs-revision-developing-countries-say-developed-countries-reluctant/

WIPO. (2004). *World Intellectual Property Organization (WIPO): Arbitration and Mediation Centre, Guide to Arbitration Centre*. Retrieved from www.wipo.int/amc/en/

Wong, R. (2012). Interim Relief in aid of International Commercial Arbitration. Singapore Academy of Law Journal, 24(499), 504.

Wong, T., & Dutfield, G. (Eds.). (2011). *Intellectual Property and Human Development.* Cambridge: Cambridge University Press.

Woods, M. (2002). Food for Thought: The Biopiracy of Jasmine and Basmati Rice. *Albany Law Journal of Science & Technology, 13*, 126.

World Health Organisation. (2000). *The World Health Report 2001.* WHO.

WTO. WT/CTE/W/156. (2009). *Protection of Biodiversity and Traditional Knowledge – the Indian Experience.* Retrieved From: https://docs.wto.org/dol2fe/Pages/FE_Search/FE_S_S009DP.aspx?language=E&CatalogueIdList=6651,53767,40823,73024,14069,45767,47562&CurrentCatalogueIdIndex=6&FullTextHash=&HasEnglishRecord=True&HasFrenchRecord=True&HasSpanishRecord=True

Wynberg, R. (2004). Rhetoric, Realism and Benefit Sharing: Use of Traditional Knowledge of Hoodia Species in the Development of an Appetite Suppressant. *The Journal of World Intellectual Property, 7*(6), 851–876. doi:10.1111/j.1747-1796.2004.tb00231.x

Yaich, R. (2007). La maîtrise des risques fiscaux. In L'impôt sur les sociétés. Les éditions Raouf Yaïch.

Yu, P. K. (2006). TRIPS and Its Discontents. *Journal of Intellectual Property Law Review,* 369.

Zip Mfg. *Co. v. Pep Mfg. Co.,* (1930) 44 F.2d 184 District Court, D. Delaware.

About the Contributors

Nisha Dhanraj Dewani has done her LL.B and LLM (corporate law) from Jamia Millia Islamia (India) and submitted her thesis on a subject of patent. She has practiced as a lawyer in Delhi High Court for 3 years. Besides she worked with reputed law firm and senior partners handling IPR matters for 2 years. In addition, she holds more than 9 years' experience in academics. She qualified the U.G.C. NET and JRF in 2010. Her major area of academic interest includes Intellectual Property rights, International Commercial Law and Public International Law. She has many research papers in various national and international reputed law journals. She has received number of letters of appreciation not only from the academic institutions but from different law journals for her contributions. She has presented many research papers in various seminars and conferences. She has worked with UNICEF and many reputed NGOs. Also she has judged many National and International Moot Court Competition. Presently she is working with Maharaja Agrasen Institute of Management Studies (School of Law), GGSIPU.

Amulya Gurtu is the Chair-Business Administration and an Associate Professor of Supply Chain Management at the Austin E. Cofrin School of Business, University of Wisconsin-Green Bay, Green Bay, WI, USA. He obtained his Ph.D. from Ryerson University, Canada, an M.B.A. from Ivey Business School, Western University, Canada. His research interests are in global manufacturing and supply chains, and its impact on the environment and society. His research has been published in Transportation Journal, the International Journal of Physical Distribution & Logistics Management, Operations and Supply Chain Management, Services Marketing Quarterly, the International Journal of Inventory Research, the International Journal of Nonprofit and Voluntary Sector Marketing, the Journal of Cleaner Production, Management Research Review, the Journal of Environment & Development, Sustainable Production and Consumption, and Applied Mathematical Modelling. He served as the Editor-in-Chief of the International Journal of Sustainable Entrepreneurship and Corporate Social Responsibility (IJSECSR) published by IGI Global and is serving as an Associate Editor of the International Journal of Systems Science: Operations & Logistics published by Taylor & Francis.

* * *

Ashita Alag completed her B.A. LLB (I) from Guru Gobind Singh Indraprastha University, New Delhi in 2018 and is enrolled with the Bar Council of Delhi. She is currently working as a Law Clerk-cum-Research Assistant at the Supreme Court of India and holds deep interest in the field of arbitration. She has represented the Moot Alumni Association of the Willem C. Vis International Commercial Arbitration Moot at the 50th Session of the United Nations Commission on International Trade Law, 2017 at Vienna and also serves as an Editor of the Vindobona Journal of International Commercial Law and Arbitration.

Balaguru Balakrishnan, is an Assistant Professor of Botany in Jamal Mohamed college, Tiruchirappalli, Tamilnadu, India. He has an experience of around 22 years in the field of research and teaching. He is also a recipient of young scientist award from DST, Indian government, He has been contributing his technical knowledge in testing the crop breeds used in traditional farming. He has field expertise in Applied Ecology, IPR and GIS. He has more than 30 research publications in indexed journals to his credit.

Anindya Bhukta is an Associate Professor of Economics, Department of Economics, Netaji Mahavidyalaya Arambagh, Hooghly, West Bengal, India. Dr. Bhukta has been writing for over three decades in different English and Bengali journals and news-papers on different issues on economics and environment. He has, to his credit, nearly sixty books and more than three hundreds articles. Recently one of his co-edited volumes by Springer Nature and one of his authored book by Emerald Publishing are at the final stage of publication. He is the editor of a Bengali little magazine 'Aryama' and an online journal named ' Economy Polity Environment'.

Moghanraj Yadhav, G., is the Managing Trustee of VAANGHAI, an NGO established for the development and sustainability of traditional crops and bovine animals in Cauvery river delta region in Nagapattinam, Tamilnadu, India. He has been coordinating the traditional farmers by conducting annual farmers meet for the past three decades. He has also been the resource person for testing new crop breeds for the agriculture department operating in delta region of Tamilnadu.

Unanza Gulzar has done her LL.B and LLM from University of Kashmir specializing in Business laws besides holding Bachelor's degree in science. She is currently pursuing her PhD from Jamia Milia. She has qualified the U.G.C. NET twice and State eligibility test for lectureship in the year 2013. She has to her credit a Book on "Money Laundering in India: Legal Perspective". She has published more than 21 research papers in various national and international reputed law journals. She has received number of letters of appreciation from different law journals for her contribution. Besides, her articles have appeared in various newspapers/ Web-portals on a wide range of subjects from politics to typical legal matters. She has presented 20 research papers in various Seminars and conferences. With over more than four years of teaching experience, she has taught in Central University of Kashmir. She has received Professional Development Training organized by National Law School University, Bangalore and Menon institute of legal advocacy training in association with SLS, CUK. currently working as assistant professor, the Northcap University.

Sebak Kumar Jana is currently Professor of Economics in the Department of Economics with Rural Development, Vidyasagar University, West Bengal, India. Dr. Jana was graduated from Presidency College, Kolkata in 1989 and did his post graduation in Economics from University of Calcutta in 1991. He obtained M.Phil. and Ph.D. degree in Economics from Jadavpur University, Kolkata. His major area of academic interest includes environmental and resource economics, rural development and economics of education. He has about seventy publications in Journals and in edited books. He, as Principal Investigator, has completed a few research projects funded by ICSSR, UGC and NABARD and IWMI.

Akanksha Jumde is Assistant Professor, Department of Law, School of Legal Studies, Central University of Tamil Nadu, and a Ph.D. Scholar at Deakin Law School, Deakin University, Australia. She received the Deakin University Post-Graduate Research Scholarship (DUPRS) for her Ph.D. She has taught at prestigious law institutions such as National Law University, Jodhpur, and Faculty of Law, Delhi University, India, as an IP law faculty. She has completed her Bachelor of Socio-Legal Sciences and Bachelors of Laws (BS.L.LLB) from ILS Law College, Pune, University of Pune, and after that, an LLM (IP law) from the USA. She has been awarded "The Franklin Pierce Law Center Certificate of Intellectual Property Laws" for excellence in the study of Intellectual Property Laws. Before joining academia, she has worked as an IP lawyer at a leading IP law firm in India, and as Head, IP Chair at Gujarat National Law University (GNLU), established by the Government of Gujarat. She has published in renowned international law journals, including Statute Law Review (OUP), and presented papers at several national and international conferences. She has also authored a booklet on 'Utility Models in India,' published by Gujarat National Law University.

Souhaila Kammoun is an Assistant-Professor at IHEC of Sfax and researcher at CODECI, University of Sfax, Tunisia. She got her Phd in Economics at the University of Social Sciences of Toulouse 1, France. She has taught Economics at the University of Social Sciences of Toulouse as a Temporary Lecturer and Research Assistant. She has also taught Economics in several university institutions in Tunisia namely Microeconomics, Macroeconomics, Management and Economy of Innovation, Immaterial Economy, Digital Economy. Her research interests focus on Innovation, Dynamic Capabilities, Corporate Social Responsibility, Foreign Direct Investment and Fintechs. She has published a number of research articles in international journals and collective books. She is also the author of a book entitled: Innovation et compétences pour innover des firmes: Modélisation du comportement innovant dans l'industrie française (Editions Universitaires Européennes, 2015). She is currently an active member of the executive board of the Association Université-Environnement, at the University of Sfax. She was a member of the PAQ-ES project committee, director of the Master's degree in Entrepreneurship and International Development (Tempus Project funded by the European Union) and member of the scientific council at IHEC of Sfax. She was also president of the teachers' association at IHEC. She has held the positions of Head of the Department of Economics, Director of Studies and Vice-Director. She was also Director of IHEC of Sfax, Tunisia.

Shaharyar Asaf Khan has completed his LL.B. from Campus Law Centre (CLC), University of Delhi and LLM in Corporate Law, with a gold medal, from Jamia Millia Islamia University, Delhi (India). He has a teaching experience of more than 8 years. He has keen interest in the field of criminal Law, Personal law and IPR. He earned more than 20 appreciation letters in his related field, 7 international and national publications and 11 presentations. Also he had judged various prestigious moots like Jamia Moot Court Competition and Amity University Moot Court Competition.

Nishant Kumar is an MGNCRE fellow currently pursuing his Ph.D. in the area of CSR and Rural Development from the Central University of Punjab. He is a recipient of Mahatma Gandhi National Council of Rural Education Ph.D. Scholarship for pursuing a Ph.D. in the area of "Possibilities of Rural Development through CSR in India." In addition to it, Mr. Kumar has also received Deakin University visiting scholarship Award from Deakin University, Melbourne, Australia. Mr. Kumar has presented his research work at various international and national platforms, including the National University of Singapore, the University of Melbourne, and the University of Wollongong. He has published his research in a few of the reputed Journals of India. Mr. Kumar is a keen learner and observer and exploring the area of CSR for the last two years in order to have in-depth knowledge of the subject matter. Prior to joining research, he has taught at Jamia Millia Islamia University, New Delhi, Nirma University Ahmedabad, and Gautam Budhha University, Greater Noida. Additionally, he has completed the course of the company secretary from ICSI, New Delhi. His area of interest includes CSR, Rural Development, IPR Laws, and Corporate Governance & Sustainability.

Claudia Masoni has a BA in Modern Languages and Literatures, specialisation in Philology and Comparative Literatures and Gender Studies (Pisa University, Italy); LLM in International Human Rights Law (London, UK); PhD in Law (Waikato University, New Zealand). Researcher in the fields of Law, Anthropology, Indigenous cultural rights and traditional knowledge, Mythology and Symbolism, Religions and Gender Studies.

Nagamurugan N. is an Assistant Professor of Botany at The Government Arts College, Melur, Madurai, Tamilnadu,India. He has research and teaching experience of around 20 years in the field of Botany, Biotechnology and Microbiology. He has expertise in application of Remote sensing and GIS in forest Management. His research contribution in recognized journals exceed 30 papers. He has also guided more than 30 M.Phil researchers.

Sudha Jha Pathak has done post-graduation in History from Jadavpur University, Kolkata and Doctorate from the M.S University of Vadodara, Baroda. She was also granted Junior Research Fellowship (JRF) by the Indian Council of Historical Research (ICHR). She taught at various colleges in Mumbai and at Amity Law School, Delhi before joining Bennett University, Greater Noida where she currently teaches. She has presented papers at several national and international conferences and seminars. She has also published articles in various journals as well as chapters in books. Her area of interest is Gender Studies. She is a Member of the Indian History Congress as well as a Life Member of the Epigraphical Society of India. She likes playing guitar and is also trained in Indian classical dance Bharatnatyam.

Chiraz Touil is a researcher in private law. She got an advanced degree in business law and criminal science at the faculty of Law, university of Sfax, Tunisia. She taught since 2000, first, at the Faculty of Law of Sfax and then at IHEC of Sfax. She has taught introduction to law, human rights law, civil law, commercial law, business criminal law, international trade law, labour and social security law, business ethics and deontology of the professional accountant, banking and insurance law, legal management of intellectual property. She has held the position of head of the accounting and tax department at IHEC of Sfax. She has been elected member of the scientific council of the same institute on two occasions. She was also one of the founders of an association called Association de Citoyenneté et de la Liberté and managed the "legal culture" committee.

Index

Ensure Quality Research is Introduced to the Academic Community

Become an IGI Global Reviewer for Authored Book Projects

The overall success of an authored book project is dependent on quality and timely reviews.

In this competitive age of scholarly publishing, constructive and timely feedback significantly expedites the turnaround time of manuscripts from submission to acceptance, allowing the publication and discovery of forward-thinking research at a much more expeditious rate. Several IGI Global authored book projects are currently seeking highly-qualified experts in the field to fill vacancies on their respective editorial review boards:

Applications and Inquiries may be sent to:
development@igi-global.com

Applicants must have a doctorate (or an equivalent degree) as well as publishing and reviewing experience. Reviewers are asked to complete the open-ended evaluation questions with as much detail as possible in a timely, collegial, and constructive manner. All reviewers' tenures run for one-year terms on the editorial review boards and are expected to complete at least three reviews per term. Upon successful completion of this term, reviewers can be considered for an additional term.

If you have a colleague that may be interested in this opportunity, we encourage you to share this information with them.

www.ingramcontent.com/pod-product-compliance
Lightning Source LLC
LaVergne TN
LVHW081248011026
849162LV00004BA/899